DALGLISH
THE BIOGRAPHY

DALGLISH
THE BIOGRAPHY

Stephen F. Kelly

This revised paperback edition first published in 2004 by Highdown,
an imprint of Raceform Ltd Compton, Newbury, Berkshire RG20 6NL
Raceform Ltd is a wholly-owned subsidiary of Trinity Mirror plc

First published in hardback in 1992 by Headline Book Publishing
First published in paperback in 1993 by Headline Book Publishing;
second revised edition 1995, third revised edition 1997

A catalogue record for this book is available from the British Library.

ISBN 1-904317-70-7

Designed by Fiona Pike
Printed by Mackays of Chatham

CONTENTS

Acknowledgements

This book was originally published in 1992. It was then updated and published again in 1995 and in 1997. This is now the third updating. During all these years I have been given valuable and generous assistance by many. It goes almost without saying that this book could not have been written without their kind help and good patience but there are some to whom I owe an especial gratitude. First I should like to thank Dennis Mooney for guiding me around the Glasgow football scene and introducing me to a number of important Celtic contacts as well as accompanying me to my first Old Firm game.

My appreciation is also due to the staff of the Mitchell Library in Glasgow, Manchester City Library, and Stockport Central Library. I am particularly indebted to Celtic historian Pat Woods for his careful reading and checking of the chapters covering Dalglish's early years and later years in Scotland. Needless to say, any mistakes are my responsibility alone.

Thanks are also due to many others for their recollections and help over the years since the mid-1990s, when the book was originally published. These include Hugh Cairns, Companies' House (Edinburgh), Professor Carey Cooper of UMIST, Bob Docherty of the Scottish FA, Les Donaldson, Sean Fallon, Cyril George for his detailed statistics covering the Celtic and Liverpool years, Ian Hargreaves, one time football correspondent of the *Liverpool Daily Post and Echo*, Dave Hill, the late Sydney Moss, the Hillsborough Advice Centre, the *Liverpool Daily Post and Echo* cuttings library, Gerry McNee, Billy McNeill, David Morris of the Scottish FA, Ian Ross, Sandy Ross, Geoff Twentyman, Ged Lalor and John Whittaker.

There were also many others who gave me considerable help, including players, journalists, and club officials, but who wished, for various reasons, to remain anonymous. My thanks to all of them for their helpful insights and suggestions. I would also like to thank the original publishers Headline and in particular Ian Marshall. My thanks also to the publishers of this latest edition including Jonathan Taylor and my agent John Pawsey.

Finally, my thanks and deepest appreciation to my family, to my mother and my parents-in-law, and especially to my wife Judith and children Nicholas and Emma who never had the pleasure of seeing King Kenny play. They have had to live with this project over many years, through its original conception and various updates to this latest edition. I hope that in the end it has proved to be worthwhile.

Stephen F. Kelly
2004

Introduction

My father had seen them all; the famed ballplayers of recent generations: James, Doherty, Dean, Matthews, Finney, Liddell, Milburn, even Shackleton, right through to the likes of Law, Best and Keegan. But the one who impressed him more than any of these memorable names was Kenny Dalglish. Week after week, we sat together at Anfield, drooling at his awesome catalogue of talents: the precise timing, his electric vision, his whippet turns and, above all, his anticipation, a sixth sense of knowing where everybody was positioned.

My father knew a thing or two about goal-scorers. He had grown up alongside Dixie Dean and they remained bosom pals throughout his life. One evening, chatting football with the pair of them, I dared to ask Dean how he rated Dalglish. As an Evertonian, I expected him to dismiss the Scot with one of his usual glares, normally reserved for rival goal-scorers. But no, this time he paused and considered carefully. Perhaps it was because my father was with me. Then he spoke: 'A wonderful player, such skill, so brave. Probably the best combination I've seen of goalscorer and goalmaker.' Then he added, typically: 'But he still wouldn't score as many goals as me.' That was enough. If Dalglish could impress Bill Dean so much, then he truly had to be someone special, Dean excepted, of course. It was as relishing a compliment as anyone could have paid the Scot.

I was fortunate to have watched Dalglish week after week during his Anfield career. I must have seen him play hundreds of times. And what I detected was consistency coupled with sublime skill. Is there a more profitable combination? And yet, on top of that, Dalglish also had a powering strength and determination that made him as brave a marksman as any. Had that been the end of the story, it would have still been worth telling. But Dalglish then took on the challenge of managing one of Europe's top clubs. In his first season, he clinched the League and Cup double. At the end of his five-and-a-half-year reign, he had won three League championships, two FA Cups, taken Liverpool to a few other finals and had come within a whisker of winning the double on two more occasions. It was an astonishing record for one so young, so inexperienced.

And then, one cold February day in the middle of a war, he caused a sensation, confounding everyone by suddenly and dramatically resigning. He had had enough, the pressure was too much. Or so he said. Few could believe him. Nobody wanted to believe him. How could so professional a player and manager as Dalglish, a man with such confidence, suddenly quit his job, leaving his club in the lurch. There had to be another explanation. Or did there?

This book, then, is an attempt to assess Dalglish's career and explore the mounting crisis in his life. But, for various reasons, it has been written without his cooperation. Some may regard it as audacious to have even considered embarking on a biography of a public figure without their prior agreement, so perhaps some explanation should be given. It was my view that Dalglish deserves better than a hagiography. He warrants a serious and detached study that attempts to place his playing career in context and, where necessary, to criticise what was at times a controversial managerial career. A book written with his cooperation would have been a very different product, perhaps with more personal anecdotes but lacking the critical edge that a more detached study can provide. Dalglish is a man worthy of respect and close analysis but as a consequence his faults too must be scrutinised. Like everyone, he has his own foibles and it is just as important that they are examined as much as his finer points are acclaimed. In the end, I hope a more balanced view will emerge.

The story of Dalglish is not just a treasury of triumph, it is also an account of pressure at the highest level, cutting down someone who seemed so invincible. There is a lesson in it for all of us. At the time, there were those who mocked Dalglish's talk of stress and who scathingly refused to acknowledge that sport can engender the same pressures as other occupations or predicaments. How could the manager of the Football League's top club be under any kind of pressure? The truth is that those who attain the highest level in any sport drive not just their bodies but their mental resources to the very limits. And managing Liverpool Football Club brought with it an unparalleled and unexpected pressure that had already affected the lives and spirit of Dalglish's predecessors.

And yet within a year of walking out on Liverpool, Dalglish was to take up what was possibly the toughest assignment of his life. He accepted a challenge to take an almost forgotten football club from the depths of the then Second Division to the top of the Premiership. Few could understand why he had taken up an offer that seemed doomed to failure. Within four years, Dalglish had guided lowly Blackburn Rovers not only into the top league but into the runners-up spot and finally to the Premiership title. It was an astonishing achievement, to rank with any in his career.

Stephen F. Kelly
Manchester May 1995

CHAPTER ONE
You'll Never Walk Alone

It was just like the Queen dying
Johnny Kennedy

Jeff Anderson slumped back into his chair and picked up the *Liverpool Daily Post*. The morning's news conference was over. There was time for a moment's break, a coffee and a quick skim through the back pages. As producer of *Granada Tonight,* the North West's local ITV news programme, he had been hard at it in the office since eight that morning. It was now shortly before 10.00am on Friday, 22 February 1991. Outside his office on Liverpool's Albert Dock, a heavy wind swirled around the Liver buildings, grey as the day itself. The Mersey was empty, a far cry from the days when the ferry boats would weave between the anchored liners and cargo ships, awaiting the next tide or a spare berth.

Film crews had been assigned their duties and reporters were scurrying across the region, gathering the stories to fill that evening's programme. A few other journalists were sitting around the newsroom chatting and drinking coffee. The production manager was on the phone arranging a link with Westminster for an interview with some politician. It looked like an average day: a visit by Michael Heseltine to Liverpool, another shooting in Manchester's Moss Side. But the news, as it had been for some weeks, continued to be dominated by the Gulf War. In particular, the question as to when the land offensive would begin filled people's minds. The challenge for a local news producer, like Anderson, was in finding a regional angle for what was the leading news story in every TV station and newspaper across the world. No doubt something else would break before the day was out, he thought, and settled down to read the paper.

He flicked through the pages, sipped on his coffee, and glanced casually at the computer sitting on his desk. There was a PA flash blinking. He leaned over and pressed the appropriate key. The message shot on to his screen: URGENT. PRESS CONFERENCE. LIVERPOOL FOOTBALL CLUB, ANFIELD 11.00AM FRIDAY. 'Christ! Why didn't they ring us and tell us yesterday?' he muttered, putting down his paper and getting up from his desk.

Mark Owen had been out celebrating his 28th birthday the night before and had strolled into Granada Television's smart high-tech news office just in time for the morning conference. It looked like a quiet day for him. He had already packaged a football roundup to go out that evening. Bob Greaves and Stuart Hall, who presented the programme, would wander into the office later, sometime after lunch, and together they would work out a few lines of chat and a script for the show. Bob, a United fan, and Hall, a City fan, would joke and tease one another as they mulled over the weekend's games and analysed the famous draw between Liverpool and Everton that week. It was their style.

Mark was chatting in the newsroom when he too spotted the PA flash blinking on a computer. He broke away from his conversation and pressed a button. The same message flashed on to his screen.

'What do you reckon, Mark?' asked Jeff Anderson, striding out of his office.

'I don't know,' said Mark.

'Did you have any idea about it?'

'No,' he replied.

'Get on the phone to them then. Find out what it's all about.'

Over at the offices of the *Liverpool Daily Post and Echo,* in a muddy brown coloured building more akin to a Crusader fort than the centre of a major news operation, a call had already arrived from Peter Robinson, chief executive of Liverpool Football Club. He was on amicable terms with the paper and was a personal friend of many on the sports desk. They would be in touch most days. The newsroom was busy putting together the day's first edition.

'We've got something big about to break,' Robinson told them. 'Hold the front page' was all that he would give away.

Mark Owen sat down, rummaged for his contacts book and phoned Peter Robinson at Anfield.

'Hello Peter. Is this right that you've got a press conference in an hour's time?' he asked. 'Why didn't you warn us about it last night?'

'Well, it's come up as an emergency. We didn't know until this morning,' replied Robinson.

'Can you tell us what it's about?' inquired Mark.

'No, sorry, I can't.'

'Hell. We've got a bit of a problem this end. We've got no crews. They've all been assigned,' pleaded Owen.

'I'm sorry. I still can't tell you. But I will warn you that it is big and if you miss it, you'll regret it. That's all I can say.'

Mark put the phone down and told Jeff Anderson the news.

'It's probably something to do with John Barnes,' added Mark. 'They'll be about to announce his transfer.' A potential deal with an Italian club had been the talk of the papers for months.

'I suppose so,' said Anderson, looking at the back page of that morning's *Liverpool Daily Post,* which Mark was pushing towards him. It was headlined: *'Barnes – I'll Keep Reds Hanging On. Wing Wonder is Holding Out For Euro Move.'* Barnes had been haggling over a new contract and was known to be itching to try Italian soccer. He was widely expected to leave at the end of the season. Anderson, a fanatical Liverpool supporter, was as aware as anyone of an impending Barnes transfer. He idolised the man.

'Right, we'd better cover it then,' agreed Anderson. 'Get Daphne to find a crew, from somewhere. You organise it. Go with them. Do a piece to camera if necessary. Depends how big it is. Keep in touch though. Maybe they've signed Gazza.' They both laughed. There had even been a rumour circulating the city about a swap with Tottenham; Barnes for Gascoigne.

In the executive suite at Anfield, home of Liverpool Football Club, journalists were milling around. Seats had been laid out and, in front of them, a table with half a dozen chairs had been arranged. Unusual. It meant that the directors would be on hand. There was only one TV crew present. Most of the national newspapers had their Liverpool stringer on hand. The talk was about what the announcement might be. The general conclusion was that either it would be John Barnes or a new sponsorship deal. But, knowing Liverpool, it could just as easily be a major signing. It was usually the case that when Liverpool dipped into the transfer market nobody ever knew anything about it until the ink was dried on the contract. The names of Mark Wright and Matthew le Tissier were mentioned. Somebody joked that maybe Kenny was about to resign after the shambles of the other evening. Everyone smiled.

From the far corner of the room, Liverpool chairman Noel White, Peter Robinson and former chairman Sir John Smith walked in and sat down at the table. Fellow directors Tony Ensor and Jack Cross sat nearby. A few paces behind came Kenny Dalglish, the Liverpool manager, smartly dressed in a double-breasted suit, white shirt and tie, his eyes empty, his cheeks hollow, like some hostage just released from a Beirut prison. He sat down at the table as well. Noel White was to his left, John Smith to his right and, beyond him, Peter Robinson. No John Barnes, no Armani-suited Italians, no new faces, no smiles. They all looked tense.

Noel White was the first to speak. A white-haired accountant and former chairman of Altrincham Football Club, he had been the Liverpool chairman for a few months only, succeeding John Smith in the summer of 1990. He was clearly not used to this kind of ordeal.

'Thank you all for coming at such short notice,' he began, fidgeting nervously in his seat. 'I have a statement to read,' he continued. 'I regret to announce that Kenny Dalglish has told the board of his wish to retire as team manager.' He paused. For a second there was a stunned silence in the room, followed by the flashing of cameras and the clicking of shutters. The journalists stared at one another in disbelief. Months earlier, they had been shocked by the sensational return of Howard Kendall to Goodison Park, but this was even more staggering. Noel White looked pale and stumbled over his words as he continued. Even he did not seem to fully comprehend or believe what he was saying.

There was little that Noel White could add. All eyes were on the man sitting next to him. Dalglish edged uncomfortably in his chair, looking impassive at first but then emotional as he began to speak, his eyes fiercely screwed into his gaunt face.

'It's the first time since I've come to this club that I have made a decision that was more in favour of Kenny Dalglish than Liverpool Football Club,' he began, his audience transfixed. 'It wasn't a decision that I woke up to one morning and thought was a good idea. It is a decision that has taken me a long time to come to. The worst decision I could have come to was not to make a decision. You can say it's not a good time, but I don't know what is a good time.'

The biggest problem had been pressure, he added. 'I was putting myself under enormous pressure because of my desire to be successful. Basically, it was just the build-up to matches and the aftermath that was a problem. People may find my decision difficult to understand, but it is one I have made. It would have been a mistake to mislead people into believing that there was nothing wrong in myself. I have been involved in football since I was seventeen. This is twenty years with two of the most successful clubs in Britain, Liverpool and Celtic. I've been in the front line throughout this time, and it is as a result of twenty years' active involvement at the highest level that a person is pushed to the limit.'

He stopped. It was as simple as that. There were few questions. Most of the journalists seemed too stunned to speak. It was all perfectly polite and dignified. Noel White added that Ronnie Moran had been asked, and had agreed, to take over as caretaker manager until a replacement was appointed. He also quickly stressed that the board had had no dispute with Dalglish and that his resignation had come despite strenuous efforts to dissuade him.

There was nothing else to be said. Dalglish stood up, refusing to answer any more questions. Mark Owen immediately rushed over to him.

'Hi, I'm Mark Owen from Granada Television,' he said. 'I wonder if we could have an interview?'

'Yeah, I know who you are,' replied Dalglish. 'You look very smart.' And with that he walked off.

He spoke a brief farewell to one or two journalists who had come to know him well over the years and then rushed downstairs in tears to drive his white Mercedes through the Shankly Gates for the final time as an employee of Liverpool Football Club.

Within minutes, the news was buzzing around Merseyside. Radio City, Liverpool's independent radio station, was the first to break the sensation. Disc jockey Johnny Kennedy, a cult figure in Liverpool since the 1960s, was on air when he was warned they would be going live to Anfield for a report. A Liverpool fan all his life, he could hardly believe his ears.

'It was just like the Queen dying,' he said. 'We were stunned. Suddenly everyone in the studio was rushing around. There was chaos. We switched from playing records to a live phone-in and, of course, the switchboard was jammed. Everyone wanted to know if it was really true and, above all, why.' It was a question people would continue to ask for many months.

Back at Anfield, the Liverpool players were preparing to board their coach, bound for Luton, where the team was scheduled to play the following day. A shocked Ronnie Moran, for so long Dalglish's number two, suddenly found himself in charge.

Liverpool were still top of the table and chasing a possible League and Cup double. Dalglish had gathered his players together earlier that morning to tell them of his decision. Club captain Alan Hansen confessed that it had come as a shock to them. 'We just couldn't believe it,' he said. Ronnie Whelan was equally bewildered. 'You would have thought he would have stayed for a good while longer but, as he said, the pressure finally got to him. It is understandable really.'

As the players climbed aboard the coach, none of them seemed much inclined to comment further on the news. Controversial new signing David Speedie would say only that he was 'gutted'. Jimmy Carter confessed that they were under orders not to talk. Ronnie Whelan was more open. 'It came as a complete surprise to everyone,' he confessed. 'The last thing we expected was the gaffer telling us he was retiring. We knew something was going on by the atmosphere around the club. He just called a meeting and said he was finished with football. It seems it got too much for him. It's a sad loss for Liverpool.'

Ronnie Moran, minus the usual smile, claimed he had had no inkling of it. 'But I can understand it in a way,' he added. 'Everyone reacts differently under pressure, but we carry on as normal. The players have reacted like good pros. They realise they can't mope about. They have to get on with the game.' With that, he boarded the coach and within minutes the Liverpool team, minus Kenny Dalglish, pulled out of Anfield bound for the M62 and Luton.

They have a word for it on Merseyside: gob-smacked. It was probably the best way to describe the reaction to Dalglish's resignation. When Mark Owen rang Granada with the news, Jeff Anderson could barely believe it. He reckoned Mark, a lifelong Evertonian, was having him on. 'Stop pissing about,' he joked. 'No, honestly, it's true,' insisted Mark. The first thing that Anderson did was to telephone his father, another dyed-in-the-wool

Reds supporter. 'But why?' was the first question he asked. It was the same question everyone asked.

Dalglish's resignation defied understanding. How could Dalglish quit the most successful club in Britain after so many years? Surely pressure alone would not make him resign just as the season was moving towards its climax? Dalglish was regarded as a thorough professional, a man who did not smoke, drink or frequent nightclubs. He was devoted to his family and, as a player, spent most afternoons resting in bed. He took his game more seriously than almost any other footballer. It was inconceivable to most fans and journalists that Dalglish, the ultimate professional, could quit soccer management when he was within a whisker of picking up at least one more trophy.

There had to be another reason for his resignation. Nobody could imagine that it was pressure alone that had made him quit. Dalglish seemed to be the last person likely to be affected by pressure. Since he had first played senior football with Celtic all those years ago, he had been at the sharp end. He was accustomed to it – league titles, FA Cups, European trophies – Dalglish had tasted soccer's hottest offerings and had grown up with them. On top of that he had been through Heysel and Hillsborough as well as the Ibrox disaster when he was at Celtic. Dalglish was the Cool Hand Luke of football: calm, calculating, decisive. He may have come in for some criticism in the back pages but surely he was not one to be swayed by what he read in the papers. Or was he? There had to be another reason for his resignation.

BBC Radio One was carrying the story on its news bulletins by 11.30am, less than half an hour after the announcement. By midday, phones were ringing all over Merseyside as astonished Liverpool supporters telephoned each other. The Anfield switchboard was jammed. Never mind the Gulf War; Kenny Dalglish had just resigned.

At the *Liverpool Daily Post and Echo* there was bedlam. It was one of their biggest news stories in years. By lunchtime, the first editions were hurtling on to the streets. 'KENNY QUITS' was the bold headline shrieking from the front page. 'Even if the land war in the Gulf had started,' claimed the editor, 'I would have led with the Dalglish story. It was that big.' In newsrooms everywhere, journalists were dumbfounded. Nor was it just the football reporters who were shocked. Dalglish was one of the biggest names in sport. After Hillsborough, his calm, dignified words had helped bring understanding to confusion, giving strength to a stunned nation. In short, his face was now as well known as any in the country. Dalglish had become more than just a football manager.

At Euston station, hundreds were pouring off early morning trains from Liverpool. Many more were waiting and queuing in the terminal's large marbled concourse area for the next trains to the North West. It was a typical, busy Friday morning, the weekend traffic already building up towards its evening peak. The tannoy was bellowing its usual incomprehensible news of delays and cancellations. Suddenly, the messages stopped and, in a clearer voice, the announcer reported that Kenny Dalglish had just resigned as manager of Liverpool Football Club. 'I just thought you'd like to know,' he added, almost apologetically. A momentary hush descended on the station.

In newsrooms everywhere, the speculation began. Even at the *Liverpool Daily Post and Echo* they could not believe it was so simple. There had to be more to it. At *The Guardian* they drew up a list of reasons. It ran to more than ten possibilities. In Glasgow, the word was that Dalglish was on his way back north. At Granada, Jeff Anderson and Mark Owen also jotted down their own thoughts.

They too wondered if he might be on his way back to Scotland to become manager of his former team, Celtic, or even his boyhood favourites, Glasgow Rangers. There was also the possibility that he might be about to take over managing the national side. Dalglish was thought to be hankering after a return north. He had even been reported to have played a game for Rangers' reserves the previous week. Or perhaps he was about to become manager of the USA. With the World Cup in America, the United States were reported to have approached him with a huge offer to manage their national side. The Scottish job, although not vacant, was always reckoned to be the one job that would tempt him away from Anfield. Maybe there had been a rift with the Liverpool board. There had been occasional whispers of conflicts. Or could it be an illness in the family? This was surely one of the few reasons that might make Dalglish resign so suddenly. And what about his wife? After 20 years of incessant football, it would come as no surprise if Marina had decided that enough was enough and he had to choose between football and her. His close friend Graeme Souness had already experienced that problem and had finished up separating from his wife. Throughout the next 24 hours, the speculation was rife. But there was never a shred of evidence to support any of the popular theories. It just seemed that no one could bring themselves to accept Dalglish's statement at face value.

That lunchtime, Granada sent a television crew out on to the streets of Liverpool. 'So, what do you think of the news of Kenny Dalglish's resignation?' asked the interviewer, stopping a group of young lads.

'Dalglish resigned? Stop having us on,' was the sharp response from a young lad with a fierce squint. 'Why would he go? I don't believe ya, come off it, Dalglish wouldn't leave Liverpool.'

'Honestly, it's true,' pleaded the Granada man.

'No way.'

May Devine was in tears. She had been a cleaner at Anfield for many years. She even remembered polishing the FA Cup after Liverpool had won it for the first time in 1965. 'I'm just heartbroken,' she said. 'I was here when Bill Shankly went and that was a shock. But this is a bigger one. We didn't have a clue, but I think you could see something at the match on the Wednesday night, the expression on his face. For us, he was a funny man, very dry. He always had the time of day for you. I took his dinner to him yesterday and I put the Scotch pies he always had at weekends on the coach for him today. I just can't believe it.'

For those with long memories, like May, it was a recurring nightmare. On 12 July 1974, the legendary Bill Shankly had walked into an Anfield press conference flanked by the same men, Peter Robinson and John Smith. After introducing Liverpool's latest recruit, Ray Kennedy of Arsenal, John Smith had read out a short statement announcing that Shankly was to retire as manager of Liverpool Football Club. It had brought the same disbelief, the same bombshell news. Like the assassination of President Kennedy, there were those in Liverpool who could still remember precisely where they were when they heard the news of Shankly's departure. It may seem trivial to some, but Shankly undeniably meant more to their lives than John F Kennedy ever did. It was to be the same with Dalglish.

Even the world of showbiz was rocked by the news. Radio One DJ and lifelong Reds supporter John Peel was almost dumbstruck. 'I can't believe it,' he said. 'It's staggering. Dalglish was the best player I ever saw. I even christened my son after him. It's like hearing about the death of a favourite uncle.' Merseyside comedian Tom O'Connor couldn't believe it either: 'I'm absolutely stunned,' was all he could muster. 'The man is a legend.' And Gerry Marsden, whose recording of 'You'll Never Walk Alone' had inspired generations of Liverpool supporters, confessed that he was equally 'shocked and stunned', adding that 'the pressures must have been enormous for Kenny to pack it in.'

Jeff Anderson's brother Steve was told the news of Dalglish's resignation by his wife that evening. He was 3,000 miles away in Saudi Arabia, covering the Gulf War as a producer for BBC Television's *Newsnight*. He had just returned from a near-suicidal mission into the northern Saudi desert where, after straying into no-man's land, he had been held at gunpoint by a 16-year-old Egyptian soldier. Steve was also a fanatical Liverpool supporter, a veteran of the Kop, Wembley, Rome and Paris, with many more years' service than his younger brother.

'I had managed to get a line through to London,' he said, 'so I rang my wife. I hadn't spoken to her for a few days. We were just chatting, she was telling me about what she had been doing, and what our little boy, Simon, was up to and then, at the end of the conversation, she said, almost casually, "Oh, and by the way, Kenny Dalglish has resigned." You could have knocked me over.

'I tried to keep it in perspective, and for a short while I succeeded. But, stuck in the middle of the Arabian desert, the news hit me with the force of one of Saddam's Scuds.

'I was determined not to get upset. I told myself to keep it in proportion. It was only football, nothing compared with what was happening here in the Gulf. But I couldn't get away from it and, by night-time, it was as if it was the only thing in the world that mattered.'

Another Liverpudlian, a leading ITN reporter accompanying Steve in the Gulf, was even more shocked when he told him the news. Within minutes, the entire news corps in Saudi Arabia were gossiping about Dalglish's resignation. Quite what the Americans made of it was anyone's guess.

'We rode into battle the next day, sitting on the top of a tank and all we could talk about was Kenny Dalglish,' remembers Anderson. Bombs may have been falling, people may have been dying, but for two exiled Scousers in the Gulf, all that seemed to matter was the resignation story. Such was the impact of Kenny Dalglish, ex-manager of Liverpool Football Club. But why had he gone?

CHAPTER TWO
Across The Great Divide

Follow, follow, we will follow Rangers
Everywhere, anywhere, we will follow on.
Glasgow Rangers song

A solitary crane casts its feeble shadow across the deserted dockyards and slips of Govan, its rusting framework silhouetted against a slatted grey sky that sweeps in from the west. It is one of the few cranes remaining in a city that once proudly boasted a jagged skyline with more cranes than any other city in the world. They say it remains in case of war, when once again it will be cranked into action to load the troops and ships that will sail down the Clyde. Others reckon it stands, deliberately, as a symbol of proud days, now long gone, when the docks heaved with ships, stevedores and sailors. Whatever the reason, Glasgow is not quite the city it once was and certainly the Govan of today is a far cry from the docklands where Kenny Dalglish was reared.

Just a stone's throw from Govan is Ibrox, where high-rise council flats gaze down over the docks and the famous football ground. It is an area of red, sandstone tenement blocks, some with neat, communal gardens, granite buildings looking deceptively grand, and wide, almost elegant, thoroughfares. Grey-bricked houses nestle around the football ground, comfortably sandwiched between the Orange Hall, the Freemasons lodge and the Rangers bars. This is unmistakably Protestant territory, where the Orange march each July sweeps arrogantly through the streets, pausing only to salute Ibrox Park. Where bowler-hatted men sporting umbrellas, sashes, white gauntlets and aprons, march jauntily behind brightly-coloured banners. Where the mace is twirled and tossed into the Glasgow sky to the rhythmic marching music of a flute band. Where young boys with flutes and the big lambeg beat out their allegiance to the rattle of the sidedrum. This is the day when Catholics are supposed to hang their heads in shame. To the Sassenach, it is the politics of a dinosaur age.

Back in the 1950s, when Kenny Dalglish lived here, it was a community still thriving around ships. Chandlers, propeller manufacturers, ships' stores, scrapyards – anything to do with boats and you could find it here, crowded among the busy backstreets of Govan and Ibrox. Almost every man laboured in the shipyards, almost every kid had sat on his father's shoulders to watch some mighty liner slide down the slipways, and almost every son imagined his own future in the same yards as his father. An apprenticeship in the yard was the best a lad could hope for, other than playing for the Rangers. In Wales, they used to say you had only to shout down the pitshaft and an international prop forward would emerge. In Glasgow, you simply yell across any patch of land where kids are playing and a future Scottish inside forward will run across. This is the heartland of Scottish soccer, where footballers are forged.

It was here that Dalglish spent his early years, romping around the streets, playing chase on the stairs of the Victorian tenement blocks, or kicking a ball around the wastelands off the Paisley Road West. And, of course, he would spend Saturday afternoon, usually with his father, worshipping at Ibrox, watching the Gers. His heroes were men like Jim Baxter, mercurial, magic; Don 'Rhino' Kichenbrand, the bustling South African (one of only a handful of Catholics ever to play for Rangers, though he was lapsed rather than active); Ian McMillan, all swank and class; and, of course, Sammy Baird, the tall powerhouse of an inside left who was equally conversant as a half back. These were the early heroes who turned his head. Little wonder Dalglish saw his role upfront, mimicking the same artistry of these legends.

On a breezy June day in 1994, the centre of attraction inside Ibrox was a steel girder being delicately hoisted high above the horizon and swung into place on top of Archibald Leitch's famed, old, red-bricked stand. It was the longest single-spanned-structure ever lifted by a crane, one of which had been specially imported from Argentina; another first for Scottish engineering ingenuity. The new girder was destined to form part of an extra deck on the stand that would eventually raise the capacity of Ibrox to just over 50,000. Of course, when Dalglish came here as a child, the capacity was nearer 100,000. Indeed, in early 1939, just over 118,000 had watched an Old Firm battle. But the conditions then were a far cry from today. The tragedy of January 1971, when 66 spectators died on the infamous Stairway 13, put an end to those decades of swaying, elbowing and shoving that had become almost the accepted part of attending a football match. After that wretched day, the directors of Rangers pledged to turn Ibrox into a stadium fit for human decency. They succeeded beyond all expectations. Today, Ibrox Park is a magnificent ground, a shrine to soccer, with seating on all four sides and amenities that any football supporters would envy. But even the Ibrox of the late 1960s would have been a splendid setting for Kenny Dalglish, the player. Yet a twist of fate was to take him from the club he had supported as a boy to their bitterest rivals, Celtic.

Culture, religion and alcohol are said by wiser men to be the three great comforters of mankind. In Scotland, they would probably add football to the list. It was George MacDonald Fraser who observed, in the *The General Danced At Dawn,* that 'the native Highlanders, the Englishmen, and the Lowlanders played football on Saturday afternoons and talked about it on Saturday evenings but the Glaswegians, men apart in this as in most things, played, slept, ate, drank and lived it seven days a week.'

Glasgow football has a culture of its own, deeply embedded in the prejudices of 19th-century Scotland. To the outsider, particularly the English, it is a curious, indecipherable and often dangerous cocktail of religion, skill and fanaticism. Where else would the tricolour wave so bravely other than in Ireland? Where else would they sing of 'Fenian bastards' other than in Glasgow? And from where else could an army be raised to make the long, arduous trek to Argentina in support of a World Cup cause, other than from Scotland. To go to Glasgow and hear men talk of football and religion as if they were one and the same is a disturbing experience, unheard of south of the border. You might expect it from boys, youths of 20 even, but to stand in the enclosure at Ibrox and see grown, mature men in their

50s screaming for the blood of the Pope is a shocking indictment of Scottish football. Yet, for anyone bred in Glasgow, it is impossible to escape football or religion. The two may seem incompatible, yet they are a marriage that has survived the years.

The Protestant Reformation was as complete and circumscribed in Scotland as anywhere. Catholic culture and worship was almost destroyed, driven out of the land by zealots, to be replaced by the equally uncompromising Calvinism of John Knox, the founder of the Presbyterian Church of Scotland. Only a handful of Catholics survived the purge, and they were in isolated pockets close to the Hebrides and parts of the Highlands around Aberdeen and Banffshire. Catholicism was all but wiped out in Glasgow, with just 39 practising Catholics in the city in the 1790s. Throughout the 18th century, the number of Catholics in Scotland was probably never more than 40,000, or just three per cent of the population. In its place had emerged the undiluted morality of the presbytery.

But all that was to change in the 19th century, as turbulence and famine triggered off a mass emigration of Irish folk from their homeland. Poverty was rife, the inevitable consequence of Ireland's rising population and its failure to industrialise. The potato famine of the 1840s added painfully to what was already a pitiful state of affairs. There was only one escape: emigration. Most made initially for the mainland of Britain, to the ports of Liverpool, Manchester and Glasgow, hoping ultimately to work a passage to Boston, New York or anywhere in the Americas. Many made it little further than Liverpool or Glasgow, settling instead for an almost equally abject poverty. But at least the industrial cities of the mainland offered some prospect of work and relief. Anything was better than Ireland.

By 1827, the Catholic population of Scotland had doubled to 80,000 and by the end of the century the numbers had reached 450,000. Conflict was inevitable. It might not have been so coarse had the newcomers spread themselves more widely throughout the land but inevitably the Irish settled where they could find work or relief. And in Scotland that meant the Clyde Valley, where the coal and iron industries offered the best opportunity of employment. In Greenock, the Catholic population peaked at 31 per cent, in Clydebank it was 24 per cent and in Coatbridge 43 per cent. The anti-Catholic societies which had lain dormant for so much of the 18th century suddenly sprang to life again, fuelled by the same cause but with a new following and fresh fears.

Equally, there were Catholic organisations. Not so much to engage in religious hatred, but rather as self-help bodies, institutions of the church. Celtic Football Club was typical. It had been founded in 1888 as a charitable organisation to raise money for clothing, free dinners and poor relief among the Irish destitute of East Glasgow, or, more specifically, in the Catholic parishes of St Mary's, St Andrew's and St Alphonsus. The inspiration behind Celtic Football Club had been a Brother Walfrid, a young, fresh-faced priest, and his assistant, Brother Dorotheus, who formed their football team in the heart of the Irish Catholic community.

In the south west of the city, a football club at Rangers had been in existence for more than ten years, founded in 1872 by a group of lads from the Gareloch. But it would be some years before Rangers could count itself among the leading clubs of the land, with Queen's Park, Vale of Leven, Dumbarton and Third Lanark monopolising Scottish football until the last decade of the old century. But the success of Celtic only spurred Rangers on to greater deeds. The rivalry gradually became intense and the Scottish League would soon become little more than a contest between Celtic and Glasgow Rangers.

Fierce though the competition may have been, initially there was little religious bickering. Prior to the turn of the century, Rangers were not so closely identified with Protestantism as they would be in later years. Undoubtedly, their geographical location, close to the distinctly Protestant shipyards of the Clyde, might have meant that their followers were largely Protestant, but there was no fervent anti-Catholic policy in operation at the time. There may have been no Catholics in their team, but that again was due more to location than any conscious decision on the part of club officials. Rather than creating sectarian divisions, Rangers and Celtic were merely the consequences of them and they acted as agents for division. The dinosaur of bigotry was evolving.

Yet it was not until the rise of Celtic, with its fervent Irish Catholic following, that Rangers began to find its own clothing, to adopt its own sectarian leanings. It was good for business and the more distinct the religious divisions, the keener the rivalry. It was an ideology promoted by the charismatic, but fiercely authoritarian, Bill Struth, who ruled over Ibrox for almost 35 years between 1920 and 1954. During that period, the antagonism and sectarianism were never more bigoted or rampant, and never closer to the Church of Scotland's own views, unashamedly spelled out in a pamphlet published in 1923 under the ominous title 'The Menace of the

Irish Race to our Scottish Nationality'. Sectarianism had at last achieved respectability.

Religion was quickly exposed by the simple question: 'Which school did you go to, laddie?' or 'Are you in the Boys' Brigade?' This sectarianism was still a powerful force when Kenny Dalglish was a young boy. Celtic had always resisted attempts to introduce a Catholics-only policy, especially in its early days, and in the 1960s could consequently afford to encourage a more liberal attitude as Scottish football faced the challenge of European competition. Rangers responded by burying its head even further into the sand. The result was that Celtic, under the visionary Jock Stein, went on to lift the European Cup, while Rangers plunged into decline, still refusing to budge from their unique sectarianism. As Denis Healey would have advised, 'when in a hole, don't dig deeper'.

Kenneth Mathieson Dalglish was born in Dalmarnock, in the East End of Glasgow, on Sunday, 4 March 1951, a stone's throw from Parkhead. He was born into a world still emerging from the ravages of the war of 1939–45, but now threatened by a more subtle, and potentially deadlier, conflict between East and West. In Korea, it was already evident, as the tiny South-East Asian country tore itself apart with more than a little outside help.

The optimism of the early post-war days that had brought Clem Attlee's Labour Government to power was visibly faltering and, before the year was out, the Conservatives would be back in office. The days of Macmillan's 'never-had-it-so-good' Britain were about to descend, but there were few signs of it in Glasgow that March Sunday. Hibernian were top of the league for a start, with Rangers fifth and Celtic seventh – and the buses were on strike. You could still travel from Glasgow to almost any port in the world, with regular sailings advertised to Madras, New York, Bombay, Holland, Canada and Australia. The Dunfermline Building Society was offering mortgages at 2.25 per cent. For entertainment, the Dalglishes might have managed a visit to see Margaret Lockwood starring in *Peter Pan* at the King's Theatre or gone to watch *Babes in the Wood* at the Pavilion. More likely, they would have been listening to the radio, scouring the airwaves for *Educating Archie,* Billy Cotton or Henry Hall.

It was a different era, a time when no lad would dare go out without a tennis ball tucked into his trouser pocket. It was a time when youngsters learned their skills in the streets, knocking the ball off the edge of the pavement as they dribbled up some imaginary wing, when a couple of coats were thrown down for goalposts. There were few cars to interfere, plastic balls had not been invented and leather balls were too expensive. There was little organised soccer in the schools; it was simply left to the communities. And in those days there were still thriving communities, with their extended families and mutual care. Dalglish was to be one of the last footballers to emerge from these solid, working-class roots. By 1966, when England won the World Cup and Harold Wilson's 'white-hot technological revolution' was in motion, working-class life, and especially football, was set to change. The commercialisation and gentrification of the working classes was under way.

The Dalglish family did not remain in Dalmarnock very long. Before the year was out, they had moved to Milton and later relocated to a flat directly overlooking the Rangers training ground, the Albion, just across the road from Ibrox itself. Bill Dalglish was an engineer; his wife Cathy looked after the two children. They were a typical, respectable Scottish working-class family, with a father and mother determined to secure the best future for their offspring. You didn't curse in the Dalglish household, you did as you were told, you respected your parents, you learned the meaning of money and you always told the truth; they did not stand for any nonsense and, in turn, they devoted all to bringing up their two children. Work was important, and Bill Dalglish knew that he was fortunate to have a job in an area of traditionally high unemployment. It provided continuity and a degree of financial stability, but the children were never allowed to forget that holding on to a job was crucial. So nothing was ever taken for granted. The Dalglish parents set the standard and the children were expected to follow. Above all, there was none of the bigotry that seemed to afflict so many Glasgow households. Protestant they might be, and Rangers supporters too, but it did not blind them to another way of life. It was a caring background, a model of order that would shape the future Dalglish, leaving an indelible image with a few lessons that would come in useful in later life.

By the age of five, like most of the kids who lived on the Milton housing estate, young Kenny was kicking a ball around. It was a comparatively new council estate, a typical post-war development, smarter in those days than it is today. Ian Ross, who later went on to play for Liverpool and Aston Villa, was a neighbour of the Dalglish family.

'I always remember my Mam. There'd be a knock on the door and she'd shout to me "That little boy's here again, wanting to play I football."'

It would be Kenny, standing there in his short trousers, football tucked under his arm, toothy smile on his face. He was always the baby. I was four years older than him. He was a small boy but he was tough, even then. We used to play football at every opportunity. All day Sunday we would play, just having a short break for lunch. But even though he was younger, he still used to play with us.'

Dalglish had a typical Protestant childhood: he went to Sunday School, joined the Boys' Brigade and the YMCA. And, of course, on a Saturday afternoon when his father had knocked off, they dashed off to Ibrox after a hurried lunch. As he played more organised football, however, his Saturday afternoons would be taken up playing himself.

There was little footballing pedigree in the Dalglish family. His father had played the game as a younger man but was never a professional, nor anywhere near such a level; he was simply as keen a fan as you could imagine. And that love of the game was enthusiastically passed on to the younger Dalglish as he encouraged him whenever he could and always went to see him play.

A team was formed called Milton Madrid. 'We played in all white, just like the great Real Madrid,' says Ian Ross. 'Because the Milton housing estate was new, there was no organised football, no set-up, no teams, so we had to organise our own games. We made nets and our own goalposts out of one-inch thick tubing so that they could be dismantled easily. Sometimes we even managed to get a roller so that we could flatten the pitch a bit. They were usually seven, or eight-a-side games, the kind of games all kids play. Anyone could join in; there were kids there of every age. We were the best.'

Kenny would play anywhere but Ian Ross recalls he always fancied himself as a bit of an inside right. 'He was a great player, even then. You could see, he was comfortable on the ball. The talent was there. I always picked him for my side and he was always wanting to play with the older lads.' And if they were not playing on grass, they would be kicking a ball around in the streets, a few jackets casually thrown down to form goalposts.

From an early age, the single-mindedness was apparent. He was dedicated, always working at improving his game, even down to forfeiting other pleasures. It was as if he was born to be a footballer, and nothing else, and that he recognised it. In later life, he would continue to forego the amusements that many of his colleagues would enjoy. There was a determination to succeed, coupled with a confidence and assuredness that he would do so. Where others strayed, Dalglish set a clear course and pursued it, irrespective of what others thought or said. It was a characteristic that would remain with him.

Like Ian Ross, Dalglish went to Milton Bank Primary School, where his footballing career first came to the attention of his elders. But perhaps the greatest surprise of all is that it began in goal. His school teachers never fancied him as an outfield player but still offered the young lad a chance to play for the school team. The only snag was that he would be between the posts. Dalglish did not complain, he jumped at the opportunity, keen to play anywhere just as long as he could have a game. But, as Ian Ross says, 'He always had too much talent to be a goalkeeper.' By the age of 12, he was at Possil Secondary School and was also playing for the Boys' Brigade. It was while he was playing for them that Possil YMCA approached him, wondering if he would care to join their team.

Possil is a tough area, close to the centre of Glasgow, now more renowned for its drug problem than anything else. But, back in the early 1960s, its YMCA was famous for its football teams. On the bus it was only ten minutes away from Milton. It had something of a reputation for churning out footballers, with a number of their youngsters having gone on to play professional soccer – Ian Ross and George Andrew at West Ham were among them. They took their football seriously at the Possil YM and any boy asked to join up was expected to have the right attitude.

'It was serious, very serious,' recalls Ian Ross. 'They used to look after the lads, though. It was also very competitive as they had good teams. They usually won everything. At the Possil, Dalglish would have been playing a year above himself.'

There was no tomfoolery here. Possil YM was run by a man called Bobby Dinnie who was something of a legend. The lads loved him, and, over the years, Dinnie was the man responsible for securing many of them trials with professional clubs. Both Ian Ross and Dalglish were to benefit from Dinnie's extensive contacts. Possil YM was a shop window and Dalglish was soon coming to the attention of other local clubs, including Glasgow United. He was also chosen to represent Glasgow Schools and helped them lift the Scottish Schools Cup in 1966, beating Ayrshire in the two-legged final.

He was now at the forefront of schoolboy soccer and before long was asked to represent Scotland Schoolboys. He made his international debut in Belfast on 6 May 1966 as Scotland Under-15s faced Northern Ireland.

They won 4–3, with Dalglish helping himself to a couple of goals. Also on the scoresheet that day was a young Tommy Craig, who went on to play for Aberdeen, Sheffield Wednesday, Newcastle United and Scotland before returning north to become assistant manager at Celtic. A few days later, Dalglish faced England at Ibrox in front of 12,000 supporters. They drew 1–1, Dalglish demonstrating enough sparkle to catch the attention of at least one newspaper: 'Scottish inside forwards Dalglish and Craig were two brilliant ballplayers making all the openings for the other forwards,' wrote *The People.*

The programme notes for that game described the five feet seven inches tall, nine stones seven pounds inside right as 'another member of the successful Glasgow team which seems likely to win the Scottish Cup. He is a strong running, difficult to dispossess inside forward with a strong shot.' It added cannily that he 'wishes to become a professional footballer'. If ever there was an invite, that was it.

The scouts were out in force, snapping up most of the England team, seven of whom went on to play professional soccer. Steve Seargeant starred with Everton, while Liverpool snapped up Paul Clarke, although he would never play for the first team. And yet, despite their attention and the praise lavished on Dalglish by the newspapers, nobody seemed in a hurry to sign up the star of the game. Dalglish has always retained fond memories of his Scottish Schoolboy days and, 25 years later, was able to astound Con Duggan, the vice president of the Scottish Schools FA, by naming every member of those teams and telling him precisely what they were doing in the early 1990s.

Les Donaldson, Scotland's goalkeeper in both those games, 'chummed up' with Dalglish from the start. They shared a cabin for the crossing to Ireland and have remained friends ever since. 'He may not have been the finished article then,' recalls Donaldson, 'but he was clearly a talented player in a class above everyone else. He and Tommy Craig ran the show. Looking back they seemed very mature even at that age.'

All the time, Dalglish was being encouraged by his father. Playing for Scotland Schoolboys naturally brought him further to the attention of a number of professional clubs. Among them were Liverpool, who wrote and asked Dalglish if he would like to come down to Merseyside for a week's trial. He readily accepted and, on 20 August 1966, shortly after England had won the World Cup, a 15-year-old Dalglish pulled on a Liverpool shirt for the first time, the number 8, as Liverpool B lined up against Southport in a Lancashire League match. Liverpool won 1–0. Ian Ross recalls his trial vividly.

'I saw him around during the week,' he says. 'I felt that Kenny looked up to me. He'd seen me go off to Liverpool and probably thought he'd like to go there as well. I'd helped fix up the trial and Kenny went home hopeful that something might happen. He waited and waited but he heard nothing. He was really disappointed. I don't think it's true that he was homesick and it is certainly not true, as some have suggested, that Shankly was ringing up his father trying to persuade him to come back. Shankly knew nothing about it.' A couple of years later, Ian Ross remembers sitting in the Hendon Hall Hotel in London with Bill Shankly.

'We were down in London for a game, and I was sitting with Bill Shankly in the lounge on the Saturday lunchtime watching the football preview on the television. Kenny had not long made his debut for Celtic and the previous week had scored a hat-trick. Then up comes this report about Celtic and Dalglish scoring his three goals. "Hey Ian," shouts Shanks, "He looks good. You must know him, he's from your part of the world."

"Oh, aye," I said. "He came down to Anfield the other year for a trial."

' "What?" screamed Shankly. "What happened?"

' "Nothing," I replied. "He just went back and nobody got in touch with him." Shankly could not believe it.'

Shankly was furious and went off to conduct an inquest into why Dalglish had never been signed. Ross always wondered if he found the culprit. From that day on, stresses Ross, Shankly wanted Dalglish. 'I remember meeting him one day outside Anfield as I came back from training. He and Reuben Bennet were in Shanks' car. He wound the window down as I walked past. "Hey Ian," he shouted. "We're off to Derby to see your pal playing in an Under-23 international." '

It was February 1972. Scotland drew 2–2 and Dalglish scored both goals. 'The next day I saw Shankly, so I thought I would tease him a bit,' says Ross. "How did you go on last night?" I inquired. "How was Dalglish?"

' "Don't talk to me about Dalglish," he moaned. "The only man on the pitch. Christ, what a player."

Shankly was still fuming, and every now and then he would put in a call to his old pal Jock Stein, but there was never any hope of business. Shankly deliberately kept quiet about the blunder, never being one to admit his mistakes, and for the rest of his days he would regret never having signed Dalglish when the man was handed to him on a plate.

So Dalglish returned home to Scotland, still a Glasgow boy at heart. He also briefly went to West Ham United, always a club to appreciate footballing skills, for a trial but became homesick and raced back to Glasgow. It was now a case of waiting to see if Rangers would come in for him. There was really no other club in his life and he was sure that someone from the Rangers was out there watching him. Someone was watching him, but it was not a man from Rangers.

CHAPTER THREE

The Quality Street Gang

Sure, it's a grand old team to play for,
Sure, it's a grand old team to see.
Celtic song

Sean Fallon had promised to take his wife Myra out for their wedding anniversary. It was late May 1967 and half of Glasgow was still celebrating Celtic's famous European Cup victory. The Fallons had been married four years. It was an event that obviously had to be observed and Sean was not one to forget the importance of such occasions. He had booked a table at the Seamill Hydro, a pleasant, friendly hotel on the Ayrshire coast, close to Largs. He knew it well. It was a regular spot for the Celtic football team. Prior to cup finals and other major games, Fallon and the Celtic team would often spend the night at the quiet hotel – ideal preparation for the forthcoming day, especially with its spacious lawns and rousing view across the Firth of Clyde towards the Isle of Arran. It was just 30 miles out of the city, no more than an hour's drive, but far enough to be away from the buzz and distractions of Glasgow. Fallon liked the hotel, and the Ayrshire coast on a late spring evening was always refreshing. He felt relaxed there, not like at some of the grander hotels in town where you were always likely to bump into people you knew and where you would have to face the cross-examination of the hangers-on, desperate for the latest snippet of news from Parkhead. What's more, the staff at the Seamill Hydro knew him and they respected his privacy.

Fallon was a popular man who had joined Celtic on, appropriately, St Patrick's Day 1950 from the Irish League club Glenavon. Three weeks later, he made his Celtic debut, though when he put into his own net after just 30 minutes it seemed his career was set to come to an abrupt end. But it didn't, and Fallon went on to play more than 250 games in the green and white hoops. He was primarily a full back, thighs as thick as bacon slabs and a face as leathery as an old blow-up football. He could even play at centre forward and in 1954, his moment of glory, he scored Celtic's winner in the Scottish Cup final against Aberdeen. He won eight caps for Ireland between 1951 and 1955, in the days of Peter Farrell and Tommy Eglington, when Ireland had a team that could match just about any in Europe. Fallon was part of the fixtures and fittings at Parkhead and it was hardly surprising when, at the end of his playing days, Celtic decided to keep him on, eventually making him assistant manager to his old chum Jock Stein.

Fallon and his wife piled their three children into his car and left their Glasgow house in good time to reach the Ayrshire coast. Their journey took them close to Ibrox and, as they drove down the Paisley Road West, Fallon, deep in thought, suddenly had an idea. It was to be an inspired moment.

'Do you mind if I drop off at someone's house for a minute?' he asked Myra. 'There's a young lad I want to see. I'd like to have another chat with his father and he might just be in now,' he said, glancing at his watch. 'We've been trying to sign him but he's a bit reluctant. I think if I can have another go at his father I might be able to persuade him. It shouldn't take long.'

The wives of football managersand assistant managers need to be patient, long-suffering and remarkably tolerant of their partners' enforced absences. Mrs Fallon had already learned in the four short years that they had been married that there was little point in arguing when it came to football. She might just as well accept that her husband was married to Celtic Football Club as well as to her. And so she reluctantly agreed, though before the night was out her patience would have been tested well beyond its tolerance level. After all, it was their wedding anniversary.

Some months before, after a particularly strenuous morning's training, Sean Fallon had walked into his Parkhead office and had sat down to open the mail. Outside the rain was beating down, sweeping across the terraces and cascading down the gutters of the stand. Inside it was warm. There was a letter from a Mrs Davidson. He had no idea who she was. 'Come and see my boy Victor,' she wrote. 'I think he has the potential to be a footballer, everyone says so and he so wants to play for Celtic.' There was nothing unusual in that. 'We received dozens of letters like that, all the time,' says Fallon today. 'But for some reason, no reason in particular, I thought we should go and take a look at the lad. We usually ignore such letters. Maybe it was the fact that it was nicely written on letter-headed paper. So I wrote back and we arranged to take a look at him.

'I went myself and saw the boy in a game against some other team, I can't remember which, but he was playing for Glasgow United. The lad was about 15 and he was impressive. I decided that I liked him and told him that I would like to see him and his father. I invited them up to Parkhead for a chat.'

Eventually, Victor Davidson signed for Celtic and went on to have a distinguished career with the club which might have been even more illustrious had it not been tragically cut short by injury.

'But while I was watching Davidson that day, I saw this other boy. He was a pal of Victor's, playing on the same side. He had magnificent balance and his attitude was unusual for one so young. Even then he was strong and the other players clearly had problems getting the ball off him.'

Fallon decided he wanted to talk to the other boy as well, so he invited him to Parkhead for some training. But the lad seemed hesitant. Nevertheless, he showed up at Parkhead one day, did a spot of training and Fallon decided to try to sign him. He asked him if he would be interested in joining Celtic, but he was non-committal. Fallon was surprised. Most lads his age would give their right arm to play for Celtic. Unless, of course, they came from the wrong side of the great divide. Fallon ought to have guessed but he didn't. Although Fallon did not know it at the time, the lad had set his heart on playing for Rangers. After all, they were his team. He had been told repeatedly that Rangers would come in for him and that one day he would wear the blue of the Gers, but so far they had failed to make a move.

Sean Fallon was not a man to be put off his stride. The more he saw of the youngster, the more he liked what he saw. He was determined to sign him and, for some weeks, had been promising himself he would go and see the lad's father as soon as he had a free moment. 'Give it one more try, see if I can't talk sense into them,' he thought. The parents are often the key in such situations and it was important to see the family in its own setting.

'I won't be long,' he promised his wife as he parked the car and slammed the door. Fallon found the flat and knocked on the door. They had just finished their tea. 'I could sense there was something wrong,' he explains. 'I don't know what it was, but I felt that maybe they had had a row. It felt awkward.' When the boy saw Sean Fallon at the house, he was petrified. His bedroom walls were covered with blue-shirted players. If Fallon should come into his room and see them, he would surely walk straight out and that would be the end of Celtic's interest. The lad sneaked into his room and, while Fallon chatted with his father, he tore down the photographs of Jim Baxter and Ian McMillan, tossing them into a drawer. And with that simple gesture he ended his boyhood association with Rangers.

'I didn't say anything about signing for Celtic,' says Fallon. 'I just sat there and talked about football, this and that, the great players – Jimmy Johnstone, Charlie Tully, Bobby Evans – even a few Rangers players – Baxter, George Young. They were clearly troubled about what the lad was going to do with his future, where he was going to work. I don't think his father was too keen on him becoming a footballer. It doesn't always work out, you know. Time went by. I didn't hurry things along.'

Mrs Dalglish made a pot of tea, the two men chatted, and the youngster hovered. Fallon needed to be sure as well, to know the boy's background, his father's attitude and the depth of the relationship between father and son. He quickly realised the closeness of the family, its respectability and he liked what he saw.

'I didn't feel it was right to broach the subject of signing for Celtic straightaway, but eventually, after about an hour and a half of all this idle chat, I finally put my cards on the table. "I want the boy to sign for Celtic," I told him. It took me two hours, but I finally got the father's agreement. He could join Celtic.'

Mrs Fallon was furious. She had been sitting in the car the whole time with three wailing bairns. They were starving, she was hungry and it wasn't exactly warm either. The spring day had turned into a chilly evening and the best part of it was now gone. Their wedding anniversary was ruined. It was pointless going to the Seamill Hydro now. When her husband returned she hit the roof.

'I want to go home,' she shouted. There was little Fallon could say to appease her and they hardly spoke the rest of the evening. She asked just one question later that night. 'What's the lad's name?'

'Kenny Dalglish,' replied Fallon.

'He'd better be worth it,' she muttered.

Sean Fallon would go down in history as the man who discovered Kenny Dalglish. Twenty years on, his wife could laugh at the memory of those hours stuck in the car. 'Aye, the sacrifice was worth it,' she said, a smile as big as Celtic Park stretching across her face.

That Rangers failed to entice the young Dalglish to Ibrox will forever remain a mystery. Over the next 20 years, the Gers would have plenty of time to dwell on the question. They would regret their error for the next ten years. As Rangers slumped to second best, Celtic continued to storm to countless titles and triumphs, one of the finest periods in their history. And the man who inspired their surge in the 1970s was none other than Kenneth Mathieson Dalglish. Ibrox should have been his natural home. Raised by his father on the exploits of Alan Morton, George Young and Jim Baxter, he should have been snapped up by the men in blue. There had been plenty of opportunity to spot him. He had played for Scotland Schoolboys Under-15s team, even playing one of those internationals at Ibrox. And yet Rangers still failed to make a move for the man Sean Fallon rates as 'the finest player I have ever worked with'.

Perhaps the explanation is buried in something a later Rangers manager, Willie Waddell, said: 'We like the big, strong, powerful fellows here,' he boasted, 'with a bit of strength and solidity in the tackle rather than the frivolous, quick moving stylists like Jimmy Johnstone, small tiptoe-through-the-tulips type of players who excite the people.' They may have excited the people, but for Rangers that was not enough. They had to be big with it. Such short-sightedness was a hallmark of post-war Rangers, confirmed by Willie Stevenson, a Rangers player of the early 1960s who was later to play with Liverpool. He talked of how the dressing rooms were built for big men, where anyone under six foot could not even reach the peg on the wall. The slight, even frail-looking Dalglish could hardly have appeared an attractive proposition to them.

It's easy, in hindsight, to claim the credit and to argue that you could spot even then that Dalglish was going to be a star. Yet Sean Fallon accepts no such plaudits. 'You can never guarantee it,' he says. 'I saw the potential in Dalglish, but you never know what will happen. Players don't always develop as you want them to. It depends on how they're trained, their attitude, whether you coax them in the right way.

'I've seen plenty or players in my day who I thought would make it, but, for one reason or another, they fell by the wayside. But the thing that impressed me about Dalglish was his spirit. He loved playing, he had perfect balance and he was a brave lad.'

Jock Stein, however, was more hesitant. He wondered if Dalglish was not too slow and wasn't so sure that he would make the grade, but once Dalglish was playing reserve team football he soon convinced Stein. Billy McNeill noticed him from the start:

'Big Jock had this policy during preseason training. He always brought the youngsters in, not just young professionals but sometimes kids at school. And I remember Dalglish coming and the thing that struck me about him initially was his self assurance; the belief in himself was an interesting thing. I've heard people say that Kenny became a player, and worked at becoming a player and I think that is contradictory. I always felt he looked as if he was a player. He always seemed so positive, even as a 15-year-old. It was inevitable he would become a good player.'

Dalglish had vowed not to follow the path of many another fine Scottish footballers, drowned in alcohol, nightclubs and women. A bit of cash in the pocket, the status of being a professional footballer, a ready-made gang of lads; it was all too easy for a working-class lad who had never even had a bank account to go off the tracks. There were plenty of glaring examples. But at Parkhead, with Stein and Sean Fallon guiding him, there was little chance for Dalglish to go astray. Fortunately, he also chose his friends carefully and, in particular, fell in with one young lad who was just as dedicated and determined to succeed. His name: Danny McGrain. It was to be an important friendship and, over the years, they would sustain each other with their commitment and discipline.

Dalglish arrived at Parkhead one morning in July 1967. He and his chum McGrain had caught the number 64 bus together from Argyle Street. It was their first day; between them they would win 164 Scottish caps. Celtic immediately farmed Dalglish out to Cumbernauld United, one of their nursery sides. In the meantime, he began to serve an apprenticeship as a joiner and, as well as training with Cumbernauld, he was also tuning up at Celtic Park once a week. He did well at Cumbernauld, scoring 37 goals for them in less than a season, even hitting four on his debut. He was the stuff of dreams and good reports soon filtered back to Parkhead. Jim Reynolds of the *Glasgow Herald* was probably one of the few journalists to see him play at this age. Some years later he recalled that moment: 'I remember Kenny as a 16-year-old playing in the tough junior grade with Cumbernauld United. Even then it was obvious one was watching a special talent – a boy destined to reach the top in his profession.'

There was no stopping the young Dalglish. He wanted to sign full-time professional forms for Celtic right away and, at the end of the season, swanned in to see Jock Stein with his pal McGrain. It was not an altogether satisfactory meeting. Stein did not share Fallon's conviction that Dalglish would go all the way to the top. He still reckoned him a little sluggish and hesitated about a contract.

'Come back in a year,' he told him. 'You're doing well, stick to the job and let's see how it develops.' But there was no budging Dalglish from his resolve. It was a characteristic that had already taken shape and was to remain with him over the years. It would infuriate others but, nevertheless, Dalglish was usually right. He was determined and managed to persuade his father to go in and talk with Stein. It worked. Stein was persuaded and, within days, Dalglish had signed full-time professional terms with Celtic. Maybe Stein was just a mite worried in case the Dalglishes went across the city and offered their services to Ibrox. It was 1968. Dalglish was on his way.

He could hardly have enrolled into a better set-up, although the Liverpool club he would join in later years boasted a similar, well-organised operation on and off the field. It was only a year since Celtic had lifted the European Cup, the first British side to do so, and Parkhead was still awash with footballing legends: Billy McNeill, Bertie Auld, Bobby Lennox, Jimmy Johnstone, Tommy Gemmell and Bobby Murdoch, all members of what was perhaps the finest Celtic side of all time. What's more, most of them set a fine example to the youngsters. Confidence was sky-high, the spirit catching. Although dreams of a second European Cup had taken an early knock, Celtic had gone on to clinch the Scottish League and the Scottish League Cup. Parkhead was the place to be, Celtic the team to beat.

'In many ways, Dalglish was very lucky,' claims Billy McNeill. 'Not just Kenny, but others such as Lou Macari, Danny McGrain. They came into a club that had a very powerful first team and their introduction was not one where they were under any pressure. They were given time to develop, to mature.'

Bobby Lennox also remembers Dalglish's early days at Celtic. 'Right from the start, when he walked into Parkhead as a kid, I knew he'd be something special. When he joined in training – and remember that was with the bulk of our European Cup-winning team – he was never over-awed. He had so much class he never looked out of place.'

Dalglish could learn from those around him. You never know more about life than when you are 18. Like all ambitious kids, he was in a hurry, but there was now ample time to develop, to sharpen his skills, and to watch the distinguished brethren of the first team. Dalglish's first appearance of any note for a Celtic side was with the reserves during the 1968/9 season. He was an immediate hit and even managed an appearance in the first team, coming on as a second-half substitute for Charlie Gallagher against Hamilton Academical in a League Cup quarter-final. The date was 25 September 1968. Celtic won 4–2, but Dalglish was unable to put his name on the scoresheet and it would be another year before he again pulled on the first-team strip.

Also that season, Dalglish was initiated into his first Old Firm battle as Celtic beat Rangers 1–0 at Ibrox in a Reserve League Cup game. It may not have had quite the glamour of a first team encounter, nor the usual 70,000-plus crowd, but it was an emotional experience nonetheless. There were three teams in the section and, with just one game remaining, Rangers looked odds-on favourites to win through. Celtic were left with the daunting task of needing to score seven goals against Partick Thistle without conceding any. Not only did they manage the seven, but they added a further five as well to win 12–0. It was a game that would go down in Parkhead folklore. Lou Macari netted four of the goals and Sean Fallon could not recall a higher score during his years at Parkhead.

The Celtic View began to take note of the young Dalglish, though for some time it would spell his name wrongly. 'Kenny Dalgleigh [*sic*] is making his mark at right half,' it reported in September 1968. 'The 17-year-old has had two really good games against Dundee United in the [reserve] league and Partick Thistle and yet he is only one of the potentially great teenagers at Parkhead.'

That season, 1968/9, he made 13 appearances in the reserve league, though he hit the net only once. But he did score three goals in four appearances in the Reserve League Cup and was a member of the side that defeated Aberdeen 4–0 on aggregate in the two-legged final. The following season, he was a regular in the reserves, playing in the midfield and scoring

19 goals, including five penalties, in 31 appearances. Celtic topped the reserve league table and also went on to defeat Dunfermline Athletic 6–5 on aggregate in the Reserve League Cup final. This time Sean Fallon could afford to be even more complimentary. 'He is a highly promising young-ster,' he wrote in *The Celtic View*, 'and this is the best reserve team at Parkhead since the Billy McNeill/ Paddy Crerand days.'

It was enough for Stein to consider him for another outing with the first team. This time he was chosen to play from the start against Raith Rovers at Parkhead. It was 4 October 1969 and he was in the side for the injured Bobby Murdoch, who came and sat next to him in the dressing room as he changed. Something of a practical joker, Murdoch asked him if he was nervous. 'No, not at all,' replied the self-assured Dalglish.

'Then you'd better put your boots on the right feet,' said Murdoch. Without thinking, Dalglish glanced down to his feet as the dressing room burst into laughter. Nervous or not, Dalglish helped Celtic to a 7–1 win, though again he failed to score. He made three more first-team appear-ances that season but still drew a blank in front of goal.

The Celtic View was impressed, with former star John McPhail report-ing that 'the boy had an outstanding debut at right half against Raith Rovers, and made a splendid impact on the Celtic fans'. Jock Stein was equally enthusiastic, telling *The Celtic View* that 'he was not carried by the big first-team names. He played an effective role in the midfield. His cross-field service to Callaghan and Hughes was quite an eye-opener to the fans.' It was the first of many rave notices he would receive from Stein.

But it was the following season that Dalglish began truly to come into the reckoning. He had now firmly established himself as a reserve team play-er and made another 31 appearances in the reserve league, scoring 15 goals as Celtic retained their title. But the result of the season was undoubtedly the 10–2 aggregate victory over Rangers in the Reserve League Cup final.

By then, the reserve side had established something of a legendary repu-tation. In Celtic circles they had become known as the Quality Street Gang, so-named after the well known TV advert for a brand of chocolates. They were about to go down in Parkhead mythology. Among them were not only Dalglish, but Danny McGrain, Lou Macari, Paul Wilson, Vic Davidson, George Connelly and David Hay. It was a team bursting with talent that would go on to win over 200 Scottish caps between them. Only Davidson, whose career was cut short by injury, failed to don the blue of Scotland. By 1970, Macari, Connelly and Hay were beginning to make their mark in the first XI, but during the 1970/71 season they all made appearances in what must have been one of the finest reserve sides ever to grace Parkhead.

Four- and even five-figure crowds regularly turned up at Celtic Park to revel in the spread of talent as they swept the board, clinching every honour and competition, most notably in the reserve league where they struck 108 goals in their 34 fixtures. In total, they hit 157 goals during the season, as they also clinched the Second XI Cup and the Reserve League Cup, averaging three goals a game. The inside trio of Dalglish, Lou Macari and Vic Davidson scored more than half their goals. Between them they struck 82 times, with Vic Davidson the top scorer on 40 goals. Dalglish shot 23 and Macari 19 in an astonishing display of powerful, attacking football that rekindled memories of Celtic's famous pre-war trio of MacDonald, Crum and Divers. The previous season they had scored 118 goals in the reserve league, with Davidson hitting 43, Macari 40, Dalglish 23 and Quinn 21. Dalglish impressed so much that he made five more first team outings that 1970/71 season, even coming on as a substitute in Celtic's European Cup clash with KPV Kokkola.

Sean Fallon, who continued to look after the reserves, was becoming increasingly impressed with Dalglish: 'He has been outstanding,' he wrote in *The Celtic View* at the time, adding that 'apart from his shooting ability, he has created many chances for his colleagues.' Even today, Fallon still has fond memories of the Quality Street Gang, calling them 'the finest bunch of lads I ever managed'.

The trouncing of Rangers secured that side's position in the club's history. On 22 April 1971, the reserves cuffed their old enemy 7–1 in a reserve league game at Parkhead. Dalglish was on target four times in a memorable display. Four days later, again at Parkhead, the reserves met Rangers in the first leg of the Reserve League Cup final. The result: Celtic 4, Rangers 1. Dalglish managed just one goal this time. Then, on 30 April, in the return leg at Ibrox, Celtic produced their finest display of the season, squeezing six goals past Rangers to win 6–1 and take the Cup 10–2 on aggregate. It was a humiliation for the men in blue, though Dalglish felt no remorse as he struck another hat-trick to give him a week's total against his former idols of eight goals. Even Stein was impressed, and Dalglish was promptly called up to play in the first team for a benefit match at Rugby Park for the Kilmarnock player Frank Beattie. It was to be a personal triumph for Dalglish, as Celtic beat Kilmarnock 7–2, with the 20-year-old scoring six times. Dalglish's apprenticeship was over. He was now ready for the big time.

CHAPTER FOUR

A Stranger In Paradise

Glasgow Celtic is not just a club, or an establishment, it is a heritage.
Malky MacDonald

There is a marked sense of tradition and history attached to Scottish football that is rarely apparent south of the border. It shapes itself in a reverence for those who have passed before, conjuring up epithets such as the Wembley Wizards, the Famous Five, the Terrible Trio and the Lisbon Lions, while the names of the elite trip off the tongue: Hughie Gallacher, Jim Baxter, George Young, Alan Morton, Billy Liddell, Matt Busby and so forth. And nowhere is this done more so than at Celtic Park, where the hallowed tradition has lingered through the decades.

'The fans talk of players of fifty years ago as if they had seen them play,' says Pat Crerand. 'So vividly have the memories been passed on from father to son.' The names are immortal – Patsy Gallacher, Jimmy McGrory, John Thomson, Charlie Tully, wee Jimmy Johnstone. Soon the name of Kenneth Mathieson Dalglish would be added to the list. At Anfield, Old Trafford and Highbury, the past has all but been forgotten by comparison.

Sociologists would no doubt argue that this sentimental obsession with history is something to do with the streak of romanticism that runs through the Gaelic character; the cynics would say it is because Scottish football has never been the same since Queen's Park were a first division side. But a former Celtic hero like Malky MacDonald will tell you that 'Celtic is not just a club, or an establishment, it is a heritage.' Even Liverpool's Bill Shankly was once overheard to confess that 'Glasgow Celtic is the most successful football club in the world. And nobody can dispute that.' Little wonder the fans called Celtic Park 'Paradise'.

The 1971/2 season firmly established Dalglish as a Celtic player. He was 20 years old; willowy but with a strength that belied his weight. He was fast, though never the speediest, but in front of goal he boasted the confidence and self-assurance of someone years more experienced. But if he still had any hankerings for Rangers, they were about to be dispelled once and for all. After helping Celtic trounce Kilmarnock in Frank Beattie's benefit game by grabbing six goals, Dalglish was promoted to the first team. In his first match, in the Drybrough Cup against Dumbarton, he scored four of Celtic's five goals. But the talk that evening in the pubs was not of Dalglish's remarkable feat but of the death of the legendary Charlie Tully earlier that day. It was now impossible for Stein to do other than pick Dalglish and in the next round he justified his selection by firing a further three against St Johnstone. Including the benefit match at Kilmarnock, he had netted 13 goals in three outings.

He had begun the season in devastating style, though arguably the competition and the tournament were hardly taxing. But next in line were Rangers at Ibrox in the sectional round of the Scottish League Cup. A packed house and the Old Firm rivalry ensured that this was no game to be taken lightly, especially with his family watching. One goal up and with 20 minutes remaining, Celtic were awarded a penalty. The ball was tossed deliberately to Dalglish. He carefully placed it on the penalty spot, began his run-up, then stopped, bent down and tied his bootlace. He retraced his steps and ran in again, calmly sending the goalkeeper the wrong way. We can only speculate on his father's mixed feelings. Celtic won 2–0 and the 20-year-old had now done more than enough to guarantee himself instant elevation to the rank of hero. *The Celtic View* was impressed: 'He might have been playing in a practice match, so cool was he as he stroked the ball home,' it wrote. John Rafferty in *The Scotsman* called him 'an old-fashioned youngster'. It was a particularly accurate assessment.

Two weeks later, Celtic faced Rangers again and, with the Parkhead ground closed due to reconstruction, were forced to play at Ibrox. This time Celtic whipped their rivals 3–0, with Dalglish again on the scoresheet. In their history of Celtic Football Club, Pat Woods and Tom Campbell reckoned it was a victory inspired by the newcomer. 'The mature play of Dalglish was a revelation,' they recounted. 'He scored the important first goal by taking his chance coolly, and set up Callaghan's volley for the second by fighting for the ball and retaining it despite fierce challenges before crossing to the tall Fifer. A new star had entered the Parkhead firmament.'

Dalglish also kicked off Celtic's league season with a goal in their 9–1 win over Clyde and, in their second league game of the season, scored yet again against his former heroes at Ibrox as Celtic strode to a third triumph over Rangers. It was still early September and the youngster had already scored three Old Firm goals. There was now no turning back.

But it might well have been very different. At the beginning of the season, Manchester United had dangled a lucrative contract in front of Stein. The Big Man pondered, and was clearly tempted, but, in the end could not bear to tear himself away from his beloved Parkhead. The players repaid him for his loyalty. Celtic were about to enjoy an outstanding season. They clinched the first division title, their seventh in succession, by ten points from Aberdeen, striking 96 goals in the process. Dalglish hit 17 of them in 31 appearances, including his first senior hat-trick, against Dundee. In the Scottish Cup, Celtic went all the way to the final where they cuffed Hibernian 6–1, equalling Renton's record score of 1888. Celtic had conceded just three goals in six games while scoring 20. In the Scottish League Cup, they also marched, or perhaps raced would be a better way to describe it, to a final where they met Partick Thistle. Celtic were expected to win the trophy with ease, yet without the thoughtful McNeill, missing through injury, they were four goals adrift inside 37 minutes. It was said that when they heard this news over at Ibrox, thousands poured out of the ground and rushed towards Hampden to witness with glee their rivals' humiliation. Celtic eventually lost 4–1. In the dressing room, Stein was furious, rounding on his players for their lack of aggression and endeavour. Even Dalglish did not escape the Big Man's famous temper despite netting Celtic's only goal.

European football has a fairy-light magic of its own. The terraces packed and swaying in the cold half-light, the fans come to gawp at the clash of continental technique against good old-fashioned English application or Scottish invention, the passion of that huge, baying crowd and the sheer excitement, novelty and intrigue of the two-legged tie. It is like a fever that envelopes you in its passion. The Scots had been the first to spot its magic, sending Hibernian into the fray a year before the English even dared. And the Scots had been the first to taste its triumphs, as the Lisbon Lions outfought, outmanoeuvred and even outroared Inter Milan. It had been the finest moment in Scottish footballing history, even Rangers had to acknowledge that, and it had given Celtic Football Club a new set of priorities. Dalglish was about to catch the bug and set himself new ambitions. But while Celtic would never quite fulfil those aspirations, they would dictate the future direction of his career.

Across the continent, Celtic were still respected, the team you had to beat to win Europe's premier trophy. In the European Cup, they came again within a whisker of another final, losing in a penalty shootout in the semi-final of 1971/2 against Inter Milan. They had reached the last four after victories over Boldklub Copenhagen, Sliema Wanderers of Malta and the Hungarians Ujpest Dozsa. Facing the team they had beaten to win the European Cup in 1967, Celtic resorted to defensive tactics in the first leg at the San Siro. Dalglish had few chances as the two defences locked horns and the game drifted into a goalless draw. In front of 75,000 at Parkhead in the second leg, it was much the same; this time Inter Milan defended resolutely, just about happy with another goalless draw and prepared to risk all in a penalty shootout. Unfortunately, Dixie Deans, with the first penalty kick, visibly changed his mind as he ran up and spooned the ball high into the night air. Inter Milan won 5–4. After reaching the final two seasons previously, it was to prove a bitter disappointment for the men in green.

At the end of the campaign, Dalglish's own statistics were impressive – 49 games played, 23 goals scored, and two medals treasured. He had even won a couple of Scottish caps; sure recognition of his impact. However, by Easter, Dalglish had been visibly tiring. His runs had all the enthusiasm of youth and the early season, but his legs in front of goal lacked strength. Yet he had begun his career as he meant to continue, by winning. What's more, the terraces had promoted him to hero.

Opposite the stand at Celtic Park was a bank of terracing, covered from the hostile elements of the Scottish weather. In Parkhead folklore it was commonly known as the Jungle. Here, the hot-headed fanatics of the green and white hoops gathered every match, roaring on their favourites; here, every Celtic fan of a certain age will have stood at some stage of his career; here was where the authentic voice of Celtic resounded. This is where heroes were created and worshipped and for the lads on the terracing the fresh-faced youngster called Kenny Dalglish was now the King of the Jungle.

He was still a boy at heart. His favourite pastime, he told *The Celtic View*, was listening to Radio One and Radio Luxembourg, though he confessed that he liked to go dancing on a Saturday night. More significantly, he added that 'I don't go out much other than that.' Dalglish was dedicated to his task. He didn't even have a flash car. Instead, he lived at home with his parents, kept his hair reasonably short and dressed conservatively. Sean Fallon also verifies that Dalglish was never one for joining in the various dressing room cliques. 'He kept himself to himself,' he says, 'and he seemed to prefer the company of his girlfriend Marina to anyone else.'

Honours would continue to drift his way during the 1972/3 season, though they were harder-earned. In the league, Celtic swept to an eighth successive title. But what had looked a gentle canter to the finishing post became a frantic scramble after the New Year. A severe bout of influenza took its toll on the club, forcing the postponement of games. Then Jock Stein was taken ill with a suspected heart attack and confined to a coronary ward for observation until mid-January. Sean Fallon took over briefly, but the spirit of Stein was missing; the Big Man's fury silent. They lost 2–1 to Rangers and then 2–1 at Airdrie, and suddenly their seemingly impregnable lead was in danger of being whittled away. Rangers dropped only two points after Christmas and almost caught Celtic at the tape, the championship decided only on the final day as Celtic triumphed 3–0 at Hibernian.

The pride of Parkhead was also disrupted by the transfer of the mercurial Lou Macari, who decided to travel in search of wealth and glory south of the border. The diehards claimed it was something that would never have happened with the Lisbon Lions, whose collective pride had kept them pinned to Parkhead. The cracks were showing. In the League Cup, they again reached the final and, for the third successive year, were defeated, this time by Hibernian. They also reached the Scottish Cup final but were unfortunate enough to face a revived Rangers, who won 3–2 (after Dalglish had given Celtic an early lead) to take just a little revenge for being pipped at the post in the league. The European Cup was also a sad tale as Celtic again faced the Hungarians Ujpest Dozsa after beating Rosenborg in the opening round. At Parkhead, Celtic squeezed a narrow

2–1 win, but in Hungary Bene and Dunai tore the Celtic defence apart to score three goals inside the first 20 minutes.

For Dalglish, however, the season was another personal triumph. He was the club's top marksman, netting 23 league goals in just 32 appearances and he even missed a couple of penalties. In the League Cup he fired ten goals, with five coming in the Scottish Cup and three in Europe to give him a season's tally of 41 goals. It was to be his highest ever total.

The 1973/4 season was not an altogether happy period for the club. Even Dalglish seemed to suffer as the goals temporarily dried up. At the heart of the problem was money and an increasing urge on the part of some players to follow in Lou Macari's footsteps by opting for the fame and fortune of the Football League. Principal among them was the steely defender David Hay, who became embroiled in a messy financial dispute with the club that dragged on far longer than anyone should have allowed. Wages at Parkhead were notoriously poor by Football League standards, and the Scotland get-togethers were renowned as a breeding ground for discontent as the Anglos turned up flashing pocketfuls of notes and boasting of match-winning bonuses higher than Celtic's weekly basic pay. The highly talented George Connelly, whom Dalglish rated as highly as Franz Beckenbauer, also had his problems and stormed out of Celtic Park for a brief time. On top of that, Bobby Murdoch was transferred to Middlesbrough and Jimmy Johnstone largely confined to life in the reserves. It was all unsettling, with players seemingly no longer prepared to devote their lives to Celtic simply for the glory. Yet despite the turmoil, Celtic strode to a ninth consecutive title, pipping Hibernian by four points. In the Scottish Cup, they progressed smoothly to the final, where they slammed Dundee United 3–0. Despite 19 goals en route to lifting the Cup, Dalglish managed only one of them. And it was very much the same story in the League Cup – 23 goals scored and only three from Dalglish. But this time there was not even a winners' medal to show for it, as Celtic crashed to the only goal of the game against Dundee.

But the 1973/4 season will be best remembered for one game, the awesome clash with Atlético Madrid in the semi-finals of the European Cup. Celtic eased comfortably through the first round with a 9–1 aggregate win over the Finnish champions TPS Turku, but then in the second round they laboured woefully against Vejle BK of Denmark, drawing 0–0 at Parkhead before Bobby Lennox fired them into the last eight. That victory set up what seemed another comparatively easy task, a quarter-final tie against

Basle. Yet in Switzerland, Basle surprised everyone, Celtic included, by winning 3–2 and that was after Wilson had given Celtic an early lead. In the return leg, Celtic stormed into attack from the whistle, with Deans and Dalglish providing the early edge. But the celebrations were soon stifled as Basle snatched a couple of goals before half time. Celtic were in serious trouble, and it took a Tom Callaghan goal to drag the game into extra time, when Steve Murray finally clinched the tie for Celtic.

Atlético Madrid were clearly more formidable opponents than either Vejle or Basle, and everyone feared the worst. They were to receive much more. The first leg at Parkhead ended goalless, yet was not without incident. Three Atlético players were sent off and seven booked as the Spanish champions hacked and clawed their way through 90 shameful minutes. Parkhead had rarely witnessed more disgraceful scenes, and it was credit to the 76,000 crowd that they did not take matters into their own hands. Nobody fancied the return leg, least of all the players. Stein protested to UEFA, but his complaints fell on deaf ears; the second leg would have to go ahead as planned, and a reluctant Celtic arrived in Madrid flanked by bodyguards and a police escort. There were threats, ugly scenes and tension, all whipped up by a scurrilous Spanish press. It brought back painful memories of Celtic's ill-tempered trip to Buenos Aires to face Racing Club in the World Club Championship. There was even a death threat levelled at Jimmy Johnstone. Little wonder Celtic took the field wondering if they would return alive. Perhaps the 2–0 defeat was a safer result. Victory for Celtic might well have sparked off a major diplomatic incident to say nothing of an immediate riot. Yet despite the hostile atmosphere, Celtic had bravely held out until the final moments when their defence eventually cracked.

It was a tie Dalglish would not forget and he had the scars to prove his part in it for some time. 'It was without doubt the worst game I have ever played in as far as violence is concerned,' he wrote in his autobiography. 'I think if they had one more player sent off then the referee would have abandoned the game and we would have been awarded the tie.' But, alas for Celtic, that was not the case. Atlético were merely fined by UEFA and went on to face Bayern Munich in the final, where, thankfully, football won the day. Perhaps more importantly, the game marked a turning point in Celtic's European fortunes.

As in the previous season, Dalglish was no longer finding the net as regularly as he had in his earlier seasons. He had been repeatedly switched from striker to midfield and back again and managed just 24 goals, 18 of those coming in the league. His reputation also marched before him. In the early days, he was an unknown quantity, rarely experiencing the man-to-man marking or the physical intimidation that was to come later. By 1974, he was finding space a rare commodity and, like all strikers, was having to adapt his game to meet the new challenges. He did it more effectively than most, learning to shield the ball with his back to the goal, allowing his team mates time and space to run off him. It was to become his hallmark. And when he did it inside the penalty area, the consequences were almost inevitable.

The 1974/5 season was to underline the problems of the previous seasons. David Hay had stormed off to join Lou Macari on the yellow brick road south, George Connelly walked out once too often and it was to be Billy McNeill's final campaign. By the end of the season, Jimmy Johnstone would also part company with the club. The Celtic dream of ten titles in succession evaporated in a 3–0 New Year defeat at Ibrox, while in Europe the largely unknown Greeks, Olympiakos, dismissed the Scottish champions in the opening round. The glory that had been Europe was over; the Lisbon Lions were a team of the past. By the end of the season, even Dalglish had arrived at the conclusion that if he wanted European honours he would be lucky to find them at Parkhead.

Back in February, Ian Archer in the *Glasgow Herald* summed up the mood of the nation when he poignantly reflected: 'The crown lies shakily on Celtic's head. One little nudge and it will roll in one huge clatter, rolling down the steps of the throne from which they have ruled this Scottish kingdom for the past nine years. There should be much sadness abroad in the land.' By the end of April, there was indeed much to mourn.

There were some bonuses. Danny McGrain was maturing into one of the sturdiest defenders Scotland had seen in years and a couple of trophies were won. Celtic beat Airdrie 3–1 at Hampden to win the Scottish Cup and destroyed Hibernian 6–3 to take the Scottish League Cup. But the success of Rangers in snatching that tenth title from Celtic hurt more than anything. It spelled an end to the European Champions' Cup, breaking a relationship with the tournament that stretched back to the Lisbon Lions of 1967. It was indeed the end of an era.

Dalglish himself was approaching his zenith at Celtic Park. John McPhail, the former Celtic and Scotland star of the early 1950s, rated Dalglish at the time as 'one of the greatest ever to wear the green and white jersey of Celtic Park.' He reckoned him 'as equal, if in fact not superior, to Jimmy McGrory, Malky MacDonald, Jimmy Delaney, Willie Buchan, Charlie Tully and Jimmy Johnstone.' There could be no higher praise. But McPhail was not alone. Jim Blair of the *Glasgow Evening Times* called him 'world class', while Harry Andrew in the *Scottish Sunday Express* predicted that he would soon 'become a midfield mastermind in the Cruyff mould, dictating play, making matches run to his pattern.' Peter Black in the *Weekly News* reckoned that he was 'one of the finest footballers it has been my privilege to see, either at Parkhead or anywhere else, and I am sure he will get better.'

Now parked permanently in the midfield, chivvying away behind the front runners, he contributed fewer goals than usual, a season's total of just 21. But he was now the orchestrator, the man who shaped the patterns of play and made the team buzz. Stein had dropped him into that position to rejuvenate him. 'There have been times,' he explained, 'when he looked as if he has been too long in the firing line. When he had an indifferent spell as a striker with Celtic, we used to drop him back into the midfield for a time.' It always worked.

But if Celtic ended the season losing their crown, they were about to suffer an even greater calamity. In July, Jock Stein, returning from a holiday in Minorca, was involved in an horrific car crash on the A74 near Lockerbie that almost cost him his life. Stein and the Glasgow bookmaker Tony Queen were both seriously injured, while the three other passengers – Stein's wife, Bob Shankly and his wife – escaped with only minor injuries. Stein's Mercedes was in a head-on collision and, for a few days, Stein lay dangerously ill in hospital. Both men would eventually pull through, but it would be many more months before Stein was fit enough to resume duties at Parkhead. In the meantime, his assistant Sean Fallon stepped into the breach.

Dalglish was becoming increasingly unhappy. He could sense the limitations at Parkhead as much as anyone, probably more so. The club was entering a transitional period, still unsure of its future direction. There was no guessing how long it would be before another outstanding Celtic side appeared, nor was there any guarantee that one day such a team would evolve. Dalglish suspected that it might never happen, that Stein's magic could not last forever. Only a handful of managers have ever created more than one outstanding side. Dalglish was now 24 years old, recently married to his 'childhood sweetheart', as the papers described Marina Harkins, and if he was to move, then he would need to make the break within the next couple of years. Stein was still recovering in hospital and the new season was about to kick off. Dalglish needed to sort something out. He went to see Sean Fallon, almost apologising as he knocked on the door. 'I'm sorry to be adding to your worries, I know you have a lot of them now that the boss is in hospital and I don't like making them worse.'

But he was, and Fallon let him know in no uncertain terms. Billy McNeill had not long retired, there were injuries, a lack of experienced players, and Stein was still desperately ill. 'This is not the time to come demanding a transfer,' he replied. With his gentle Irish brogue and supportive arm, Fallon was an impossible man to contradict. 'I talked to him like a father talks to his son,' he says. 'I was simply honest and straightforward.' It would have taken a brave and stubborn man not to have caved in under such emotional blackmail.

Dalglish left Fallon, his tail between his legs, and went home to consult his wife. They both agreed that it was probably not the moment to pursue the matter any further, especially with their first baby due. Celtic had, after all, been good to Dalglish and he genuinely felt that he could not leave them in the lurch. So, reluctantly, he agreed to sign a new one-year deal. Fallon was delighted and offered him the club captaincy as a reward. 'I felt that he was entitled to it anyway, but I also reckoned it might give him some incentive.' Dalglish was thrilled; Fallon even promised to see if the board would give him more money. Dalglish readily accepted his new job; it was a role he would relish.

But Fallon was no Jock Stein. Nobody could replace the Big Man, though arguably even he would have had problems that season. Steve Murray was absent for most of the campaign through injury, George Connelly yet again stormed out, while others, like Dixie Deans, struggled to find form. The first league match of the season seemed to set the tone, a 2–1 defeat at Ibrox, although through to Christmas Celtic made the running in the new premier division. Then, on New Year's Day, Rangers again stole two points from them as Celtic's challenge began to wilt. At Easter it slumped. Defeats against Dundee United, Hibernian and Ayr United, plus draws with Aberdeen and Rangers at Parkhead, settled the matter. Celtic had not simply lost the championship, they had carelessly tossed it away. Fallon fumed. We can only imagine what Stein would have said.

Nor was there relief elsewhere. In the Scottish Cup, Celtic crashed at the first hurdle, going down 3–2 at Motherwell. The League Cup looked more promising as Celtic gradually edged their way towards the final, only to be beaten by Rangers, now very much the top dogs of Scottish soccer. Dalglish was already regretting his decision to remain at Parkhead. They could hardly have done any worse without him.

'During the latter part of his Celtic days, there was no doubt that he was single-handedly carrying the team,' says Billy McNeill. Tommy Burns agrees, 'But for Kenny Dalglish and Danny McGrain, Celtic would have had to face up to certain harsh facts a long while before they had to confront the truth. They carried Celtic on their backs.' Celtic were in decline and the insiders knew it.

In the European Cup-Winners' Cup, they progressed smoothly through the early rounds with wins over Reykjavik of Iceland and Boavista of Portugal, but then ran up against Sachsenring Zwickau, the little known East German side. The latter having knocked out Panathinaikos and Fiorentina, Celtic should perhaps have given the Germans more respect, but they were about to enter their spring slide and carelessness was in the air. The East Germans scraped a last minute draw at Parkhead after Dalglish had given Celtic the lead and then won 1–0 back home.

The cupboard was bare. For the first time in 12 years, Celtic Football Club had failed to win a major trophy. For the Celtic fans, the 1975/6 season had been a disaster, a humiliation. A generation had grown up knowing nothing but success and now they had to get used to being second best. It came hard, even for an ex-Rangers boy like Dalglish. One season as skipper and they had won nothing. But at least there was hope on the horizon, with Jock Stein returning to Parkhead after his long convalescence. Surely he could sort it all out.

Dalglish had been offered a new contract, but his reservations still lingered. He figured it was time for another chat with the manager. But if Fallon was a difficult man to contradict, Stein was impossible. He would hear nothing of Dalglish's transfer demands and instead persuaded him that there was a rosy future at Parkhead, that trophies would soon be shining once more from the shelves and that he had his eyes on a couple of new signings. Besides which, Celtic was the greatest football club in the world and he simply could not understand why Dalglish should wish to go anywhere else. Privately, he was convinced that the Anglos in the Scotland squad were turning his head. Dalglish denied this and still refused to sign the contract. He went away to reconsider. The negotiations continued for some time, well into the following year, 1977, when Dalglish's hand was finally forced. Celtic were due to play Rangers in the Scottish Cup final and Dalglish needed to reregister with the Scottish FA in order to be eligible to play. A refusal to sign a new contract would clearly have splashed his name across the back pages. So far he had managed to keep the lid on his dispute, but if it was to leak out it would only add to the problem. As club captain he had a responsibility. Once more, Dalglish had to climb down and re-sign but he promised himself that there would be no more debate; he was going and would not be persuaded otherwise.

Dalglish had been about to begin his final season at Parkhead when Stein, as promised, immediately moved to improve the side. Pat Stanton from Hibernian and Joe Craig from Partick Thistle were both enlisted, with former Rangers boy Alfie Conn joining up later in the season. Stein even consulted Dalglish about the Conn signing, wanting to know what the dressing-room reaction would be to signing an ex-Rangers player. Dalglish told him to go ahead. It was to pay dividends. After a sluggish start – just five points from their opening five fixtures – Celtic eventually settled to produce an impressive run of 13 victories in 14 outings. By the time Alfie Conn arrived in March 1977, they were well on their way to snatching the League title. In the League Cup they had raced to the final, only to be beaten 2–1 by Aberdeen. It had been their 13th final in succession. But there was better fortune in the Scottish Cup, and the sweet smell of revenge, as Celtic sneaked a 1–0 victory over Rangers in the final, Dalglish having re-signed in time for the clash. Celtic had completed the double for a remarkable sixth time in Stein's 12 years at Parkhead.

The Scottish Cup final was to prove almost Dalglish's final game in the green and white hoops of Celtic. It was fitting that he should have skippered the side to the double and, as the final whistle blew, the first men to throw their arms around each other were Stein and Dalglish, master and pupil. At that moment they could celebrate but in a few months' time Stein would have to accept that their long and fruitful association was about to end.

Ironically, Dalglish almost lost his Cup final medal within minutes of receiving it. As he trotted around Hampden celebrating, he stopped to show it to some disabled children near the touchline. Just as he held it up to them, someone jolted his arm and the medal flew out of his hand. He immediately started scrambling around looking for it, but nowhere was it to be found. Peter Latchford, joined him as did trainer Neil Mochan, and, convinced that it had fallen behind the advertising hoardings, they began to tear them apart. Finally, the police intervened and, with Dalglish almost in tears, they persuaded him to get on with his lap of honour and leave it to them. The medal was eventually retrieved and returned; it had fallen into the umbrella of one of the fans in a wheelchair.

Given Celtic's return to fortune, and the promise of European Cup football, Dalglish might have been expected once more to reconsider his threat to leave, but a first round exit in the UEFA Cup earlier that season had only underlined Celtic's shortcomings in Europe. Winning trophies in Scotland was one thing, winning them in Europe was another. That result merely strengthened his resolve. Both Stein and Dalglish were honest and astute enough to realise that Celtic fell some way short of being a good European side. Stein called it 'a blessing in disguise'.

Tommy Burns spotted it just as clearly. 'Kenny was absolutely correct to get out when he did,' he says. 'He had done all he possibly could with Celtic and I think he knew that. At the time, Celtic simply could not provide him with the quality of fellow players to complement his skills and Liverpool were also making a considerable impression on Europe, something we were far from up to at Celtic Park.'

In many respects, Dalglish had had a mixed season. He had captained Scotland and led Celtic to the double, but he had also been unusually inconsistent, switched from midfield one week to up front the next. It resulted in his lowest league tally of goals since he had become a regular, just 14, although his ten in the League Cup more than compensated. Even Stein described his year as 'patchy'.

During the season, Dalglish talked with a number of Anglo Scots, trying to fathom where best he should rest his skills. Liverpool were always top of that list. Twice winners of the UEFA Cup, they were about to lift the European Cup and were without any doubt the strongest side in British football. 'What impressed me most about Liverpool was that they were still ambitious and greedy,' he later said.

Manchester United remained another possibility. Lou Macari recommended United and his old Scotland boss, Tommy Docherty, was still in charge at Old Trafford, though not for much longer. United were always likely to be engaged in European soccer and in Dalglish's book, European football was a key factor. The money would probably be better at Old Trafford as well, although wages were not a motivating factor in this instance. Tottenham Hotspur were also considered, but they looked to be heading for the second division, making European football an unlikely possibility. Elsewhere in London, there was Arsenal, winners of the double in 1971, but not quite so successful by 1977 and certainly not likely to achieve much in Europe. There was also the option of Liverpool's neighbours Everton, once known as the 'Millionaires' club' but very much in Liverpool's shadow in recent years. That left one other club – Nottingham Forest. Managed by Brian Clough, they were an intriguing possibility but Clough was not then renowned for forking out huge sums of money for players, preferring instead to develop homegrown talent. He might baulk at the kind of fee Celtic were bound to ask, In the end, Billy McNeill reckons it came down to two clubs – Liverpool and Manchester United, and, ironically, the two sides lined up against each other in the 1977 Cup final. Manchester United with their glamour, ambition and smattering of Scots – Buchan, Macari and Docherty; Liverpool with their pedigree and guile.

Dalglish did his homework on the leading English sides and talked to a few friends, and Liverpool began to emerge as favourites. It was not an easy decision, though if he had any doubts they would have been resolved by July. By then Docherty had been sacked by United and Liverpool were the European champions with a spare £500,000 in their pockets from the sale of Kevin Keegan. What's more, they were in the market for a player to replace Keegan and had earmarked Dalglish for that role.

Dalglish arrived back from Scotland's summer tour of South America convinced he had to leave Parkhead. His future had still not been settled. Celtic were about to undertake a pre-season tour of Australia and the Far East and, as club captain, Dalglish was expected to lead that tour. Dalglish knew he could not go. His absence was bound to lead to speculation and cause a furore. Neither Celtic nor the fans would like it. But the time had finally arrived for a showdown.

CHAPTER FIVE
From Paradise To Paradise

*Sailors love this Liverpool; and upon long voyages to distant parts of the globe, will
be continually dilating upon its charms and attractions, and extolling it above all
other sea ports in the world. For in Liverpool they find their paradise.*
Herman Melville, *Redburn*

It all began in Barcelona, the night Kevin Keegan's head was turned. The
date, 30 March 1976. Liverpool had just delivered an Oscar-winning performance against the might of Barcelona beneath the glittering lights of
the Nou Camp Stadium. It was the first leg of their UEFA Cup semi-final
and Liverpool had stormed to a famous 1–0 victory, thanks partly to a John
Toshack goal but mainly to the tireless efforts and bubbling enthusiasm of
one man – Kevin Keegan. Almost alone the little man, who had cost
Liverpool a mere £35,000, had destroyed a team that boasted two of the
finest and most expensive players in Europe, Dutch internationals Johan
Cruyff and Johan Neeskens. A crowd of 85,000 watched in awe as Keegan
and his team-mates overwhelmed one of the greatest clubs in European
soccer. By the time the two teams met again, a fortnight later at Anfield,
the Barcelona manager, Hennes Weisweiler had been sacked.

As Keegan returned triumphantly to the dressing rooms, clutching his souvenir Barcelona shirt, it dawned on him that Liverpool, and in particular Kevin Keegan, were not out of place in such stately surroundings. The dressing rooms were almost as huge as Liverpool's training ground, there was even a chapel, and the stadium and its facilities were something to behold. The press were in raptures, surrounding Keegan, who was the centre of attraction. The following morning his photograph would be splashed across every sports page in Europe. 'You would have thought he was the only player in our team,' recalled one of his colleagues cuttingly, some years later. But there was no denying that Keegan's performance against one of Europe's finest clubs had catapulted him on to the world stage.

The contrast with English league soccer could not have been more harshly exposed. 'This was something else,' he thought. 'Suddenly my eyes were opened. I felt envious of the Barcelona players, enjoying such facilities and glamour every day of the week. For the first time I felt "I want to be part of this." And then I realised there was no reason on earth why I should not be a part of it,' he recalled.

Keegan's conversion to continental football was under way. Early in 1977 the Liverpool striker finally made up his mind: he wanted to try his luck on the continent. After six glorious years at Anfield that had brought League championship, FA Cup and UEFA Cup honours, as well as the title Footballer of the Year, he felt it was time to broaden his horizons. Keegan informed the Liverpool manager Bob Paisley of his decision early that year. His mind was set: he and his wife had decided that they would like to taste European soccer at the highest level. Keegan knew he would be able to take his pick of any number of clubs – Real Madrid, Barcelona, Juventus, Inter Milan – they were all likely to come in with an offer.

Paisley was hardly surprised. It had been the talk of the back pages for several months and a number of European clubs had already made tentative inquiries, including Barcelona's illustrious rivals Real Madrid. The Spanish giants had even agreed a £650,000 fee with Paisley and John Smith after a secret meeting during the 1976 close season. Keegan mulled over the offer but eventually decided to give Liverpool a final year in the hope that they might capture the coveted European Cup, the one trophy above all others that Keegan wanted to lift. Paisley now knew he had to find a replacement, although of course he would continue to try and dissuade Keegan from moving abroad.

Keegan was a vital component to the Liverpool goal-scoring machine, having formed a formidable striking partnership with the tall Welshman John Toshack. Paisley could barely afford to let him go but he was faced with little alternative. Replacing him seemed an impossible task that could spell the end of Liverpool's astonishing reign of supremacy. For Paisley, it was to be the biggest test of his managerial career.

Paisley seemed to have been at Anfield most of his life. He had joined the club shortly before the outbreak of war as a tough half back, forged in the traditions of North East football with the famous Bishop Auckland side. The then Liverpool manager, George Kay, decided to throw him a chance in professional soccer but war intervened and Paisley did not make his Football League debut until September 1946. In between he helped liberate Rome. Also making his Anfield debut that day in September 1946 was Billy Liddell and Liverpool ran riot, hitting seven goals against Chelsea, before going on to clinch the League title.

Paisley may not have been the most stylish back of the post-war era but he was indefatigable and reliable. Few forwards managed to get the better of him yet he was never honoured by his country, nor featured on cigarette cards. Quiet and evasive, he always shunned the limelight. The highlight of his career came in 1947 when Liverpool clinched their fifth championship and his greatest disappointment came in 1950 after he had scored against Everton in the FA Cup semi-final at Maine Road to give Liverpool a Cup final clash with Arsenal. It should have earned him a place in the team for Wembley but sadly he had been deputising that day for the injured Laurie Hughes. When Hughes was fit again, Paisley found himself dropped. It was a bitter frustration but he accepted it graciously.

When Paisley's playing days came to an end in 1954, he was immediately invited by manager Don Welsh to join the backroom staff. After Welsh's departure two years later, Phil Taylor took over, and Paisley hung on to his precious coaching job. When Shankly arrived in 1959, he was more than delighted to have Paisley as his number two. Throughout the Shankly era, Paisley was at his side, his ears and eyes on the training field, his spy on continental expeditions, his scout on transfer missions, his physiotherapist in the treatment room. And when Shankly sensationally resigned in 1974, Paisley was not only the obvious choice but by far the most popular. Paisley was everyone's favourite uncle, although, as they were to discover, he also had a ruthless streak in him.

Kevin Keegan's dreams finally came true. On the evening of Wednesday, 25 May 1977, Liverpool, already League champions, added the

European Cup to their growing collection of honours when they defeated Borussia Moenchengladbach 3–1 in one of the most exciting European
finals in years. The bustling Keegan even had his own personal moment of
glory when Berti Vogts, finally despairing of his unceasing trickery, upended him as he powered into the penalty area. Phil Neal converted the
penalty for Liverpool's third goal.

Long before the final, Keegan had agreed a £500,000 transfer to
Hamburg, a move which surprised many who had expected him to opt for
the glamour of Spain or Italy. Keegan had played his final game for
Liverpool. As Paisley soaked in the atmosphere on that gloriously warm
night in Rome, his mind turned once more to thoughts of a replacement.
Liverpool had promised their supporters someone of the highest quality. If
necessary, they were prepared to spend the entire record £500,000 they
had received from Hamburg. The supporters, showering in the Trevi foun-
tain and snaking their way around the Eternal City in an ever-lengthening
conga, deserved the best. But the question was 'Who?'

Bob Paisley had long been an admirer of Kenny Dalglish. He had no
memories of the scrawny teenager who had turned up at Anfield for a trial
back in the mid-60s, and would no doubt have preferred to forget that they
could have signed the promising 15-year-old for a few pounds. Instead,
Dalglish had returned to Glasgow, and the chance of a Dalglish-Keegan-
Toshack partnership never materialised. Along the football grapevine, Paisley
had heard whispers that Dalglish was unsettled.

It was also known that Dalglish had wanted to leave Celtic earlier but
the serious injury to Jock Stein following his car crash had made it a difficult moment to demand a transfer request as Dalglish felt a sense of
loyalty to the club. It was hardly the appropriate time to leave. However,
Paisley did make an initial inquiry to Celtic, hoping that he might be able
to partner the young Scot with Keegan, but he was given a firm rebuff.
Dalglish was not for sale. 'But if he ever is, I'll let you know first,' promised
Stein.

It came as something of a surprise to Paisley, when he returned home
from Rome a year later to receive a call from the Celtic manager. Stein
told him that Dalglish wanted away from the club: 'I can't understand why
anyone should want to leave Celtic,' Stein told Paisley. 'Perhaps he needs
the money.' It was the only rationale Stein could put behind Dalglish's rest-
lessness. But the fact was that Dalglish wanted a move and the Celtic board
had agreed to his request. Stein was not happy. 'I don't want to let him go,'

he told Paisley, 'and I shall continue to try and keep him here. But in the event of my failing you can have first choice.'

Paisley asked if anyone else was interested. 'Only if I announce it,' he replied. 'But I don't intend to telegraph it.'

Stein's phone call was the spark and Paisley lost no time in informing John Smith, the Liverpool chairman, of his interest in the Celtic player. Smith, similarly, had no hesitation. He trusted Paisley's instincts and knew enough about football himself to agree that Dalglish was a big name, big enough to appease the Liverpool fans, disappointed at losing their favourite, and big enough to continue Liverpool's glory roll. A meeting was set up in Glasgow between Stein, Paisley and various club representatives.

It soon emerged that Dalglish was indeed happy to play for Liverpool. But it was also clear that Stein was stalling. He was reluctant to lose Dalglish and was doing everything in his power to hold him at Parkhead. He even asked Billy McNeill to have a quiet word with the young man. Stein wanted further time to consider and, as Paisley guessed, further time to keep coaxing Dalglish to stay. Their first meeting broke up unsatisfactorily, and Paisley returned to Liverpool still not sure whether the transfer was on or not. He waited patiently but there was no news from Parkhead; no telephone call as promised. The only item of interest was that Dalglish had decided against joining Celtic's summer tour to the Far East and Australia. Instead, he was remaining at home. It did not make him popular with the fans. He had only recently returned from a tour of South America with Scotland and although this provided a convenient excuse, the word around the Glasgow pubs was that Dalglish had again asked for a transfer.

Paisley guessed, and rightly, that Stein had failed to make any headway in persuading his protégé to stay. The Liverpool manager immediately contacted John Smith and advised him to telephone Jock Stein in the Far East to see if they could finalise a deal. Smith spoke with Peter Robinson and they tried to contact Stein and his party. When they eventually tracked him down in Singapore, they discovered him in low spirits. The news could hardly have been worse. Celtic, without Dalglish, were having a dreadful tour. 'If this is the way they're going to perform without Dalglish, then we are going to have to do all in our powers to hang on to him,' he told Liverpool. The loss in 1974 of David Hay to Chelsea and Lou Macari to Manchester United a season before that had been a bitter blow and had taken its toll. The Far East tour had been designed by Stein to find a settled team in time for their first European games. It was not working.

Stein was far from happy. He could not understand why his skipper should want to leave Celtic; in his eyes the greatest club in the world. What could any player hope to find elsewhere that could not be found at Parkhead? 'Let me have one more try at persuading him,' pleaded Stein. 'I need to talk to him again when we get home.' Paisley reluctantly agreed but began to wonder if he would ever get his man. 'If we are going to sign him,' Paisley told him, 'we need to have his signature before 'the European deadline.' The two men agreed that a final decision needed to be made but it had not been a satisfactory telephone conversation.

By now, Paisley had set his heart on signing Dalglish and was not going to be fobbed off by Stein. As soon as Celtic returned home from their tour, Paisley decided to give Stein another call. 'Bob, if I can, I'll try to keep him,' Stein repeated again and again, still refusing to accept the inevitable. Paisley, Smith and chief executive Peter Robinson conferred. They needed a decision soon. The August deadline for European registration was nearing and the papers were linking Liverpool to just about every unsettled player in the Football League. The three men decided on a different tack. They would go back to Parkhead and talk with the Celtic directors to see if they could upstage Stein. Paisley cancelled his holidays and the three men made their way to Glasgow for a make-or-break session with Celtic.

Much to their surprise, they discovered that there were no problems as far as the board was concerned. Dalglish was going and that was it. Stein might like to keep him, but it was clear that Dalglish did not wish to stay and there was no point in hanging on to a man who no longer wanted to play for Celtic. The board had made their decision. All that needed to be agreed was the fee. Stein was asked to join them. He was not happy. He was losing his finest player and would fight to the bitter end to keep him. He scowled and fidgeted, making his distaste all too obvious.

No fee had been mentioned during their previous meetings, so Liverpool threw in the figure of £300,000, a fee that would have been close to breaking the British transfer record, and considerably more than Celtic had received from Chelsea for David Hay. The directors were almost rubbing their hands with glee, but Stein shook his head. 'No way,' he said, knowing full well that Liverpool had more than £500,000 sitting in the bank after the Keegan deal. The Celtic board called for an adjournment and both sides broke for ten minutes. When they returned, the Celtic directors informed Liverpool that the £300,000 fee was not enough. Smith and Paisley were hardly surprised and had agreed during the break to continue upping the price at ten per cent increments until they reached £400,000. That would be their top price. When £330,000 was offered Celtic still refused to budge. Then it went to £360,000. Still they said no. Finally Liverpool offered £400,000. The Celtic directors looked delighted, but Stein, who by now was conducting the negotiations on Celtic's part, shook his head. They looked to have reached a deadlock. Stein sensed that Liverpool were at their limit and did not want to jeopardise the entire deal.

'I think if you were to suggest another ten per cent we could agree,' he urged. There were gentle nods from the Celtic officials. Paisley looked at Smith. This was it, make or break. Smith knew Paisley wanted Dalglish. Smith also knew that Liverpool needed him. They would still be making a small profit after the Keegan deal. If he refused, another club might be in like a shot. For the sake of £40,000, he nodded.

Liverpool had their man. It was almost midnight. Celtic Park was deserted save for the bright light still burning in the boardroom. The British transfer record had been smashed. All Liverpool had to do now was agree personal terms with Dalglish but nobody anticipated any hitch there. Celtic were not renowned as particularly generous employers and there would be no problem in more than matching their terms.

Dalglish was finally tracked down at his father-in-law's pub in Rutherglen, where he was chatting with goalkeeper Peter Latchford. His wife called him and told him that Stein had been trying to get hold of him; he was to call Stein at Parkhead immediately. All day, rumours had been flying around Glasgow. Bob Paisley had been reported to have visited Parkhead, watching Dalglish from the stands, but when their game against Dunfermline had ended there had been no contact. Dalglish had lingered, wondering if something was about to break, waiting anxiously for someone to tell him some news. But there was no official word from anyone until he spoke to Jock Stein late that evening.

'Liverpool are here,' said Stein. 'They've made an offer and want to speak to you, unless of course you've changed your mind about going.' Dalglish had not. He had his wish. He had single-mindedly pursued a move. He had talked with other players and knew that Liverpool was the club he wanted. He quickly left his father-in-law, saying little, and jumped into his car. As he drove to Parkhead through the quiet streets of Glasgow, he knew that his career at Celtic was over. He was about to change the green and white hoops of Celtic for the all red of the European champions, Liverpool.

He realised that he was taking a gamble but there are times when you know that the risk has to be taken. He was confident that he could succeed and there were few doubts in his mind that he would make the transition. He could not face the prospect of remaining at Parkhead for the rest of his career. Dalglish recognised that to make any progress he had to accept a new challenge. It was time to say goodbye to their bungalow in Newton Mearns and to Paradise. He couldn't help but keep his fingers crossed and hope that Liverpool would be another paradise.

It took a mere five minutes for Liverpool's chairman John Smith to outline the terms. Dalglish listened carefully, digested them and agreed. Hands were shaken and it was decided that Dalglish would travel down to Liverpool the following day, where he would formally sign following a medical.

After Dalglish had departed, the Celtic directors produced the traditional bottle of malt whisky to seal the deal. Even Jock Stein managed a smile but deep down he was angry. He knew the value of Dalglish. Celtic might have £440,000 in the bank, but they would not have Dalglish and he knew which he would prefer. The Celtic directors had virtually signed their own death warrant.

To this day Sean Fallon remains convinced that Stein could have kept his man. He was astonished at Stein's climbdown. Both he and Stein had been determined to keep Dalglish at Parkhead but in the final round of talks Stein had capitulated. 'Celtic,' insists Fallon, 'could have held on to him. He could have been pressured to stay.' There had been much talk at Parkhead about Dalglish and his business venture. Dalglish had been a non-executive director of the Albyn Bonding Company, a whisky-bonding business based in Airdrie which had found itself in severe financial difficulties that year and in May had been placed in the hands of a receiver.

'Celtic could have solved that problem,' maintains Fallon. 'After all, ways were found of sorting out Jock Stein's enormous gambling debts.' Fallon reckons they could have held a testimonial or given Dalglish a substantial rise. But perhaps that is all wishful thinking. There is no evidence to suggest that a pay-off from Celtic would have kept him at Parkhead. He was determined to leave; he was ambitious and ready for a bigger stage.

The deal undoubtedly made Dalglish richer, as he would have received a cut of the transfer fee. 'It never at any time had anything to do with money,' he told Hugh Keevins of *The Scotsman*. 'I had to know if I could make it somewhere else, and I wanted that place to be England. What I did not want was to go through the rest of my life wondering what might have been without putting myself to the test.'

'He had achieved all he could at Celtic,' says his former colleague Billy McNeill. 'He was ready for a new challenge.' Although McNeill was no longer part of the Celtic set-up, Jock Stein had called him one day and asked him to have a chat with Dalglish, to see if he could persuade him to stay. 'I tried,' says McNeill. 'But it was almost as if he had chosen Liverpool. He had decided where his next career move lay. Liverpool had just won the European Cup and that was where he wanted to be. There was no persuading him to stay. It was almost as if Liverpool didn't pick Kenny Dalglish; Kenny Dalglish picked Liverpool. Why not pick Manchester United, Arsenal or Tottenham? It was instinctive. They were made for each other. He had mapped out his career.'

McNeill comments, however, that Dalglish was not the most popular player on the terraces. 'I was surprised when he went. Astonished. But he had never been accepted by some. Possibly because he was a Rangers boy. Maybe he just wasn't flamboyant enough. They like their stars to be flamboyant at Celtic. He was never accepted to the degree he should have been by Celtic fans. It was always a grudging appreciation. I remember going to see Celtic play at Motherwell once and they lost. I was up in the stands and I ended up in a heated exchange with people around me who were blaming Kenny. If things went well, it was great, but if they didn't, they would say it was Kenny's responsibility.'

There will probably always be speculation over Jock Stein's role in the affair. For a period, Stein and Fallon fell out over the deal. 'I don't know what happened,' says Fallon. 'I just believe that Jock could have kept him at Parkhead.' A year later, Jock Stein was given a testimonial match against, of all clubs, Liverpool. A crowd of 60,000 turned up, raising more than £150,000 and no doubt helped to pay off more of Stein's gambling debts. By then, Stein had handed over the reins of power to Billy McNeill and taken a commercial job with the club. In effect, his new job was a snub from the board, who had had more than their share of problems from the Big Man. Stein could never reconcile himself to the new post and, before the new season was even under way, departed for the lucrative managerial chair at Leeds United.

Bill Shankly, for one, was astonished that Stein could even consider selling Dalglish. The man who had discovered Kevin Keegan, the player Dalglish had been bought to replace, reckoned it was a resigning matter. 'It is the most unbelievable thing I have ever known,' he said. 'It took my breath away. I understand that, like Kevin Keegan, Dalglish wants to get on but I would have moved heaven and earth to keep him. I would rather have quit and got out of the game altogether than sold a player of his brilliance.'

Whether or not the Jock Stein testimonial was connected with Dalglish's departure, the former Celtic star's return to play in that game at Parkhead was not a happy affair. Long before he arrived in the city, there was a whisper of a concerted campaign against him. The word circulated that he would be booed from start to finish. And that was precisely how it turned out. Dalglish had heard of it and was prepared, even warning his fellow Liverpool players of what might happen. The long tradition of courtesy and respect for former Celtic players when they return to Parkhead was suddenly forgotten. To the final whistle, Dalglish had to endure the taunts of the crowd, the bitterness of the fans left ringing in his ears. It could not have been a pleasant occasion, although it seems to have done little to affect his relationship with Parkhead.

Ironically, 12 months after Keegan had departed these shores for Hamburg, he too returned to Anfield to face Liverpool in the European Super Cup. Hamburg were destroyed by Dalglish, losing 6–0, with Keegan booed every time he touched the ball. Both sets of fans were bitter at the departure of their favourite gods. It was perhaps understandable. The rifts with Parkhead and its terraces were eventually healed, so when Dalglish took a Liverpool side to Celtic to play an emotional first match after the Hillsborough tragedy, he and his team were given a moving welcome, the tears welling in Dalglish's eyes as the vast crowd chanted his name over and over again.

But the truth was that Dalglish needed to leave Parkhead to achieve the kind of success he craved. It may irk Celtic fans to admit it but it is doubtful that Celtic would have achieved much had Dalglish remained with them. Dalglish and Stein knew it. So did the more astute fans. Celtic historian Pat Woods says: 'You could see the writing was on the wall.' The club was in a transitional stage, many of the great names had retired, others had moved south and the younger players had yet to make an impact. The season after Dalglish left Parkhead, Celtic finished fifth in the premier division, going out of the European Cup in the second round and the Scottish Cup in the fourth. Their only success was to reach the League Cup final, where they were beaten by Rangers. It was Celtic's worst season in years. Jock Stein was set to quit. Kenny Dalglish had unwittingly helped bring about the end of an era.

CHAPTER SIX
Kenny's From Heaven

We speak with an accent exceedingly rare,
Meet under a statue exceedingly bare
And if you want a cathedral
We've got one to spare
In my Liverpool home.
Modern Liverpool folk song

Liverpool is a city not unlike Glasgow. Ships, the smell of sea and salt, unemployment, deprivation, grey, anonymous tenement blocks towering across scarred wastelands. In places, even the colour of the stone looks familiar. Only the accents are different. Glasgow today may be slightly wealthier, more active and certainly grander but a decade or two ago, you would have had trouble telling them apart. Generations have sweated in these Liverpool docks building ships, loading cargo, sailing the seas, only to find that in recent years the trade that once reaped fortune and reputation has swung from the Americas to Europe. With the lowering of the Union Jack over the Empire came depression. The busy docks and the lofty warehouses of Jesse Hartley that had once flourished slid into silent decline. The

Pier Head, and its Liver Buildings, no longer welcomes travellers or waves a last, sad farewell to those bound for the New World. And yet, despite all, there remains a municipal pride, an irrational and overpowering conviction in both Glasgow and Liverpool, that their city is better than any other.

Just as Glasgow frowns down on the rest of Scotland, so Liverpool cocks a snook at the South. There are five countries in Great Britain, joke Liverpool comedians – England, Ireland, Scotland, Wales and Merseyside. No doubt Glaswegians claim much the same about their city. There is also little doubt that Liverpudlians revel in the image of themselves as a set apart from the rest of the nation, something special. It's an extravagance which others misinterpret as 'a chip on the shoulder', though there is more than an ounce of truth in the suggestion that Liverpudlians have a persecution complex. It has been finely developed after years of hardship and bad deals from Whitehall. To survive in either city you need a sense of humour and, if it's not there to begin with, they soon drum it into you. You have to learn to give and take. Taking the piss they call it.

It's all connected with the Celtic nature, the Irish influence, call it what you will. You can't mistake it. It dwells in the soul of the city and its people. Liverpool is as much governed by its Irish roots as Glasgow. In 1780 there were barely 5,000 Irish in the city. By 1820, the numbers had doubled and even before the Great Famine it already stood at 35,000. But as the terrible events of 1847 took their toll, so the Irish fled in their hundreds of thousands across the Irish Sea. In January 1847, they were pouring off the boats at the rate of 900 a day; by April the numbers peaked at 3,000 a day. Half a million had arrived. Most moved on, many returned home but more than 100,000 remained in the city of Liverpool, forming almost a third of the population. They brought with them their Celtic heritage, their Catholic culture, their naked emotions.

It's long been claimed that Glaswegians feel more at home in Liverpool than anywhere else. Perhaps for that reason alone, Scottish footballers have been more attracted to Merseyside than anywhere else. London has a reputation for destroying talent, with its proliferation of bars, nightclubs and flashy girls playing on many a Scottish weakness. Newcastle is too near home; Manchester is fine if you come from Irish Catholic stock; and Birmingham… well, Birmingham is Birmingham, anonymous and unfriendly. Liverpool is more like an extended family; a welcoming and supportive arm. There's safety here, they'll look after you, make sure you don't get up to too much mischief. And if you do, they won't desert you like the others.

Anfield has always attracted the Scots. The first ever Liverpool team, taking the field for a friendly against Rotherham Town at Anfield in September 1892, was composed entirely of Scotsmen. It went down in history as 'the team of the Macs'. Following the cataclysmic split in the club that led to a majority of members storming out and forming a new club which they called Everton, the new secretary/manager John McKenna had been sent on a recruitment drive north of the border. That was where the skilled ballplayers were found, at clubs such as Queen's Park, Renton and Dumbarton. In all, McKenna signed 13 Scots. Later, he returned north again, signing the enigmatic George Allan, the first Liverpool player to be capped by Scotland and then bought the elegant Alex Raisbeck from Stoke, one of four outstanding Scots to be associated with Liverpool.

The tradition lingered. During the 1920s, the club brought Scottish international goalkeeper Kenny Campbell to Anfield along with four other Scots, all destined to become internationals. In February 1936, they brought another distinguished Scot to Merseyside, Matt Busby, signing him for £8,000 from Manchester City and immediately resurrecting his flagging career. Two years later, Liverpool had signed another Celt who was to have an important influence on the club's fortunes: Billy Liddell, a frail-looking winger who hailed from Dunfermline. Although he did not make any appearances until peace had returned after wartime, Liddell was to become not only one of the finest wingers ever to emerge from north of the border but one of the most loyal servants Liverpool Football Club ever employed.

But if Raisbeck and Liddell ranked among Anfield's immortal Scots, one was to arrive at the end of 1959 who would surpass even their fame. Yet he was not a player, he was a manager and his name was Bill Shankly.

Shankly joined with Liverpool's fortunes at their lowest ebb. They were a second division side, performing in a first division stadium in front of first division crowds. Yet what Shankly discovered was a club lacking ambition. They had suffered five seasons scrambling to escape the second division, and at one point had gone six months without a win at Anfield. Even more humiliatingly, in the previous season's Cup they had crashed at the first hurdle, beaten 2–1 by non-league Worcester City. After a 1–0 defeat at Huddersfield Town they spotted the man they thought could rescue them from further catastrophe. Over the next 14 years, Shankly would transform Liverpool from a slumbering giant into League champions, Cup winners and one of the finest teams in Europe. Shankly brought Scottish pride, providence, flair and fanaticism to Anfield. He understood the people of Liverpool, their hopes, their suffering. 'Liverpool was made for me and I was made for Liverpool,' he once boasted.

It was hardly surprising, then, that Shankly should venture north of the border for his first, and probably most important, signings, Ron Yeats and Ian St John, and build his team around them. Liverpool, at that time, were not renowned for their big spending, unlike Everton. Liverpool had broken the bank to pay for Yeats and St John. But Shankly promised it would be worth it and they quickly recouped their outlay. They were soon joined by other Scots: Willie Stevenson, Ian Ross, Bobby Graham and Peter Cormack. All came and gave outstanding service. He tried to buy Denis Law from his old club Huddersfield but the Liverpool board gave an emphatic 'no'; they could not afford him.

Within a couple of seasons Shankly was guiding Liverpool back towards their rightful home in the first division. These were the days of the Mersey sound: the Beatles, Gerry and the Pacemakers, and the Searchers. The eyes of the nation were focused on the city and, almost as if they were drawing strength from Merseyside's newfound fame, Liverpool Football Club began their climb back to division one. The crowds were even larger, flocking in their thousands towards Anfield as Liverpool clinched the second division championship.

In 1964, just two seasons back in the first division, Liverpool were champions. Everton had already caught a whiff of the excitement sweeping Merseyside by capturing the League title the previous year. In 1965, Liverpool added the FA Cup to their honours, the first time they had ever won the trophy in their history. Shankly went on to win two more League titles and a second FA Cup, as well as the UEFA Cup, before he sensationally resigned as manager in July 1974 at a press conference that would bear an uncanny resemblance to Dalglish's resignation. The impact of both resignations was much the same.

Nobody could ever take the place of Shankly. He was unique. But into his shoes stepped his number two at Anfield; Bob Paisley. It proved to be an inspired choice. He was the wise old man of Anfield, a sage who might have had difficulty communicating his ideas to the press but somehow managed to get most things over to the players, though one or two of them confessed they could never understand a word he was saying. There were no upheavals, everything continued in much the same way, following the pattern that Shankly had painstakingly laid down. But Shankly had left another rich legacy: two players who would guarantee the fortunes of the club for the next five years: Kevin Keegan, a young forward signed from fourth division Scunthorpe for a mere £35,000; and the record-breaking signing Ray Kennedy, bought from Arsenal for almost £200,000. Paisley failed to win any silverware in his first season in charge but nobody fretted or panicked. The next year, Liverpool were champions again, their ninth title win, and they added a second UEFA Cup to their blossoming European reputation.

Like Matt Busby, the one trophy Shankly had always aspired to win was the European Cup. In 1965, they had reached the semi-finals and looked to be on the verge of the final after a thrilling 3–1 victory over holders and world champions Inter Milan. But, a week later, in the tense cauldron of the San Siro Stadium, Inter won 3–0

It was Paisley who turned the dream into reality. What's more, it was achieved in Italy, in Rome's Olympic Stadium. It was a night when British soccer stood proud, and no one was more pleased than Dalglish when Liverpool stormed to a memorable 3–1 victory over the German champions Borussia Moenchengladbach. Dalglish was about to decide where next to rest his head. He liked what he saw. Liverpool had already won the League championship and had narrowly missed out on clinching a unique treble, having lost to Manchester United in an FA Cup final they ought really to have won.

So it was to this city, and this club with its rich Scottish traditions, that Dalglish fittingly arrived in the summer of 1977. Shankly, then in cosy retirement, had one small piece of advice for Dalglish. 'Never lose your Glasgow accent, son,' he ordered. They were wise words. But there would always be enough Scots around him to ensure that Dalglish remained true to his heritage.

Dalglish had been handed an onerous task; more of a poisoned chalice, reckoned one newspaper. To take over from Kevin Keegan, Anfield's favourite son, might be beyond even Dalglish's capabilities. Keegan had been the hero of the Kop, the last piece in Shankly's jigsaw, and his departure had not been received with much enthusiasm by the club's greatest critics, the massed ranks of the Kop. Had any player ever been given a more difficult task? Certainly not since poor old Hugh Baird took over from the mighty John Charles at Leeds United or those unfortunate souls who had to follow on after Stanley Matthews, Tom Finney and Jimmy Greaves.

But at least the signing of Dalglish had been greeted with almost unanimous approval among the fans. That was half the battle. The club and its supporters needed a major signing and Dalglish fitted the bill. The question now was whether he could live up to a reputation built solely in Scotland and at a club that had only one genuine rival in the Scottish League. Transferring those talents south of the border would not be the easiest of tasks. Many had gone before him – banner headlines, expensive fees, huge reputations, much expectation. And many had failed. Jim Baxter, Joe Harper, Peter Marinello – none of these had quite made it in the rigours of the English first division. Even Liverpool had their own Scottish failure in Frank McGarvey, a record signing from St Mirren who never even managed one first-team appearance, though the Scots still rated him highly enough to cap him twice while he was at Anfield. McGarvey ended up returning to Scotland, ironically to Celtic, three years after the arrival of Dalglish. There was little doubt who got the better of that exchange.

Within a couple of days of completing his medical and signing the necessary forms, Dalglish was pulling on a Liverpool shirt to make his debut, fittingly, at Wembley. Liverpool were League champions and had been losing FA Cup finalists, but now there was a chance for some small revenge as Liverpool faced United in the traditional preseason Charity Shield fixture at Wembley. It took only a few touches for Dalglish to demonstrate that he was a player amply qualified to wear the number 7 shirt that had once belonged to Kevin Keegan. He may not have scored, nor even created many opportunities, but he performed well enough to win over the Liverpool supporters among the 82,000 crowd.

'Dalglish,' wrote David Lacey in the *Guardian,* 'moved on the ball confidently near goal and struck up a good rapport with those around him.' He added prophetically that Dalglish was 'a more deliberate player than Keegan, he may give the side better balance in the long run.' Bob Paisley was his usual reticent self. 'He'll do for me,' was all he would say.

But, as was his wont, Dalglish, ruddy faced, faded as the second half wore on. It was a perennial problem, noted by more than one manager, especially at international level. Already 26 years old, there were those who wondered if he would ever generate the stamina to survive the tough English first division, particularly at Liverpool, with its fixture list of 50 games and more a season. In the Scottish League there was always the chance for a breather, and not every game demanded the maximum input. But, as Dalglish soon learned, the Liverpool training system had been specially designed to increase stamina. Within six months, any doubts about Dalglish's staying power had been finally dispelled.

The Liverpool side that Dalglish lined up with was well established. There was only one other newcomer to the Anfield training ground, another Scot, Alan Hansen, who had arrived from Partick Thistle in April, just months ahead of Dalglish. Ironically, 14 years later they would both quit the club in the same week, their careers running parallel for much of that time. In goal was Ray Clemence, thoughtful, dependable, quick off the mark, while in front of him was Phil Neal, Bob Paisley's first slice of business in the transfer market and already an England international. Alongside Neal was Joey Jones; a Welsh lad of never-say-die spirit; Phil Thompson, gangly, fearless, a speedy defender; and Emlyn Hughes, enthusiasm, boyishness, all power.

The midfield was composed of Ray Kennedy, inspirationally converted from an Arsenal striker into an authoritative half back who frequently sneaked into the penalty area to steal a crucial goal; Terry McDermott, a local boy, supple and full of running; Ian Callaghan, the old man who had seen it all, the last link with the second division days. Out on the flanks was Steve Heighway, a greyhound of a winger, sinewy, swift, and just as capable of operating on the right or left. Upfront was David Johnson, assiduous, suddenly anxious about his future and threatening a transfer; and David Fairclough, already dubbed 'Super Sub'. John Toshack was also around, though not for much longer, visibly mourning the loss of his partner Keegan; and there was Tommy Smith, who had intended to retire after the European Cup final but had been caught up in the glory of Rome after heading a spectacular, Roy-of-the-Rovers second goal. He was going to give it another season. It was into this mix of outrageous talent, experience and individualism that Dalglish moved. Tommy Smith, who had played in Keegan's debut, years before, also played in Dalglish's first game. Comparisons were inevitable but from the beginning Smith had no doubts about who was the master. 'He was the best player I ever lined up with,' he says. 'He came with an international pedigree and from the word go you knew his talent was heaven-sent.'

Liverpool and Dalglish kicked off the new season at Middlesbrough on a sweltering August afternoon. Middlesbrough, a typical middle-of-the-table outfit, attracted what was for them a bumper gate with just over 30,000 showing up, their best crowd of the season. The Middlesbrough side also had a debutant that day, manager John Neal, who gave the job of stalking Dalglish to a gritty young midfielder by the name of Graeme

Souness. Within a few months, Souness would also be part of the Anfield set-up, signed for a £350,000 fee.

It took Dalglish just seven minutes to make his mark, thanks to Terry McDermott. But one goal was not sufficient to give Liverpool a win as Middlesbrough equalised in the second half. It was a useful, if unspectacular, start to Liverpool's campaign and was particularly pleasing for Dalglish.

Liverpool's first home league game, and Dalglish's Anfield debut, came three days later when another North East team provided the opposition, this time Newcastle United. Dalglish was given a rapturous welcome by the Kop, 'reckoned by local observers,' wrote Patrick Barclay in the *Guardian,* 'to constitute the strongest expression of feeling since the heyday of Ian St John, surpassing even that shown to Keegan and Toshack.' Anfield would not be disappointed. A minute after half time, with Liverpool thundering forward, Ray Kennedy fed a long, speculative ball downfield, but with Irving Nattrass several yards ahead of Dalglish it seemed the Scot had little hope. But suddenly, with an astonishing spurt of pace, he attacked the ball, leaving Nattrass floundering. Then, with exquisite timing, he flicked the ball beyond the advancing keeper. Dalglish had made his mark.

At one end of Anfield is terracing that climbs from the back of the goal on a dramatic scale to tower over the ground and the Walton Breck Road behind. The view from the top can be frightening. It is entirely covered, its enormous roof adding strikingly to the skyline and acoustics. It is a banking known as the Spion Kop. It was built in 1906 as a reward to the fans just after the club had lifted its second League championship. A local journalist, Ernest Jones, suggested naming it Spion Kop after an infamous battle in South Africa where a local regiment had suffered severe losses during the Boer War. The name stuck and in the 1960s it became renowned throughout the football world. The vast swaying crowd, as many as 25,000, gathered under its canopy to sing the chart-toppers that had made the Merseybeat so popular. The legend of the Kop had been born. Here the fanatics gather at each home game to voice their allegiances. Here, where the entrance fee is cheaper than anywhere else, is the authentic, knowledgeable voice of Liverpool Football Club. Tommy Smith, Jimmy Case, John Aldridge and Steve McManaman all had their first glimpse of Anfield as supporters on this impressive banking. Ian St John was its first hero, his name chanted in rhythmical style. Then there was Kevin Keegan.

But now the Kop had a new hero and the chant 'DAL-GLISH' echoed around Anfield for the first time. Dalglish was King of the Kop.

Dalglish scored again in Liverpool's third league match as they notched up an impressive 3–0 win at West Bromwich Albion. They were off to a flying start, not losing a game until they faced Manchester United at Old Trafford in early October. But Nottingham Forest, now under the scrupulous tutelage of Brian Clough, had set an equally sprightly pace and by Christmas they had carved open a six-point gap at the top of the table. Liverpool probably relinquished their title in a disastrous six-week spell between mid-January and March when they lost four games. With Forest still racing away, Liverpool could not, at that stage, afford to squander any points. They were also dismissed from the FA Cup almost before it had begun, beaten 4–2 at Chelsea. It was the first time anyone had squeezed four goals past Liverpool in years. A few weeks later, Chelsea slammed another three past Clemence in a league match and suddenly everyone was asking questions about the European champions, wondering if the transfer of Keegan had really been wise.

These were unusually barren days for Dalglish. After his spectacular opening to the season, the goals had all but dried up; only two in the league in three months between early December and early March. Some pundits were even questioning the wisdom of buying the Scot. Dalglish's problem was probably quite simple. He was living in an hotel in the centre of the city, unable to find suitable accommodation. Marina and the two children were still spending much of their time in Glasgow, waiting to make the final move to Merseyside. It was a particularly difficult period, especially for a man like Dalglish, so dependent on a settled background and home. It took them eight months to find the right house, but by the beginning of the next season Dalglish was comfortably settled.

But if Liverpool were struggling in the league, the same could not be said of Europe. Dalglish had long lived in the shadow of Celtic's Lisbon Lions, having joined the club soon after the famous 1967 triumph. The key factor tempting him to Anfield had been Liverpool's successes in Europe. They had just captured the European Cup and had twice carried off the UEFA Cup. Liverpool were a major force on the continent; feared, respected and expected to lift further trophies.

Dalglish's first taste of European soccer in a red shirt came at Anfield on 19 October against the East German champions Dynamo Dresden. Liverpool ran out 5–1 winners, with Steve Heighway jinking his way through Dresden's iron curtain defence time and again. Also embarking on his European debut that night was Alan Hansen, stepping in for the injured Phil Thompson. Although the result was more than satisfactory, it was not a particularly pleasing personal debut for Dalglish. He was given little space by his East German minders and, when he did squirm free, he was usually hauled back illegally. It was a problem he would have to learn to live with. The second leg was barely better from his point of view, nor from Liverpool's, as they went down 2–1. But with such a comfortable lead from the first leg, they cantered easily enough to the quarter-finals, where they faced Benfica.

It was, of course, a far different Benfica from the side that had glided so gracefully across Europe during the early 1960s, spearheaded by the elegant Eusebio, to claim two European Cups. But with 14 league titles in the previous 18 seasons and an awesome stadium crammed with 70,000 fanatical supporters, they were still a tricky proposition. But in the driving rain and on a waterlogged pitch more akin to the Mersey than sunny Portugal, Liverpool produced a sparkling performance to win 2–1, and that after being a goal down in only 13 minutes. It was a foul on Dalglish just outside the area that led to Liverpool's first goal, Case firing the ball in from the free kick. In the return leg at Anfield, Dalglish finally made his European mark for Liverpool, bagging their second goal in a thrilling 4–1 rout of the Portuguese.

The draw for the semi-final could hardly have been more unkind, with Borussia Moenchengladbach, Liverpool's victims in the Rome final, their opponents yet again. There is nothing like hurt pride to spur the opposition, especially when it is German, and Liverpool must have felt that this time it would be near impossible to defeat the Germans. In the first leg in Dusseldorf, it certainly proved to be the case as Liverpool slumped to a 2–1 defeat, Dalglish largely anonymous. But in the return leg before a packed Anfield, the Scot finally found the room to demonstrate his complete repertoire. He was everywhere, a constant worry, even scoring Liverpool's second goal, which as good as sealed their passage to the final. Jimmy Case added a third in the second half and Liverpool were 3–0 winners on the night.

Another trip to Wembley beckoned, as the London ground was to be the venue for the 1978 European Cup final. It was to be Dalglish's third appearance at the famed stadium since joining Liverpool. Apart from the Charity Shield, Liverpool had also reached the League Cup final, where they had faced Nottingham Forest. Liverpool had never lifted the League Cup and 1978 was to be yet another disappointing year, with Forest eventually winning the replay after a goalless draw. Even the presence of Dalglish could not deter Forest, who also went on to capture the title from Liverpool by seven points. Perhaps it would be fair to claim that Liverpool's minds were on higher matters: retaining the European Cup.

Juventus had been the sure favourites to join Liverpool in the final. Yet against a particularly adept Belgian side, Bruges, the Italian champions had been surprisingly beaten. Bruges had also brushed aside Atlético Madrid and Panathinaikos en route to Wembley, but it still left Liverpool favourites to lift the trophy for a second successive year. By now the Liverpool side had begun to take on a new shape. Tommy Smith, Joey Jones, Ian Callaghan and Kevin Keegan had all either moved aside or been transferred, and only six members of the European Cup-winning side of 12 months previously lined up against Bruges at Wembley. Into their places had stepped Dalglish, Alan Hansen and Graeme Souness to give the team a Scottish backbone that would power them to infinite glory during the next decade.

Sadly, the final, which promised an exhibition of flowing football in front of a Wembley crammed largely with Liverpool supporters, was a dour affair. Bruges came to defend, missing two of their key men in Lambert and Courant and only emerged from their defensive shell in the final moments after Liverpool had gone ahead. By then it was too late. The final would be remembered for just one incident – a goal by Dalglish. It arrived in the 65th minute and fittingly it was the new Souness/Dalglish link that provided the key to unlock Bruges's tightly knit defence, Souness chipping a delicate ball into the area for Dalglish to chase. The young Scot seized his chance, measured his pace, waited for the goalkeeper to commit himself and then fired the ball into the net. It was his 30th goal of the season. He turned and in a memorable gesture raced towards the fans, leaping the advertising hoardings and sprinting towards the fence. It was, admits Dalglish, one of the greatest moments in his career. And what a grin. Dalglish had quit Celtic in search of European glory and, within one season, he was clutching his coveted medal. He could glance back on his first campaign in English football with some satisfaction: three Wembley appearances, a European Cup-winners' medal, runners-up in the first division, 30 goals and, finally, a house. He had made the transition from Scotland to England much more smoothly than either he or anyone, with perhaps the exception of Bob Paisley, could have dared imagine.

Liverpool kicked off the following season intent on recapturing the title, winning their opening five games in some style, including a 7–0 defeat of Tottenham at Anfield that many still recall as one of the most memorable in the club's history. Dalglish struck the back of the net twice, with Terry McDermott heading Liverpool's final goal in a four-man build-up, reckoned by Bob Paisley to be the finest he had ever seen at Anfield. Time and again it was Dalglish who carved Tottenham apart. In their first five fixtures, Liverpool had scored 20 goals and conceded just two. A draw at West Brom was then followed by four more victories, which left Liverpool in late October 1978 heading the table having dropped just one point, 35 goals in credit and only four conceded. Dalglish had more than played his part, notching up ten of those goals.

It was inevitable that somebody would eventually get the better of Liverpool and, of course, it had to be Everton, 1–0 winners at Goodison. It heralded the beginning of a dismal six-week spell, a hangover from their first round defeat in the European Cup to Nottingham Forest. It had been Liverpool's wretched luck to draw Forest out of the bag and a 2–0 defeat at the City Ground virtually sank any hopes of a third successive Cup victory. At Anfield a fortnight later, they battled grittily but Forest slammed down the shutters and the game petered out into a goalless draw. It was the first European tie they had lost in four years. Misery set in at Anfield. Dreams of emulating Bayern Munich, Benfica, Inter Milan and Ajax had been dashed. In the subsequent weeks, Liverpool lost not only to Everton but also at Arsenal and Bristol City and threw away further points against Leeds and Spurs.

But on Boxing Day, a 3–0 walloping of Manchester United at Old Trafford raised everyone's spirits and began a run that would steer them to the title and a record points haul. They lost only one more game all season, at Aston Villa, and rounded off their campaign with the most impressive first division record in history. At Anfield they had won 19 games, drawn two and lost none, with 51 goals scored and a mere four conceded. Away from home they had won 11 games, drawn six and lost only four, netting 34 goals with 12 against. Their total of 16 goals conceded remains the lowest in the history of the Football League, while their 68 points haul was the highest ever achieved by any team under the old rule of two points for a win. Ray Clemence had kept a clean sheet on 27 occasions. In the end, they raced away with the title, eight points clear of Nottingham Forest. Dalglish had more than played his part in their triumph, scoring 21 league goals and, despite David Johnson's reservations about the arrival of Dalglish, the two had linked up to form an effective goal-scoring partnership, with Johnson firing 16 league goals himself. Dalglish added a few more in other competitions to give him a campaign tally of 25 goals. Two years in England and he had already struck 55 goals in 111 appearances. Everyone was impressed, especially the football writers; they voted him their Player of the Year.

It was one of the finest of all Liverpool sides and, although it may not have been quite so exhilarating as the Barnes/Beardsley force of later years, it boasted an iron wall of a defence, now improved further by the addition of Alan Kennedy. The crowds loved them, particularly at Anfield where 50,000 regularly flocked through the gates. In the FA Cup they seemed at one stage on the verge of the double, reaching the semi-final where they faced Manchester United. But after drawing 2–2 at Maine Road, they crashed 1–0 at Goodison in the replay. The double would have to wait a few more years.

The 1979/80 season was to be almost a repeat of the previous campaign. There was a surprisingly early exit in the European Cup, as Liverpool faced Soviet opposition for the first time. Dinamo Tbilisi were still something of an unknown quantity when they arrived on Merseyside. But within minutes of setting foot on the Anfield turf, even before kick-off, it was apparent that Liverpool were up against an elegant team. They even had the temerity to hold the kick-around in front of the Kop where they gave an elegant display of fast-moving passing. The Kop watched in awe. Liverpool won the first leg 2–1, but the writing was clearly on the wall. In the return leg in deepest Georgia, Liverpool crashed 3–0 in front of 80,000 and for the second successive year they been eliminated from the European Cup at the first hurdle. It was one of Liverpool's worst defeats in Europe, but there could be no excuses. Dalglish was philosophical. Tbilisi were an outstanding side, it was pointless denying it. For once, Liverpool had been bettered. Soviet soccer was finally emerging from its defensive shroud and Tbilisi, with their flowing football, neat passing and inventive tactics, won many admirers on Merseyside.

It had been Liverpool's misfortune again to draw such opposition at so early a stage in the competition. In the previous season, Liverpool could at least argue that Nottingham Forest had stormed on to win the trophy and had not faced a tougher game throughout the competition. But, much to everyone's surprise, Tbilisi were eliminated in the next round of the tournament by Kevin Keegan's Hamburg, although Tbilisi did stride on to win the European Cup-Winners' Cup the following season.

Dumped out of Europe's premier competition, there was little Liverpool could do other than concentrate on the domestic honours. In the league, they made a shaky start to the defence of their title. An early defeat at Southampton and then at Nottingham Forest, plus a clutch of draws, left them adrift of the leaders. It was December before they eventually clambered back to the top of the table but once in place there was little doubt who would end up champions. Five consecutive victories in March virtually guaranteed them the title and, against Aston Villa at Anfield, Liverpool wrapped up their 12th championship in style with a 4–1 win. The goal-scoring mantle passed from Dalglish to David Johnson, with the former Ipswich Town and Everton player hitting 21 league goals. Dalglish himself struck 16 and claimed a further six in other competitions.

Four of those goals came in the League Cup as Liverpool marched on to another semi-final but, yet again, Nottingham Forest proved their downfall, edging Liverpool out of the competition over the two legs. Liverpool also reached the semi-finals of the FA Cup where it took four games with Arsenal before the Gunners finally succeeded in battling their way through to Wembley.

So tantalisingly near and yet so far, the following season, 1980/81, Liverpool would finally make the breakthrough in the two cup competitions. But in doing so they would forfeit their first division title, winding up a miserable fifth, their lowest league position since 1971. There were problems in defence. Injuries cost Alan Kennedy, Phil Thompson and Alan Hansen well over 50 games between them. And, at the other end, the goals did not materialise with quite the regularity and ease of previous seasons. Dalglish had his most unrewarding season so far in English football, scoring only eight league goals and missing eight league games through injury. After November, he failed to score in the first division. Terry McDermott was the leading league marksman with 13 goals. Dalglish had more luck in the other competitions, striking another ten in all to give him a more respectable end-of-season total.

But if there was disappointment in the league, Liverpool struck gold elsewhere. They lifted the League Cup for the first time, beating West Ham 2–1 in a replay at Villa Park, Dalglish volleying Liverpool ahead mid-way through the first half. But even more satisfying was another European triumph. After two disappointing seasons of being eliminated at the first hurdle, they finally drew easy opposition, this time in the shape of Oulu

Palloseura, the Finnish part-timers. In the first tie, played at Oulu's friendly little ground close to the Arctic Circle, Liverpool scraped a draw. But at Anfield a fortnight later, the full power of the Liverpool machine was on view as they rattled in ten goals. Astonishingly, Dalglish never managed to get on the scoresheet. The next round took Dalglish on a rare footballing trip north of the border with his new club as they faced, and easily defeated, the Scottish champions Aberdeen. The gulf in class was there for everyone to spot, only confirming in Dalglish's mind the wisdom of his move south. In the quarter-finals, Liverpool comfortably disposed of the Bulgarian champions CSKA Sofia and then faced Bayern Munich in the semi-finals. At Anfield, Liverpool scraped a goalless draw that looked as if it would not be enough but on a warm, spring evening in Munich, the German champions were run ragged by the unknown Howard Gayle, who came on in place of the injured Dalglish after just five minutes. Liverpool's late goal was enough to guarantee a place in the final against Real Madrid.

The next six weeks were to be a particularly anxious time for Dalglish. He was still nursing a bad injury from that Bayern game and it was touch and go whether he would eventually make it for the final. He did, though only just, and then did not play the full 90 minutes. But his presence in the side was enough to boost everyone's morale.

It was Liverpool's sternest test since Rome, yet they were to emerge from what was later dubbed 'a game for the connoisseurs' with considerable credit. Dalglish was a constant thorn in the Spanish defence and might well have been on the scoresheet in the first half. As it was, he was eventually substituted and was a spectator as Alan Kennedy careered down the left flank in the 81st minute to drill in an unstoppable shot from the acutest of angles. Four seasons at Anfield and Dalglish had already picked up two European Cup-winner's medals. Towards the end of the season he had also welcomed a new partner up front, a young lad recently signed from Chester. But the youngster, Ian Rush, did not look too promising after failing to score in his first seven outings.

The 1981/2 season was to be the first of three successive title wins for Liverpool that equalled Huddersfield and Arsenal's pre-war triumphs. Yet, early in the season, few would have bet on a Liverpool championship. In late October, they were in the lower half of the table but an inspired surge after Christmas brought a staggering 18 victories in 20 games to clinch the title for Liverpool.

Liverpool also added a second League Cup to their collection, beating

Tottenham 3–1 in extra time. Dalglish was an ever-present in the league, shaking off his injury of the previous season, though it was not until October that he managed to score. He had gone almost 11 months without a league goal. Eventually he notched 13 in the campaign. But in Europe, after a promising start, Liverpool were eliminated in the quarter-finals by CSKA Sofia, the side they had so contemptuously disposed of the previous season.

The turnabout in Liverpool's fortunes after their elimination was almost entirely due to Ian Rush, who, after his disappointing start, suddenly found a perfect foil in Dalglish. Over the next few years, they were to establish one of the most formidable goal-scoring partnerships seen in British football since the War. Dalglish's early partner at Anfield had been David Johnson who, like so many strikers, had found that Dalglish's presence only added to his fortunes. Dalglish had now become the provider and Rush was to be the principal benefactor, whipping in 30 goals that season.

The early 1980s were savage years for the city of Liverpool. Wracked by acute unemployment (more people were jobless in the area than in the whole of Wales), the politics of the city hit the headlines. In July 1981, rioting in Toxteth sparked off a nationwide reaction. CS gas was used for the first time on the mainland of Britain and the once-grand boulevards of Liverpool 8 blazed dramatically. You could understand the frustration. Almost 20 per cent of the city's working population were unemployed; in some areas, such as Toxteth, one in two men were on the dole. And, if you added the non-working population – old-age pensioners and youngsters – to the total, then at times it seemed as if hardly anyone in the city had a job. There was little to be proud of in Liverpool, except for its football teams, which seemed to belie the chaos and deprivation elsewhere. For many, the hopes and glories of a Saturday afternoon were all they had to keep them going.

The following season, 1982/3, would be just as profitable for Rush as Liverpool gave what was virtually a repeat performance, snatching the championship again and beating Manchester United at Wembley to take their third consecutive League Cup, but in Europe they were again eliminated in the quarter-finals. Dalglish struck 18 goals in the league as he and Rush chalked up 42 between them. The Football Writers' Association again honoured him, naming him Player of the Year, while his fellow professionals in the PFA also voted him their best player.

There will long be debates in bars around the city over which was

Liverpool's most accomplished side and which their finest season. Among the contenders will always rank the 1983/4 campaign. It was the season Liverpool lifted three trophies, the season they captured their third successive title and the season they first faced Everton at Wembley. It was as memorable a time as any. The only blot for Dalglish was a tally of just seven league goals, although injury had robbed him of a number of appearances.

Dalglish, 33 years old by the end of the campaign, had dropped into the midfield to make way for Michael Robinson up front but while Rush struck 32 goals Robinson managed no more than six. Rush was still dependent on Dalglish for his chances; Robinson floundered in the wilderness, never able to understand Dalglish's game. By the end of the season he would be gone. The partnership between Rush and Dalglish was proving not only the most potent in the Football League but perhaps the most effective Anfield had ever seen. Strikers hunting in pairs had long been a tradition at Anfield, with Shankly forging the link between Ian St John and Roger Hunt before bringing Kevin Keegan and John Toshack together. But the Dalglish-Rush partnership had the added spice of excitement and innovation. There was no telling what they might do next. Rush seemed to read instinctively Dalglish, while Dalglish similarly knew that a ball into open space would be seized upon by the gangly Welsh striker. 'I just made the runs knowing the ball would come to me,' says Rush.

Under new manager Joe Fagan, wrapping up their third consecutive title was a formality and they could even afford to throw away points at the end of the season as they began to concentrate their attention on Europe. Less of a formality was a record-breaking fourth consecutive League Cup. This time they were taken to a replay after neighbours Everton held them to a goalless draw in the pouring rain of Wembley. It was an unforgettable occasion where civic pride probably got the better of the day as the fans stood, danced and sang alongside each other in Wembley's friendliest-ever final. But in the replay at Maine Road, there was no room for sentiment and Liverpool sneaked a famous victory, thanks to a Graeme Souness strike.

As if that were not enough, they then faced AS Roma in the European Cup final on Roma's home ground, the Olympic Stadium. It was to be another memorable evening in Rome. Liverpool edged into an early lead through Phil Neal, but late in the first half Roma snatched an equaliser. And that was the way the score remained after 120 minutes. Dalglish, tiring in the warm Rome evening air, had eventually given way to Michael

Robinson and was consequently ineligible for the dramatic penalty shootout. But he was not needed. Alan Kennedy, who had missed every penalty during practice the day before, finally got it right on the night. It clinched a fourth European Cup for Liverpool and a third European champion's medal for Dalglish.

When Dalglish kicked off his footballing career at Parkhead back in 1967, he could never have imagined picking up three European medals himself and being part of a club that had now won more European Cups than any side other than the immortal Real Madrid. Dalglish had more than played his part in those successes and, although he would be the first to deny the importance of any one individual to the club's success, there is no doubt that without Dalglish, Liverpool would not have been the force they were in both European and domestic competition. In the Football League he was unrivalled, honoured by his fellow professionals, the most-capped Scot of all time, the scorer of 100 goals in both Scottish and English football. And yet, for all his domestic honours and European medals, he was never feted in the same manner outside of Britain. His best performances were undoubtedly reserved for the Football League. In Europe, he never dominated with quite the same style; he was often marked tightly, usually playing more deeply than he would at home and rarely scoring with the same freedom. His tally for European games was a mere ten in 46 appearances. And while Graeme Souness had been snapped up by Sampdoria and Ian Rush was being earmarked for a similar move to Italy, there were surprisingly few serious inquiries from the continent about Dalglish.

Dalglish's final season as a player, 1984/5, began with an early goal and ended in the sad chaos and confusion of Heysel. In between there was little that was memorable. Liverpool were pipped to the title by neighbours Everton, while in the FA Cup, after four depressing seasons, Liverpool finally battled their way to the semi-final, only to be beaten in a replay at Goodison by Manchester United. The League Cup also offered no compensation, with an early exit at Tottenham. But in Europe, the champions marched on, defeating Poznan, Benfica, Austria Vienna and Panathinaikos on their way to what should have been a distinguished final against Michel Platini's Juventus.

Earlier that season Dalglish suffered the indignity of being dropped for the first time in his career. 'He's not been at his best,' claimed Joe Fagan, the manager at the time. 'And there's no room for sentiment.' Dalglish was disappointed but typically accepted the manager's decision without question. He was soon back and Fagan later described his decision to drop him as 'daft'. Dalglish's best playing days may have been behind him, but he was still an effective cog in the Anfield machine. At 34, he was clearly in the twilight of his playing days and was already being excused some of the heavier training schedules. Most of his training seemed to be confined to a Thursday, with the remainder of his time spent either on the treatment bench or simply resting. Some of the other professionals, particularly the older hands, found this galling, yet it made sense. There was also a long-term injury to be cared for and the need to avoid further exacerbation.

Dalglish's mind was beginning to turn towards the future. At best, he guessed, he had two more seasons at Anfield but more likely just one. As he grew older, the pace was only going to get harder, especially in the first division. He also reckoned that Joe Fagan would not remain in the hot seat for more than another season and a new manager might not want his services. He could, of course, drop down a division or two, but that was never really the Dalglish style. When he retired, he wanted to go at the top. He had seen too many players destroy the legends they had carefully created by attempting to remain in the game too long or by dropping a division.

Dalglish had no fixed plans. Management was a possibility, and doubtless somebody would tap him for a job if he let it be known that he was keen on following that path. But as he looked around him, he could see former stars such as Bobby Moore managing lowly Southend United and Billy Bremner at ramshackle Doncaster Rovers. Was that what he really wanted? As a rookie manager, he could probably expect no better than a third or fourth division club. Then, of course, there was always Scotland, but that might mean Dumbarton or Stenhousemuir, rather than Rangers or Celtic. And anyhow he had been so long, probably too long, out of Scottish football. If soccer was not to hold him, then he might have to rely on his business interests. He had a pub up in Scotland with his father-in-law and there were other possibilities, maybe in the media. Then, one day, shortly before the European Cup final of 1985 he received a phone call from John Smith. He could barely believe his ears.

CHAPTER SEVEN
The Man With The Midas Touch

'Y've never seen me play, have yer? Y' don't know what y've missed.
I'm sort of a combination of Bobby Moore and Stanley Matthews, with
a touch of the Kevin Keegans as well.'
'Sounds too incredible for words,' Sluggy said.
Alan Bleasdale. *Scully*

Comparisons may, as the scurrilous Doctor Johnson once suggested, be 'mischief making', but alas they are also inevitable. Though why should we apologise? It may be unfair to compare men who are not contemporaries but who is ever going to cry foul as fathers and sons argue the toss between generations of sporting heroes? Who was the best? Who was the fastest? Who was the most skilful? Let the argument commence.

Comparisons with Kevin Keegan were unavoidable once Dalglish had arrived at Liverpool. Yet in a short time he had proved his mettle. At first, few thought that he could ever be as good as Keegan, but in the long term there was never any debate. Dalglish had won the battle hands down. As a contest, it was virtually decided the evening Keegan's new club Hamburg came to Anfield to play the second leg of their European Super Cup final. The first game had been drawn 1–1 in Germany, but at Anfield on a chilly December evening, Dalglish and Liverpool destroyed the European Cup-Winners' Cup holders 6–0. Keegan, a lone forager up front for the Germans, looked pitiful. At one stage, with hands on hips, he trudged despairingly towards his own half, another attack broken down, glaring in disbelief as red shirts swarmed past him towards the Kop.

It was a scintillating performance, with Terry McDermott stealing the show with a glorious hat-trick. Yet it was Dalglish's inspiration that engineered Liverpool's red machine, his running with the ball, his neat, sharp passing, his ability to hold the ball under threat. And, of course, he rounded the evening off by scoring Liverpool's sixth goal. Keegan had been gone only six months.

Bob Paisley, always reluctant to be drawn into the debate, nevertheless plumped wholeheartedly for Dalglish. 'Of all the players I have played alongside, managed and coached in more than forty years at Anfield, he is the most talented,' he once said. 'When Kenny shines the whole team shines.' It was almost the cue for a song. The former Liverpool chairman Sir John Smith adds his weighty testimony: 'The best player this club has signed this century,' he claims without hesitation.

Tommy Smith similarly has no reservations: 'They were like chalk and cheese. Dalglish was the best player I ever lined up with. Kenny was a complete one-off, a football genius. His passes inside the full back were devastating. Keegan was also a great player in his own right, but I would put his successor slightly ahead of him. Kenny's talent was heaven-sent. Kevin's qualities were man-made.'

Ian St John also supports this view. 'Kevin Keegan was a buzzy little player. He was manufactured. Dalglish had the football brain. He was an old-fashioned Scottish inside forward. You can't manufacture that. You've either got it or you haven't.'

Next to Paisley only one other man has managed Dalglish at club level for any length of time. That was Jock Stein. Although Stein had his early doubts about Dalglish's abilities, he was soon converted. 'I think Liverpool bought a better player than Keegan. They bought a better club man,' he once said, adding sardonically, 'they also made a profit on the deal.' His assistant at Celtic, Sean Fallon, rated Dalglish 'as good a player as I have ever seen'.

Fallon it was who discovered Dalglish, as well as Ronnie Simpson, Paul McStay, Paul Reaney, Pat Bonner and Bertie Auld. So what would he list as his attributes? 'First,' says Fallon, 'he had two good feet. He was capable of scoring instinctively with either his right or left foot. Second, he had so much confidence. Rarely have I seen that much confidence in a player. Not cocky you understand, just self-assured. Third, he had balance. Watch him move, his arms splayed out like a bird. He could ride tackles and still come up with the ball. Fourth, his attitude, always positive. Fifth, he was competitive. I've never met a more competitive player. And finally, his professionalism. He always looked after himself. No drinking, smoking, always early to bed, training hard. Put those together and you have the perfect player.'

Fallon also picks up on another aspect. 'How often did you see him have a bad game?' he asks rhetorically. 'Rarely. I could probably count the bad games he had at Celtic on one hand. And even when he did have a bad game, he still contributed. He didn't sit around up front waiting for things to happen: he would try to play himself into the game, go looking for the ball.'

Dalglish may not have been the fastest player on the park but, as Paisley once pointed out, the Scot's first five yards were in his head. 'What made him unique was his vision. He had this rare quality of being able to know where the other players were without even looking – and to find them with a perfect pass.' He could pace his game. That was one reason why he survived longer than others. With one pass he could take three or four players out of a game.

His favourite manoeuvre was to receive the ball with his back to the goal, then pirouette while shielding the ball, before threading the subtlest of passes into open space. Has anyone ever done it better?

International defender David O'Leary, while acknowledging Dalglish's skill, also points out that he had the biggest backside in football. 'Trying to take the ball off Kenny once he's got it, is almost impossible. He crouches over the ball, legs spread and elbows poking out, and defies you to try and get it off him. Whatever angle you come in from, you're liable to find his backside in your face, and if you commit yourself too soon, he'll twist and turn right past you. You never seem to get a free header because he's so good at backing into you.' Phil Neal, who faced him in many a five-a-side or training match, agrees wholeheartedly: 'No one had a bigger bum than him,' he says amusingly.

Sean Fallon also regards his ability to guard the ball as the most important aspect of his game. 'He was the best shielder of the ball I've ever seen. It was so difficult to take it off him once he had it. He would take the ball right up close to defenders, and then beat them, and when that happens opponents have no chance of recovering.'

Standing behind him week after week at Anfield was goalkeeper Ray Clemence. 'You cannot anticipate what he is going to do,' he explained. 'He was born with a great gift. You can't define it. He was three or four moves ahead of everyone. Sometimes I felt so frustrated for him, because other players were not able to read what he was doing.'

Although Dalglish will be best remembered in later years as a goal-maker, in his early days it was his goal-scoring talents which excited so many, particularly Sean Fallon. 'He was never an outstanding header of the ball,' recalls Fallon, 'but when the ball was at his feet there was nobody to touch him. He was greedy in the box. I think he counted every goal he scored. He and Lou Macari used to compete and argue over who got the final touch. I've never seen a more confident player in front of goal. Give him a half chance and I'd bank on him taking it.'

In a Scottish career that spanned 322 games, Dalglish scored 167 goals. In the Scottish League Cup alone, he hit the net 35 times in 56 appearances. In the Scottish league, he scored 112 goals in 204 games to join Bobby Lennox, Steve Chalmers and John Hughes as the only Celtic players since the War to have scored over 100 league goals. It was a rate of a goal every other game. He was the leading marksman at Celtic in three seasons, 1972/3, 1974/5 and 1975/6.

At Anfield, Dalglish's goal-scoring record was almost as phenomenal. In 355 first division appearances he scored 118 times, a rate of one every third game. Adding his other Liverpool appearances to that gives him a total tally of 498 games and 168 goals. He became the first player ever to score more than a century of goals on both sides of the border. In his first season at Anfield, he blasted 30 goals in 59 appearances and managed a total of more than 20 goals a season on five occasions. For Scotland, he heads the all-time goal-scoring charts, alongside Denis Law, with 30 goals in 102 games. He has also scored more European Cup goals than any other British player. Wherever Dalglish has played he has scored goals; wherever he has travelled he has smashed records. They came from everywhere. Like snooker's Steve Davis, he could pot them from impossible angles. He could clip them in off the bar and cue the ball perfectly for an incoming team-mate.

But it is probably those who played closest to him, up front, that we should heed most of all. And, more than anyone, it was Ian Rush who would benefit from Dalglish's presence. With Dalglish alongside him, Rush developed into the most formidable striker English soccer had seen for many years. Together they formed a partnership that became the scourge of the Football League and Europe. 'He gave me enormous confidence,' claims Rush, 'which was precisely what I needed. I would make the runs off the ball knowing that Kenny would be aware and that the ball would eventually come to me.' But it took time for the young Welshman to attune himself to the Dalglish style.

'I had to be ready to receive the ball when I least expected it,' he says. 'It took time to get accustomed to.' After a few glares from the Maestro, it finally clicked. They were on the same wavelength and one of football's greatest double acts was born. It sounds simple. It was. But only Kenny could do it.

I can recall it as if it were yesterday, a moment of genius indelibly etched in the mind. It is a Saturday afternoon at Anfield in lukewarm spring weather. Liverpool are leading 1–0. They are kicking towards the Anfield Road end, working their way downfield. Dalglish takes a pass inside the penalty area with his back, as usual, to goal. Then, turning, he faces his defender, shimmying one way, then the other, not sure where to go. Instead of releasing the ball quickly, he hangs on to it while the defence gathers its wits. The opportunity has surely passed. Dalglish is surrounded by defenders. Someone must snatch the ball from him. We are all on our feet, urging him to release the ball. But no, the moment has slipped away, Dalglish annoyingly clinging to the ball too long. Then suddenly, out of nowhere, he chips the ball into open space and into the path of Ian Rush who has raced all of 15 yards into the penalty box undetected. The ball is in the back of the net. We can only gawp in disbelief. It was not a spectacular goat by any standards, but the skill and the vision involved in its execution summed up Dalglish at his finest. It was all thanks to his confident awareness that Rush was awaiting his move. He instinctively understood space and its importance. He knew also that Rush would arrive. It was part of the complex understanding they had formed. Instead of a goalscorer, Dalglish was now a king among goalmakers. The man with the Midas touch.

David Johnson, whose sagging career was resurrected rather than destroyed by the arrival of the Scot, was also an admirer. 'He had an incredible will and desire to succeed,' he says. 'He didn't even have to work at it.

He could always make something from nothing. He had tremendous vision and could turn a game on his own by producing the unexpected. Defenders would think they had him covered and suddenly he would wriggle clear and bend one into the top corner. He was supremely confident with an unquenchable belief in his own ability.'

Bob Paisley once made a pertinent, though often overlooked, point about the importance of Dalglish's strength to his play. He explained that Dalglish was playing in the hardest position of all. 'He takes all the knocks that are handed out. Yet he never retaliates, he just gets on with the game. He takes some whackings from defenders and yet he had that wonderful record for us of not missing a game in something like three seasons. That's a miracle, playing in the position he plays in. He is the target for all the hitmen in the game. He is the man they are after yet few of them can kick him out of the game.' It was the killer instinct in Dalglish, the ability to ride tackles, the refusal to let defenders get the better of him, the strength to give as much as he received. It was part and parcel of the battle between defenders and attackers and Dalglish made sure that he won that battle. He may not be tall and may look willowy, but do not be deceived. He is as strong as an oak.

Former Celtic star Bobby Lennox is unreserved in his praise of Dalglish. 'At the peak of his powers with Liverpool,' he argues, 'Kenny was the best player in the world. Zico was around then and he was outstanding – but Kenny had everything. Dalglish played every game of football as if it was his last. He had such an appetite for the game.'

His skill was daunting and just as spectacular as the Brazilian's. One morning, when Dalglish was manager at Liverpool, he decided after a drawn 11-a-side training match that they would have a penalty shootout to decide the winners – but with a difference. To win, you had to hit the crossbar with a chipped shot from 25 yards. Everyone had to try. John Barnes stepped up confidently and missed, so did Peter Beardsley, then Jan Molby. Both sides tried, but all failed. Finally, up strolled the manager for his turn. He placed the ball and began his run up, the players hurling mud and grass at him. Then, as he kicked the ball, he slipped. But it made no difference. He still struck the ball and it sailed gracefully through the air and bounced against the crossbar. Dalglish was ecstatic. 'It was as if he had just won the FA Cup,' said one of his players. 'None of us could believe it.'

'Mind you,' says Sean Fallon. 'He could give you the occasional trouble. He was stubborn, stubborn to the point of being obstinate. The only problem was that he was usually right.' Fallon recalls one occasion when they fell out. 'We had a row, something to do with team tactics. He didn't agree with me, told me so. We shouted and he went off in a huff, didn't speak to me. I went away, thought "sod you". Then I thought about it. "He's right, you know," I said. "Damn it, he's right."

Football writer Ian Archer also caught an early glimpse of Dalglish's self-conviction. Walking down Glasgow's Buchanan Street one day, he bumped into Dalglish, then a young player with Celtic. 'Wisnae,' Dalglish muttered to him. 'Wisnae whit?' asked a perplexed Archer. 'Wisnae offside,' replied Dalglish and strolled off to do his shopping, leaving Archer stumped. What did he mean? Then Archer remembered. Dalglish was referring to a match report Archer had written four weeks previously when he had dared suggest that a Dalglish goal might have been offside.

'In retrospect,' said Archer, 'it was just about the most piercing, informative and lengthy interview Dalglish ever gave me. It was clear then, that Dalglish was going to become a pretty singular footballer, not part of the noisy boisterous brigade who could play from a three o'clock kick-off until the early hours of a Sunday morning.' Even George Best had to agree with that. 'His attitude was tremendous,' he says. 'If I was a manager, he'd be the first name on the teamsheet week after week.'

Dalglish was reckoned, rightly or wrongly, to be a moaner, always complaining about plastic pitches, such as the one at Luton, refereeing decisions and anything that seemed to go against him. Birmingham manager John Bond once called him 'the moaningest minnie I've ever known'. Such descriptions may have been applied more often during his managerial days, but even as a player he had finely tuned his reputation. 'But he was always like that,' insists Sean Fallon. 'Even at Celtic, he was continually talking to referees. But he did know how to talk to them decently. They understood him. He was just being competitive. That's the way he is. He was the same in training, mouth all the time. It didn't matter if it was a five-a-side match, a reserve game or the Cup final; he would still argue with whoever was in charge.' But after snapping at a referee he would sink back into his usual concentration.

Competitive nature or not, it hardly won him many friends on opposition terraces up and down the country. Not that it ever bothered Dalglish. Yet he was soon stamped with the label 'whiner' and it occasionally got him into trouble. Yet he was sent off only once in a long career.

The public and the press saw one face of Dalglish; his colleagues saw a very different man. He had a wicked sense of humour that could just as easily be turned on his team-mates as on the press. Steve Nicol, as a young player not long arrived at Liverpool from Ayr United, was told by Graeme Souness and Alan Hansen one day that Dalglish was seriously ill. The team were on a tour of Israel and Dalglish had retired to bed for his usual afternoon nap. Nicol clearly did not know about this ritual and thought it strange that Dalglish should be in bed in the middle of the afternoon.

'Have you noticed he doesn't train every day,' they pointed out 'and goes home to sleep in an afternoon.' Nicol nodded. 'That's because he's got leukaemia,' added Souness. 'What's more, it's terminal.'

'Ah dinnae believe ya,' said Nicol.

'Well go and ask him yourself, ask any of the lads,' suggested Souness.

They were staying in an hotel at the time and Nicol raced off to Dalglish's room, checking first with a few other Liverpool players who, of course, had been primed. They all confirmed the tale. In the meantime, Ronnie Whelan rang Dalglish's room to put him in on the joke. Nicol knocked gently on Dalglish's door.

'Come in,' answered a quiet voice. Dalglish was lying there in bed doing his best to look ill.

'I've just heard about your illness,' said Nicol almost in tears. 'I'm really sorry, I didn't know.'

'Aye, I'm afraid it's true,' confessed Dalglish. 'Hadn't you noticed how badly I've been playing recently?'

'Well, yes I had, actually,' began Nicol. But Dalglish could contain himself no longer, especially after Nicol's effrontery to suggest that he had not been playing particularly well. In a flash, Dalglish was out of bed and ribbing Nicol for accusing him of playing badly.

Steve Nicol was frequently the butt of Dalglish's and Souness's humour. On another occasion, Nicol, Dalglish and Souness were travelling up to Scotland in Souness's car for an international. The weather was atrocious, snow, sleet and bitterly cold, but Nicol, as was his wont, came dressed in only a tee shirt. Dalglish and Souness ribbed him for some time about his lack of clothing, but Nicol insisted that he was not at all cold. Finally, they decided to teach him a lesson. Souness stopped the car and asked Nicol to go out and wipe the back window as it was getting snowed up. Nicol happily piled out of the back and got on with it. But no sooner had he started scraping the window than Souness slammed his foot down and tore away, leaving the young Scot stranded by the roadside yelling after them. Half an hour later they returned. Nicol was almost frozen solid but had learned his lesson.

Dalglish may have been unpopular on terraces up and down the land, but with his own breed at Parkhead and Anfield he was a god, developing an instant rapport, as long as he wore their colours. King of the Jungle at Parkhead, he was equally King of the Kop at Anfield. If he was on your side, you loved him. 'He knows nothing who does not mix with the crowds,' runs the Spanish proverb. Dalglish knew where his loyal support lay.

Footballers are often slated as uncaring, greedy, unprofessional. But it is not always true. Much good work that they perform is ignored or unreported. Dalglish was no exception. Hospitals, boys' clubs, all benefited from him, not just financially but with his time as well. Any sick child writing into Liverpool Football Club would be almost certain of a visit from one, of the players, maybe even Dalglish himself.

Dalglish was dedicated from his earliest days, kicking a ball about from morning until night as a youngster. It was the same at Celtic. One of the first points Billy McNeill noticed was that Dalglish used to return to Parkhead every afternoon to practise his ball skills. To the majority of players it was puzzling, even something of a joke, that anyone should be so keen to train one minute longer than necessary. 'But there was Dalglish putting in the extra hours, perfecting his control and shooting,' says McNeill.

Graeme Souness, who succeeded Dalglish as Liverpool manager and was a playing colleague of his for many years with both Liverpool and Scotland, argues that there is no praise too high for Dalglish. 'I never saw anyone in this country to touch him,' he claims. 'I can think of only two players who could go ahead of him – Pele and possibly Cruyff. He was better than Maradona, Rummenigge or Platini. I would say that on his day he was, without any shadow of a doubt, the best player in the world.' Another Liverpool colleague, Mark Lawrenson, has also called him 'one of the greatest players of the last twenty-five years'.

His former Celtic skipper Billy McNeill endorses that view. 'He was the best Scottish player I ever played with,' he says. 'He could hold his own in any company and go anywhere in the world. He was a genuine world-class player.' Another manager, and former England full back, Jimmy Armfield, is equally flattering. 'Jimmy Greaves and Kenny Dalglish have similar know-how, but Dalglish's knowledge and reading of the game are far superior. He is the most complete footballer in British soccer.'

And then there was that smile, the grin as wide as the Mersey tunnel itself, the sheer boyish delight, as he pivoted, arms raised aloft and wheeled away from the goalmouth. This is the Dalglish to remember. The man who is doing what he likes best, scoring goals.

Perhaps the final word should rest with the one other outstanding British player of post-war football – George Best. Of Dalglish he says simply: 'He is on a par with Di Stefano. And that is the best compliment I can pay him.'

CHAPTER EIGHT
Flower Of Scotland

O Flower of Scotland When will we see your likes again.
Scottish anthem

Tommy Docherty was a cavalier. If for nothing else, he will always be remembered for his flamboyance. His life was never anything but colourful, fraught with boardroom conflicts, dressing room rows, sackings and even a marital break-up that was to grip the front pages for days. And, on the field, his teams always displayed the same brand of hedonistic, couldn't care less football. Attack first, think about defence later, toss caution aside. It was the Docherty philosophy of life.

At Old Trafford, the Stretford Enders still recall his reign with affection and, even though honours have come their way since, they still hanker for that brash brand of Scottish flair, dashing wingmen and arrogance. It often got him into trouble. United were relegated before they stormed back to division one with record attendances. But the boardroom boys never really appreciated him. They wanted success, trophies in the cupboard, a manager they could respect, but in Tommy Docherty found nothing but trouble, and trouble with a capital T. He crossed swords with them and refused to kowtow. In the end, Docherty boasted he'd had more clubs than Jack Nicklaus.

When Tommy Docherty became manager of Scotland, Scottish football was in yet another of its deep depressions. They had lost six of their previous seven games and drawn the other and had scored only three goals in 12 internationals. Paranoia had well and truly set in and Docherty was just the kind of self-confident quack needed to restore its dignity and pride. Yet again Scotland had failed to qualify for a major tournament, this time the European Championship finals. There were two remaining games in the competition and the results hardly mattered. So the Scottish FA offered him a temporary contract, giving him charge for just those two games. It was to be an inspired move that would bring about a renaissance in Scottish football that was to yield a crop of youngsters for the future. For a short time, the Hampden crowd would have had you think Scotland were the world champions.

Docherty's first game in charge, against Portugal in October 1971, brought a 2–1 win and one of Hampden's best crowds in years for an international, with almost 60,000 turning up for what was essentially an irrelevant fixture. Irrelevant or not, it fired the Scottish imagination. Docherty's next fixture, against Belgium at Pittodrie, resulted in a 1–0 victory but perhaps more importantly it marked the beginning of Kenny Dalglish's record-breaking career in a blue shirt. 'Quite honestly there was no way that I could ignore him,' Docherty once said. 'He forced his way into that team and it's significant that he has never been out of Scotland's plans since.'

Dalglish was abroad when he heard of his selection, sunning himself by a Maltese swimming pool, as Celtic prepared to face Sliema Wanderers in the second round of the European Cup. Jock Stein was the first to break the news. He wandered over.

'You're in the pool, Kenny' he shouted.

'I know,' replied Kenny, mystified.

'No, I mean the Scotland pool,' laughed Stein. Dalglish took the news calmly.

It was November 1971. Dalglish had already turned out for the Scottish Under-23 side when it was managed by Bobby Brown the previous season, but he had barely been in Celtic's first team five minutes and could hardly have expected a place in the full squad with so little experience under his belt. His call-up was a surprise, catching even the football writers off guard. But Docherty was looking to Scotland's future.

'I could have gone for the likes of Denis Law and Frank McLintock,' he told the papers. 'But I feel it is an ideal opportunity to try a few new faces. The youngsters have to be blooded some time. And, with nothing at stake, this is the ideal moment.'

So, into the squad came Dalglish, goalkeeper Alan Rough, Aberdeen's Steve Murray, John Hansen of Partick Thistle and Jim Steele of Dundee. They didn't all make the team. Hansen, the older brother of Alan Hansen, was to be capped only once and Jim Steele was never capped while Alan Rough would have to wait a little longer before he pulled on the Scottish goalkeeper's jersey. But once he did, he and Dalglish would go on to earn more than 150 caps between them.

Docherty had spotted the potential in Dalglish. He was gambling and needed fresh blood in the side. There was little to lose and Dalglish did not let him down. Over the next few months other youngsters would be given their chance, including Alex Forsyth, Willie Morgan and Martin Buchan. Denis Law even made a brief return. Docherty also spotted enough flair in that Scotland side to bring, later Macari, Buchan and Forsyth to Old Trafford to give United half a dozen of his Scotland team. He even tried to take Dalglish to Manchester, but Jock Stein would have none of it. No way was he going to part with his jewel.

But for Dalglish it was a fairly uneventful debut. He came on as substitute just after the interval to replace Alex Cropley of Hibs. A 1–0 win and a packed house at Pittodrie was enough to send the fans home singing Docherty's praises. It was also sufficient to impress the Scottish FA who immediately offered him a four-year contract and a free hand to shape Scotland's future. He readily accepted.

Dalglish had also done enough to warrant selection for the future and had impressed one or two experienced commentators. John Rafferty of *The Scotsman* called it an 'extraordinary' debut. 'Then there was Ken Dalglish to surprise the manager by the calm way he picked up the rhythm of the game,' he wrote, 'and the way he started to link the passes together. His was an extraordinary performance in moving so easily into this new class of football with such assurance and effectiveness.'

Typically, Scotland lost their next fixture 2–1, against Holland in Amsterdam, though considering the Dutch would be appearing in a World Cup final within three years it was, in hindsight, not such a poor result. Scotland matched them ball for ball, Dalglish toiling relentlessly, but a goal in the last minute robbed them of a deserved draw.

Dalglish skipped Scotland's summer tour to Brazil for the mini World Cup, even though invited. Jock Stein warned that it would be debilitating and the young Dalglish still needed to be carefully nurtured. Dalglish took his advice and remained at home, anxious that his absence might jeopardise his Scotland career. Docherty was renowned for falling out with players and extracting his revenge. But there was never any danger of that happening with Dalglish. When they returned from what was generally regarded as a fairly successful South American trip, Dalglish was back in the squad for the World Cup qualifier against Denmark in Copenhagen. Scottish hopes were high and they would be even higher by the end of the evening, Scotland winning 4–1 with Dalglish coming on as substitute. Then, a month later at Hampden, Dalglish consummated his marriage with the blue shirt, scoring in the second minute as the Scots romped to a 2–0 victory. It was to be the first of many goals, but the last match of Docherty's short reign. Old Trafford beckoned with its glamour and fat salary; an even more challenging task. Docherty was away.

Dalglish has always been magnanimous in his praise of Docherty, 'the man who gave me my chance'. In particular, he points to Docherty's reorganisation of the national team at all levels, including a team comprised solely of second division players. 'He recognised lads in the second division and gave them a chance when other managers would have concentrated their talent spotting only on the glamour games,' he once remarked, adding that Docherty 'looked at some of the unfashionable clubs, saw players with ability there and brought them into the limelight.' It was a policy long espoused by Bill Shankly, who had always scoured the lower divisions to find new talent, emerging with players such as Kevin Keegan, Ray Clemence, Gordon Milne, Peter Thompson, Chris Lawler and many more. Yet, surprisingly, it was not a policy Dalglish was to adopt in later years when he became manager at Liverpool. Only a handful of players were ever signed from the lower divisions and few ever made it to the first team as Dalglish preferred to concentrate on expensive, quality signings.

Dalglish and Docherty had just one disagreement. Dalglish was on the verge of the full squad and had already been on the bench as a reserve. Then, surprisingly, Docherty left him out of the Under-23s side. Dalglish was furious. 'Not that he was worried from an egotistical point of view,' says Docherty. 'No, it was simply that he wasn't going to be playing. He lives for playing the game. That's all he wants to do.'

Docherty may have given back to Scotland some of its pride but it instantly disappeared when his successor, Willie Ormond, was appointed. In his first game in charge, Scotland crashed 5–0 to the Auld Enemy in a Scottish FA centenary celebration match at Hampden. It was humiliating. Ormond was a total contrast to the swashbuckling Docherty; withdrawn, thoughtful, unassuming, his managerial career had thus far been effective rather than glorious. If Docherty was the cavalier, Ormond was a round-head. He had taken St Johnstone to within striking range of the more fashionable clubs and the League championship, but when it came to inter-national football he was a novice. He knew little of the English first division and had not even seen most of the Anglos play other than on television.

But while Dalglish still had much to learn at an international level, many of the older heads showed little respect for Ormond. The exciting days of Docherty had suddenly been replaced by a period of austerity that was not always popular with the ranks. But Dalglish sat and listened, learn-ing with every game. The respect between Ormond and Dalglish was mutual. Yet the results were hardly impressive. After the England fiasco, Scotland went on to beat Wales but then slumped to seven defeats in their next ten games. It was hardly much fun playing in a side that was contin-ually losing, but gradually results improved, team spirit lifted, and the Ormond knockers were sidelined.

Scotland found themselves in the autumn of 1973 needing only to beat Czechoslovakia at Hampden to reach the World Cup finals. A 100,000 crowd turned up, but when Scotland fell a goal behind on the half-hour it looked as if the evening might be about to turn into disappointment. Dalglish, lining up alongside an ever youthful Denis Law, played his heart out. Scotland pulled a goal back but with Dalglish tiring, Ormond replaced him with the formidable Joe Jordan. It was an inspired move. With a quar-ter of an hour remaining, Jordan, near the penalty spot, dived bravely to head Willie Morgan's cross into the back of the net. Scotland had won 2–1 and even the usually critical Hampden crowd was ready to forgive Ormond his mistakes. Bremner recognised the mood and, at the final whistle, dragged Ormond on to the pitch to receive his encore. But the real hero of the hour was Denis Law.

At the time, Dalglish was so in awe of his fellow Scot that after a testi-monial against Manchester United at Old Trafford, he raced up to Law and swapped shirts immediately the final whistle blew. Later, in the dressing room, Jock Stein demanded all the shirts back for a charity auction. But Dalglish clung on to Law's shirt, refusing to hand it over. 'If necessary I'll buy it myself,' he pleaded. 'I'm sorry,' he added, much to the surprise and amusement of his team-mates. But no one is going to take it away from me.' It spoke volumes for Dalglish's reverence for his international colleagues.

Scotland's failure to reach the World Cup finals since 1958 had reached desperation point. Suicide had been on the menu and, had Scotland not qualified, a whole nation would have sunk into an appalling decline and depression. But they had been rescued and instead of depression there was hysteria, especially with England not making the trip to West Germany.

Scotland, as ever, travelled full of confidence. The mood was exuberant, expectations were high and the fans were as fanatical as ever. But the more sober analysts had only to examine Scotland's record to realise that it was a false dawn. England may have been beaten 2–0 the previous month but the fact was that England had not even qualified for the finals and Scotland's results prior to that were a miserable litany. A 1–1 draw with World Cup favourites West Germany was much to blame for the hysteria as Scotland played some of their best football in years. The German manager, Helmut Schoen, was impressed, rating Scotland the best side they had played that year and Dalglish the pick of their men. Unfortunately, the praise went to Scottish heads.

Scotland had been drawn in a difficult World Cup group, though it did little to dampen their spirits. It comprised everyone's favourite team, Brazil, the unknown Africans of Zaire and the always tough competitors from Yugoslavia. The group opened with an unexpected goalless draw between the Brazilians and the Yugoslavs, which did much to boost the confidence of the watching Scots. With the top two teams qualifying for the next round, it was becoming increasingly obvious that the group would be decided on how many goals each could score against Zaire. And Zaire were Scotland's first opponents. It was an ideal opportunity to put everyone else under pressure. All began promisingly, as Peter Lorimer and Joe Jordan put them two goals ahead within half an hour and everyone waited for the Zaireans to crumble. Then, astonishingly, the lights went out and everyone gathered in the centre circle while someone was sent to find an electrician. When light was eventually restored Scotland had gone off the boil. Zaire gritted their teeth and battled back courageously, almost scoring on more than one occasion. Scotland hung on to their lead but, try as they might, could not add to their scoreline. As the final whistle blew, a mood of despondency settled over the Scottish camp.

A few days later, Yugloslavia slammed nine goals past Zaire and virtually booked their passage to the next round. Scotland now needed to beat Brazil to guarantee qualification and that was an awesome task. But, typically, with all the odds stacked against them, Scotland produced one of their finest performances in years, holding the mighty Brazilians to a goalless draw and almost sneaking away with a victory themselves.

That draw had suddenly given Scotland a flicker of hope. They had expected to lose against Brazil, but it was now clear that the group would be decided by the last two games, with goal difference certain to play a key factor. If Scotland could beat Yugoslavia they would be through, but a draw would leave Brazil needing to score only three goals against Zaire. Defeat would all but eliminate Scotland. A mighty effort was demanded and Scotland gave it, against a side that was fancied by many to go all the way to the final. No goals arrived until the final ten minutes, when Karasi put the Yugoslavs ahead, but just when it looked as if Scotland were on their way home, up popped Joe Jordan to level the scores.

Scotland returned to their dressing room and then had to sit out an agonising three minutes awaiting the scoreline from Gelsenkirchen as Brazil and Zaire played out the last few moments of their contest. Of course there was never much doubt that the Brazilians would score three, yet they only just managed it, their third goal sneaking in under the belly of Zaire's fumbling keeper 11 minutes from time, a goal that raised one or two suspicions in minds north of the border.

Scotland were out of the World Cup and were left kicking themselves for failing to take advantage of Zaire. Dalglish had not played well. He had laboured, perhaps inexperienced at such a high level, perhaps too in awe of some of the finest defenders in world football, perhaps a shade too reserved when a little more adventure was called for. He was still only 23. Whatever the reason, it left him dispirited for some time. Much had been expected of him and he had failed to deliver. He had twice been substituted, with Tommy Hutchison replacing him as the expected goals failed to arrive. It was the first time a question mark had been raised against his ability in a blue shirt, but it was a doubt that was to remain attached to him for much of his international career.

Dalglish was the first to accept that much of the criticism being directed at him after the World Cup was fair, but added that 'no one was more disappointed than myself'. He told journalist Roger Baillie in 1975 that he didn't think it was because he was trying too hard. 'I've never really believed you can try too hard,' he claimed. 'Maybe it's because I have a bit of an infe-riority complex when I am with the international team. There are so many big names around I sometimes wonder what I am doing there.'

His Scotland team-mate at the time, Sandy Jardine, tends to agree and reckons it had much to do with age. He remembers him in that World Cup as a quiet, self-effacing youth. 'Kenny would not push himself while in the company of those Scotland players who were regarded as elder statesmen. At Celtic Park he would be familiar with everyone on a daily basis, but when it came to the business of the irregular international get-togethers Kenny was inclined to say nothing and think a lot.'

Yet Dalglish was just as committed when it came to playing for Scotland as he was with Celtic. 'With Kenny it was always early to bed and look after yourself,' recalls his former Scotland team-mate Denis Law. 'When we went out on our pranks, the one person missing was always Kenny. He'd be back in bed fast asleep.'

Dalglish had only one disagreement with Ormond. It came in May 1976 when he looked set to win a 34th consecutive cap for his country, breaking George Young's longstanding record. The game against Wales had been her-alded in the press as a milestone in Scottish international football and Hampden was well primed for the occasion. But when the team was announced there was no Dalglish, he was named merely as substitute. Still, it seemed certain that he would come on at some point to claim his record. But no; he remained on the bench even though a couple of players took knocks and Scotland were cruising to a comfortable victory. There was a stony silence between the two men. Dalglish was bitterly disappointed and the celebrations had to be abandoned.

Willie Ormond's departure was probably inevitable, though it took longer than expected. The 1974 finals had not been a total disaster. Scotland were the only unbeaten side, even holding the mighty Brazilians to a draw, as well as winning their first ever game at that level. And, judg-ing by the 10,000 fans who turned up to greet the team's return, the fans clearly reckoned they had done a reasonable job.

Eventually, Hearts lured Ormond off to Tynecastle and, with the 1978 World Cup finals just a year away, Ally MacLeod, the Aberdeen manager, was handed the poisoned chalice of guiding Scotland to Argentina, leaving him precious little time to prepare his troops. It was the summer of 1977 when MacLeod took over. His first game in charge was a dour goalless draw with Wales that left a number of his squad wondering if he really was the man to inspire Scotland into the next World Cup finals. But if a 3–0 win over Northern Ireland (Dalglish scored a couple) at Hampden in their next game raised spirits, a 2–1 victory at Wembley resulted in mass hysteria. With Brooking and Keegan absent from the England line-up, Scotland, inspired by Danny McGrain, tore England apart, with Gordon McQueen and Dalglish doing the damage in front of goal. Only an 87th minute penalty from Mick Channon brought some respectability to England's afternoon. It was only Scotland's fifth win on English soil since 1938 and it seemed just cause for celebration, as Scotland's Tartan Army invaded the sacred pitch at the final whistle and tore down everything in sight. It was not a pretty sight. Hugh McIlvanney in the *Observer* was damning, calling them 'the tribe that lost its head'. It was a description that could equally have applied to the entire Scotland team a year later in Argentina.

The famous victory over England was followed by an equally encouraging acclimatisation tour of South America, embarked upon even though Scotland had yet to qualify for the 1978 World Cup finals. A 4–2 win against Chile, followed by an ill-tempered 1–1 draw against Argentina and the sending off of Willie Johnston and then a 2–0 defeat at the hands of Brazil left Scottish optimism sky-high.

The game against Chile had been played against a howl of protests from the Labour government and the Scottish TUC, angered that the fixture would be interpreted as a friendly gesture towards General Pinochet's military dictatorship. Worse, the match was scheduled to be played in the national stadium, scene of some of the most horrific crimes and where thousands of President Allende's supporters had been incarcerated, tortured and murdered following the coup of September 1973. Even some of the players had questioned the wisdom of the Scottish FA in arranging such a fixture. But football is football and the team duly travelled without too many divisions among their ranks.

Equally, they were not going to be fobbed off by a blast of propaganda, not from anyone. Lounging by their Santiago swimming pool one morning, a silver haired gentleman wandered over to the Scottish players and began to chat with them. BBC commentator Archie MacPherson, sitting close by, spotted the man as he walked over towards Dalglish. MacPherson overheard him pontificating about how wonderful life now was in Chile and how the facts were being distorted. Everyone in Chile was happy and settled now that they had a stable government. But Dalglish was clearly not impressed. 'You're talking a load of crap,' he snapped. 'We'll make up our own minds about what we see. We don't need you to tell us. It was the voice of working-class Govan talking. The silver-haired man stormed off angrily.

A mixed bag of results in the World Cup qualifiers had left Scottish hopes for Argentina depending on the outcome of their final match, away to Wales. By then, Dalglish had moved to Liverpool and, with Cardiff Arms Park restricted to a mere 10,000 capacity, the Welsh FA decided to transfer the game to, of all places, Anfield. It suited Dalglish perfectly. Even fervent Liverpool supporters had to admit that Anfield had never seen anything quite like this. By the end of the evening, Scotland's Tartan Army was probably wondering why they did not play all their fixtures at Anfield rather than Hampden.

It seemed that somehow almost all the 53,000 tickets had found their way north of the border for what was supposed to be a home game for the Welsh. The Kop end of the ground, which had been allocated to Wales, was instead a sea of tartan, with the Welsh supporters occupying a small enclave somewhere in the top left corner of the Kop. Elsewhere was nothing but tartan. A Scottish victory was inevitable, yet it took a hotly disputed penalty plus a stunning Dalglish goal to send Scotland on their way. Don Masson put away the penalty in the 79th minute after Joe Jordan and Dave Jones jumped to reach Willie Johnston's long throw in. Someone's hand looked to have touched the ball; the referee reckoned it was Jones's, but many others suspected it belonged to Jordan. The Welsh protested furiously but it made no difference and, after what seemed an eternity, Don Masson stepped up and coolly sent the goalkeeper the wrong way. It was enough but with three minutes remaining, Dalglish sealed Scotland's victory with a goal that will always live in the memory of Scottish fans, a goal that would rank among Scotland's greatest. He raced into the box to meet Martin Buchan's cross with a glancing header that soared into the back of the net. It was Dalglish's 50th international cap and, fittingly, a game he will always be remembered for. Scotland were on their way to Buenos Aires or, to be more exact, Cordoba.

Argentina was to provide a salutary lesson for Dalglish and he was not slow to take on board its message. It began with Ally MacLeod boasting to the Scottish press that his team would return jangling with medals. Expectations among the public were raised to fever pitch and when Scotland returned humiliated, MacLeod was to be the scapegoat. The players knew better, they understood the quality of the opposition they would be facing as well as the unfriendly conditions. Some, including Dalglish, thought it perverse to be telling the public one thing when the players knew different. In his autobiography, written some years before he became a manager, Dalglish warned: 'I'm a great believer in talking about something only when you've done the job. Looking back, I feel that he placed a lot of unnecessary pressure on the players when he talked of winning medals in Argentina. People began to believe that all we had to do was turn up.'

Nor was it helped by a famous lap of honour aboard an open-topped bus at Hampden in front of 35,000 fans before the team departed for Argentina. Never before had so many football fans gone to Hampden not to see a game of football. The former travelling salesman Ally MacLeod knew a thing or two about selling a product but he should also have remembered that enthusiasm for the product needs to be matched by the quality. If the fans had been enthusiastic in 1974, they were hysterical now, and all thanks to MacLeod's brand of marketing. Dalglish had recently helped Liverpool to their second successive European Cup where the preparation had been as low-key as imaginable, yet here were Scotland about to go to Argentina and celebrating even before they had played a game. It was tempting fate.

Dalglish was also to learn another lesson. For the first time he was exposed to the cruelties of Fleet Street. England had failed to qualify for Argentina and the English press as well as the Scottish press were sent in their droves to cover Scotland's fortunes. But, given the previous World Cup, they were clearly more interested in what happened off the field than on it. Tales were flashed back to London and Glasgow of drunken binges, womanising and gambling. Facts were rarely checked (why spoil a good story?), players were mistakenly identified and the innocent were often accused of the most outrageous behaviour. Nor was it all helped by some Scottish players selling their stories to the ever eager tabloids. But back home it all made good reading, sold more newspapers and no doubt thrilled a few editors. Scotland were sinking into a quagmire of disasters.

Although Ally MacLeod had jumped for joy when he heard the draw, Scotland had in fact been given a far from easy group. Holland were the automatic favourites, favourites even to win the tournament, while Peru were reckoned one of the weakest South American sides. But at least they were not playing 15,000 miles away from home. Iran were the unknown and least fancied of the four. But then Scotland should have remembered Zaire. In Scottish eyes, all they had to do was overcome Peru and they would be through to the next round.

As it happened, their first game was against the Peruvians. 'Poor poor Peru if only you knew what the boys in blue are going to do to you too true' penned Scottish poet Alan Bold.

Dalglish pulled on the Scottish shirt for the 55th time to break Denis Law's record as the most-capped Scottish player of all time. Within half an hour Scotland were ahead, thanks to Joe Jordan. But then Peru began to find their feet and by the second half were cutting through the Scottish defence like a knife through butter. By full time, the Scots had crashed to a 3–1 defeat and disgrace number one had struck. Worse was to follow. After the game Dalglish and West Brom's Willie Johnston were picked out to supply random dope tests. It seemed a mere formality but later that evening the news broke that Johnston's test had proved positive. It was disgrace number two. Johnston immediately admitted to taking a drug, Reactivan, purely for medical purposes, but had failed to notify the doctor despite all the players being repeatedly asked to disclose any medicines they were taking. Johnston was on the next plane home. Had Scotland won then, they would have had to forfeit the game anyhow.

But all was not quite lost. Scotland could still pick up the advantage by defeating Iran handsomely. But, unfortunately, Ally MacLeod paid the Iranians little respect, barely bothering to read Andy Roxburgh's carefully prepared spying reports. Iran would be easy; the players were simply told to go out and win. But in World Cup finals, rhetoric alone is hardly sufficient. By now the world's sporting press had fixed their gaze firmly on Cordoba and the Scottish camp.

Iran were a handful. Scotland opened the scoring courtesy of an Iranian own goal but then tragically gave away an equaliser as they laboured woefully. The game ended in a wretched 1–1 draw. Disgrace number three. Scotland were all but out of the World Cup. Dalglish was devastated. He described it as the worst day of his footballing career. He had even been substituted in favour of Joe Harper and, as a striker, had to take much of the blame for the lack of goals. The press were hardly generous towards him and his team-mates. 'We were so bad, the sooner Scotland get home the better,' raged the *Daily Record*. 'Shamed. Humiliated. And shown up to be fourth rate in front of the world,' it screamed.

Lou Macari called it a 'nightmare' as the party rolled from one disgrace to another. Heads hung in shame, players locked themselves away. Sponsors Chrysler dropped the team from its advertising campaign and Ally MacLeod wisely stayed in his hotel room. Back home in Scotland, Mrs

MacLeod was being hounded by the press.

There was one final chance to redeem themselves. Scotland had not even expected a draw from the Dutch, but when the odds are stacked against them the Scots come out as bonny fighters. Astonishingly, they won 3–2. Dalglish had a goal disallowed early on and when the Dutch scored from the penalty spot it seemed that the expected was about to happen. But on the stroke of half time Dalglish atoned with an equaliser. Three minutes after the interval, Scotland were themselves awarded a penalty and suddenly they were ahead, thanks to Archie Gemmill. Gemmill, in the 68th minute, jinked his way past the Dutch masters to fire in one of the most memorable goals in the competition. Scotland were 3–1 up but a goal from Johnny Nef brought the scoreline back to 3–2 and the Scots exited on goal difference. The Scots were left wondering 'if only'.

The Argentinian flop left a bitter taste in Dalglish's mouth. Scotland had travelled ill-prepared, hawking around their arrogance without sufficient homework. And they had paid the price. Few players, with the notable exception of Graeme Souness, came out of the experience with any credit. Dalglish had at least applied his usual professionalism to the task but on an international stage wearing a blue shirt, he was again found to be wanting.

Soured by their Argentinian experience, Scotland cowered back into their self-protective shell. By the autumn and after another defeat, this time in Austria, Ally MacLeod was gone, his reputation destroyed; at least Dalglish could return to the cool-headed atmosphere of Anfield with its glorious winning ways and a couple more European triumphs. In England he was set to become Footballer of the Year and one of the post-war period's finest players, yet his international career looked at a crossroads. It seemed that after more than 50 caps it might even be about to draw to a close. After the World Cup trauma there were calls for a clean sweep and it might easily have been the appropriate moment to thank Dalglish for all his services. Names and reputations counted for little: Lou Macari, Don Masson and Bruce Rioch were all shown the door along with the disgraced Willie Johnston. Dalglish must have wondered if he might be next.

Ally MacLeod partly blamed himself for failing to reap the best from Dalglish. 'He hasn't always been played in his best position for Scotland and I blame myself for that as much as anyone,' he admitted. 'He has been played off someone like Joe Jordan or Andy Gray, when at Liverpool they play off him. I tried it that way twice. When we played friendly games in

Chile and in Argentina before the 1978 World Cup finals, I used Kenny as a target man up front with little Lou Macari playing off him. It worked in both games, and I'm only sorry that I didn't persist. I thought of doing it against Iran for instance, and then changed my mind. It might have made all the difference.'

But MacLeod had no complaints about Dalglish as a Scotland player. Writing some time before Argentina, MacLeod reminded his readers that the Scots were quick to forget how they treated many a romantic hero of the past. 'People say he does more for Liverpool than Scotland. Maybe there is a grain of truth in that. But in my time as a manager I can remember some outstanding performances from him. I think that he has been sadly underrated by some of the Scots fans. It makes me laugh to hear them in the pubs talking about the great performances of Denis Law or Jim Baxter. They forget that these two players got a lot of stick too when they had bad games for Scotland. Dalglish is one of the finest players ever to wear a Scottish jersey. He will be a legend in years to come, mark my words.'

For once, MacLeod was right. But then in Dalglish he was selling a quality product. Into MacLeod's chair came Dalglish's old mentor Jock Stein. It was the wisest decision the Scottish FA had taken in years and indeed it might have come earlier had Stein not been so severely injured in his car crash. But with Stein forced out at Parkhead and now in control at Elland Road, it was the ideal moment to tempt him back north of the border. Changes were about to be wrought but Dalglish would be safe. In his first game under his new charge, Dalglish twice equalised as Scotland defeated Norway 3–2 in an exciting European Championship qualifier. In their next game, they lost 1–0 to Portugal and shortly afterwards Stein took Dalglish aside. Was this the moment when Stein would break the bad news to him that his international career was at an end? No, the very opposite. Stein asked him to take over as captain.

It was an honour and a move greatly appreciated by Dalglish. But Scottish results barely improved. They were beaten 3–0 by Wales, 3–1 by England and then 3–1 at Hampden by the reigning World Champions Argentina with an 18-year-old Diego Maradona putting on the kind of scintillating individual performance that had once been the prerogative of Scottish football. But it was not a happy game for Dalglish, who was about to become a victim of the Hampden boo-boys. Alan Hansen recalled Dalglish's treatment with some bitterness in his book *Tall, Dark and Hansen*:

'He suffered really badly. From the start of that game the fans were on his back. Every time he touched the ball he was booed and, of course, Kenny, being the kind of person he is, simply tried harder and harder. It was sad to be there and see the torment he went through. In fact it was even worse to be on the field with him because we all suffered with Kenny that day.'

After that there was a weary 1–0 victory over Northern Ireland. Dalglish's four games as captain had hardly inspired the side. He looked to be bearing the responsibilities heavily. Stein realised his mistake and quickly stepped in to lift the burden. The captaincy eventually reverted to Gemmill and Dalglish was given a freer role. It was immediately followed by a 4–0 win over Norway, with Dalglish hitting Scotland's second. Dalglish completed the year with draws against Peru and Austria before two disastrous defeats by Belgium in the European qualifiers made 1979 a year to forget.

However, 1980 was barely better, another undistinguished year, culminating in a 2–0 defeat by England at Hampden. Dalglish had played in all eight games. But success was to follow as Scotland qualified for their third successive World Cup finals after overcoming a powerful preliminary group that included Northern Ireland, Portugal and Sweden. Jock Stein was determined that there should be no repeat of the Argentinian nightmare. Stein was not the kind of manager to allow the money wrangles, inadequate hotels and the ill-prepared tactics that had dogged Scotland in Argentina to be part of his administration. He was far too wise and Scotland travelled to Spain, this time without a Hampden farewell, but with tempered optimism. They had a wretched draw, perhaps the toughest of all, alongside Brazil, New Zealand and Europe's in-form team the Soviet Union. They all knew it would be difficult and there were no boasts about medals. The money problem was solved by appointing a committee, including Dalglish, Asa Hartford and Willie Miller to sort the arrangements out long before they stepped on to any aeroplane.

Stein was also a disciplinarian and would never tolerate misbehaviour, disloyalty or disrespect. He knew everything that was going on and was not averse to sitting in hotel foyers late at night carefully logging his players. There was no taking liberties with the Big Man. He ruled, as Graeme Souness once said, borrowing from Jack London, 'with a rod of iron, an iron fist without a velvet glove'. Dalglish for one felt the lash of his tongue during those Scotland days. Prior to a game in Brussels against Belgium, he and

Souness had been given permission to go out shopping with a friend but were told to be back in time for the team meeting. The only problem was that they forgot at what time the meeting had been scheduled. Dalglish was convinced that it was at 5.00pm; Souness was not quite so sure but Dalglish seemed so certain that it was hard to disagree. So, they rolled back to the hotel at five to spot Stein waiting and raging at the hotel reception desk. Before they were through the door, the wrath of Stein descended on them. Dalglish tried to shoulder the blame but Stein lashed out at them both, reserving the greater invective for Souness, who was by then captain. The abuse ensued as they strode down the corridors and into the team meeting where it was repeated just so that everyone else could realise that reputations and captaincy meant added responsibilities and that everyone was treated just the same. Both men had an anxious wait when the next Scotland squad was announced, wondering if they would be part of it.

But if everything off the field was in order, the same problems lingered on the field. Scotland's opening game in Spain against New Zealand looked a simple enough task but it was a case of not simply winning but needing to win handsomely. Scotland soon swept into the lead, thanks to Dalglish, plus a couple from John Wark, but then astonishingly they contrived almost to surrender the game by conceding two goals. Sense returned eventually and Scotland finally ran out 5–2 winners, but there were enough cracks in the Scottish defence to suggest that a more capable attacking side would rip through them. Dalglish later admitted in one newspaper that he 'had played badly against New Zealand in the opening World Cup game. I had frozen. I scored the first goal in the 5–2 win but my play was terrible.' For Dalglish the writing was on the wall.

Scotland's moment of truth came three days later against Brazil. Stein decided to leave Dalglish out of his line-up, preferring instead Steve Archibald. He guessed that Dalglish could not perform in the sizzling heat of southern Spain, that he did not have the stamina to play for a full 90 minutes. He might also have recalled his days at Parkhead when Dalglish was reckoned a 60-minute player. Dalglish was deeply upset. It was a controversial decision yet it looked to be fully justified when David Narey fired Scotland into a sensational lead after just 18 minutes. But 12 minutes from half time, Zico equalised. After the interval, a revitalised Brazil cut through Scotland, scoring three times before the final whistle. Dalglish was sent on after the third rattled the back of the net but it was too late for him to rectify the shambles. The fact was simple; Brazil were a far better side than Scotland, probably the best, certainly the most flamboyant, in the competition.

Scotland could hardly complain, but they still had an opportunity to redeem themselves. A 3–0 win by the Soviet Union over New Zealand now meant the Scots needed to beat the Soviet Union to grab second spot in the group. They ran out determined to battle all the way. Dalglish was again omitted from the line-up, this time losing out to Joe Jordan. And this time his omission hurt even more. It was not that Dalglish was questioning the wisdom of Stein leaving him out of the side, but the manner in which it was done. Dalglish was given no forewarning and was not even included among the substitutes. Worse, in Dalglish's books, he was given no explanation. Later he lashed out at Stein in the *Sunday Mirror* arguing that 'it would have been good manners to have a word with me but I wasn't offered any explanation.' He added that Stein had 'left me out of a World Cup qualifier against Portugal earlier on and I had to ask him why. Otherwise I would never have known.'

Scotland shot into the lead against the Soviet Union, Jordan sending Scottish hearts back home pounding 20 to the dozen. But it did not last long. The Soviets were soon leading 2–1. The game finally petered out into a 2–2 draw, Scotland's equaliser coming from captain Graeme Souness late in the match. Dalglish was not even given an opportunity and returned home knowing that he had barely played a part in Scotland's campaign.

There could be no criticism this time of the organisation, the players' discipline or the preparation. Scotland were simply unlucky to have drawn two outstanding nations in their group. Yet they still returned home to a barrage of abuse, much of it directed towards Dalglish. The *Daily Record* was scathing, though not just of Dalglish. 'He had a disastrous World Cup,' it raged. 'Against New Zealand he didn't show anything like his real ability.' The newspaper gave him an overall rating of five out of ten. The World Cup it reckoned 'could spell the end of Danny McGrain's international career,' adding that 'the same could go for Kenny Dalglish and Alan Rough.'

If, four years earlier, Dalglish's international career had faced a crossroads after Argentina, his future was now in severe doubt. At 31, he could hardly be expected to continue forever and, with 80 odd caps behind him, it was possibly time to step aside. 'Has my international career ended,' he wondered in the *Sunday Mirror* when the team returned home. 'I don't know,' he wrote. 'That is not for me to decide.' He added poignantly that 'I cannot see myself taking part in Scotland's next World Cup qualifying rounds.'

But Stein remained loyal to his former Celtic star. Dalglish missed the next two Scotland games through injury but was back to face Belgium in Brussels, scoring two of his finest international goals. It was the beginning of a renaissance in Dalglish's international career.

Scottish football journalist Gerry McNee, for one, reckoned it was a turning point for Dalglish. 'He had not lived up to his reputation in his first 60 or so caps but in his last 40 he began to flower into the player we all knew he was. His hunger for the game seemed to increase.' And yet he would never bask in the same adulation that was given Wee Jinky Johnstone, the Lawman or Slim Jim Baxter. Even less would his name stand alongside Alex James, Hughie Gallacher or Alex Jackson. Perhaps he just lacked the flair for the Scottish occasion, the one-liners, the rapport with the Hampden terraces.

Dalglish's Scotland career seems to fall into three phases. Initially, in his early years, there was a time when he showed promise; then, in a middle period with the three important World Cups, he failed to deliver. Finally, in a third period covering his later years, he eventually flowered into the player all Scotland knew he could be. Sadly it was too late for him to affect or influence the course of Scottish international football. Dalglish's greatest failure had been his inability to perform at the highest level, in the World Cup. It may only have been a four-week tournament, but it was the world's shop window and quality players were expected to excel and delight in its surrounds. Dalglish's failure to do so meant that he would never be as highly rated on the continent as he was in Britain. The Real Madrids and Milans of Europe never made Liverpool an offer for his services. Perhaps, in the end, Dalglish simply did not like being away from his family for so long. He was known to get homesick, he would miss Marina and the children, feel more insecure and it would show.

The goals may have been. hard to come by, they always are at an international level, but when they did arrive they were spectacular. None more so than his stunning goal against Spain at Hampden in November 1984 when he waltzed across the area, sidestepping the Spanish defence, before blasting a rocket of a shot into the corner of the net. It was not just Dalglish's finest goal for his country but one of the most memorable struck by anyone in a Scottish shirt. The *Scottish Daily Express* labelled it a 'wonder goal'. It was his 30th goal for Scotland and equalled Denis Law's longstanding scoring record. It was also to be his last.

But in the European Championship neither Dalglish. nor any of his esteemed colleagues could rescue Scottish fortunes as they sank miserably, finishing bottom of their group with only four points from six games. It was an appalling indictment of Scottish football to reflect that, within the space of 18 months, they could beat Holland 2–1 at Hampden and Uruguay 2–0 yet could not overcome the under-resourced footballers of Switzerland.

And in the World Cup qualifiers Scotland's dreams were on a knife-edge. It all came down to the final game and, yet again, the opposition was Wales. Defeat at Cardiff would mean Scotland would be eliminated, a draw would mean a play-off against Australia, while a win would also mean a play-off with the Australians. Dalglish and most of his Liverpool colleagues were absent through injury. Now player/manager of Liverpool, Dalglish had instead gone on a spying mission to look at a player they were interested in signing. In a tension-packed match, Scotland, a goal behind after 13 minutes, equalised from the penalty spot ten minutes from time to earn themselves a final eliminator with the Socceroos. Mexico looked a mere formality that left the crowd singing 'Que sera, sera, we're going to Mexico'. Yet minutes before the final whistle, unknown to most of the 40,000 crowd, Jock Stein had collapsed on the touchline. He was rushed to the dressing rooms after suffering a heart attack. Resuscitation was tried, but it was too late. Minutes later Jock Stein was dead and a veil was cast over Scottish football.

Stein's death that tense evening at Ninian Park was a desperate blow to Dalglish. He was told about it when he rang his wife and could barely believe it. There had been few differences between the two men over the many years they had been associated. Dalglish had learned much from Stein and had come to look upon him as a father figure. Similarly, Stein took pride in watching his young protégé mature into the finest Celtic and Scotland player of all time. Dalglish knew that if he was ever in trouble he would have to face two men – his father and Jock Stein. There could be no higher praise. Any initial doubts Stein had once harboured about the youngster had soon given way to unreserved admiration. For Dalglish, international life would never be quite the same again. He was now 34 years old and could hardly expect a new manager to persevere with him. He had been capped 97 times by his country and not unnaturally was keen to reach his century of international caps.

The incoming manager, Alex Ferguson, could perhaps have been understood had he ignored Dalglish, though one half of Glasgow would never have forgiven him. As it was, Dalglish made a welcome return to the team for the goalless draw against East Germany at Hampden in October 1985. He was also at Hampden for the 2–0 win over Australia but did not travel down under for the return leg. Dalglish, with too many responsibilities at Anfield, decided to skip the journey, needing instead to remain at home to help Liverpool's assault on the double. Just one more cap was needed to reach his 100 and, fittingly, it came at Hampden in March 1986 against Romania. Dalglish was made captain for the evening and the Scottish FA acknowledged his contribution to Scottish international football by awarding him a solid silver cap before the kick-off, presented by West Germany's manager Franz Beckenbauer. Within a minute of the whistle, Dalglish had almost provided an opening goal for Eamonn Bannon. 'Dalglish's touch, vision and control were still there in abundance,' reported the *Liverpool Daily Post*. Scotland eventually scored three times through Strachan, Gough and Aitken, but the evening belonged to one man, Kenny Dalglish, holder of 100 Scottish caps.

Injury and commitments at Anfield would limit Dalglish's international appearances for the remainder of the season but, not surprisingly, he was named in the Scotland squad for the World Cup finals. More surprisingly, however, his Liverpool team-mate Alan Hansen was omitted. Dalglish was quietly fuming, astonished that Alex Ferguson could leave out one of the most experienced defenders in the British game, a man who was captain of Liverpool, among the most honoured players of all time and who had graced four European Cup finals. After the news reached him, Dalglish turned up at Hansen's house clutching a compensatory bottle of champagne.

Yet within ten days, Dalglish, who had just led Liverpool to the League and Cup double, was out of the World Cup himself, sidelined by a knee injury. It would have been his fourth appearance in the World Cup finals, a record for a British player and an achievement which only eight players had ever matched. The news caused a sensation. Even in England it was the lead story in most of the tabloids. The headline in the *Scottish Daily Express* told it all: 'DALGLISH OUT'. Ferguson was devastated. 'He was to be our linchpin,' he despaired.

It was probably just as well that Dalglish missed Scotland's trip to Mexico. Drawn in the same group as West Germany, Uruguay and Denmark, they never really had much chance and managed only a goalless draw with Uruguay, scoring just one goal in their three games. Dalglish's international career was virtually at an end now. After the World Cup he returned briefly to the side, coming on as a substitute against Bulgaria and lining up for his final cap in the 3–0 win against Luxembourg at Hampden. It was November 1986 and he was 35 years old. He had scored 30 goals for his country and had won a record 102 caps.

CHAPTER NINE
The Right Stuff?

That crazed hour of the night when it came time to prove that
the right stuff works in all areas of life.
Tom Wolfe, *The Right Stuff*

Kenny Dalglish harboured no overwhelming desire to become a football manager. It was always an option at the back of his mind. But, given his business interests and other possibilities such as television and newspaper columns, it was nothing more than that. He had even recently tried a spot of acting, playing himself in a television adaptation of Alan Bleasdale's *Scully*. The producer, Sandy Ross, was full of praise for his performance, calling it thoroughly professional. 'He learned his lines and always turned up on time. Nothing was too much trouble,' adds Ross.

However, you cannot become a manager until someone offers you employment. Dalglish was 33 years of age. Old, perhaps, for a footballer, but he had always taken care of himself and was still as fit and healthy as anyone on the staff. He reckoned he had a few more years of football left in him and thoughts of retiring and taking up management were still some distance from his mind.

When John Smith casually asked him one day what his thoughts were for the future, Dalglish answered that he was keen on management but he was more than happy to play for a few more years, hopefully at Anfield. He assured the chairman that he would not be looking for a job yet but expected to be playing for Liverpool for some time. A seed had been planted in John Smith's mind.

Joe Fagan had always been a short-term appointment as Liverpool manager; he was already 62 years old when he took over from Bob Paisley. Fagan was a popular character, his round, rubbery face ready to be twisted and pulled into any emotion or exclamation. Everybody loved Joe and Joe loved everybody; the only thing he hated was dropping players. He had joined the club in 1958, shortly before Bill Shankly's arrival and, like Paisley before him, had tried his hand at every job in the bootroom. Joe was as Scouse as they come yet had never actually played for the club. Instead, he had enrolled at Manchester City a year before war broke out but had to wait until January 1947 before making his league debut. He left Maine Road in August 1951, spending a short time with Nelson before making a brief return to league football with Bradford Park Avenue. Two years later, he left Park Avenue to become trainer at Rochdale and then moved to Anfield to join its famous bootroom staff. But in 1985 he was 64 years old. He had tasted life at the top and been hugely successful but clearly he could not be expected to continue for much longer. The strain was already telling and had even been noticed by some of his players. Early in the 1984/5 season Fagan decided to tell John Smith that he felt this ought to be his final campaign at Anfield. It was time to retire; he would like to go at the end of the season.

It must have come as something of a surprise to Dalglish when John Smith rang him at his house one day towards the end of that season. He was brief and came directly to the point. He and Peter Robinson wanted to come and see him immediately at his house. 'Sure,' replied Dalglish, 'no problem.' Joe Fagan was retiring, said Smith, they needed a new manager, was he interested? 'You can still come,' was all he could say. Dalglish was flattered. Above all he was dumbfounded. He had never in his wildest dreams expected such an offer. To be asked to take over the reins of Britain's number one football club was an honour. At the very least, he would have expected to enter football management at the bottom, perhaps in the third division if he was lucky. But to take over at the top was astonishing. Of course he was interested. 'Then Peter Robinson and I had better come to your house and talk it over,' said Smith.

On the evening before Liverpool's ill-fated European Cup final with Juventus, John Smith sat down in his Brussels hotel room and picked up the telephone. He rang the various members of the board in their rooms and asked them if they would come up to his suite as he needed an urgent meeting with them. When they had all gathered, he began by announcing that Joe Fagan had decided to retire after the following day's game. That did not come as a surprise to any of them. For some time they had known that Fagan was keen to go, although no specific date had been set. Most assumed, however, that it would be at the end of the season. Fagan had always been regarded as a stop-gap manager. Now 64 years old, it was clear that he could not soldier on indefinitely. He had spent 27 years at Anfield and it was not unreasonable that at his age he would soon wish to relinquish the highly pressured job of managing one of Europe's top football clubs. Like the players, the directors too had sensed a change in him since he took over.

'I also wish to tell you,' added Smith, 'that in his place I have appointed Kenny Dalglish as player/manager.'

There were gasps. Few had had any inkling. One or two directors nodded approvingly. They knew Dalglish as a popular player, courteous, professional and, of course, one of the finest players ever to wear the red shirt of Liverpool. It was John Smith at his most brilliant.

John Smith then announced that he had also appointed Bob Paisley on a two-year contract as Dalglish's adviser. Dalglish, he said, had particularly asked for Bob's help. It was his condition for accepting the job – and Smith had agreed to it.

The discussion was over before it had barely begun. Fagan was going and the succession had been decided. The King is dead, long live the King.

The decision had been ratified. Dalglish was to be the new manager of Liverpool Football Club and an announcement would be made following the European Cup final. But, sadly, events did not turn out quite as smoothly as hoped.

The news inevitably leaked out. The following morning, the day of the European Cup final, Dalglish and his fellow players awoke to find the back pages full of speculation. Fagan was going and the rumour was that Dalglish would be taking over. Craig Johnston was the first to get hold of the English papers and break the news. 'JOE SET TO GO' was the headline splashed across the *Daily Mirror*. His successor would be found from within the club, predicted the paper, with Ronnie Moran, Roy Evans and Chris Lawler lining up as possibilities, but the name of Kenny Dalglish was the hot favourite. Ronnie Moran and Chris Lawler, Fagan's bootroom assistants, first heard the news while watching BBC Television in their hotel bedrooms on the morning of the game. At first they did not believe it. After all, Fagan had not told any of them about his impending departure and surely they would be the first to know. Ronnie Moran was deeply upset that Fagan, with whom he had worked for so many years, had not confided in him. It was the same with the players. Phil Neal and Mark Lawrenson similarly heard the news on TV and were dumbfounded. Neal, for his own reasons, was deeply upset. Dalglish was tight-lipped, his wife equally noncommittal when confronted by some of the players' wives. It was all a mystery.

Fagan was furious that the news had leaked out. This was the most important day in the club's season, the moment when Liverpool could stand above all European clubs, with the exception of Real Madrid, as five times winners of the trophy. The news had distracted his players and staff. He had been awaiting his moment to tell them. Now they were standing around gossiping in corners when they should have been concentrating on that evening's game. The press were also milling about, trying to find out what was happening. It did not make for good preparation.

Fagan quickly decided to hold a meeting with the players and his staff in an attempt to scotch the rumours. Unfortunately the get-together only added fuel to the speculation. Fagan said merely that an announcement would be made after the game and he refused either to confirm or deny the stories. As everyone filed away he added, 'After tonight you can call me Joe.' The older hands looked at him knowingly. Given what he had just said, it should have been obvious to all the players that something was in the air. Most, rightly, concluded that Fagan was quitting, but they also believed that there was still some uncertainty about his successor.

In a more receptive frame of mind that afternoon, Fagan confessed everything to one journalist, Chris James of the *Daily Mirror*. 'I'm too old and tired,' he told him. 'It's a job for a young man's brains and energy.' He admitted that he had decided to quit back in February. He had met with John Smith and Peter Robinson and they had agreed that he would go after the final game of the season. When he was appointed he had always insisted that it would be only for two years. 'I wanted to give them plenty of time to find a new manager.

'It's not an eight hours a day job, it's 24 hours a day,' he admitted. 'And there's no way you can get away from that.' Fagan too had felt the pressures, although what stress he had experienced would be nothing to what the next 24 hours were about to bring.

'You can't just wipe away all the pressures when you wake up in the morning,' he explained. 'The pressures are enormous. I've worked under managers like Harry Catterick, Bill Shankly and Bob Paisley and seen how they had to live with the pressure.'

Chris Lawler, from his seat in the bootroom, had noticed the marked change. 'During that last year,' he says, 'Fagan changed dramatically. You could see it in his physical appearance. He suddenly grew old. There was an enormous change over the few years I worked with him. You could see the pressure was getting to him.'

Mark Lawrenson also tracked the decline in Fagan during his second season in charge. 'Certainly he was not the same man,' he says. 'He started to look old, and age was something you never associated with him. The enjoyment seemed to have gone out of the job in the second year. Something happened to Joe in that second season, and it happened long before the Heysel disaster.'

The pressure had got to Shankly, now it had struck at Fagan. He had been unable to take any more. The daily strain, the relentless quest for success, the continual limelight, the buying and selling of players, making decisions. Liverpool had become almost unmanageable. One day it would even claim his young successor. And some years later the strain would even bite at Graeme Souness, leading to a heart attack and triple bypass surgery.

The news was eventually confirmed the following day, in the wake of the Heysel disaster. But, after the previous evening's events, not surprisingly, nobody really wanted to talk about the new manager. The football lobby had moved aside while the newshounds dissected and analysed the tragic events at Heysel. The eyes and ears of the nation were tuned to the disaster and the way Downing Street was talking some even wondered if football would ever be welcomed again in England.

Even the players did not know how to respond. They of course congratulated the new manager, but with the weight of 39 deaths on their minds, nobody could even consider any celebrations. It was a muted succession. Only Jimmy Murphy of Manchester United, after Munich, could have known what it was like to take over a football club in such desperate circumstances.

Fagan returned to Merseyside a broken man, openly shedding tears as he stepped from the plane at Speke Airport, his young assistant Roy Evans lending a comforting arm. Together they crossed the tarmac to face the world's press. His career, which should have ended on a glorious note had instead culminated in shame and turmoil, the saddest day of his life. It was hardly an ideal moment for Dalglish to be taking charge.

In the lounge at Speke Airport, the cross-examination of Liverpool Football Club began. The questioning was intense, the response muted and confused. Television cameras and microphones battled with each other beneath glaring lights. Blame was laid at the door of extremists in the National Front, the poor standard of the Heysel Stadium and the disastrous failure to properly segregate the fans on the ill-fated sectors X and Z. But while the news journalists battled with each other at the airport, the footballing press had been tipped off that there would also be a press conference at Anfield later that day to announce Dalglish's appointment as manager. The club felt, correctly, that it would have been insensitive to announce their decision at the Speke Airport press conference. Yet dragging the footballing corps off to Anfield was equally crass at a time when Liverpool and its supporters were the focus of the world's press.

Later that day, Dalglish, flanked by his mentor, Paisley, and his chairman, sat in a daze, not quite sure how to respond to the questioning as the club announced his promotion to player/manager. Dalglish had never been one for courting journalists, even the tame ones who tracked Liverpool's daily progress. Friendly to journalists but never a friend, was how one reporter summed him up. Now he was facing questions from distinctly unfriendly reporters and, like everyone else at the club, was understandably having difficulty in knowing how to cope. There was no one to shield him and nobody properly equipped to help guide him in his new role.

John Smith pulled on a brave face. 'Kenny is entering the managerial side for the first time,' he told the gathering. 'And we have every reason to believe he will have a successful period in office. We feel we have a man of great ability on the field who has got an old head on young shoulders.' An old head on young shoulders. It would make a fitting epitaph for Dalglish.

Dalglish was equally reticent. What will be the hardest part of the job? asked someone. 'Divorcing myself from the lads,' came the reply, though he added quickly that he didn't think it would be a long-term problem although it might be initially.

Meanwhile, the bodies of 39 victims were being returned to their bereaved families back in Turin.

'Life has to go on,' he added, and there were three immediate jobs. He and Bob Paisley would be contacting Ian Rush and Craig Johnston about their contracts. He was hopeful that they might be able to hang on to Ian Rush for another year. They would also be holding talks the following afternoon with Paul Allen, the £650,000-rated West Ham midfielder who was considering a move to Anfield.

In the event, Paul Allen settled for a transfer to Tottenham, but Ian Rush remained at Anfield for another two years as Juventus and other interested Italian clubs cooled on the idea of a frantic scramble to sign a Liverpool player in the wake of the Heysel disaster. As an added bonus, Craig Johnston also opted to stay put. Earlier in the season, his failure to secure a regular first team spot had caused considerable friction with manager Joe Fagan, culminating in Johnston demanding a transfer. Fagan was happy to see the headstrong Australian leave, but Dalglish wasted no time in tracking him down and offering him a fresh start. It was clear that Johnston was part of his plans. The two had always had a friendly relationship rather than a warm one; Dalglish's dressing room hanger was next to Johnston's and over the past few years he had closely monitored Johnston's clashes with the club. Johnston had often mulled his problems over with the Scot; Dalglish sometimes sympathetic, occasionally chastising. But Dalglish recognised Johnston's abilities and did not wish to begin his managerial career short of a player. Yet in time even Dalglish would be unable to discipline the wayward spirit of Johnston.

Graeme Souness, unlike some, was not surprised at the appointment. A year before, he had predicted to Scottish journalist Gerry McNee that the next Liverpool manager would be Kenny Dalglish. McNee remembers it well. 'I was slightly taken back by his prediction. I thought it was a bit off the mark. I was inclined not to take it too seriously,' he says. At that time it was highly unlikely that Souness would have had any indication. It was probably just Scottish canniness on his part. Shortly after Dalglish's selection, Souness seconded his appointment with the astute observation that 'people are a bit frightened of him. He growls at them. He makes them jump.' These were the essential ingredients of a good manager, he added.

The former Liverpool striker Ian St John was not as convinced as Souness. He too had tried management, but without much success. 'He'll find his playing days are his best days,' he insisted. 'Once you stop playing that's when the worries start. As a player you only have to worry about yourself. As a manager you have to worry about everyone. You're carrying the can for the whole of the club.' His remarks were to prove perceptive, as was his warning that 'nobody likes criticism, but as a manager Dalglish will have to get used to it.'

Dalglish's most taxing problem, as is inevitable with anyone switching from employee to manager, was how to deal with those who have previously been colleagues. Dalglish recognised the dilemma from the start and decided to meet it head on. Mark Lawrenson was probably the first to feel the wind of change. In his autobiography he recounts that moment:

> It can't have been easy for him, probably harder than it was for us, but he clearly decided he would do it his way right from the beginning. I had been recuperating all summer from my shoulder operation and I had been told that I would not be ready for preseason training, so I arranged to do a couple of days' coaching in Dublin, when the lads reported back. I rang Vanessa at home to see how things were and she said that Kenny had been on the phone all day wondering where I was. She suggested that I get back to him straight away, which I did, to face a carpeting from the new manager. Not the best way to get started. We had been next door neighbours in Southport, and had taken it in turns to drive for training, but that relationship had changed, which was only right and proper. I was left in no doubt that he considered I was in the wrong and I did not forget it.

After the tragedy at Heysel, the footballing spotlight blazed on Liverpool. The club and all other English clubs were banned from European competitions, the police began a painstaking investigation into the riot, the politicians began to interfere and the pundits wondered if Liverpool Football Club could ever overcome the trauma and shame of the disaster. And there was the added question mark over the new player/manager. As Liverpool kicked off the new season, the tension inside Anfield was at boiling point. Mark Lawrenson recalls that the first game, against Arsenal, was as nerve-racking as any game he had ever played in. 'I cannot recall a more tense occasion,' he said. 'It seemed the world's press was at Anfield that day. I wondered how Kenny was feeling for his first game in charge. We were all churning inside but if he felt the same way, he did not let on to any of us.'

But if the players were anxious, they did not show it on the field. Liverpool won 2–0 but then dropped points with a draw at Aston Villa and a defeat at Newcastle. Press tongues were soon wagging although a 5–0 defeat of Ipswich halted any sustained questioning of the new pilot. The principal difficulty facing Dalglish was off the field – the presence of Phil Neal, still bitter and angry after being overlooked for the manager's post. That problem, however, was resolved by mid-October as Neal wisely read the runes and opted for the chance to manage Bolton Wanderers. Neal, with 50 England caps, was one of the most honoured players in the game and was virtually impossible to replace. And when his partner at the back, Alan Kennedy, decided to return to the North East, Dalglish faced a potential crisis. As it was, he re-jigged the format, dropping Steve Nicol into the back four and introducing young Jim Beglin to the number 3 shirt. Alan Hansen was also handed the captaincy. That still left him short of a midfield general, a role never ably filled since the departure of Graeme Souness to Italy. A solution had to be found outside of Anfield and so Dalglish dipped into the transfer market for his first slice of business when he signed Steve McMahon from Aston Villa for £350,000. A local lad, McMahon had originally been at Everton but had left them for Villa. At that time Liverpool had been interested in signing him but instead he chose Villa Park. The signing of McMahon was to prove an inspired piece of business, among the best that Dalglish ever executed. Six years later, Liverpool were able to sell him for £900,000.

From the beginning, Dalglish shifted the team around at his whim. And often nobody, not even the players, knew if they were in or out until the last moment. He would not even tell the television producers who needed ample warning to sort out their captions. One television production assistant recalls being sent down to the dressing rooms at Anfield spot on 2.00pm on derby day to find out the teams. At the Everton dressing room Howard Kendall generously supplied the information with a smile; at the Liverpool dressing room the door was slammed in her face.

But worse, even his staff did not know. 'We were just as much in the dark,' says Chris Lawler. 'The clock would be ticking towards two and we still did not know who was playing.' Many of the players testified that it took some getting used to. Under previous managers, the team was always the same, the manager keeping faith with the same men as the previous week. Shankly always picked the same side and let the opposition do the worrying. Even if you played badly there was still room for you. Continuity was the key word.

There were also early questions about Jan Molby's role. When the Dane arrived at Anfield from the Dutch club Ajax, Joe Fagan had immediately given him an opportunity in the first team. But he was overweight, reluctant to tackle and Fagan relegated him to the reserves. Dalglish, however, was clearly an admirer of the Dane and promptly gave him another opportunity. But there was always a doubt over his role. One week he was in midfield, the next he was acting as a stopper in what became a five-man defence. It intrigued the pundits.

With a dozen games gone, the title race, according to Fleet Street, was all but over. Manchester United had swept into an astonishing, ten-point lead after winning their opening ten fixtures. Yet, by the end of November, Liverpool's patient plodding had pulled the gap back to within a couple of points. But then a sequence of poor results in February, following a shaky December, allowed Everton to gallop ahead of the field by eight points. In February, Everton came to Anfield and won 2–0. One paper labelled Dalglish's men 'Liverpool's worst side in twenty years.' It looked a hopeless cause for Liverpool and at times they barely looked championship winners. They had set themselves an almost impossible task. Yet an astonishing end-of-season flurry saw them drop only two points in their last 12 games.

Dalglish's own appearances in his traditional number 7 shirt had been limited. After a couple of early season outings he had left himself out of the side, much to the chagrin of the supporters. By Christmas, the press were screaming for his recall, yet he continued to restrict his appearances, only donning the famous shirt for a sustained run as Liverpool rallied themselves for the final burst. It was an inspired piece of timing and it was fitting that it should be Dalglish who memorably chested the ball down in the Chelsea penalty area before firing home Liverpool's title winner. His smile said it all. The same boyish grin, the joy of scoring. It would contrast sharply with the agonised frown of later years. It had been a game Liverpool simply had to win to secure the title and it had been Dalglish who had stolen into the area to clinch the championship. In his first season as manager, Dalglish had won the League title. He had also twice been named Bell's Manager of the Month and was set to become Manager of the Year. But there was still more to come.

Liverpool had already won the Screen Sport Super Cup, an irrelevant though innocuous enough trophy, but, more importantly, they had reached the semi-finals of the League Cup. Although beaten 1–0 by Queen's Park Rangers at Loftus Road, Liverpool were quietly confident of the second leg but, in front of a packed Kop, they not only missed a penalty but contrived to give QPR two own goals. Liverpool had scored all four goals in the game and had finished up losing the tie. It was a nightmare that left Dalglish raging in the dressing room.

In the FA Cup, Liverpool opened with a warning to all and sundry: a 5–0 thrashing of Norwich. They then beat a lively Chelsea side 2–1 at Stamford Bridge and drew one apiece at York before winning the replay 3–1. In the quarterfinals they faced Elton John's Watford at Anfield but could manage only a goalless draw. Suddenly everything began to look ominous, especially with Watford a goal ahead in the replay and only a minute remaining before a packed Vicarage Road. Dalglish had returned to the side and, just as it seemed they were about to crash out of the Cup, Rush was conveniently felled in the penalty area. Molby promptly tucked away the resulting penalty and in extra time Ian Rush pounced to shoot Liverpool into the last four. In their semi-final at White Hart Lane against Southampton, it was Rush again who was the destroyer, firing two extra-time goals to book Liverpool's passage to Wembley. Even if Dalglish's season had come to an end at White Hart Lane it would still have been a famous campaign. Meanwhile, in the other semi-final, neighbours Everton lined up against Sheffield Wednesday and again in extra time settled the contest. As Dalglish trudged wearily off the field he was told they would be facing Everton at Wembley. The season was building towards an undreamed-of climax.

There had never been a Cup final quite like it. Everton, champions the previous season as well as European Cup-Winners' Cup holders, had already beaten Liverpool 2–0 at Anfield back in February only to see Liverpool pip them to the title by two points. It was the first ever Merseyside Cup final and the entire city was scrambling for tickets. The pressure of trying to win the league had been intense enough, but now there was the added drama of a Wembley Cup final, plus all the inevitable talk of a double by either side and a final against the club just a stone's throw away across Stanley Park. It was like living in a goldfish bowl. This was the testing time when nerves jangle, fingers twitch, and you wonder if you really do have what Tom Wolfe called 'The Right Stuff'.

Craig Johnston testified to the strain when he spoke of the 'unrelenting passage of pressure for the players and management of a club used to the demands of being on top. It would,' he added, 'take us a long time to unwind.' To win the double, Liverpool had slogged through the back end of the season playing 19 games without defeat.

Dalglish picked himself for the final even though he was experiencing some trouble with his knee. This was one game he certainly did not want to miss, and he proved that he was well up to playing the match. On a glorious summer's day that befitted the occasion, he led Liverpool down the famous tunnel and on to the sparkling green turf, Howard Kendall alongside him. In many ways it was a game Everton ought to have won. They led 1–0 at half time and for all but 20 minutes they were undeniably the more impressive side. But during those 20 minutes Liverpool destroyed their neighbours, scored three classic goals, and became only the third side this century to lift the double. 'Playing like this Liverpool compared with the cream – the Real Madrid of Di Stefano, the Ajax of Cruyff, the Bayern Munich of Beckenbauer,' wrote David Emery in the *Daily Express*. It was perhaps a little excessive; once the euphoria had dissipated, even the most diehard Liverpool supporter had to admit that for most of the season Liverpool had hardly looked potential champions, let alone winners of the double. And they would also be forced to admit that of all the Liverpool sides since the mid-1960s there were others far more deserving of the distinction than the 1986 side. But, at the end of the day, Dalglish had proved that he really did have The Right Stuff.

CHAPTER TEN
What Next?

First is first, second is nowhere.
Anfield saying

As Liverpool lifted their first European Cup in Rome's Olympic stadium an excited television journalist caught up with Emlyn Hughes. 'So, what do Liverpool do next?' he asked the Liverpool captain as he hoisted the massive trophy aloft to the cheers of the ecstatic fans massed behind the goal. 'I don't know,' replied Hughes. 'Win it again, I suppose.' Had the question been asked of Kenny Dalglish after winning the double, the same answer would probably have been forthcoming. It was, after all, a stock Liverpool response.

Liverpool had indeed, as Hughes rashly predicted, gone on to capture a second successive European Cup. They had even done it with a little help from Dalglish. But Dalglish was about to discover that a second double was beyond even him, although over the next few years he came very close. It had been an astonishing year for Dalglish: the double in his first season as manager, the first player/manager to appear at Wembley, the first Scot to win 100 international caps, a testimonial at Hampden Park, Manager of the Year and a Freeman of the City of Glasgow.

Craig Johnston recalls Dalglish putting an arm around him during the evening of their double celebration. 'Make the most of it, son,' advised Dalglish. 'It doesn't get any better than this.' It wouldn't. Liverpool had beaten their keenest rivals to clinch the double. Nothing could surpass that moment. It could only go downhill from now on. Dalglish was about to learn that Liverpool was almost an ungovernable club. Success reaped its own problems, its own demands.

After their double triumph the 1986/7 season turned out, by comparison, to be disappointing. A £3.2 million deal with Juventus for the transfer of Ian Rush was eventually agreed, with Liverpool negotiating a compromise that would keep Rush at Anfield for a further year. But although Rush would bag a total of 40 goals that season, they would not help add any trophies to the Anfield sideboard. Dalglish saw little reason to dash out and spend all the money on an immediate replacement. He could afford to wait, size up the possibilities and make a considered decision later in the season. Barry Venison was the only surprise signing during the close season. A full back with Sunderland, he had written to every first division club offering his services when his contract had come to an end. A few clubs expressed interest, but Dalglish was the only manager to pursue the offer. It was a canny piece of business.

During the summer, however, other changes were made which sent reverberations through Anfield. For the first time in living memory, a member of the sacred bootroom was sacked. The unlucky man was Chris Lawler, the former Liverpool and England full back, who had been recruited by Joe Fagan to look after the reserves but was discarded that summer. Also shown the door, after almost 20 years' service to the club, was chief scout Geoff Twentyman. Into their places stepped two former Liverpool stalwarts, Phil Thompson, as reserve team coach, and Ron Yeats as chief scout. Tom Saunders, the youth development officer, also moved aside voluntarily. After 16 years, he had decided to retire and Malcolm Cook was appointed in his place.

The 1986/7 season kicked off to a promising start, with Rush scoring both goals in Liverpool's 2–0 win at Newcastle. After just three games they had shot into top spot and were already the bookies' favourites to retain the title. But they then went down to Leicester before bouncing back with a 5–2 thumping of West Ham. Dalglish even netted a couple that day to earn himself the man of the match award. He had confined most of his early-season appearances to the substitute's bench, but after his goals against West Ham he decided that he was the in-form player and began to pull on the number 7 shirt more regularly. But at Southampton in mid-September, a second defeat left Dalglish fuming. Not only had they thrown away vital points but Kevin MacDonald had broken a leg, bringing his season to a premature end. It was to be the first of a number of distracting injuries over the year.

The highlight of Liverpool's early season was undoubtedly the 10–0 thrashing of Fulham in the second round, first leg of the Littlewoods Cup. It was the club's highest ever win in domestic football, bettered only by the 11–0 hammering of Stromgodset in 1974. Ten goals and Dalglish couldn't manage one of them. It must have been something of a personal record for the Scot and he certainly took some ribbing from his colleagues after the game as they sat in the dressing room working out who had scored and how many. But what Dalglish would have given for some of those goals to be spread among the other matches. Aston Villa battled back bravely at Anfield to snatch a 3–3 draw but the biggest surprise of all was the 4–1 hiding by Luton on Kenilworth Road's plastic surface. Liverpool had suddenly slumped to fifth in the table with four defeats already to their name. But, as is their normal style, Liverpool surged back from that defeat with due revenge. The victims were second-placed Norwich City, hammered 6–2, with Paul Walsh bagging a hat-trick and Ian Rush a couple more. By Christmas, Liverpool were still in contention, with Arsenal, Everton and Nottingham Forest looking to be their chief rivals. After five defeats and five draws, they faced a long haul to retain their title.

The one trophy Liverpool did look set to win was the Littlewoods Cup. They had reached the final after opening their account in the competition by winning their two-leg-tie against Fulham 13–2. They then beat Leicester 4–1 before overpowering Coventry after a replay. The quarter-finals brought them up against Everton and although Liverpool won 1–0 at Goodison on a bitterly cold January evening they lost the services of their young Irish defender Jim Beglin with a broken leg. He would never again play for Liverpool. That win put Liverpool into the semi-finals for the eighth time in ten years. The first leg against Southampton was a dour, goalless draw, although after their earlier league defeat at the Dell it was generally regarded as something of a triumph. The second leg turned out to be a memorable occasion, particularly for Dalglish who returned to the side, on his 36th birthday, and celebrated by scoring Liverpool's second in a 3–0 win that catapulted them into a Wembley clash with Arsenal.

Liverpool had never beaten Arsenal in a Wembley final and the Littlewoods Cup was to prove no different from their previous battles. Rush edged Liverpool into a 20th-minute lead but Arsenal fought back, equalising minutes later. Shortly before full time, Perry Groves' fresh young legs provided a cross for Charlie Nicholas to hit Arsenal's winner. Liverpool had performed well enough, but the luck was with the Gunners. It was the first time in 144 games that Rush had scored and Liverpool had lost. Dalglish had come on as substitute late in the game but was virtually ineffective. The years were now beginning to tell. He had kicked off the season in a Liverpool shirt and had played in seven of their opening nine fixtures, but as the season wore on, his appearances were becoming less frequent. He made just 18 league appearances in all, scoring half a dozen goals and notched up five appearances in other competitions with two goals. Yet, for a 36-year-old, eight goals in 23 games was not a bad average.

Back in the league, the New Year shot off to a bright start, although there was an early exit against Luton in the FA Cup, after two replays. The first replay at Anfield had to be postponed when Luton failed to turn up. Atrocious weather had left them stranded in a snow storm. Meanwhile, at Anfield where the conditions were much better, the meat pies were warming up, the television cameras had been switched on and the Kop was eagerly awaiting the arrival of Luton; When they failed to show up, Dalglish was not amused and everyone was left wondering why Luton had not looked at the weather forecast. But the FA would have none of Liverpool's complaints. The tie was eventually settled back on Kenilworth Road's plastic pitch, with Liverpool crashing to a 3–0 defeat.

Dreams of another double had been shattered. It was Dalglish's first setback since taking over. He shrugged his shoulders, his poker face hiding his own disappointment, and talked about getting on with the job of winning the League. He hardly needed reminding of the Anfield saying: 'First is first, second is nowhere.' After the Luton Cup exit, all seemed to go well. Even high flyers Arsenal were beaten 1–0 at Highbury. Liverpool, six points ahead of Everton at the top of the table, looked odds-on favourites to retain their title. But then came a spring slump of catastrophic proportions. First they lost 1–0 at Tottenham, then they were beaten 2–1 at Anfield by Wimbledon, next came a 2–1 defeat at Norwich, with their Littlewoods Cup-final disappointment sandwiched in between.

After the Norwich game, the team were locked in the dressing room for an hour while Dalglish and Moran ranted and raged at their lack of endeavour. Some players had not been pulling their weight, screamed Moran, his sergeant major voice booming down the corridors of Carrow Road. But it was to no avail. With those three defeats, Liverpool handed the initiative to Everton. Craig Johnston remembers it well. 'For some weeks there had been a few not pulling their weight. We might have had the same collection of players as the previous season, but it wasn't the same team. The unity was gone.' They were telling words.

Chris James, writing in the *Daily Mirror*, was perhaps the harshest of Dalglish's critics, giving public vent to what many outside of Merseyside were privately hoping: 'Kenny Dalglish is facing the grim spectre of failure. Liverpool will finish empty-handed for only the third time in fifteen seasons. It is not a prospect which will go down well on the terraces or in the boardroom, where chairman John Smith has often been quoted as saying: "Winning is not the most important thing, it is the only thing."'

James was possibly being a little unfair on Dalglish and had failed to realise the close rapport he had developed with the terraces. They at least were more understanding, but he did make one pertinent point when he noted that 'it is not just the recent defeats but the *performances.*' He ended his two page piece by suggesting that Dalglish, like his predecessors Shankly and Paisley, should be rebuilding his team. 'They need to do it again and the ball is at Dalglish's feet. The pressure on him is increasing because the Kop are not used to the sour taste of defeat.'

There was a further defeat at Manchester United and even though Everton then came to Anfield and lost 3–1, it was too late. Everton still led the table by three points with a game in hand. Liverpool were running out of games. The title race finally turned Everton's way the following week when Everton sneaked a fortunate draw at Maine Road while Liverpool went down by the only goal at Coventry.

Dalglish would have to be content with second place, neighbour Howard Kendall this time scooping the prize. Dalglish was annoyed that Liverpool had failed when the title was within their grasp. There were excuses. Injuries had tested his resources. Steve Nicol did not play in 1987, while Mark Lawrenson limped away towards the end. of the season with an Achilles problem that would end his Anfield career. Bruce Grobbelaar had also missed a number of games, while Kevin MacDonald and Jim Beglin's playing days at Anfield were also to end after the injuries they had sustained that season. To counter the injury crisis, Dalglish had dipped into the transfer market, signing Nigel Spackman from Chelsea for £400,000 but his impact was limited; always promising, never quite fulfilling.

Joe Fagan had left Dalglish with a rich heritage and a team worthy of the Liverpool tradition. But as every successful manager learns, all outstanding sides eventually grow old and stale. Moulding a second championship team is the real test of an eminent manager. And few had ever successfully passed that examination: only Chapman, Busby, Nicholson, Shankly, Paisley and perhaps one or two others. Not that Liverpool looked that weary, though perhaps they lacked a little motivation after the honours of the previous year. Dalglish could have kept much the same format together for another season or more and they would have always been among the challengers in any competition. But that was accepting second best and that was not the Liverpool style. On top of which, Dalglish was losing his chief goalscorer to the Italians.

It was a critical time for Dalglish. Cynics could point to the double side and say: 'Well, that was really Joe Fagan's team.' Of course, given that logic, the same judgement applied to the side that had failed to win anything the following season. It was time for Dalglish to become his own man. He had already taken tentative steps in that direction by removing Twentyman and Lawler, but in doing so had ruffled a few feathers. In his first season, he had rarely been criticised but now you could hear whispers on the terraces, read about it in the papers. The media were growing increasingly impatient with him for one reason or another. Much of it was uncalled-for, most of it inaccurate. What's more, there were even a few comments being made along the corridors of Anfield and in the plush dining suites. But he was as aware as anyone that changes were needed.

Dalglish had already spent £750,000 on a replacement for Ian Rush. John Aldridge, a local lad who had supported Liverpool from the Kop as a youngster, had been exiled to Oxford United after a spell with Newport County. Now he was back, signed from Oxford with the unenviable task of replacing Ian Rush. Wherever he had travelled, Aldridge had seemed to score goals but there was still a question as to whether he could bag them at the highest level, at Anfield. Only time would tell. He had already had a few outings and the signs were not optimistic with him, having scored just two goals in ten appearances, most as substitute. One paper was already calling him 'a £750,000 misfit'. Looking like Rush was one thing, filling his boots was another.

Dalglish himself was now past his sell-by-date as well. His appearance at Wembley in the Littlewoods Cup final had underlined his fading abilities, a damaged knee having restricted his recent appearances. Many expected him to announce his retirement during the close season. Whether or not he did, he would still have to find someone to replace him, someone to create the opportunities for Aldridge. It was going to be a difficult close season. The realities of being manager of Britain's most successful football club were beginning to hit him. But he already had his eye on one or two possibilities.

CHAPTER ELEVEN
Better Than The Brazilians

The finest exhibition of football I have ever seen.
Tom Finney

The signing of John Barnes was a prolonged and tortuous business, overly messy and enough to test the patience of any manager. Nor was it much appreciated by Liverpool fans, who expected their heroes to leap at the opportunity of performing in front of the Kop each week. It was a privilege, an honour, never to be questioned. Dalglish had set his sights on the Watford winger as early as the spring of 1987, detecting in him a calibre not always appreciated by others. Barnes may have imprinted his name indelibly on the game with a goal in Rio's Maracana Stadium of such startling quality that even the Brazilians described it as the best ever seen at that ground, yet he had rarely lived up to his promise. Even by his own admission, he could be frustratingly inconsistent, sometimes lazy, visibly growing bored if he did not see enough of the ball. He could be infuriating; enthralling one moment, sloppy the next. Someone even described him as 'athleticism masquerading as talent'. Dalglish knew better.

At the end of the 1986/7 season, Barnes's contract with Watford was due for renewal, but long before its expiry date the player let it be known that he wanted a move from Vicarage Road. Watford manager Graham Taylor was well aware of Barnes's ability, having carefully nurtured the Jamaican-born winger from early days. There was little he could do to stand in his way, nor indeed was there much he could offer in the way of money or incentive. Taylor was resigned to losing his man. A move was inevitable.

Dalglish initially appeared on the scene with an offer that was immediately acceptable to Watford. The deal seemed straightforward, yet Barnes hesitated. He was given a deadline of 8 June. In private, he longed for a move to Italy where he felt his unusual flair would be best appreciated. He was keen on Italian soccer and, along with his agent, had even compiled a video which had been distributed to a select group of Italian clubs. Some scouts had turned up dutifully at Vicarage Road to satisfy their bosses back home but although there were rumours that Fiorentina, Roma and even Napoli were interested, their curiosity never went any further. Real Madrid and Barcelona made no move either, though a few French clubs were reported to be showing signs of interest. Yet there were still no firm bids from the continent.

It became increasingly obvious to Barnes that his future lay in the Football League. Next best in the Watford player's mind was a London club. 'If I cannot go abroad, I would prefer to stay in London with a club like Arsenal or Spurs, and I simply cannot believe they are not interested in signing me,' he told the *Liverpool Echo*. He was convinced that some club other than Liverpool would come in with a bid. He had never seriously considered a move north and needed time to evaluate the implications.

Barnes's hesitation eventually alerted Arsenal, but again he dithered, still hankering for the sun and the San Siro. Arsenal angrily withdrew their offer. Barnes had been assured that one of the giant Italian or Spanish clubs would make their move before the summer was out. But no offer seemed forthcoming and the new season was drawing closer. His deadline was now past and still no deal had been finalised. Dalglish was growing impatient. He warned Watford and Barnes of their deadline and that if a deal was not sorted quickly the transfer would be off. The truth finally dawned on Barnes: no other club wanted him – it was Liverpool or Watford. The Anfield machine had timed its ultimatum carefully. Barnes duly travelled to Merseyside and signed for £900,000, and made all the right noises. 'When I realised I was not going to Europe, there was only one English club for me and that was Liverpool,' he assured the *Liverpool Daily Post*.

Yet the drawn-out kerfuffle surrounding the Barnes transfer angered and puzzled many. There were those furious at his indecision, angered by his apparent reluctance to join what they considered the finest football club in Europe. Equally, there were many who questioned Barnes's ability and wondered if he could adapt his skills to the Liverpool style. Was he capable of sharing the burden of defending or would he stand idly by on the touchline waiting for the ball to be played to his feet? Was he really a team player? And how long would Liverpool be able to hold him at Anfield if Sampdoria or Milan came in with an offer? More significantly, there were also those who questioned the signing of a black player.

Liverpool Football Club's record of employing black players was one of the poorest in the Football League, rivalled only by Merseyside neighbours Everton. During the early 1980s Howard Gayle, a local black lad, had played just a handful of games for Liverpool before being transferred to Birmingham City. Yet Gayle had written himself a short chapter in the history of the club after a remarkable performance in the semi-final of the 1980/81 European Cup. Coming on as a substitute early in the game for the injured Dalglish, Gayle had torn apart the Bayern Munich defence with his powerful, dangerous runs, helping turn a desperate situation into a passport to the European Cup final. After that display, many thought Gayle would be given an extended run in the first team. He was, making three more appearances before the end of the season, even scoring. But, ultimately, with so many outstanding players at Anfield there was no place for him in the European Cup final team and at the end of the season, he was offered a meagre pay rise, a clear indication that he did not figure in the club's plans for the future. He went to Fulham on loan and never reappeared at Anfield.

The Howard Gayle affair had left a bitter legacy. There were accusations that Liverpool Football Club was anti-black and not doing sufficient to encourage the city's black population through the turnstiles. Why did so few blacks ever travel to Anfield, even though many lived close by? Black players were still subjected to the most appalling racist taunts and barracking from the Kop, with the club seemingly doing little to curb the extremists. It was a long time before there was ever anything in the programme requesting fans to desist from these practices. Racist graffiti decorating the walls outside the ground was ignored for many years.

Dalglish may have had some fears that the transfer of Barnes would unleash a new deluge of racist hatred. Letters began to arrive at the club, and there was fresh graffiti on the walls. The club hushed it up and for a time buried their heads in the sand, adopting what one journalist called 'the colourblind position'. Nobody seemed prepared to confront the problem. Eventually, it took a protest from a bunch of school kids from the University School protesting to the club and the local papers to elicit a satisfactory response. John Smith ordered a clean-up while telling the *Liverpool Daily Post* that he did not believe it was as bad as claimed. Afterwards there was a much more positive attitude at the club.

'He's not a black player, he's a player,' snapped Dalglish when somebody plucked up the courage to ask his opinion about Barnes. In his ghosted diary, *The Liverpool Year,* he argued that 'the fact that John happens to be the first black player Liverpool have bought was something that had not crossed my mind until it was pointed out to me. At Liverpool we are not concerned with race, creed or the colour of a person's skin.'

If religion was the great divide in Glasgow, then race was the great barrier in Liverpool. One commentator wrote that for Liverpool to sign a black was the equivalent of Rangers signing a Catholic. The parallel would not be lost on Dalglish. Religion has only ever played a minor role in Merseyside football. The borders are blurred and even to this day nobody is quite sure which is the 'Catholic club'. One person will tell you that it is Liverpool, another will insist it is Everton. And yet the roots of both clubs stem back to the same man, John Houlding. 'King John', as he was fondly known, was a Conservative councillor and an Orangeman who became Lord Mayor of the city in 1897. Houlding was the force behind Everton Football Club, but when most of its members angrily stormed off to form a new club, retaining the name Everton, he remained at Anfield, setting up a rival club and giving it the name Liverpool. Throughout their histories, the two clubs have been strongly connected. For many years, they shared the same programme and when Houlding died his coffin was borne by players from both clubs. In more recent years, the pools magnate John Moores has been the largest shareholder in both clubs.

Rivalry between the city's two clubs may be intense and passionate, but it holds none of the bitterness that exists north of the border between Celtic and Glasgow Rangers. What divisions there are cut across religion and geography. Families and friends can be split over support for the Reds or the Blues, but the differences go no deeper.

There are those who have tried to create a religious gulf between the city's clubs, but it has never been wholly successful. During the late 1940s and 1950s, Everton forged strong links with Eire, importing a host of players, which helped form the impression that Everton was a Catholic club, but it was unfounded. They may have had a substantial number of Catholic players on their staff but they did not pursue a Catholics-only policy. In more recent years, Liverpool has similarly forged bonds with Eire through an influx of Irish players such as Ronnie Whelan, Steve Staunton and Jim Beglin, plus those who played for Eire but were never really Irish – Steve Heighway, Ray Houghton and John Aldridge. But that in no way suggests that Liverpool are a Catholic club in the way that Celtic could be defined. The declining influence of religion as an issue can be seen by the traditional annual march of the Orange Lodge, which is now a pathetic event, supported by few, loathed by many more.

But if religion was not an issue in post-1960s Liverpool, the same could not be said of race. The desperate rioting during the summer of 1981 highlighted, possibly for the first time, the undercurrent of feeling in the black community. And yet Liverpool's black community is as indigenous to the city as its Irish population. It was not some new West Indian community that had suddenly poured into the city with the mass influx of the late 1950s and 1960s, but an Afro-English population that stretched back as far as the early years of the century, with the Chinese community going back even further. Indeed, it had been there almost as long as Liverpool Football Club itself. The race issue was fermenting beneath the surface of politics in Liverpool and has continued to do so ever since. In 1987, there were still nightclubs in Liverpool where blacks were discreetly banned, while job opportunities for blacks scarcely existed either then or now. The most telling remark during the riots came from a Conservative Liverpool councillor who confessed that he did not realise there was a black population in the city until they started rioting. Ghettoised in Toxteth, the black population had kept to its own territory and if you did not live in dose proximity, it was possible to go a lifetime without ever coming into contact with the black community.

If Dalglish had not realised the implications of signing a black player, he soon would. Within 24 hours of finalising the deal, the racists had attacked. Daubings appeared overnight on the walls inside Anfield. The club continued to keep it quiet and the cleaners were busy first thing the following morning. But news eventually leaked out, though the full extent of the daubings was never revealed. Perhaps the club assumed that by keeping it low-key, the issue would simply disappear. It would not be a successful ploy, and club officials were forced to confront the delicate question of racism at

Anfield. By signing John Barnes, Dalglish had taken a major step in the reconstruction of his team, but he had also unwittingly unleashed a debate that would eventually help improve race relations in the city, even if it could not solve the problems.

Having achieved the double in his first season as a manager, Dalglish had the problem of maintaining the same level of excellence – an unnerving task. Nevertheless, he had already set out with the intention of improving on Liverpool's double performance. The addition to the squad of Kevin MacDonald, Nigel Spackman, Barry Venison and John Aldridge was not enough, especially with the transfer of Ian Rush to Juventus and his own imminent retirement. It was evident that massive reconstruction was called for if the club was to maintain its phenomenal success.

Barnes was the first gesture in rebuilding the creative department of the side. Liverpool had money to play with from the £3.2 million they had received for Rush. The loss of the ever-popular Rush was a devastating blow, not just to the club and its playing staff but to the fans who regarded the Welshman with a special affection. His final appearance in front of the Kop was testament to that popularity. Rush's transfer demanded the import of more than one star name. But the arrival of Aldridge and Barnes was only the beginning. Dalglish had not finished there. For two seasons he had managed a team that he had largely inherited. Save for one or two transfers, in particular Steve McMahon, the side remained that of his predecessors, Bob Paisley and Joe Fagan.

Next in line for Anfield was Peter Beardsley, the restless Newcastle United forward, once a Manchester United player but discarded for next to nothing only to re-emerge in the North East with qualities undetected at Old Trafford. Beardsley showed none of the hesitation of Barnes. He could not sign fast enough and had long hankered for a move to Anfield. Yet it took a record-breaking fee of £1.9 million to bring the 26-year-old England international to Merseyside.

There was to be just one further addition to the side, in mid-October, when Ray Houghton, the Oxford United and Eire midfielder, arrived for another fat fee, extending Dalglish's expenditure to £5.5 million on the nine players he had signed since his appointment. All the pieces were now in place, ready for Dalglish to begin his assault on Everton's League title and a second double.

The campaign began at Highbury, with a curious press gleefully watching, eager to analyse the new-look Liverpool. How would they cope without Ian Rush? Would Barnes prove too much of an individualist and was Peter Beardsley really worth his gilt-edged fee? After 90 minutes, some of the answers were becoming clearer. John Aldridge had opened Liverpool's account, Barnes had grafted unselfishly in defence as well as up front, and Beardsley had shown more than a few promising touches. Above all, Liverpool had won 2–1, Steve Nicol striking Liverpool's second late in the game. But the jury, rightly, was still out.

In their second match, Liverpool won 4–1 at Coventry City, with a preformance described by Coventry manager John Sillett as the finest performance he had ever seen in the first division, and then drew at Upton Park before they finally appeared in front of a packed Anfield. A collapsed sewer under the Kop had meant the postponement of their three opening home fixtures and it was 12 September before Merseyside had its first glimpse of Barnes and Beardsley. They were not to be disappointed as Liverpool beat Oxford United 2–0. Dalglish was delighted. His faith in Barnes was beginning to pay dividends as the England winger took on a new lease of life. He looked more confident than at any time in his career, prepared to take on players, set off on exciting runs and was as subtle a crosser of the ball as anyone at Anfield since Peter Thompson. On the Oxford side, Dalglish had been impressed by the hustling midfielder Ray Houghton, whom he would soon sign.

Charlton Athletic were next at Anfield and they even had the temerity to go in front as Garth Crooks lobbed the ball over a stranded Grobbelaar. Rogan Taylor remembers the moment vividly and the reaction to a black player scoring in front of the Kop. 'Normally they would have given him all hell, but this time they didn't know what to do. Some racist shouts began, then they realised that they couldn't call him because Liverpool's best player also happened to be black.' It was a turning point.

More victories followed and the goals flowed. Four against Newcastle, Derby and Portsmouth and then, at Anfield against Queen's Park Rangers, Barnes consolidated his arrival with a goal of breathtaking quality. Collecting the ball just inside his own half he began a run that took him half the length of the pitch and into the opposing penalty area. He curved nonchalantly past player after player before neatly sliding the ball into the corner of the net. Long before he had reached the penalty area the entire ground was on its feet marvelling at his skills and willing the ball into the net. Dalglish called it one of the finest goals he had seen at Anfield. Barnes had arrived in splendid style. The racists on the Kop were silenced.

The arrival of Ray Houghton in October posed a delicate problem for Dalglish. Who to drop? The obvious candidate was Craig Johnston, whose career had been briefly resurrected by Dalglish following his earlier exile by Fagan. Johnston, hardly surprisingly, did not take kindly to Dalglish's decision and by the end of the season had decided to quit Anfield and football altogether. But Dalglish had recognised that Johnston, for all his enthusiasm, lacked certain essentials, most notably he seemed unable to cross the ball accurately which often rendered his dizzy efforts down the flanks ineffective.

The problem of racism reared its ugly head again as Liverpool faced the League champions Everton in what were to be two memorable dashes. Sadly, they will be remembered not solely for the football. The first dash was marred by what was probably the worst racist chanting ever heard at Anfield. Barnes was barracked at every touch of the ball and, whenever he courted the sidelines, a barrage of bananas was hurled in his direction. The abuse came almost solely from the Evertonians. The Liverpool supporters were gradually changing their attitude, as Barnes had more than proved his ability by early November. It may have been a change of convenience, as there was still some abuse being hurled at black opposition players. Had Barnes failed to make an impact, they may have reverted to norm. But now they took up the cause on his behalf. The barracking was a disgrace, and could be heard quite distinctly on both television and radio. Radio Merseyside and Radio City were besieged with phone calls that demanded a response. The *Liverpool Daily Post* and the *Liverpool Echo* also took up the cause. Fortunately, both clubs by now recognised the need for firm action. The Everton chairman Phillip Carter, then President of the Football League, made a direct appeal to the fans, threatening to eject anyone inciting racial hatred. This time their positive steps were effective. When the two teams lined up a few days later in front of the TV cameras at Anfield for a league fixture, the first hint of racist taunts was met with a hail of abuse. The racists soon cracked.

Liverpool had lost the first game against Everton, a Littlewoods Cup tie, 1–0. After the match, Dalglish lost his temper for the first and only time that season: 'They wanted to win more than you. Their hearts were in it, yours weren't.' The dressing room was like a morgue. But Liverpool did not repeat the same mistake in the league, winning 2–0 to consolidate their grip at the top of the table. Liverpool looked as impressive a side as any seen at Anfield since the war. By the end of the year, unbeaten and still leading the first division, they had scored 51 goals and conceded just 11. As the New Year kicked off, Peter Beardsley also began to demonstrate why he was the most expensive footballer in Britain. He had so far struck only four goals, but a brace against Coventry on New Year's Day began a sequence of goals that would bring him a season's tally of 18, his most spectacular coming against Arsenal as he burst through the Gunners' defence in front of a live audience of 250 million.

There were further wins against Charlton, Watford, Portsmouth and QPR, before Liverpool travelled to Derby needing only a draw to match Leeds United's record of 29 unbeaten games since the start of the season. Nerves were beginning to show, the back pages were headlining Liverpool's feats, and although Liverpool dominated the game they could only draw. But in doing so, they had equalled the Leeds record. What's more, they had won more games, claimed more points and scored more goals than the great Leeds side of the 1970s.

Suddenly, Liverpool were the darlings of the back pages. It had long been a whine of Liverpudlians that, despite umpteen championships and sundry European honours, they had never been given the recognition they deserved. Manchester United, with just a handful of titles and one European trophy, remained, for some inexplicable reason, the most romanticised club in the Football League. It was part of the Liverpudlian persecution complex. It had irked Liverpool supporters for years and had much to do with the increasing tension between the two clubs. But suddenly the press were beginning to talk of Liverpool in revered tones.

Even Dalglish had to admit he was impressed by his side. 'What do you say to them in the dressing room?' he was asked. 'Nothing really,' he replied. 'Most of the time I don't even know what they are going to do myself.' It must have been even more frightening for the opposition.

To everyone on Merseyside it was always clear what was going to happen next. There is a sixth sense about these things. A freak in the fixture list had pitted Everton as Liverpool's next opponents. If Liverpool were to continue their unbeaten charge and claim a 30-game record run for themselves, they needed to beat the current League champions on their own territory, Goodison Park. It was inevitable that against their oldest enemy they would finally slip. After all, Everton had already shown in the Littlewoods Cup that they could beat Liverpool; if they could do it once, they could do it twice. Dalglish warned his men to forget about the record, but there was so much newspaper speculation, some even foolishly suggesting that Liverpool might end the season without losing a league game, that it was impossible to put such thoughts aside. The nation sat glued to its TV screens watching, waiting. It was a safe bet that sooner or later Liverpool would have an off day and, sure enough, it duly arrived at Goodison. Everton won 1–0, Grobbelaar dropping the ball tantalisingly at the feet of scorer Wayne Clarke.

Dalglish was as disappointed as anyone, but in a dressing room of slumped shoulders and long faces, he bravely tried to revive their spirits. Typically, he pointed out to the press that what really mattered was winning the championship, not setting records. In some respects, he explained, it was just as well. The pressure had been mounting with every game. The players had been thinking more about the record than winning the title. Perhaps they could now relax a little. He could probably have afforded to show more public disappointment as there was never any question of who was going to wind up League champions.

Any doubts the press had harboured back in August about Liverpool's potential had by Christmas long dissipated. By the spring, they were reaching for their dictionaries. Dalglish could do no wrong; Barnes was a revelation and Beardsley was emerging as a potent force in European football. The full-up sign was posted at Anfield virtually every week. But injuries were about to strike. Mark Lawrenson, on his comeback from a serious Achilles tendon problem, promptly limped off again and never returned. It was to be a loss the club would never really overcome, with their vulnerability at the back rudely exposed in the years ahead. Ronnie Whelan was also injured and missed the remainder of the season, while Gary Gillespie and Barry Venison also joined those on the treatment bench.

With the arrival of so much new talent on the scene, some of the older hands decided to try their luck elsewhere. John Wark told Dalglish that he was unhappy and a return to his old club Ipswich was quickly arranged. The maverick Paul Walsh moved to Spurs. He was a frustrating player, much admired by Dalglish, but lacking discipline and endeavour. On the field he was unpredictable, capable one moment of an incisive twist, a backheel or a blistering run; off the field he caused more than his share of headaches. The club had stood by him during a well publicised and messy court case also involving Sammy Lee and reserve player John McGregor. The three men had been charged with inflicting grievous bodily harm on a 17-year-old youth outside a Liverpool nightclub known as the Coconut

Grove. The three were finally acquitted but not before the press had had a field day. Walsh had also been banned from driving after racing his car up the M6 at 100mph. Nor was that his first speeding offence. It all added up to the kind of indiscipline that angered Dalglish, to see so talented a player failing to fulfil his promise. With Beardsley and Barnes now firmly in place, a parting of the ways was inevitable for Walsh.

John Aldridge had also given Dalglish a disciplinary problem earlier that season when he was thrown out of a Liverpool nightclub accused of threatening a bouncer and swearing at a barmaid. He too was eventually found not guilty and, although Dalglish stood by him, he warned him to be more careful about where he did his drinking in future.

In the FA Cup, Liverpool looked just as invincible as they did in the league. Wins against Stoke, Aston Villa, Everton and Manchester City swept them towards the semi-final and a clash with Nottingham Forest. But before that they faced Forest in a league encounter at the City Ground. Forest were still, theoretically, in contention for the championship but were so far in arrears that they simply had to beat Liverpool in order to have any hope of remaining in the race. Dalglish opted for a surprise change of tactics. Instead of picking his strongest line-up, he decided to leave Beardsley and Houghton on the bench, choosing instead a five-man midfield. Even the players were surprised. It was to prove a disastrous error, although there was a suspicion that Dalglish simply did not wish to reveal his hand, preferring instead to save his trump card for the Cup semi-final. In effect, Forest were given the all-clear to attack. They did, and the Liverpool defence buckled under the pressure. Forest won 2–1. It was Liverpool's second and last defeat of the season. The players had been unsettled by the change and never had time to adjust. In the dressing room after the game, Dalglish privately admitted that it never paid off. But in the back pages he came in for some rare criticism. Forest's morale had been boosted by their victory with just days to go before the semi-final clash. 'Why change a winning formula?' demanded the press. In hindsight, however, it could be argued that it was the appropriate tactic and one which encouraged Dalglish to experiment further.

A week later, this time with Houghton and Beardsley restored to the line-up, Liverpool took their revenge, winning 2–1, both strikes coming from John Aldridge. The second goal was a classic Liverpool move with Aldridge volleying in Barnes's neatly chipped cross. Liverpool were through to another Cup final, Dalglish's second as manager. The odds on Liverpool winning a second double were dramatically slashed.

Four days later, Liverpool faced Forest yet again. If Brian Clough's young side were not demoralised when they arrived on Merseyside after the semi-final defeat they certainly were by the time they boarded their coach to leave. In between they had conceded five goals as Liverpool produced one of the most dazzling performances ever seen in the first division. Liverpool were simply breathtaking, seeing off their closest rivals for the championship with contemptuous ease. The legendary Tom Finney, watching from the stands, was mesmerised.

'In all my time as a player and as a spectator that was the finest exhibition of football I've ever seen,' oozed the former Preston North End and England winger after the match. 'Everyone will be left believing that they have seen something that will never be bettered. It could have been seven or eight quite easily.' He reckoned that neither the Busby Babes, nor the Tottenham Hotspur side that had won the double, nor even the glorious Brazilians would have been a match for Liverpool. 'I've never seen skill at that pace,' he enthused.

Forest had begun impressively and for half an hour they matched Liverpool blow for blow, but by half time were already two goals in arrears. Ray Houghton began the rout in the 18th minute, trading passes with John Barnes before neatly slotting in the return. In the 36th minute, John Aldridge made it 2–0 after Peter Beardsley had sent him clear with an exquisite pass. In the second half, the tension evaporated and, as Liverpool visibly began to enjoy themselves, Anfield took on a carnival atmosphere. Gillespie added a third from a short corner in the 57th minute and then, 20 minutes later, John Barnes summed up Liverpool's season when he turned Forest's defence inside out before setting up Beardsley. By then Forest had given up, sensibly caving in to the inevitable. Two minutes from time, Nigel Spackman created enough space to offer Aldridge the kind of opportunity he laps up. The Kop was delirious. And on top of all that, Liverpool had struck the woodwork on three occasions and had been denied by the Forest keeper, Steve Sutton, as many times.

John Aldridge, in his book *Inside Anfield,* rated it 'the greatest team performance I have ever experienced. It was exhilarating, pulsating football at its best.' He added that 'if the crowd at Anfield and the millions who experienced the highlights enjoyed it, just imagine what it was like to play in.' Even the Liverpool captain Alan Hansen could not recall ever playing in or seeing such a sustained show of brilliance.

Within a few weeks, a video of the game was selling like hotcakes on

Merseyside. Like Finney, Dalglish watched mesmerised, calling it 'a great exhibition of football. The double may have been the pinnacle of Dalglish's achievements at Anfield, but the 5–0 drubbing of Forest would go down in folklore as the night Liverpool reached a new zenith.

Forest had been crushed and were lucky to escape so lightly. With that win, the League championship was virtually sealed. A fortnight later, with Spurs the visitors at Anfield, Liverpool were crowned champions; their 17th League title.

Liverpool's winning margin in the league eventually stretched to nine points over their nearest rivals, Manchester United. It was Dalglish's seventh title victory since arriving from Celtic in 1977. Forest had fallen away at the end, finishing in third place 17 points adrift. Liverpool had also equalled Everton's record haul of 90 points even though they had played two games fewer. They had won 26 games, drawn 12 and lost just two, scoring 87 goals and conceding 24. John Aldridge had justified Dalglish's faith in him, scoring 29 goals in all competitions, while his other signings, Beardsley and Barnes, had scored 18 and 17 goals respectively.

At Wembley, Liverpool were the hottest favourites to lift the FA Cup in years. Defeat was inconceivable. The opposition, Wimbledon, were a kick-and-run team, not long out of the fourth division. It was impossible to imagine how they could survive against the sophistication and guile of this Liverpool side. Dalglish was on course for a famous, second League and Cup double and the Scousers were gathered in strength to salute the occasion. There seemed only a handful of Wimbledon supporters inside Wembley, mustering somewhere down by the halfway line. Everywhere was a sea of red, all drawn there in anticipation of an historic moment. But of course it all turned out very differently. Yet how different it might have been had Peter Beardsley's early goal stood after he shrugged off a tackle to push the ball into the area, before stroking it past Dave Beasant. But, instead of playing the advantage, the referee indicated a foul on Beardsley, a decision he later acknowledged was wrong. It was the turning point. Wimbledon grew in confidence, Liverpool's defence failed to deal with a simple-looking cross, Lawrie Sanchez glanced a header beyond Grobbelaar and then, late in the game, John Aldridge missed the first penalty of his Liverpool career. From that moment on, Wimbledon were destined to win the Cup. Not even an Algonquin rain dance would have saved them. Liverpool had been denied their second double. At the end of the afternoon, Dalglish, along with his Red army, could only shrug his shoulders.

It was that kind of result. But the sight Dalglish would never forget was the look of disappointment on his own son's face.

Over the years, so many championship-winning Liverpool sides had been described as pragmatic, utilitarian. They seemed to lack the gusto of Revie's Leeds United or the individualism of the Best/Charlton/Law Manchester United side of the 1960s. Nor did they have the style of Blanchflower's Tottenham. You may not have hated the Liverpool sides of the 1960s and 1970s, but you hardly warmed to them. They just seemed to grind the opposition down with their relentless pressure and accurate passing. It had been a formula that worked. But now everyone was forced to admit that Dalglish had brought a flair and imagination to Anfield that had previously been absent. Here was a team that could run with the ball, a team that had broken out of the Liverpool tradition of deliberate passing. It was a side to admire, be proud of, go out and watch, a side where individualism was encouraged. It was even exciting, a rare commodity in English football. What's more, they were also obliged to concede that this team was Kenny Dalglish's and not Joe Fagan's or Bob Paisley's. And it was playing in a style that mimicked its new manager's. If only they had been able to show Europe. The one problem was that Dalglish had now set himself a standard that would be impossible to follow. In the years ahead, that evening at Anfield when Liverpool became the new Brazil would come to haunt him.

CHAPTER TWELVE
The Unmanageable Club

It's the plugging away that will win you the day,
So don't be a piker, old pard!
Just draw on your grit; it's so easy to quit:
It's the keeping-your-chin-up that's hard.
Robert Service

Goalscoring is a capricious business. Even the most fluent marksmen can find themselves scratching through barren patches when the flow seems to dry up altogether. It had happened to Dalglish and now it was happening to Ian Rush in Italy. At Anfield, Rush had been one of the most prolific goal-scorers in the club's history, forming a partnership with Dalglish that was the scourge of the Football League. 'Painful to watch but beautiful,' was David Pleat's summing up after Rush had fired five goals past his Luton Town. He had scored 139 goals in 224 league appearances and another 50 in all cup competitions, a record that very soon had every leading continental club knocking on the Anfield door. Juventus won the race with a £3.2 million offer that Liverpool could hardly refuse.

And so Rush packed his bags, bought a dictionary, found himself a bride and flew to the land of pasta and sunshine. But it was not a happy time. A bad car crash when the season had barely kicked off and then hepatitis left him drained and lost. Coupled with the usual acclimatisation problems and the notorious iron wall defences of the Italian league, his romance with Italy had turned into a nightmare. Rush also cried out for the services of a dynamic midfielder and at Juventus the loss of the elegant Michel Platini and the flame-haired Pole Ziggy Boniek left Rush a desperate figure up front.

During the spring of 1988, gossip began to filter back to Anfield about Rush's unhappiness with life in Turin, but a return was thought unlikely. That is, until Peter Robinson went on holiday. Sitting in a Spanish cafe one early August morning, he spotted a story in a local paper about Juventus signing the Dynamo Kiev striker Alexander Zavarov. It dawned on him that this meant Juventus now had four foreign players in their squad, one more than was permitted. Somebody was bound to go and as they had just bought a striker, he had a good idea who it might be. He knew that Rush was unhappy and had scored only seven league goals all season. Equally, both the Italian press and Juventus supporters had picked him out for some scathing criticism A clause in the original contract with Juventus allowed Liverpool first offer if he should ever become available. It was worth a call. Dalglish was alerted to the possibility of a Rush return and relished the prospect.

And so, precisely one year after Ian Rush had flown off to Turin, he was on his way home to Anfield. The deal was kept under wraps and Rush was proudly presented to astonished journalists at an Anfield press conference on Thursday 18 August, two days before Liverpool were due to play Wimbledon at Wembley in the Charity Shield. No one was more thrilled than Dalglish. Barnes, Beardsley and Aldridge had generated so much excitement that the prospect of Rush linking alongside this formidable trio rekindled fading memories of another football era.

On the debit side, Dalglish lost Craig Johnston when the maverick Australian returned home to care for his paralysed sister. The news of Johnston's split with the club was revealed in a *Sun* exclusive on the eve of the Cup final against Wimbledon. It did not go down well with Dalglish. It came as a surprise to him and he was angry that Johnston had chosen to tell the papers before even discussing it with him. At the very least, he thought he should have kept quiet until after Wembley. Dalglish respected Johnston's decision but was annoyed that he should have allowed his own predicament to distract the team at so delicate a stage of the season. Johnston, who claims he expected to be in the starting line-up at Wembley, instead found himself named as substitute.

But if Ian Rush thought his return to first-team football was a mere matter of course, he was in for a rude awakening. To the astonishment of many, Dalglish kept Rush sitting on the bench as the season kicked off, and remained loyal to the previous season's line-up. Aldridge, who had been depressed by the news of Rush's return, responded by hitting a couple of goals at Wembley in the Charity Shield before striking a hat-trick in the opening game of the season against Charlton. The Charlton manager Lennie Lawrence despaired. 'We may be in the same division as Liverpool,' he sighed. 'But we are trying to do different things. There are two leagues in one division.' Yet even with Aldridge in such devastating form, it was impossible to keep Rush glued to the bench forever. Within a few games he had been tossed the number 9 shirt.

The season began well enough but by September the injury list was growing. Hansen was to be sidelined for much of the campaign, then Steve McMahon and John Barnes joined him on the treatment table to be followed by Bruce Grobbelaar. On top of the premature retirements of Mark Lawrenson, through injury, and Craig Johnston, Liverpool began to look vulnerable. Newcastle United came to Anfield on the first day of October and inflicted a rare home defeat on the champions. A week later, Luton Town did the same at Kenilworth Road. Barnes returned in that game only for Gary Gillespie to limp off, his season ended. And Rush's Italian form continued to haunt him. He had failed to score in seven outings, his worst run at Anfield since his earliest days. There was even rumour of him being dropped.

Dalglish was not one for excuses, but it had to be admitted that the club's injury crisis was worse than anyone could recall. When Liverpool crashed at Nottingham Forest in late October it was already their third defeat of the season, one more than they had suffered in the whole of the previous campaign. It was so bad that even Dalglish had been forced to pull on a shirt again for the Centenary Cup semi-final against Arsenal earlier in the season. It was the first of a number of meetings with Arsenal that autumn, as Liverpool again faced them in the third round of the Littlewoods Cup. In the first game at Anfield, Liverpool could count themselves fortunate not to have ended up with a good hiding let alone escape with a 1–1 draw. Everyone expected the worst in the replay at Highbury but, instead, Liverpool managed a goalless draw. In the second replay at Villa Park, Liverpool produced an outstanding performance that Dalglish rated the best he had ever seen from a Liverpool side, including the 5–0 thrashing of Nottingham Forest. Liverpool won 2–1. Former Gunner Alan Ball reckoned the only way to beat Liverpool was to let the ball down.

The one blot on the evening involved Dalglish and some Arsenal fans. An object had been thrown at Dalglish as he stood by the dugout and Dalglish, in return, was said to have hurled something back. It did not go down well either with the Arsenal fans or the police but in the event the police decided to take no action after he had apologised. Previously, in March, he had been spoken to after complaints about using foul language as Liverpool lost 1–0 to QPR at Loftus Road.

The following month there was an incident at his luxury Southport home when his Alsatian dog terrorised a woman and her one-year-old grandson. The woman had just posted a Spastics Society collecting envelope through the Dalglishes' letterbox when the dog suddenly appeared and confronted her in the garden. The woman rang the doorbell, but nobody was in. It was some time before a neighbour finally came to the rescue, backing a car into the drive so that the woman and baby could scramble in. The police later warned Dalglish not to let his dog roam in the garden when nobody was around. The incident highlighted Dalglish's commitment to privacy and protecting his family.

Having successfully battled their way past Arsenal in the Littlewoods Cup, Liverpool then crashed 4–1 to an improving West Ham United at Upton Park in the next round. The *Daily Mirror* described it as 'one of the most humiliating defeats in Kenny Dalglish's reign as manager'. It was their biggest domestic cup defeat since losing 4–1 to Wolves in 1939. Dalglish lost his temper in the dressing room after the match, accusing players of bottling out and not fighting. A couple of weeks later, Norwich inflicted a second home defeat in the league although Dalglish, ill at home with the flu, was fortunate enough to miss it.

Like the autumn leaves, Liverpool were being blown away. There were also problems off the field that were just as frustrating. Following a report in one of the newspapers, alleging that Bob Paisley did not rate John Aldridge, the Liverpool striker launched a scathing attack on the former manager in another newspaper article. It was unprecedented and unheard of to speak ill of a man held in such veneration at Anfield. Nobody at Liverpool could recall anything like it. The normally private world of

Anfield was suddenly splashed across the back pages. The row threatened to get out of hand, but Peter Robinson intervened swiftly enough to limit the damage. Unfortunately, neither he, John Smith nor even Dalglish were able to do anything about the next public exposure of Liverpool Football Club.

Over the years, as former scout Geoff Twentyman testifies, Liverpool always looked closely at a player's character before they made any approach. 'This was particularly important with Shankly, he says. 'Any lads had to have the temperament as well as the talent.' But, in more recent years, this rule no longer held such force, with players signed solely on the basis of their playing ability. It inevitably brought its problems. Paul Walsh had proved troublesome and in Jan Molby Liverpool had signed a player of extraordinary perception on the field but with difficulties off it. During his few years at Anfield the Danish international had appeared a number of times before the courts on various charges connected with driving. In mid-October 1988 he appeared again, on this occasion for reckless driving. He had been chased in his BMW by three police cars through the streets of Wallasey one night at speeds of up to 100mph. Molby was duly sentenced to three months' imprisonment, although, with good conduct, he was to be released after 45 days. For Dalglish, it was not just that he was temporarily losing an outstanding player when he could ill afford it, but the club was yet again being tarnished.

'Dalglish is facing the first serious crisis of a brief and golden reign,' warned the *Daily Mirror*. 'It has nothing to do with the uncharacteristically uncertain start his side have made in defence of their first division title. It has everything to do with that one quality that has always seemed the cornerstone of the Anfield success story – discipline. Would this have happened under Shanks? The answer invariably is No.'

The Molby and Aldridge affairs were dealt with in more typical Liverpool fashion, privately. It was not in the Anfield tradition to fine players, but Molby's wages were docked while he was in prison and Aldridge was dropped to reflect on his outburst.

For a time it seemed that the black cloud was lifting from Anfield, but then on New Year's Day in front of the TV cameras at Old Trafford, Liverpool were trounced 3–1. Dalglish was fuming. Ray Houghton claims he had never seen him so angry. The dressing room was locked, there was screaming, shouting and a great deal of finger-pointing. Harsh words were spoken and when a grim-faced Dalglish finally emerged he was forced to admit that United deserved to win. 'Our problem is not down to any one individual player,' he claimed. 'It is a collective thing.' Liverpool had stolen the lead early in the second half but time and again their defence had been exposed, particularly by high crosses. The team travelled in silence on the coach back to Merseyside. Liverpool had now slumped into seventh spot, nine points adrift of Arsenal at the top of the table. The newspapers had just about written them off and the instant quip 'crisis, what crisis?' was beginning to sound hollower with every game. Yet Liverpool were about to begin a charge that would once more take them to within a whisker of the double.

As the players arrived at Melwood for training the following morning, Dalglish ordered them into a team meeting before any training, unusual in Liverpool tradition. The normal practice was simply to brush aside defeat without turning it into too much of an issue and to concentrate instead on the next game. But this time it was different. Dalglish was looking for help. He told them his patience was running out and that he would not tolerate another display like the one at Old Trafford. They had to thrash out a solution there and then. Everyone had their say. A number of players later testified that the meeting marked a turning point in the season and that Dalglish's strategy had worked.

There was no single, simple solution to the crisis, although the signing of full back David Burrows from West Brom for £500,000 brought some much needed sting to the defence, while Steve Staunton also came in to show some quality touches. Molby eventually returned but on the debit side Rush was injured and missed a substantial part of the rest of the season. If there was an instant solution to Liverpool's dilemma, it was probably more to do with spirit and confidence and the clear-the-air discussion at Melwood. A few useful wins, particularly in the FA Cup, seemed to do the trick, but with only one league game played in the whole of February, Liverpool looked, at the end of that month, to be well out of contention, an astonishing 19 points adrift of Arsenal. Yet within six weeks, Liverpool would not only close the gap but actually overtake the Gunners at the top of the table, albeit momentarily. Liverpool had begun a run that would take them 24 consecutive games without defeat. They would not be defeated until the final game of the season, though by then the thoughts of many were no longer on football. It was to be the most painful spring in the club's history.

Liverpool's problem in the early part of the season had been their lack of goals. Once into 1989 they arrived in abundance: five against Luton, West Ham and Sheffield Wednesday, four against Middlesbrough and Brentford, the latter taking Liverpool into their 17th FA Cup semi-final.

A 2–1 win at Millwall in early April, their ninth consecutive league win, finally saw Liverpool clamber to the top of the table to open up a slender gap on Arsenal. Into the last four of the FA Cup and top of the league, it was the ideal boost for their semi-final battle with Nottingham Forest at Hillsborough.

The events at Hillsborough are dealt with elsewhere but suffice it to say, at this point, that it was to cast a shadow over everyone associated with Liverpool that would take many months, even years, to disappear. It was a day nobody would want to remember but a day nobody would ever forget. Indeed its scars would be there forever. Liverpool had arrived in eager anticipation of their clash, but after six minutes a lone figure in Liverpool colours racing on to the field heralded the worst sporting tragedy in British history. Liverpool Football Club would never be quite the same again.

By the end of April, some of the players had eased their way back through international duty, but the club decided that its first game should be a friendly, against Celtic. About 60,000 turned up at Parkhead and if Dalglish ever thought that bad feelings still lingered among the fans he was mistaken. Dalglish even appeared, and opened the scoring as Liverpool swept to a 4–0 win. At the end of the game, the name of Dalglish echoed around the terraces. The Jungle had not forgotten their former hero.

Liverpool's return to competitive football began with a goalless draw at Goodison Park. It was perhaps not the result Liverpool wanted, but everyone was glad to have got their first serious game since Hillsborough out of the way. On reflection, that result cost Liverpool the League title. Dalglish seemed back to his usual self, talking football, desperate to win the double. A 3–1 win in an emotional, replayed semi-final against Forest at Old Trafford helped put him on course for it as they picked up where they had left off. Liverpool were through to their third final in four years. But Liverpool's enforced absence from league football had seen Arsenal soar off into the distance and catching them would require an almighty effort. But everyone at Anfield was determined to give it a go for the sake of those who had so tragically died.

The final itself turned out to be another all–Merseyside clash. Everton had beaten Norwich in a semi-final that had been overshadowed by the events at Hillsborough and all but forgotten. Out of consideration, Wembley tore down the fences for the day, nobody was bothered about segregation, the sun cracked the flags and Gerry Marsden led the singing of 'You'll Never Walk Alone'. It was a highly charged afternoon, a family affair, rather than the nation's greatest sporting day. With Rush still shaking off his injury, Dalglish decided to keep the Welsh international on the bench and handed the number 9 shirt instead to John Aldridge. After five minutes it looked a masterstroke as Aldridge slammed Liverpool ahead. But that was to be the only excitement for the next 80-odd minutes. It was a dour affair, both teams labouring in the torrid heat, the occasion looking to get the better of them. But suddenly, in the final minute, it exploded back into action as Everton dramatically equalised. Extra time was needed. Dalglish decided that now was the moment to introduce Ian Rush to the proceedings. It was to prove a canny substitution. Within minutes of the resumption, Rush had swept Liverpool back into the lead. Suddenly the game had sprung into life. A minute later, Stuart McCall added a second for Everton. But almost before there was time to breathe, Rush had pounced to make it 3–2, beating Dixie Dean's record of goals in Merseyside derbies. There was no coming back for Everton. Dalglish was thrilled to have won the Cup for the Hillsborough victims. 'Sometimes you have to wait for the satisfaction to sink in,' he said. 'But this was immediate and emotional.' Liverpool had clinched the first part of the double. All they had to do now was win their remaining two league games.

Liverpool's fixture list had piled up, an inevitable consequence of their long layoff after the Hillsborough disaster. It meant that in their final run-in they faced three crucial games in six days – and one of those was a Cup final that had gone into extra time. Their two other games, both at Anfield, were equally important. In the first, three days after the Cup final, they faced a West Ham United side that needed to win to avoid relegation while Liverpool equally needed to win to maintain their challenge on the title. Three days later they were due to line up against Arsenal in what would be a title decider if Liverpool beat West Ham. It was an end-of-the-season climax as potentially dramatic as any in the history of the game. With Everton accounted for, Liverpool lined up against West Ham on the following Tuesday evening. Dalglish decided to go for goals and left Beardsley on the bench in favour of Ian Rush. It proved again to be a wise decision as Liverpool stormed to a 5–1 victory. The clutch of goals from that game also gave Liverpool an extra cushion. All they had to do now was to avoid losing by more than one goal against Arsenal – and the double would be theirs.

Rush was again preferred to Beardsley, Anfield was packed and more than 15 million sat at home glued to their televisions. They would never see a more dramatic finish to a football match. From the start, Liverpool looked weary. It had been predicted that at some point the after-effects of Hillsborough would strike. Everyone had expected that occasion to be at Wembley. Yet, on the contrary, Liverpool had shown astonishing resources, even battling their way through an extra 30 minutes of sizzling heat to win the Cup. Liverpool needed only to draw with Arsenal and, for most of the 90 minutes, seemed content to let the game drift towards a draw. At half time there was still no score. 'Just keep it tight,' urged Dalglish in the dressing room. 'We're doing alright.' Then in the 52nd minute, Arsenal were awarded an indirect free kick just outside the area. Nigel Winterburn stepped up and promptly slammed the ball into the net. It looked as if it had not touched anyone but the referee ignored the linesman's flag and ruled that the ball had been helped on by Alan Smith as it sailed into the net. Smith claimed the goal despite Liverpool's vigorous protests. Yet, even a goal down, they were still safe.

As the second half wore on, so Liverpool resorted to dwelling on the ball, stroking it back to Grobbelaar and across the back four, reluctant to go forward for fear they might surrender possession. It had been the same at Wembley and had almost had dire consequences, with Everton equalising on the stroke of full time. For the second time in less than a week they would make the same error of judgement. There was just one minute left. As John Barnes hung on to the ball near the corner flag, Kevin Richardson stole it from him and quickly pushed it back to his keeper. Lukic threw it out to Lee Dixon who played it on to Alan Smith who in turn knocked it on to Michael Thomas. Suddenly Thomas was charging into the box, in space, and the ball flashed into the back of the net. Arsenal had snatched the double from Liverpool in injury time with almost the last kick of the season. It was unbelievable, the most dramatic conclusion to an already dramatic season.

As Michael Thomas leapt for joy, Dalglish, standing on the touchline, looked on horrified, his hands clutching his head, visibly in shock at what he had seen. He was not alone. John Barnes had collapsed full length, John Aldridge was kneeling as if in prayer, his head buried in his hands. Another 36,000 Liverpool fans watched in disbelief, stunned into silence. The unthinkable had happened. Dalglish turned and looked at Moran and Evans, his face taut, mouth half open, you could see the despair in his eyes. Yet again he had been robbed of a second double. It was almost certainly the most disappointing night in the history of Anfield.

'The next morning I refused to even look at the newspapers,' moaned one Koppite. 'In fact I've still never read any match reports or seen a video of the game. That's how much it hurt. Imagine how Dalglish must have felt.'

There were no celebrations in Liverpool that evening. Few even went for a drink to drown their sorrows. Everyone simply wanted to go home and be left in peace. Outside Anfield the streets were filled with thousands slowly walking back to their cars, still in stunned silence, shaking their heads in disbelief. Nobody needed to say anything.

There were moments when Dalglish must have wondered if he really enjoyed being a manager. But Dalglish was a professional; he had to get on with it. Like all professionals there was little room for sentiment. The nightmare of that balmy evening when Dalglish was outgunned by the Gunners had to be put aside. But it had been a mentally and physically draining year. The legacy of Hillsborough still hung darkly over Anfield. Nobody could be quite sure how it would affect them all. No manager in the history of football had ever experienced so traumatic and pressured a season as Dalglish. Hillsborough, a replayed semi-final, an FA Cup final against their closest rivals and then the torture of that evening against Arsenal. It had taken its toll. Liverpool Football Club was proving to be too big a job for any one man. It was almost unmanageable.

At the start of every season, Ronnie Moran always reminded the players that the previous campaign counted for nothing. 'Let's go out and do it all again,' he would urge. It was part of the Anfield ritual. After 1988/9 his words were difficult to digest. But somehow Dalglish and his backroom staff managed to motivate them, though on the first day of the following season, as they lined up against Manchester City at Anfield, you could sense the lack of enthusiasm on the terraces. It was as if it had all been too much for everyone.

The only urgency for Dalglish during the close season had been to find a tall, experienced centre back. The man who fitted the part was Glenn Hysen, the Swedish international playing in the Italian league with Fiorentina, who was cheekily stolen from the clutches of Manchester United as Alex Ferguson hesitated over the asking price. Dalglish was in like a shot and Hysen was on his way to Anfield before Ferguson could respond. It was also inevitable that John Aldridge would seek another challenge. Dalglish had tried to satisfy his demands, but Rush and Aldridge were too similar in style and there was simply not enough room for both strikers in the same line-up. Aldridge found himself on the bench just once too often and reluctantly decided to try his luck elsewhere, joining Real Sociedad in Spain.

Dalglish started his career with Possil YMCA. Here he is sixth from the right in the second row [© Daily Mirror].

A youthful Dalglish apparently enjoying his football as a teenager [© Daily Mirror].

A fearsome sight for defenders: Dalglish on the charge, May 1972 [© MSI].

1975: as proud to wear the green and white hoops of Celtic (below) as to represent his country (above) [© MSI].

With Graeme Souness, anticipating the 1978 World Cup finals [© MSI].

Turning on the style for his country against Holland in Argentina [© MSI].

Looking pensive during his first game for Liverpool, August 1977 [© Getty Images].

Receiving the 1979 Footballer of the Year award from Stanley Matthews [© Daily Mirror].

At full stretch, blasting home against Swansea City in 1981 [© MSI].

Dalglish (far left) joins his Liverpool team-mates in celebrating their 1983 League Cup final victory against Manchester United [© Sunday Mirror].

At home with his wife, daughter and Scotland caps [© Sunday Mail].

Leading by example: as ever, Liverpool's player/manager has the ball under his complete control, 1985 [© MSI].

Golf has always been a major Dalglish obsession [© Daily Record].

The highlight of the early season was the 9–0 blitz of newly promoted Crystal Palace to equal Liverpool's best ever score in the league. By the end of September, Liverpool had already climbed to the top of the table. They would remain there for much of the campaign. The arrival of Hysen looked a winner as the team conceded only six goals in their first ten fixtures. But then against Southampton they came unstuck, losing 4–1, their biggest league defeat since 1986. The *Daily Mirror* called it a 'humiliation', while the *Daily Express* talked of Liverpool being 'ripped apart'.

A few days later, with Hansen, Hysen and Gillespie absent through injury, they lost again to Arsenal in the Littlewoods Cup and were then beaten 1–0 at home by Coventry. Dalglish was furious, lashing out publicly at his players. 'We won't accept that standard of performance at this club,' he raged. 'Our attitude wasn't right.' One of the problems was that Ian Rush was not finding the net with the same regularity since his return from Italy. The transfer of Aldridge to Real Sociedad, where he was the new goalscoring hero, meant that Liverpool did not have a substitute striker. There was talk of dropping Rush but it was impossible when there was no replacement. Some papers wondered if Dalglish had not been a little premature in selling Aldridge. But it was all very well to say that in hindsight. The back pages were full of speculation, linking Liverpool to any number of strikers, including Roy Wegerle of Luton Town and particularly Marco Gabbiadini of Sunderland. But Dalglish was in no hurry to gamble.

The following week, Liverpool crashed 3–2 at Queen's Park Rangers, their fourth defeat in five games, and the tabloids were awash with crisis stories. 'KENNY ON THE RACK' was the headline in the *Daily Mirror*, while the *Daily Express* reckoned 'Liverpool must be facing some kind of a crisis.' But if there was a crisis, and there rarely is at Anfield, it was quickly resolved. The goals began to come in a flood: four at Maine Road, then five against Chelsea before another record was set, this time in the FA Cup as they slaughtered Swansea City 8–0 after a goalless draw at Vetch Field. Liverpool cantered to the title, losing only one league game after November.

However, there were moments when Liverpool looked lethargic. They may have been winning, but it was rarely with the panache and style of true champions as in 1987/8. Their victories were wrung out of the opposition, seldom convincing and often in the balance until the final whistle. When it seemed they might stumble, the inspired signing late in the season of Ronnie Rosenthal added some much-needed zest to the attack. Rosenthal, an Israeli, had been on loan from Standard Liege to Hibernian,

Brighton and Luton Town before Liverpool jumped in with an offer he could barely refuse. Everyone had seemed reluctant to make a definite bid and the Israeli was on the brink of returning to Belgium until Liverpool jumped in. It was another masterstroke by Dalglish, turning a player nobody had wanted into a title winner. Rosenthal became an instant hit. He may not have shown the delicate touches of a Dalglish or the speed of an Ian Rush, but he was an awkward, bustling player, difficult to dispossess, and could carry the ball into unknown territory. He was to be the difference between Liverpool winning the title and finishing as runners-up.

Until April it looked as if Liverpool might also go the distance in the FA Cup to give Dalglish that coveted second double. After disposing of Swansea City so emphatically, they defeated Norwich, Southampton and Queen's Park Rangers to reach the last four.

But if any game that season was to underline Liverpool's increasing vulnerability, it was their FA Cup semi-final against Crystal Palace. Earlier in the season they had drilled nine goals past Palace. The game seemed a mere formality. Liverpool looked odds-on to win another double. But Palace, under their astute young manager Steve Coppell, had learned their lesson well. Admittedly, injuries during the match to Ian Rush and Gary Gillespie disrupted Liverpool's flow, but twice they tossed away a lead to lose 4–3. It had been one of the most exciting semi-finals in years, but in the full glare of the television cameras the cracks in the Liverpool defence had been there for all to examine. The *Daily Mirror* called it 'the biggest FA Cup semi-final upset in history.'

When they returned to the dressing room, there was an ominous silence. Nothing was said for 15 minutes. Dalglish calmly showered and changed; everyone bit their lip. Then Dalglish let loose. He called it the most unprofessional performance he had ever seen. 'How could they give away such silly free kicks, where was the defence?' He stormed across to Steve McMahon, blaming him for one of the Palace equalisers. Then he tore into the defenders, letting them know that they had let everyone down. He was furious.

It was not normally the Liverpool style to hold inquests, the rule was to put a defeat behind you and get on with the next game. But this time, as after the New Year's Day game the previous season, it was different. Dalglish gathered them all together after training and went through each of the four goals in detail, pointing out the mistakes and trying to thrash out the solutions. Once more, it was to be effective. The following weekend they beat Charlton 4–0 as they ploughed on towards their 18th championship.

Dalglish had collected his final honour with Liverpool but the pressures seemed to mount with every day. New players had to be found, money had to be spent wisely, and as manager he had discovered that there were as many problems off the field as there were on. As a player, one could not know half the problems and worries that were being taken to the manager by the rest of the team. There were more than a few people ready to offer their advice, either from the back pages or the terraces. As a player, Dalglish knew that he could contribute as much as anyone to resolving any problem on the pitch, but sitting on the bench he was impotent to help. All he could do was shout and worry. More than 20 years at the top and still they expected the trophies to roll in. Since returning to the first division in 1962 they had won 13 League titles, four FA Cups, four League Cups, four European Cups and two UEFA Cups. They had also reached several other finals and, since 1972, had only once finished out of the top two. It was a phenomenal record, without equal in the Football League. Dalglish had been fortunate to have had his share of those honours both as a player and as a manager. But for how much longer could he weave his magic spell?

CHAPTER THIRTEEN

Hillsborough

There is nothing worth one death, let alone one hundred.
Kenny Dalglish

It was Liverpool's 17th FA Cup semi-final; Nottingham Forest were the opposition, Hillsborough the venue. By the end of the evening the name Hillsborough would have taken on a new meaning. Top of the first division and just one game away from Wembley, Liverpool stood on the verge of another double. Long before the game kicked off, questions had been raised about the allocation of ground ends. Liverpool, the better supported club, had been given the smaller Leppings Lane end of the ground while Forest had been allocated the large Kop end at Hillsborough. The Football Association had argued that this was in accordance with a police request. To allocate the larger Kop end to Liverpool would have meant fans crossing each other on their approach to the ground, and that might have led to violence. The FA also pointed out that the allocation was precisely as it had been the previous year when Forest and Liverpool had met at Hillsborough in the Cup semi-final. At the time it seemed to make sense.

The game was barely minutes old. A Peter Beardsley shot had already cannoned off the bar and Liverpool were beginning to surge forward when a few figures spilled on to the pitch. The next moment a policeman was racing towards the referee; something was happening behind the goal at the Leppings Lane end where all the Liverpool supporters were massed. Another fan wearing the colours of Liverpool was spotted sprinting towards Ray Houghton and shouting at him. 'Ray, they are dying in there.' Steve Nicol was seen pleading with the referee. Nobody seemed to know quite what was happening. The commentators assumed it was crowd trouble. Over the next few hours, the most horrific tragedy in British sporting history unfolded before the TV cameras.

As the referee brought the game to a halt, Dalglish quickly ushered his players back to the dressing room. 'Keep warm lads, we'll be back on in a few minutes,' shouted the referee. The players sat around, some reading the programme, others doing a few gentle exercises. Dalglish walked around nervously. The dressing room door had been left ajar and they could see fans being helped down the tunnel towards a small first aid centre. A couple of fans sitting on the floor outside the dressing room were in tears and Dalglish stepped out for a few moments to console them. The manager then went back out on to the pitch to find out what was happening and when the game would continue. Back in the dressing room, little was said. They all knew that there were serious injuries and possibly even deaths, but there was still confusion. Someone suggested the club had another Heysel on its hands. There was a stunned silence. At 3.30pm the referee popped his head around the door and told the players to be ready to come out again in a few minutes. Little information was being relayed back to the dressing room. At 4.00pm the players were finally told that the game had been abandoned. By then it was apparent that there had been a terrible loss of life. John Barnes was in tears, inconsolable; it would take a little longer before the enormity of the disaster would hit others. They all changed and went upstairs to the players' lounge to join their wives as the full extent of the tragedy was becoming clearer. The official death toll continued to rise, eventually reaching 95.

Dalglish was stunned. For the second time in less than four years, he was at the centre of a disaster with Liverpool Football Club and for the third time in his footballing career he had been present at a sporting tragedy. He had not been playing the day Rangers met Celtic at Ibrox in 1971 when a last minute equaliser led to the deaths of 66 fans on the infamous Stairway 13. He was still only 19 years old and had yet to make the breakthrough into the first team but he had gone along with the Celtic party to Ibrox. Yet, over the next few weeks as Scottish football mourned, he would be as involved as anyone in the depressing rituals. His family was Protestant and Rangers, his own career was at Catholic Parkhead. Dalglish was in a unique position, with a foot on each side of the Great Divide. Then at Heysel in May 1985, set to become player/manager of Liverpool, there had been the deaths of 39, mainly Italian, fans. It was more than enough for any man.

And yet in his most painful hour, Dalglish mustered the resources to carry on. When leadership was most needed, he was able to provide it. When the hour came, the man emerged. The following morning, he and Marina were on the phone to all the Liverpool players telling them to report to Anfield. There would also be a special mass that evening at the Catholic cathedral and they were all expected to be there. At Anfield, Dalglish was comforting the players, particularly those born in Liverpool like John Aldridge and Steve McMahon, as well as many of the younger players still with the reserves. They were all deeply shocked. Bruce Grobbelaar volunteered to read the lesson at the mass. 'What is called for now is dignity,' Dalglish told them. 'We need to set an example.'

And no one set a finer example than Dalglish. Here he was, a man said to be shy of the press, stepping forward into the limelight to answer the barrage of questions. Here was a man, said to have no public relations skills, answering with dignity, honesty and patience as many press questions as could be fielded. And here was a man said to have no interests other than football, refusing point blank to talk about the game. With quiet, but firm, leadership Dalglish was trying to steady the floundering ship.

On the Sunday morning after Hillsborough, Liverpool was a ghost town. The streets were almost deserted, the buses empty, the normally busy lunchtime pubs silent, many of them closed. Even the paper shops were quiet, nobody being inclined to pore over the details, or with the courage to look at those terrifying photographs so insensitively and sensationally splashed across the front pages. Too many tears had already been wept.

The previous evening at Anfield a few scallies had gathered and had tied their scarves to the Shankly Gates. It was a simple gesture, the only way they knew how to say 'goodbye' or 'sorry' to their pals, a last sad farewell. Yet its simplicity struck a chord. The word spread and later that day many more wandered up to the ground to place flowers, scarves, hats, anything they could find that had Liverpool attached to it, at the Shankly Gates. By the Monday the Shankly Gates were awash in red scarves and flowers. Someone then asked if they could place a wreath on the Kop. The club flung open the gates to admit them. By the end of the week, Anfield had been turned into a shrine as thousands came to pay their respects. Flowers covered half the ground, a thousand scarves and more hung from the barriers of the Kop. Nobody who saw it will ever forget it. It was the most extraordinary and moving sight. A city was in mourning.

In the days that followed, Dalglish and his wife organised a rota. Dalglish dealt with the players, Marina with their wives. Anfield became almost an open house. The bereaved were welcomed, Marina and the wives brewed pots of tea and tried to give what comfort they could. On the Monday morning, the players journeyed to Sheffield to visit the hospitals, taking programmes, books, autographs, anything that might help the injured. It seemed trivial but the visits and gifts brought enormous pleasure and help. On his first visit, John Aldridge and Dalglish were taken to see a young boy still in a coma. When the doctor announced 'Kenny Dalglish is here to see you,' the young fan promptly opened his eyes and emerged from his coma. The story only added to the legend of Dalglish. They were also asked to visit another youngster on a life-support machine who had no hope of recovery. The mother had asked for the machine to be switched off but as a final request wanted Dalglish and some of the players to visit her son. They did so without question. But it was a gruelling experience for all of them. Ray Houghton later spoke of how he 'had never been so upset in my life'. Alan Hansen was visibly shaking.

For Dalglish, having young children of his own, one can only guess at the effects and the scars that Hillsborough and the subsequent weeks must have left. There is a photograph of Dalglish taken at the scene of the disaster that afternoon. He is clearly distraught; a police officer has his arm around him. At his other side is the Nottingham Forest manager Brian Clough, a comforting arm gently touching him.

Nor was it just the injured and the bereaved who needed comforting but thousands of fans who had witnessed the disaster. Some had seen friends and relatives die, others had given the kiss of life, while others had raced across the pitch with their makeshift stretchers. Everyone at the Leppings Lane end of Hillsborough had gone through a traumatic experience. They wanted and needed to talk about it. Dalglish and the players were always available.

'We were just trying to help people,' Dalglish told one reporter. 'They have always helped us as supporters. We supported them when they needed us. It's what families do. This club is like a family. It was 95 members of a family we lost. When you lose people in a family you all help each other.' The city of Liverpool can rarely have known such suffering, yet it found its strength in belonging. There were those outside of Liverpool who expressed disdain for this morbidity and length of grieving, who could not understand. It was a typically English response. What they did not understand is that Liverpool is not an English city: it is a Celtic city.

The players decided that at least one of them should be assigned to each bereaved family to help with the counselling. They took it upon themselves to visit the families in their homes and made themselves available for any telephone calls. John Barnes, for one, chatted for hours on the phone to one family he helped comfort. The families did not always want to talk about the disaster, some just wanted to gossip about football, about Liverpool, the outstanding players, the great games. The bereaved needed to chat. Marina was even said to have been answering the phone at two in the morning. Her role would not be forgotten. Years later, she was invited to open the Hillsborough Advice Centre, a small token of the appreciation felt by many.

The hospital visits were followed by the funerals, with the players again agreeing that at least one of them should be at each funeral. They drew up a list and over the next week or so gathered at cemeteries all over Merseyside. And at the lectern they bravely read the lesson. For the Scousers like John Aldridge and Steve McMahon it was a particularly gruelling time. Both had known fans who had been killed or injured and being Liverpool-born themselves felt the tragedy as deeply as anyone. Not surprisingly, Aldridge wondered if he could ever play football again. Bruce Grobbelaar also pondered his future.

'We were all seeing an additional dimension to Dalglish which we had not seen before,' says Rogan Taylor, of the Football Supporters' Association, who was closely involved with the club after the disaster. 'It was a glimpse into the inner chamber that showed Dalglish was more than just a footballer. His shyness was cracked open by the tragedy. The man was clearly emotional in a way that we had not imagined possible.'

Barry Devonside, who lost his son at Hillsborough, had nothing but praise for Dalglish. 'Kenny Dalglish did a wonderful job of lending support,' he says. 'Though I respect him even more for the level of feeling he has shown since.' Mr Devonside, who got to know Dalglish well, adds that 'I think Hillsborough caused him to re-evaluate his already treasured family life and the fact that it is far more important than football. I believe that has been a big factor in Dalglish's resignation.'

From all over the country, football fans, politicians, royalty, even people who had never seen a football match, came to pay their respects. Anfield became an awesome sight. Dalglish put into words what everybody thought: 'The saddest and most beautiful sight I have ever seen,' he whispered. He would often arrive at the ground early in the morning, before anyone else, and steal into the stands where he would sit for a few minutes in the early spring sunshine, alone and silent with just the rustling of cellophane and the fragrance of the flowers.

Dalglish admitted to the *Daily Mirror* that he had shed tears during those difficult weeks. 'I realised that in all my years as manager and player,' he explained, 'that I had miscalculated the importance of the club to the people. It was a mistake. I never fully appreciated the part we played in their lives. It's not we and them, it's us.' Undoubtedly, the board, the players, even the fans had never fully appreciated just how important the club was in the lives of Liverpool people. For many, it was their only gratification. Unemployment, urban deprivation, poor housing, mortgages, rents, these were problems they had to cope with day in and day out. Liverpool Football Club was the one distraction in their lives, the one thing that made them feel happy, the one success with which they could be proudly associated.

Dalglish was also the first to leap to the defence of the fans when certain newspapers, the *Sun* in particular, made allegations about drunkenness and loutish behaviour at Hillsborough.

A year after Hillsborough, some of the players were still visiting patients in hospital, nearly everyone kept up the friendships that had been formed with the families and even two years after the tragedy, Dalglish was still sending Christmas cards to those who had suffered.

Dalglish initially campaigned for Liverpool's withdrawal from the FA Cup. Twice the board deferred a decision, believing it important that whatever the final outcome it should have general approval not only within the club, but throughout the city as well. The board judged that more time was needed before they could truly reflect those views. Yet once the initial shock of Hillsborough began to fade and the funerals were over, it became clear that most fans wanted the club to replay the semi-final. Dalglish acquiesced.

Prior to Hillsborough, grumblings about Dalglish had been heard along the corridors of power at Anfield. Dalglish's position was being questioned, although the directors were still some way from taking the ultimate measure. But he emerged from Hillsborough in an impregnable position thanks to his handling of the situation. More than anyone at the club, he had shown dignity and control. It was Dalglish who had been the spokesman for them all, Dalglish who had faced the cameras, Dalglish who decided when to start playing, Dalglish who had organised the players to help the bereaved. And he had carried all those burdens without any consideration for himself. And yet, as later events would prove, he probably needed as much help as anyone in overcoming the terrible pain of that tragedy. No institution, no city could have asked for a finer ambassador in their greatest hour of need.

Dalglish had forged a rare relationship with the people of Liverpool, not seen since the days of Shankly, and one that extended way beyond the gates of the Kop. He was a spokesman for the whole city, indeed for the whole game of football. Even those outside of Merseyside who had previously sniped at his surliness and his success were forced to admit that without his calm handling of the situation the game might have gone into terminal decline. Instead, Hillsborough was to act as a catalyst, putting the game back on the road towards sanity. Dalglish was expected to provide the answers, know all the solutions. He was no longer a mere mortal.

Even the media latched on to his new role, though promotion to the deity was something Dalglish would have resolutely resisted. A national radio opinion poll to choose the person of the year voted him into second place, just behind Chinese student Wang Weilin who had stood defiantly in front of Chinese Army tanks in Tiananmen Square. Soviet leader Mikhail Gorbachev was third.

Leading trauma psychologist Doctor James Thompson of University College, London, warned at the time that Hillsborough could turn out to be, in psychological terms, Britain's worst disaster. So many people had witnessed it at close quarters. 'The effects on some people may take anything up to five years before they appear,' he warned, adding that nobody should plunge themselves into work, seeing it as a remedy.

Hillsborough changed many people, not least Dalglish. Players openly wept and had to face up to the rituals of mourning. It was the first time some of them had experienced bereavement. Their involvement with those who had lost relatives and friends forced them to respond emotionally and to analyse their own reactions and feelings. It was no bad thing, turning many of them from boys into men. Steve McMahon, for one, admits that he grew up almost overnight. For once, the normally macho world of the football dressing room began to take on a more compassionate image as they realised that football was not everything. Bill Shankly would always be remembered for his famous quip that 'Football is not a matter of life and death. It's much more important than that.' Merseyside had readily agreed with him. But Hillsborough changed that attitude. Dalglish summed it up more neatly than anyone, cleverly moulding the famous Shankly quote to his own words. 'The FA Cup isn't worth it,' he said. 'There is nothing worth one death, let alone one hundred.'

Like the others, Dalglish had suddenly come to realise that there were other important factors in life. For more than 20 years, all he had cared for had been soccer and his family but Hillsborough opened up a new perspective. Nobody could have experienced such a tragedy without it having a profound effect. Dalglish was to be no exception. Could he ever be quite so single-minded again? Football would never have quite the same hold for him. Hillsborough was to mark a turning point.

CHAPTER FOURTEEN

The Corridors Of Power

You gotta stand and fight for the price you pay.
Bruce Springsteen

As you climb up Everton Valley past narrow streets of back-to-back Victorian houses you could almost be forgiven for failing to notice that there is a football ground here. It's a poor area of litter-strewn alleys, corner pubs, rundown shops, tumbling walls and endless graffiti. You can almost hear the cry for help. Only the mighty Spion Kop, rising majestically above the rooftops, gives any hint that this is the home of Liverpool Football Club. Everything about Anfield is modest. It's always been a homely club, the local shop rather than the supermarket. They don't employ many people here, they shut down at four, lock the doors and all go home for their teas. But go to Old Trafford at almost any time of the day and you can smell the wealth; there will be dozens of cars parked there, people milling around and an organisation that clearly employs hundreds. But not at Anfield.

Hidden deep beneath the main stand at Anfield, along a corridor close to the dressing rooms, is an unassuming door. It might be just another office, a junk room or simply a door that leads to a further labyrinth of passageways. But it is none of these. It is in fact the most important door in the club. This is the bunker, the Anfield bootroom, where the downfall of many a club has been plotted. As you pass it, club officials proudly point it out. 'That's the bootroom;' they whisper, but they never let you look in. Entry is by invitation only. The bootroom is hidden well away from the public, the press, football's groupies and even most of the Anfield staff. It would be easier to secure an invitation to Buckingham Palace than to the bootroom.

Liverpool's success story has been founded on its bootroom, an institution almost as legendary and beloved in soccer as the Spion Kop. Throughout football they talk in revered and hushed tones of Anfield's bootroom. The occasional visiting manager is invited in after a game where he might be offered a cup of tea or, if he's lucky, something a little stronger. But what the visiting managers don't realise is that they are only being welcomed so that the back-room boys can tap their knowledge. 'Been to see any third division football this season?' they ask innocently, knowing full well that their guest was spotted somewhere unusual the other evening. 'Aye,' replies the unsuspecting visitor. 'I went to see Reading the other day. Went to look at a young lad, full back, very promising he was.' Ronnie Moran takes note and by the end of the week someone from the club will be at Reading watching the young full back. In Whitehall circles they would call it intelligence gathering.

Lawrie McMenemy recalls with amusement many a visit he paid to the bootroom during his days as Southampton manager, especially the first one:

'I went down this corridor at the back of this magnificent stand expecting to find something special but there it was, tucked away, just an old bootroom. "Come on in, Lawrie," says Bob. "Sit yerself down." I looked around but there wasn't a seat to sit on, just an upturned beer barrel or a crate. I was all dressed up in my suit and best coat; they were in tracksuits. But you daren't dust your coat down or wipe the beer barrel or they'll slaughter you. "Have a drink," they say. And you look around but there's no bar. Then they open a cupboard here and produce a can of lager or a cupboard there and produce a bottle of scotch. You daren't ask for a glass either or they'll think you're a cissy. They're testing you, all the time they're testing you.'

The bootroom stretches back more than 30 years to the arrival of Bill Shankly in 1959. It is, as the name suggests, just an ordinary room where the players' boots are stored. Shankly and his backroom staff made it their base. They would gather here after training or on match day for a cup of tea and a chat. It was their den and it soon became part of football's folk-lore. Since then, it has become the design office for countless championships, European triumphs and much Wembley glory. This is where Liverpool's success over the decades has been planned.

Its inhabitants have changed little over the years. You can almost sense the ghosts. At first there was Shankly, Paisley, Fagan and Reuben Bennett. Then Ronnie Moran joined them, followed by Geoff Twentyman and Tom Saunders. Even later came Roy Evans and Chris Lawler. And then Phil Thompson, Steve Heighway and Ron Yeats.

The Anfield bootroom may be unique in football, yet there must be a hundred other similar rooms in British soccer. Wherever a former Liverpool player is managing you will find a bootroom. So if the bootroom is the key to Liverpool's success, why have other imitations failed so miserably? Perhaps the secret has been in the continuity of its staff. The same faces, the same jokes, the same pooling of knowledge over the years. All of which adds up to confidence. They know that when there is a problem they can look back and say: 'Yes, we had a similar situation three, five, ten years ago and we got over it.' Experience, confidence and continuity. When someone retired, a new face appeared, though usually it was one of the players and so not really new at all. They've all been at Anfield, man and boy, all their lives. They don't like outsiders here, they interfere, change things. Even the players are not welcomed. They might pop their heads around the door to pinch a sandwich after a game, but they certainly never sat down and chatted to Ronnie Moran or Roy Evans. It was not the done thing. Change at Anfield has to be evolutionary, not revolutionary.

And yet, when it comes to diplomas, they are probably the most unqualified bunch of coaches in soccer. If, as has been suggested, only qualified coaches will in future be allowed to coach in the Football League then practically the entire Liverpool bootroom are likely to be made redundant. Not one of them has ever been awarded a coaching' diploma between them over the past 30 years. Liverpool have proved that qualifi-cations count for nothing.

Over the years the bootroom boys have built up a collection of dossiers unrivalled in the Football League. There are volumes currently in use and sitting on the shelves, kept up to date daily. And there are further volumes, now stored away in some broom cupboard gathering dust, detailing events since 1959. These are the Anfield bibles that provide all the answers to their prayers. They contain every detail of every player, their eating habits, fitness record, injuries, weight and state of mind – all carefully noted and entered. Even the condition of the ground is recorded and the temperature as well as the training schedule for that day. Every injury is logged, every treatment noted and every recovery analysed so that they always know how best to deal with any injury. They can even tell you what type of training to do in certain weather conditions. It means that come some crisis, some problem, they can refer back to how they responded the last time. There are said to be volumes and volumes of these black dossiers that would no doubt make compulsive and instructional reading to anyone outside of Anfield's inner circle. Even a few people inside Anfield would not mind a sneak at them too. But only those in the know get to see the dossiers. Take them away and maybe the Anfield magic would disappear. The bootroom boys have almost become obsessive about their dossiers, each day recording the smallest incident knowing that some day it might just come in useful. If there is a secret to Liverpool's success then it probably lies somewhere in the bootroom, in its continuity, its experience, its mutual trust and its dossiers. But much of that was to change with the elevation of Dalglish to soccer's top job. If the bootroom had been legendary, it was about to become a myth.

Chris Lawler was one of the finest full backs in the history of post-war Liverpool. If you had to pick an all-time Liverpool XI, Lawler would always be a contender for one of the full back spots. He played 546 games for the club between 1962 and 1975 and scored 61 goals, winning countless medals as well as four England caps. But even that summary barely describes Lawler's contribution. It is his European record which perhaps more than anything underlines his role. In 66 European games he notched 11 goals, stealing into the area on so many occasions to strike crucial goals for the club. Time and again Lawler saved Liverpool from a European exit. Shankly called him 'one of the greatest servants of all time'. After Liverpool he joined other clubs as first a player then as a coach before Joe Fagan brought him back to Anfield in 1983 to join the bootroom staff. His principal job was to look after the reserves, but there were always other tasks. He would cast an eye over any players the club was interested in signing, he was involved in training and, on a Saturday, if the reserves were not playing, he would be in the dressing room or on the bench with the first team. Everyone mucked in at Anfield.

When Fagan announced his retirement, Lawler was as surprised as anyone, though he had seen the strain tell on him. He was equally surprised when Dalglish was named as manager. Like so many others, Lawler had assumed that Ronnie Moran would be next in line. Tom Saunders had engaged them one relaxed evening after a European game in a light-hearted discussion, sounding them out about the future, about whether they might be interested in the top job when it arose. Looking back on it, Lawler wonders if Saunders was perhaps quietly sounding out the potential candidates.

Lawler was possibly a candidate. He had, after all, been successful during his brief period in charge of the reserves. He was calm, thoughtful, respected, just the kind of image the club appreciated. But even Lawler would admit that he was never a serious candidate. He certainly felt no bitterness when Dalglish was appointed, simply surprise. But after one season of working with Dalglish, Lawler was sacked.

It was the close season. Liverpool had just won the double and Lawler and the bootroom boys had celebrated with Dalglish at a London hotel. But when Lawler returned for preseason training, he noticed that had not received any bonus. He mentioned it to Ronnie Moran and Roy Evans and they both confirmed that they had received their money. Lawler was puzzled and went to see Peter Robinson, but Robinson suggested he saw the manager. So he traipsed off to see Dalglish.

'I asked him what was going on, why I had not received a bonus. He simply told me that he did not want me anymore. Phil Thompson was taking over the reserves,' Lawler says. 'I could have hit him.' With the new season impending, it was too late to find a post elsewhere. Dalglish did then offer him a stay of execution while he found a new job. Lawler had won two Central League titles and had been runner-up in his three years in charge. But reserve team honours count for nothing in football, especially at Anfield. It was the first sacking of a bootroom boy in living memory.

Dalglish felt that Lawler was not the right man for the job. He was quiet, self-effacing, and known around Anfield as 'the silent knight', a title bestowed upon him by Shankly. In his autobiography, Shankly tells a story about Lawler which probably says as much about Shankly as it does about Lawler:

'My team in the five-a-side was claiming a goal and I said, "Just hold on, Chris, you were watching."

'"Yes," he said.

'"Speak up, Chris," I said. "I can't hear you. Did you think that was a goal Chris?"

'"No," he said.

' "Good God, Chris," I said. "This is the first time I've heard you speak to me and you tell me a bloody lie!" '

Similarly, Dalglish reckoned Lawler too quiet. He shied from arguing a forceful case on behalf of his reserves, some of whom might be worth a tryout in the first team. But if the sacking of Chris Lawler was to hit the headlines, there was worse to follow.

Geoff Twentyman had devoted his life to Liverpool Football Club. As chief scout he was, arguably, just as responsible for the club's phenomenal success as anyone. Managers can only mould riches out of potential. Someone has to spot the promise in the first place. Twentyman's record spoke for itself. Over the years, he had first spotted and then encouraged the club to sign a list of players that would have given any team in the world a game. Men like Ian Rush, Steve Nicol, Alec Lindsay, Steve Heighway and Terry McDermott were all Geoff Twentyman protégés. Some were bought solely on Twentyman's recommendation, without the manager even seeing them.

Twentyman had begun his playing career with Carlisle United, a young, local centre half, powerful and with a ferocious shot. Liverpool signed him in December 1953 for a substantial fee and Twentyman was cleverly converted to left half. For a short spell, he was even captain of Liverpool but during the 1959/60 season, shortly before Shankly arrived, Twentyman was transferred to the Irish league club Ballymena. It was not until 1967 that he returned to Anfield as chief scout. He was to become one of the finest scouts in the business, given credit for much of the Anfield success. Yet now Dalglish had also handed Geoff Twentyman his cards. Two bootroom boys gone and Dalglish had been in the job barely a year.

The dismissal of Twentyman is harder to understand than the firing of Lawler. He was replaced by Ron Yeats, a former Liverpool captain but a man with no experience of scouting. But, as Dalglish, pointing to his heart, told one former player, 'Yeats has it here.' That may have been the case but so too did Twentyman. The truth was that Dalglish wanted his own men around him. John Smith called Twentyman into his office and told him that he was not looking too well. It was the lead up to the sack. Twentyman was devastated. It had come out of the blue.

Both Lawler and Twentyman were bitter about their treatment and had little compunction about spilling their tale to the tabloids. Twentyman's last act at Anfield had been to make reports on the opposition while Tom Saunders was in hospital. He saw Newcastle against Birmingham and, in his report, waxed lyrical about Peter Beardsley, 'the difference between the two sides.' He then went to see Watford, Liverpool's opponents in the FA Cup, play Bury. Again, one man took his eye, John Barnes, and his report was devoted to extolling the virtues of Barnes. 'In both cases it was a clear recommendation from me that the club should buy them,' he says. A year later, Beardsley and Barnes had been signed But if Dalglish and Liverpool were happy to dispose of Twentyman, others were quick to sign up their cast-offs. Within weeks, Twentyman's services had been snapped up by the new manager of Glasgow Rangers, Graeme Souness.

The traditional bootroom atmosphere of Shankly, Paisley and Fagan had already disappeared. Dalglish was not consulting his colleagues in the way that his predecessors had. After matches at Anfield he would often spend his time in the dressing room and in the players' lounge rather than join Moran, Evans and company in the bootroom. Chris Lawler saw at close hand how it changed. 'Joe Fagan spent a lot of time with us in the bootroom,' he says. 'But Dalglish never bothered very much. He rarely consulted Ronnie Moran and even more rarely did he talk with me, though he was close to Roy Evans. I suppose Fagan was always part of the bootroom, he'd been there so long, whereas Kenny had never been a member. Dalglish was his own man.'

The fact was that Dalglish had not graduated through the bootroom. If anything, it was alien to him. As a player, he would not have spent much time in there chatting with its inmates. His background was the dressing room. Of the backroom staff, Dalglish was probably closest to Tom Saunders, the onetime youth development officer and former headmaster. Saunders was the man everyone could talk to, from directors to players. He was, and still is, one of the most respected men at Anfield. Everyone trusted him and Saunders justified their loyalty. Dalglish gave him a chair in his office and Saunders would often wander in, answer the phone for him, open his mail and even chauffeur him around. Dalglish found him easy to discuss things with.

Bob Paisley had been appointed to help and guide Dalglish whenever he felt the need for advice, but he soon became irrelevant. Ian Ross, the former Liverpool player of the 1960s, recalls bumping into Paisley one evening some months after Dalglish had been appointed. 'I asked him if he was busy.

"No," he replied. I was surprised and said "I thought Kenny would have had you hard at it." "Nah," he said. "I've been his assistant for six months now and he hasn't consulted me once."'

'Paisley was not angry,' points out Ross, 'and his remarks were in no way meant to be derogatory. He simply saw Dalglish as being his own man and not needing much advice from anyone.' But Paisley did have his uses and it would be wrong to suggest that Dalglish never listened to him. But once Dalglish had proved himself by winning the double there is little doubt that Paisley played a diminishing role behind the scenes. When Paisley's contract came to an end, it was not renewed.

Chris Lawler, in his one year under Dalglish, also had little involvement with him. 'There were few players being promoted from the reserves,' he says. 'So contact was kept to a minimum. I would write my reports and he would occasionally ask me how someone was doing, but I was never what you would call close to him. It had been very different, however, with Joe Fagan.'

Perhaps the most visible change came with the team selection: nobody ever knew who would be playing. Team news was released at the last moment and everyone, including players and press, was kept waiting. 'I could never quite see the sense in it,' says Lawler. 'He obviously knew who he was choosing and I'm sure the opposition had made contingency plans anyhow. Shankly would never have worried about the opposition.'

Ronnie Moran, however, reckoned it a brilliant move and told Ian Hargreaves of the *Liverpool Daily Post and Echo* that it had really shaken everyone up. There were now 14 or 15 players training every week, all hoping to be part of the team and not knowing until the last moment if they would be playing. It kept everyone keyed up and sharp. Ray Houghton has also testified to its effectiveness in keeping players keen and committed until the last minute.

Even Alan Hansen was never certain of a place. 'I once asked him how he would be marking a certain player,' recalls Hargreaves, 'and he reminded me that he did not know if in fact he would be playing. "Oh, come on," I said. "Surely you will be in the team."

'"With Dalglish, you never know," he replied.'

There was a joke doing the Anfield rounds that for each game the players had a sweep on naming the correct starting line-up. It was said that at one point the kitty had risen to £50,000 because nobody had ever managed to guess right.

Dalglish, also contrary to bootroom tradition, began to tailor his side to match the opposition. In his final season, he employed the tactic more than ever. At Tottenham and Arsenal he played six men at the back, moving players up-field as the game progressed; he was successful against Spurs but came unstuck at Highbury. For the most part, however, his careful manoeuvring worked and, given his astonishing record of success, it seems churlish to criticise his team selection. Besides, despite popular myth, Shankly was not averse to a little caution as well, particularly when it came to European games. On many occasions he too tailored his side to suit the opposition, dropping a striker in favour of an extra defender. It was perhaps more understandable for those vital away legs. Dalglish was merely extending the method to its logical conclusion.

Dalglish's relationship with the press was also a source of friction. He could be remarkably offhand with journalists, not only reluctant to reveal his plans, but equally evasive when it came to explaining his tactics or providing post-match comments.

One of the first journalists in Liverpool to feel the cold stare of Dalglish was Stephen Boulton. Then a young cub reporter on the *Liverpool Daily Post and Echo,* he had been sent to cover the Dalglish signing. He was not normally a football reporter and had been told to write a colour piece that tried to give a glimpse of the new man's personality. His first question to Dalglish had the football reporting fraternity cringing. 'What do you intend to do with the money?' he asked.

'It was an innocent enough question,' he remembers. 'I was just interested and thought it might tell me something about him. I'd asked Bob Latchford, Everton's record signing, the same question a few months previously and he answered quite politely, telling me about how he'd always had the ambition to buy a shop for his Dad. I thought maybe Dalglish might have a similar interesting answer.'

But no. Instead Dalglish stared at him and snapped back: 'The money disnae matter.' There was a stony silence, so Boulton decided on a different tack. 'He was wearing all blue that day – blue suit, tie, shirt – so I made a joke about how he'd have to change the colours of his clothes now he was in Liverpool.' Dalglish just grunted at him. It was not the perfect beginning to his Anfield career.

Others complained that when he did cooperate, they could not understand him anyhow. They joked that his accent was impossible to follow and that he had a barbed sense of humour, reserving it exclusively for journalists.

The accent was hardly his problem, the dry sense of humour was no doubt cultivated. 'How did you see the game?' inquired one reporter at the post match get-together. 'From the dugout,' answered Dalglish. And then there was silence, no smile. Sean Fallon reckons Dalglish picked up the style from Jock Stein, who could be equally waspish. It was a sense of humour so dry it was rarely understood south of the border, not even in Liverpool. After a round of golf with Peter Alliss for BBC Television in which he had played particularly well, Alliss suggested he throw the ball to the crowd. 'What? At these prices!' he exploded with barely a hint of a smile on his face. Dalglish was a master at winding up people.

The tabloid journalists, hunting in packs, relied on him for their head-lines, but Dalglish had little time for them. The quality papers were different. They occasionally attempted some analysis yet found him at times unnecessarily belligerent. The club even organised a lunch with the press at a Swiss Cottage hotel that was the team's usual London retreat. There was plenty of backslapping and Dalglish went out of his way to be as friendly and helpful as possible, but come the following afternoon, Dalglish had reverted to self. Brian Glanville of the *Sunday Times* even suggested that, like Brian Clough, he should perhaps be exempted from press conferences.

At times it was easy to understand Dalglish's reluctance to play the game with the press. The Koppites loved it. They held little respect for the back pages anyhow and as long as Dalglish was successful, it hardly mat-tered whether or not he cooperated with the press. The Liverpool media, always a close knit group, gave Dalglish few problems, refusing to report tittle tattle, criticise or speculate, even in that final season when there was much to debate.

Despite all the changes, as Dalglish looked to assert his control, train-ing remained as it was before. Dalglish would turn up, usually joining in the traditional five-a-side games rather than exerting himself with too many exercises. And there was no doubting the popularity of the change which brought back the lunchtime meal, slashed in a cost-cutting exercise some years previously. It was not a slap-up lunch, more a chips with every-thing menu, but it allowed the players to get together and relax back at Anfield after training. Dalglish saw this as crucial to morale and all his play-ers appreciated the move.

At board level, there were worries. It did not need an astute eye to spot that things were no longer what they used to be and change always brings concern to some. Although the board was prepared to go along with the sacking of Lawler and Twentyman, they did not like to see the story splashed across the tabloids. They would have preferred to see better relations between Dalglish and the press as it only put the club in a bad light. What had always seemed a content ship to the public was beginning to look less happy. The more conservative members began to hanker for the days of yesteryear when there was little for the papers to reveal, but that was always going to be difficult given the growth of a more intrusive press than in the past. Shankly, Paisley and Fagan had been their men, the old breed of manager, who were loyal and never even bothered about a contract, yet they had a friendly relationship with the press. But Dalglish was much more of the modern world.

There was a feeling among the board that things were spinning out of their control; they could see some of their authority slipping away. In the corridors of Anfield there were whispers. Napoleon had always advised that when you choose your generals, make sure they are lucky. There was no doubt that in Dalglish Liverpool had chosen a lucky general. It posed a dilemma: how could you be critical of Dalglish when he was so successful? Other board members welcomed the new style, seeing it as part of the modern game. Differences or not, they all basked in the glory of winning trophies. There may have been some who would have liked to oust Dalglish, but whether the gossip would ever have translated itself into action is a far different matter. As long as Dalglish won trophies he was safe, even if his methods were different from his predecessors'. It was only 30 years since Bill Shankly had told the Liverpool board that he would only accept the post of manager if he was allowed to choose the team. It seems inconceivable today, but prior to Shankly it had been the board who picked the side.

Dalglish combined both mastery and mystery; they came hand in hand. Dalglish knew what he wanted. The job had to be done his way. And that meant that if you wanted his successes, you had to accept his style.

CHAPTER FIFTEEN
Typhoon

*Facing it – always facing it – that's the way to get through. You are a young
sailor. Face it. That's enough for any man. Keep a cool head.*
Joseph Conrad, *Typhoon*

It was a golden summer, the best anyone could recall. The nation basked
in a fermenting heatwave that seemed to burn on forever. The temperature in Gloucestershire topped a sweltering 98.9 degrees Fahrenheit, the
highest in Britain since records had been kept. At Heathrow, one of the
busiest runways melted and had to be closed to air traffic. Elsewhere forests
caught fire and tempers flared. In the City, the financial whizzkids boiled
in their smoked-glass office blocks, while up at St John's Wood Graham
Gooch set about a mammoth knock of 333 in the first Test against India
and then added a further 123 in the second innings. At St Andrews, Nick
Faldo stormed to a five-shot victory in the Open. It was hardly the summer for watching television, yet on a warm July evening more than 20
million tuned in to watch a football match. England had reached the semi-
finals of the World Cup and, but for a ballooned penalty kick, might well
have gone all the way to the final.

Back in Liverpool, Dalglish was pondering his future. He was weary. Hillsborough had taken its toll and even though it was more than a year since 95 had died on the Leppings Lane terrace, it seemed he had barely had time to reflect. So much had happened since. Managing Liverpool was more like steering a ship through a storm. At times, Dalglish must have felt like Conrad's Captain MacWhirr, lashed to the wheel, being tossed about the China Seas as they lurched headlong and blind into the eye of a typhoon. And like his fellow Scot MacWhirr, Dalglish appeared just as determined, just as single-minded, just as sure of himself. But, like MacWhirr, he too had his secret doubts.

In his four years as manager, he had three times steered Liverpool to the League title. They had also won the FA Cup twice and been losing finalists, as well as losing finalists in the Littlewoods Cup. What's more, he had been within a minute of a fourth League title and second double. It was an astonishing record, but he must have wondered what more he could achieve. His contract was at an end and Liverpool, not unnaturally, were hankering after a three-year extension. As he later admitted, he could so easily have quit then, but instead he signed on the dotted line and decided to take on the challenge of another storm.

His final season in charge at Anfield began, as it usually had over the previous ten years, at Wembley with the annual showpiece, the Charity Shield. Liverpool drew 1–1 with lively Cup-winners Manchester United and then, the following Saturday, set about defending their first division title. There had been no new additions to the squad, though there was one notable absentee from the players' pool – Dalglish himself. After 23 years in the professional game, he had finally decided it was time to hang up his boots. He had played just one game the previous season, coming on as a late substitute in Liverpool's final home game, against Derby County, when the League championship was safely locked away. Dalglish was approaching his 40th birthday and it was obvious he could not play forever. Typically, he consulted nobody and news that he would not be registering as a player almost slipped out unnoticed. There was no fuss, everyone had guessed his playing career had drawn to a close with the appearance against Derby. Even the Kop had given a knowing cheer to him that evening, delighted as he demonstrated one or two of his old touches. But Dalglish the player was to be no more. His family aside, he had given up what he loved best in life – playing football.

His playing career was formally closed with a testimonial in April 1990 against John Aldridge's new club Real Sociedad at Anfield. A crowd of just over 30,000 turned up, netting him £150,000. But in a city of high unemployment and desperate poverty, the decision to give him a testimonial was not greeted with universal enthusiasm. It was pointed out that Dalglish was already a rich man and more than well paid for doing his job. What's more he had already been given a testimonial by Scotland. Dalglish helped appease any protests by donating some of the proceeds to Liverpool's Oxford Street Maternity Hospital where Lauren, the latest addition to the Dalglish household, had just been delivered.

The season kicked off with a flourish when newly promoted Sheffield United were beaten at Bramall Lane, thanks principally to an injury to their goalkeeper. Then Nottingham Forest, Aston Villa, Wimbledon, Manchester United, Everton, Crewe, Sunderland, Derby County and Crewe again were all brushed aside before Liverpool dropped their first points of the season in a 1–1 draw at Norwich. They had swept to the top of the table and would stay there as long as Dalglish remained manager.

Yet even before the early October winds had blown in, Dalglish was facing his first test of the season – a catastrophic defeat at Old Trafford that had the football writers pitching some delicate questions in his direction. Liverpool had been overwhelmed by a rampant United in the Rumbelows Cup, losing 3–1. In the first half they barely mustered one attack as United, egged on by an ecstatic crowd, pegged them into their own half and stormed into a 2–0 lead. It was a dire, confused performance by Liverpool and although they improved after a half time carpeting, they still looked a shadow of the side that had so convincingly clinched the League title earlier that year. 'NIGHTMARE FOR KENNY' sneered the headline in the following morning's *Daily Mirror,* reporting that 'Kenny Dalglish's team were outplayed, outfought and outmanoeuvred.'

Dalglish was furious. 'We have a talented squad and we should be able to handle any player being out. We should produce better performances than this, with or without John Barnes.' To lose before a baying Old Trafford crowd brought humiliation enough but to be dismissed with so little fight was hardly in the Liverpool tradition. The evening's embarrassment was also compounded for Dalglish when he casually attempted to volley a loose ball back into play from his vantage point on the touchline. But he missed, much to the delight of the partisan audience, which hooted its derision for the man they loved to hate. Dalglish sank back into his dugout.

By the end of the week, however, Liverpool were back on track with a robust performance at White Hart Lane in front of the TV cameras. Yet even as the two sides lined up, doubts were again being raised about Dalglish's team selection. Out went Beardsley, the first division's leading goalscorer, and Ray Houghton, both mysteriously relegated to the substitutes' bench, and in came two defenders, Molby and Ablett. Dalglish, clearly determined not to lose this particular battle, was fielding a side which included seven players who usually played in defence. Spurs, lying third in the table, unbeaten and not having conceded more than one goal in any game, were shown the utmost respect – perhaps too much respect. Dalglish was tailoring his selection to a particular job, rather than simply choosing his best 11 players. In the event, Dalglish's tactics paid off handsomely. David Burrows blotted the ebullient Paul Gascoigne out of the game and, as Liverpool's confidence grew, Peter Beardsley emerged from the bench to add a third goal to Ian Rush's brace. The doubting pundits had been confounded in emphatic fashion and Dalglish could allow himself a faint smile.

By the following Saturday evening, everyone's confidence had been fully restored as Liverpool dashed to a 4–0 win over Luton at Anfield. 'The best first half performance I've seen all season,' Dalglish claimed after the game. It was hard to disagree. What's more, the result had been achieved without Barnes and Whelan, both temporarily injured. Chief title contenders Arsenal were suddenly six points adrift of Liverpool, with Manchester United trailing by an astonishing 16 points. When the Football Association deducted points from both sides following an ill-tempered clash at Old Trafford, the gap was even wider by the following weekend.

Another win followed, this time at Coventry, and then Liverpool entertained a Manchester City side still reeling from the dramatic resignation of manager Howard Kendall. Into his shoes had stepped Liverpudlian Peter Reid, once the doyen of an arrogant Everton midfield, now tasting management for the first time. City were inspired, Liverpool lethargic. In the first half, they were outclassed and were lucky to turn around without their goal having been breached. Midway through the second half, City got their reward, edging ahead from the penalty spot only to see their hopes dashed as Ian Rush equalised with eight minutes remaining. Then, with just a minute on the clock, Ronnie Rosenthal seized on an unforgivable error in the City defence and lobbed his gifted ball over Andy Dibble to give Liverpool what seemed a hardly-deserved victory. That should have settled matters, but immediately from the restart City forced a corner and the gangly Niall Quinn rose above a watching Liverpool defence to give City a point. It was scarcely credible. Ronnie Moran was livid at Liverpool's undisciplined and carefree attitude. Traditionally so confident in the final minutes, Liverpool had recklessly dropped their guard and proved vulnerable yet again to the high cross. They now seemed to be making a habit of conceding last minute goals. However, both Gillespie and McMahon had limped off with injuries, leaving the defence flatfooted and exposed to City's enthusiastic youngsters, thus destroying the balance of the side.

Once again, the newspapers went on the attack but having leaked only nine goals in 14 league games and with only four points dropped all season, some of the criticism of the back pages seemed a touch harsh. But it was not only the pundits who were growing increasingly restless; the fans were also despairing. Success had gone to the heads of the Anfield faithful. A new generation had grown up knowing nothing but one triumph after another. Liverpool had not been out of the top two in ten seasons and had won six titles during the 1980s as well as half a dozen other trophies. There were fans standing on the Kop who had been supporting Liverpool since they were 13-year-old lads and they were now in their mid-20s, married with children, and had never known Liverpool out of the top two. Even when Liverpool were winning, you could hear the groans around the ground at missed chances. The Kop, once the inspiration behind the team, had become depressingly quiet, reluctant to break into song unless the situation was desperate. It was as if they needed a handicap before they could find their voice. 'You're supposed to be at home,' became the derisory chant of visiting supporters, astonished at the Kop's silence. It was impossible for the players not to notice.

Lifelong Koppite Rogan Taylor also spotted a changing attitude: 'There was a time during the late 1960s and 1970s when you cheered and were delighted as long as Liverpool won. But during the 1980s it began to change. Nobody was satisfied unless they won by at least three clear goals, and with a certain style. Even then people would come off the Kop moaning because they had missed so many chances. It was a case of footballing gout. The fans at Anfield had been fed on the richest diet of footballing triumphs in the entire history of the Football League.' It was another off-shoot of the success Dalglish had brought the club.

The following week, Liverpool had the chance to redeem themselves, as they travelled to Highbury for what was being billed as the clash of the season. Arsenal had just been cuffed 6–2 in midweek by Manchester United in the fourth round of the Rumbelows Cup. It was the Gunners' heaviest defeat at Highbury in 70 years and raised as many doubts about their defence as had Liverpool's defeat by United in the previous round. Both sides were suddenly under the spotlight. Yet Arsenal were a formidable outfit, well drilled by manager George Graham and with a handsomely talented squad. Indeed, there was a streak of Graham himself running through the side: tough, disciplined, conceding little, hardworking and beneath it all a fair smattering of artistry. It was typical of the man who had formed the backbone of Arsenal's double-winning side in 1971.

Gillespie had recovered from his knock against City but, with McMahon still sidelined, Dalglish reverted to the style he had employed so successfully at Tottenham and opted for a six-man defence. What's more, he decided to leave Beardsley, still the division's leading scorer with ten goals, out of the squad altogether. There was not even a place for him on the bench and although Beardsley shrugged his shoulders dispassionately, he was clearly not a happy man. He even showed up in the TV commentary box to offer his opinions on the game, carefully sidestepping any criticism of Dalglish's selection. Ray Houghton was also omitted, although he was named as substitute. In their places stepped full backs Barry Venison and David Burrows, alongside Ablett, Molby, Hysen and Gillespie. Ronnie Rosenthal was named as the other substitute.

Dalglish's selection surprised everyone, especially Arsenal, who hurriedly called a last-minute team talk when they discovered the Liverpool line-up. Graham's plans had in no way accounted for so defensive a cast. It was clear that Dalglish had come to Highbury to defend his six-point advantage at the top of the table. Previous Liverpool managers would simply have named their usual team and left Arsenal to fidget with the worry beads.

The tactic had worked at Tottenham but this time the ploy backfired. Perhaps Dalglish was a little unlucky. By their own admission, Arsenal were confused and nervous in the early stages as they anxiously tried to work out the Liverpool tactics. And yet Liverpool failed to take advantage of it, still holding men back in defence when a little more daring might have paid dividends. For much of the first half, Liverpool gave a confident performance and it seemed as if Dalglish might yet again prove the tactical master. But a disputed goal on the stroke of half time was to leave them 1 goal down at a crucial moment. The Liverpool defenders claimed that Paul Merson's header had not crossed the line but, under orders from Dalglish not to argue with referees, they barely contested the decision. They traipsed in at the interval, clearly upset and quietly fuming.

The second half was barely a few minutes old when a second questionable refereeing decision put them further behind. This time, a penalty was awarded as Anders Limpar crashed to the ground as he sprinted into the penalty area. Liverpool argued that the Swede had dived but referee Allan Gunn still awarded a penalty. Liverpool's heads went down. They could sense it was not to be their day and it was hardly surprising when the Gunners added a third goal. Rosenthal and Houghton tried to initiate some fresh ideas, but what was lacking was a midfield general and a goalmaker. Sadly, the midfield general was injured while the goalmaker was watching from the stands.

It had been Liverpool's heaviest defeat for over a year and the finger was being pointed at one man – Kenny Dalglish. Yet Dalglish seemed unprepared to accept any blame. Instead, he was uncharacteristically critical of his own players. 'Even if we had twelve players we wouldn't have won,' he claimed. 'We didn't do ourselves justice. We're still three points ahead and in the position everyone wants to be. But we have to do better than that.'

It was unlike Dalglish, who had always disapproved of managers who chided their players in the media. 'Kenny always made a point of not criticising any of us in public,' says Mark Lawrenson. 'I can remember when we would drive in together as players for training and he would always say that the worst thing a manager could ever do was to slam his players in public. If we ever heard it happening on the radio, Kenny would shake his head and say: "You should never do that no matter what the circumstances."'

The next morning, the press went for the jugular. 'The Reds boss must also be held responsible for Liverpool's substandard performance,' insisted the *Daily Mirror*. 'He picked a safety-first team and saw Arsenal swarm all over them.' The *Daily Mail* was just as scathing. 'Dalglish gave us negative virtues and his side paid a heavy price.'

But the most eloquent summing up came from Brian Glanville in the *Sunday Times*. 'Is Kenny Dalglish too clever by half, or just not clever enough?' he demanded to know. 'Dalglish deployed the kind of formation which might just have been valid against Real Madrid in their prime. How Liverpool's players must have writhed, knowing they might have done so much better if they had only been allowed to.

'Quite what is it that makes managers and coaches commit so many crass, basic tactical errors, flying in the face of all common sense. If war is too important to be left to the generals, is football too important to be left to football managers?'

Former Arsenal manager Bertie Mee was also tracked down to give the sage's view. He argued that Liverpool had only themselves to blame. 'How could anyone leave out Beardsley?' he commented, adding pointedly: 'The rest of the players wouldn't approve of that selection, and it is going to be very difficult to regain that trust, that respect.' When Dalglish's tactics paid off, there was grudging recognition of a canny move; when it failed, there was only criticism.

Liverpool had to wait a fortnight before their next game, the miserable weather thankfully causing the postponement of what might have been a tricky fixture at Nottingham Forest. It also gave Liverpool's limping wounded the chance of a more leisurely recovery. Their next opponents looked almost handpicked – bottom-of-the-table Sheffield United – now in sight of a record nobody wanted, the worst start to a season. It was just the kind of game Liverpool needed to boost their confidence after the traumas of Highbury. And not only did McMahon return to the line-up but Peter Beardsley was also recalled. Yet what should have been an afternoon stroll for them turned out to be a hard-earned three points, Liverpool eventually winning 2–0. Liverpool gave as miserable a performance as they had against Manchester United and any thoughts that Dalglish might have recanted after dropping Beardsley were dispelled when the England man was substituted, and that after he had helped mastermind Liverpool's first goal. Into his spot stepped young Steve McManaman, a teenager making his debut just one week after playing for the England Under-21 side.

It was something of a humiliation for Beardsley, who was beginning to wonder if his days at Anfield were numbered. Dalglish could no doubt point to a few poor performances from the England man, a reluctance to run with the ball, or to try and take players on; but his reasons for dropping Beardsley were more to do with tactics. During his first season at Anfield, Beardsley had looked almost as impressive as John Barnes. He was hardworking, with the ability to drift past players and he had the confidence to carry the ball into the opponents' penalty area. He was also a proven goalscorer with 60 goals to his credit in 174 games, surprisingly good figures for someone who was not a marksman in the mode of Ian Rush. Even at the beginning of this, his third season at Anfield, he had been scoring goals at a remarkable rate, with 13 already to his credit. But Beardsley was clearly losing confidence and dropping him didn't help. It began to show in his play. The player who had once moved forward so effortlessly was suddenly nervous, collecting the ball with his back to goal and merely returning it timidly to his midfielders. Beardsley was a player moving backwards, not forwards.

For someone like Dalglish, a player who had filled a similar role to Beardsley, it must have been a painful sight. George Best had long warned that Dalglish would find it frustrating as a manager to watch players who did not quite possess his own ability. 'To sit there and see these people make mistakes will drive him nuts,' he claimed, pointing out that this was the one reason why he could never have become a manager.

Beardsley stormed into Dalglish's office on more than one occasion to demand an explanation. But according to the England international, Dalglish simply argued that he had picked the team he thought could win. Beardsley is philosophical about it in retrospect and concedes that 'nine times out of ten they did win. You can't criticise that.' But it still left him unhappy. 'I was left out mainly for tactical reasons. That was sad. Fifteen or twenty years ago they would have chosen the best team and I thought I was good enough for the best team.'

Dalglish had originally spotted in Beardsley a player with the potential to carry his mantle. Strong and resourceful with a natural first touch and a surprising turn of pace, Beardsley had repaid Dalglish's investment during his first season at Anfield. He delighted in taking on defenders, as he did when scoring a memorable goal against Arsenal at Anfield. Dalglish tried desperately to shape him and to maintain his progress, even giving him personal coaching, but in the end Beardsley lacked one essential quality – the killer instinct. It was a skill Dalglish had perfected north of the border, the cunning to hold on to the ball, no matter what the provocation. Intimidation was part of the game and a forward had to learn to be just as robust as a defender. Beardsley was not that kind of player. Dalglish had the reputation of being an awkward player, niggling, always complaining. Yet all he was doing was to give back some of what he received. It was an essential quality and one that helped distinguish him from so many other goal-scorers. Denis Law was another cultured inside forward who could return the compliments given by defenders.

Over the Christmas period Liverpool, without Beardsley, had a mixed bag of results. They beat Southampton 3–2 at Anfield, then held QPR to a draw at Loftus Road before they went down 1–0 at Crystal Palace in front of a live television audience. Liverpool had formed something of a losing habit every time the TV cameras turned up, adding further to the public pressures, fuelling the speculation and criticism. Again the press were unremitting. 'The turn of the year leaves Liverpool asking searching questions of themselves,' read the *Daily Mirror*. 'Kenny Dalglish has mocked the critics who suggest that cracks are beginning to show in the Anfield armoury. But Dalglish cannot ignore that Liverpool have suffered capital punishment – with eight out of a possible 12 points surrendered in the capital'.

Dalglish sloped gloomily back to the dressing rooms. 'We are not firing on all cylinders' was all he would say. He was only too aware of the problems. But unearthing the remedy was another matter. The typhoon was gathering pace.

Yet Liverpool had lost only two games and still clung to their spot at the top of division one. Their winning ways returned in the New Year with a surprisingly comfortable 3–0 win over an increasingly impressive Leeds United. But in the third round of the FA Cup at Blackburn, Liverpool were exposed and only an own goal in the dying seconds saved them from an early exit and humiliation.

It was not just Beardsley who was now the focus of attention but almost the entire team. Question marks were being placed over a number of players, some of whom were visibly showing their age. Alan Hansen was the old man of the side at 36, with Bruce Grobbelaar not far behind. The Swede Glenn Hysen was almost 32 and Gary Gillespie was 31, while Peter Beardsley, Steve Nicol, Steve McMahon, Ronnie Whelan and Ian Rush were all pushing 30. Ronnie Rosenthal's age was anyone's guess. Ten players in the squad were either over or close to 30. It was not ideal and as Dalglish well knew there was a shortage of young players ready to make the breakthrough. Steve McManaman, Mike Marsh and Nicky Tanner had all managed an outing with the first team, but were still waiting their turn in the wings.

Dalglish faced a dilemma, the sort of problem Captain Yossarian would have appreciated. It was Catch-22. The problem of being in contention for honours season after season only added to the difficulty of blooding youngsters. Dalglish had to choose his best and most experienced side. Every game Liverpool played was vital; they had to win to stay in contention. There was rarely a fixture when they could relax and perhaps experiment with some of the inexperienced, younger players. Many of the Liverpool youngsters of the past, like Tommy Smith, Phil Thompson,

Sammy Lee and Brian Hall, had been given their baptism in a red shirt during the early rounds of European competitions when Liverpool would have a four or five goal cushion and could afford to take risks. But now there was no Europe and virtually the only opportunity to gamble on youth was in the second round of the Rumbelows Cup when they would usually be facing third or fourth division opposition. If Dalglish experimented and it went wrong, then neither the supporters nor the club would be ready to forgive him. It was a dilemma few seemed to appreciate, especially the press, who were now campaigning for him to try out the rookies.

As ever there was a tendency to exaggerate the number of young, home-bred players who had emerged through Liverpool's youth policy over the years. It was largely a myth. Shankly had been more inclined to dip into the lower divisions to buy his future stars, paying a small fee and then moulding them in the reserves until they were ready for the big time. Kevin Keegan, Ray Clemence, Larry Lloyd, Alex Lindsay, Phil Neal, Steve Nicol, Alan Hansen, Emlyn Hughes, Gordon Milne, Ronnie Whelan and Ian Rush had all followed this route through Anfield.

Dalglish had recognised the club's shortage of quality youngsters during his first season in charge and had set in motion a youth scheme that would in time pay dividends. Steve Heighway, the former winger who had blossomed under Bill Shankly, had been brought in to mastermind the plan. A number of his players were maturing quickly and showed all the signs of making the first team, but none was quite ready. The search for young talent in the lower divisions also went on and already that season Dalglish had dipped into the transfer market to sign the Irish Under-21 striker Tony Cousins from Dundalk as well as the Hartlepool midfielder Don Hutchison.

There was also another factor at play. New European rules meant that Football League clubs would be restricted to a maximum of four non-English players in their squad of 16 for European competitions. For a club like Liverpool this controversial ruling was to have devastating consequences. In recent years they had scoured the world in search of talent, drafting in players from as far away as Australia, South Africa, Israel, Denmark and Sweden as well as Ireland and the home nations. When they clinched the double at Wembley against Everton in 1986, not one player in the side was eligible to play for England. In their current squad Steve Nicol, Ian Rush, Bruce Grobbelaar, Jan Molby, Alan Hansen, Gary Gillespie, Glenn Hysen, Ronnie Whelan, Ray Houghton, Ronnie Rosenthal and Steve

Staunton would all be competing for four places. If Liverpool were to participate in Europe, as seemed increasingly likely the following season, then there was now an urgency to buy in English players. But this in itself was difficult, narrowing his field of choice.

On top of that, Dalglish knew that money would not be so readily available as it had been in the past. Following the Taylor Report after the Hillsborough disaster, the club had committed itself to a major redevelopment of Anfield. The ground was to become an all-seater stadium and, with the capacity of the Kop being greatly reduced, the directors had given the go-ahead for the rebuilding of the Kemlyn Road stand to maintain a 40,000 capacity. The cost of all this was estimated at £10 million.

The money had to come from somewhere and some of it was coming from the transfer fund. It was just another pressure on the successful manager. The man with the Midas touch was being swamped with problems.

Within a fortnight of the Blackburn embarrassment, Dalglish decided he had to move into the transfer market again, this time signing Jimmy Carter, the Millwall winger, for £800,000 and young Jamie Redknapp, the highly-rated, teenage Bournemouth midfielder and son of manager Harry Redknapp. At £350,000 Redknapp was one for the future, but Carter was quickly plunged into the fray, making his debut at Aston Villa in an exciting goalless draw. A week later the problems reappeared as Wimbledon came to Anfield and struck an equaliser in the final minutes. Then it was into the FA Cup again, this time with a comparatively easy home draw against second division Brighton. Although the south coast club had been showing useful form, few expected them to take anything from Anfield. Liverpool grabbed a comfortable two-goal lead and the game appeared to be petering out into a mere formality when, in the final 26 minutes, Brighton dramatically struck twice and almost wrenched a third in the dying moments. There were red faces all around. Liverpool's normally solid defence was now leaking goals like a sieve, especially late in matches.

The replay against Brighton was almost as reckless, with Liverpool trailing for much of the game and only unearthing an equaliser on the stroke of normal time, just as the home fans were beginning to break into celebratory song. Eventually, they scraped through with a goal in extra time.

Liverpool had begun the season with a swing but had now lapsed into unforgivable habits. They were out of the Rumbelows Cup and had been lucky to survive a beating in the FA Cup by two second division sides. Criticism in the press was growing and, although Dalglish was never one to pay much attention to what journalists wrote or thought, none of it helped ease the mounting burden on Dalglish's back. Nor did Jimmy Carter look to be a Liverpool player. He was fast, but showed none of the control or strength of John Barnes or Steve Heighway. Geoff Twentyman believed 'he was no better than any number of players lurking in the reserves'. And Steve McManaman would soon emerge to prove his point.' Carter's inadequacies were there for all to spot from the beginning. Glenn Hysen was also looking unusually suspect, a shadow of the calm, elegant Swede who had stood alongside Alan Hansen the season before. Hysen was suddenly beginning to show his years, with clumsiness replacing control.

On top of all that, Dalglish knew that John Barnes was still itching for a transfer to the continent. At the end of every contract there was speculation of a move abroad. Dalglish had so far managed to keep Barnes pinned to Anfield, thanks to the generosity of the board, but with his contract due for renewal at the end of the season the usual speculation was again surfacing. This time Barnes seemed more adamant than ever about a move, or maybe he was simply casting bait into the water to see if any Italian or Spanish clubs might bite. If Barnes did go, then Dalglish knew he would have a major problem. Could anyone in English football replace him?

Replacements would be necessary no matter what and £5 million had already been earmarked for summer deals. The names of Derby County's England defender Mark Wright and striker Dean Saunders had been pencilled in, but there was no possibility of a deal until the season was ended. Despite all this, Liverpool were still ahead of the chasing pack even though they were dropping points at an alarming rate.

As a remedy Dalglish once again plunged into the transfer market, this time gambling on the Coventry frontrunner David Speedie. It was to be his final transaction for Liverpool, a last throw of the dice, and one of his most controversial signings, though it was less puzzling than that of Carter. Nevertheless it smacked of panic. Speedie was not only 31 years old but also a Scot and he cost the club almost £700,000. Dalglish said he had been tracking Speedie for years and had tried to sign him when he was on the point of leaving Chelsea but no deal had been agreed and Speedie had settled instead for Coventry. The Kop also had a love/hate relationship with the fiery little Scot. In his days at Chelsea, the Anfield crowd always picked him out for special abuse, a sure sign that the Kop secretly appreciated his commitment. He was a hard player with a quick temper, not unlike Steve McMahon but without the ability to win the ball and hold it in midfield.

For all the criticism of the deal, Speedie was an instant success, scoring on his debut at Old Trafford to give Liverpool a well-earned draw. A week later he struck two memorable goals on his Anfield debut against Everton as Liverpool stormed to an impressive 3–1 win. Speedie was suddenly the toast of Anfield, the man designed to solve all their problems. In the space of a week he had fired three goals against Liverpool's two keenest rivals. It seemed as if Dalglish had again come up trumps, defying all his critics with an inspired signing.

Although Dalglish could afford to smile, the criticism was impossible to ignore. It had been painful and was perhaps even taking its toll on his health. He could hardly pick up a newspaper without being given columns of advice from a coterie of untutored football writers. Even his own fans on the Kop were beginning to write in to the local papers questioning his defensive tactics and the omission of Peter Beardsley – a state of affairs that would have upset Dalglish far more than any tabloid criticism.

Dalglish was said to have come out in a nervous rash. He had become withdrawn and found sleeping difficult. Ian Hargreaves of the *Liverpool Echo* found him 'more tetchy than usual' and, instead of looking forward to match days, Dalglish was privately dreading them. The team had become unpredictable, immediate solutions were not obvious and the long-term problems looked, at times, almost insurmountable. Dalglish could cope during the week, enjoying the training and the day-to-day running of the club. But on Saturday afternoon came the most frustrating aspect of a manager's job; sitting back and letting others do the job for you. Perhaps what Liverpool really needed was a year in the wilderness to sort themselves out but neither the fans, nor the board, was ever likely to tolerate that luxury. Dalglish was becoming a victim of his own success.

Liverpool were three points clear at the top of the division but a televised league fixture against Everton had produced a further casualty. Ronnie Whelan limped off after returning to the side following weeks of injury and now looked set to be confined to the sidelines for another lengthy spell. A fractured fibula was diagnosed and an urgent operation was required, plus further recuperation that would eventually mean him missing a year of football. Although Whelan was not always the most popular player with the Anfield crowd, Dalglish recognised his key role in the team. He had a binding influence, latching on to loose balls in the midfield, feeding McMahon, and then lurking threateningly around the edge of the penalty area, ready to size up any opportunities. But, above all, Whelan was a midfielder who could race back quickly into his own penalty area, tackle well and bolster the back four. He brought an added confidence and experience to the defence that would be sorely lacking in the months ahead.

During Whelan's previous absence over Christmas and the New Year, the team had struggled and, as Dalglish surmised, it was probably as much to do with the loss of Whelan as anything else. Now they would have to face life without him again, probably for the remainder of the season. Steve Staunton had been tried in Whelan's role, and although he had asserted himself well, he was still relatively inexperienced and more at home as a full back than as a left-footed midfielder. The pack was shuffled and eventually the job was handed to Jan Molby, but he lacked the mobility of Whelan and rarely managed to get into the opposing penalty area. And when he did, it usually meant a breathless sprint back into defence.

The draw for the fifth round of the FA Cup came up trumps, with Everton obliged to cross Stanley Park to Anfield. Most of Merseyside rubbed their hands at the prospect, but one man at Anfield knew it would provide a far sterner test than either Blackburn or Brighton had been able to muster. And they had been tricky enough. Liverpool may have beaten Everton with comparative ease in the league, but to face them in the Cup a week later was a far different proposition. Ian Rush came back into the side, which, given his goal-scoring record against Everton, had to be welcome news and Venison was the man left out, while Jan Molby stepped into the injured Ronnie Whelan's boots. It was not a classic, traditionally these games rarely are, with neither side managing to mount many penetrating attacks. Everton had done their homework well, learning much from the previous week and with a goalless draw, the pendulum had swung in their favour.

But if the first game was to be remembered for anything, it will always be recalled for one incident: a reckless challenge by Steve McMahon on Everton's John Ebbrell which left the Liverpool man writhing in agony on the floor. McMahon had torn his knee tendons, a serious injury which was about to wreck Liverpool's season. It had been a foolish tackle and McMahon could only blame himself for the consequences. He had unwittingly added a further burden for Dalglish to carry.

Jimmy Hill, long an admirer of Liverpool, was unusually harsh in his summing up to seven million television viewers: 'What we've got now is a very unbalanced Liverpool team. The great stylish midfield players of

Liverpool will be turning over in their graves to see the orthodox and very average way in which they are performing.' Wherever Dalglish turned, the brickbats were pouring in, from the newspapers, television, other managers and even from his own kith and kin on the Kop. At Anfield, rows simmered about his team selection and within days John Barnes would go public. But by then Dalglish would have made his momentous decision.

Some 76,000 fans had watched the first two encounters and a further 37,000 turned up at Goodison on a cold evening three days later to watch what would be not only Dalglish's final game in charge at Anfield but perhaps the most memorable clash ever between the Merseyside rivals. Some even called it the finest cup-tie seen since the war. With mounting calls for the return of Peter Beardsley, Dalglish finally relented and the England international was once more handed the number 7 shirt, with Speedie relegated to the substitutes' bench. For a time it seemed an inspired move.

With just 32 minutes gone, Beardsley was on the scoresheet, slamming in a right-foot shot. Fifteen minutes later, Scottish international Graeme Sharp equalised. Beardsley added his second in the 71st minute and Liverpool were suddenly playing with all the passion and style that had been absent in recent weeks. But their concentration lapsed and within the minute Everton were back on level terms thanks to Graeme Sharp again. Five minutes later, Ian Rush, with yet another goal against Everton, looked to have put the tie beyond doubt. With just one minute remaining on the clock, Liverpool seemed all set for the quarter-finals, but with almost the final kick of normal time substitute Tony Cottee blasted the tie into extra time. Dalglish was furious: to have given away another last minute equaliser was unforgivable. Liverpool now had to do it all over again. The typhoon was raging.

The tension inside Goodison was unbearable. Dalglish, as usual, was off his bench screaming at his defence. He stood perched in the dugout like MacWhirr aboard his *Nan-Shan,* his face screwed up, eyes blazing as they tore into the storm. Yet there was more drama to come. In the 102nd minute, John Barnes, with a flash of genius, hit a spectacular goal to make it 4–3 and once more Liverpool had the edge. But Everton were not finished and yet again just as it seemed Liverpool would be through to the last eight Tony Cottee leaped to their rescue with a last-second equaliser. Goodison erupted. But in the blast of noise, Dalglish had rarely felt lonelier. You could see the weariness in his eyes. The entire Liverpool bench was horrified. Dalglish slumped to his seat, Moran buried his head in his hands, Roy Evans looked devastated.

Everton were elated. Howard Kendall, not surprisingly, described it as 'one of the greatest cup-ties ever'. Dalglish grudgingly agreed. 'I don't think I've ever been involved in a derby match like that. If there have ever been any better cup-ties, I wish somebody would send me a video of them.' But he was devastated by the result, adding that 'We gave four great examples of how to score goals, and four bad examples of how to defend.' Somebody jokingly asked him how his heart was after such excitement. 'Still the same,' he quipped. 'It's stopped.' Perhaps they should have asked about his blood pressure as well.

In the dressing room there were angry words. Moran was fuming. 'As angry as I've ever seen him,' said one player. But his rages were hardly new. He was the sergeant major of the outfit, ready to blast anyone who stepped out of line. Evans, usually the more thoughtful and calm of the two, was subdued but still lashed out at the defence for twice conceding late equalisers. A fearful row was set to break out as accusations were hurled from one side of the dressing room to the other. The forwards were livid with the defence: 'For Christ's sake, we're scoring the fucking goals and you bastards at the back are letting them in. Get yourselves sorted out,' screamed one. The anger was barely contained, some feared the recriminations would turn into a fight. Outside the dressing room, the yelling and screaming could be heard by everyone. The news soon filtered back to the Everton dressing room that all hell was being let loose down the corridor.

John Barnes confirmed that there had been 'screaming, ranting and raving'. The racket went on for 15 or 20 minutes. It was not the first blow-up after a game, but it was one of the bitterest anyone could remember. While the slanging match raged, one man remained silent, his back to the wall, head bent slightly forward, staring at the floor, almost in a daze. Dalglish had barely spoken a word. He stood dumbstruck, almost oblivious to the hurricane that was raging around him, unable to find words to contribute. The situation was clearly beyond him. That moment was a catalyst when Dalglish finally cracked under the pressure. He had already made his decision to go, but in the Goodison Park dressing room that decision was certainly confirmed. It was the moment Dalglish finally lost control of Liverpool Football Club.

The dressing room eventually calmed down and the players slunk away for a beer with some of the Everton players. But there were few smiles. There was little doubt that Liverpool had thrown away a game that had been won on more than one occasion. It was becoming a habit.

The cracks were finally showing among the players and the following day John Barnes, in an unusually frank interview, gave his full backing to Beardsley. 'I would have him in my side,' he argued, but added that 'Kenny Dalglish is the manager and picks the best team for Liverpool Football Club.' Yet it was perfectly clear where Barnes's loyalties lay. 'I think Peter improves the fluidity of Liverpool's play. If Liverpool are going to play the type of football they are used to, they have to have a Peter Beardsley type player.' It was the first time anyone could recall a player being so openly critical of a Liverpool manager.

The pressure on Dalglish that week had been excruciating and he knew that, for the sake of his family, as well as himself, he could take no more. He needed to talk to his wife again. As he drove through the quiet streets of Liverpool that night towards his home in Southport, he knew in his own mind that it was time to see the chairman. He could go on no longer. The drama was about to unfold.

CHAPTER SIXTEEN
Paradise Lost

When you walk through a storm
Hold your head up high
And don't be afraid of the dark.
Liverpool anthem

Once a month Dalglish would meet with chairman Noel White and high-ly respected chief executive Peter Robinson to mull over various problems. It was a longstanding arrangement designed to suit the members of the board rather than the manager, though there were clearly benefits for both sides. Under the previous chairman, John Smith, the meetings had grown increasingly irregular in recent years, something which had been a cause for concern among some board members. Smith was often unavoid-ably absent on other business either at the Sports Council, of which he was chairman, or running his own company. There were moments when it seemed nobody upstairs was helping Dalglish and that advice he might be seeking was not forthcoming. Similarly, the directors were not always able to maintain a close check on their manager. But new chairman Noel White was determined to keep the monthly date and to make sure that he was always available to assist Dalglish should he require advice or help.

Since the days of Bill Shankly, there have been strict demarcation lines at Anfield between the tasks of the manager and those of the board. It had been Shankly's one condition for accepting the job. The rule was simple: the board did not interfere with team affairs. Team selection, the choice of coaching staff and the buying and selling of players were the manager's decisions alone. If the manager thought he could do a deal on a player, he would inform the chief executive of his interest and the board would then take over and settle a deal. It was the same with players' contracts. If the manager wanted to extend someone's contract, he informed Peter Robinson, who would then set about the business of seeing the player and negotiating a new deal. Finance and the day-to-day running of the club were the business of the chief executive and board. The directors were always free to question the manager, but only at the monthly board meeting when he would appear to give his report, and they would only interfere if they felt the manager was usurping their powers. Board members might have their own views on team selection – who doesn't? – and once or twice under Dalglish there were grimaces when the teamsheet was produced shortly before kick-off, but nobody ever questioned Dalglish's authority.

In close-knit Anfield circles it was thought that John Smith had become exasperated with Dalglish. Relations had cooled considerably since Smith had, almost unilaterally, appointed the Scottish international as manager. Smith felt that Dalglish was running out of control, or at least their control. He had become the most powerful manager in the club's history. Yet Smith's involvement with the Sports Council had meant he could no longer monitor the situation as closely as in previous times. While new to the job, Noel White needed to keep a closer rein on Dalglish without ever inhibiting the man who had so quickly become one of the most successful managers in the Football League. Dalglish had never expressed any distaste for the regular meeting with White and Robinson and appeared to regard it as a useful means of communicating with those who pulled the strings at Anfield. It was an opportunity for any of them to air their problems, thoughts, or suggestions, rather than having to wait for the monthly board meeting.

On the morning of 21 February, just hours after Liverpool's tumultuous 4–4 draw with Everton, the three men gathered in the boardroom. There seemed nothing unusual that Thursday morning. They sat surrounded by portraits of the club's directors and began to work their way through a rough agenda. Dalglish seemed no different from usual. Perhaps a little more tense, maybe more tired. The previous evening's excitement had been enough to take its toll on anyone. The meeting began with a few wry references to the draw with Everton. Liverpool may have conceded four goals, yet there were no accusations being hurled about the room although it was clear that even Dalglish himself was not happy with the Liverpool defence. After their brief discussion about the Everton game, they moved on to a few other topics and the meeting remained amicable.

Then suddenly, 20 minutes into the meeting, Dalglish looked up at both men and calmly announced: 'I want to resign as manager of Liverpool.' Its effect was devastating.

Noel White and Peter Robinson glanced at one another. Had they understood it right? 'Pardon?' said White.

'I've decided to quit Liverpool. I'd like to go,' replied Dalglish, his face showing barely a flicker of emotion. 'I simply can't take it any more,' he added. 'I want to resign.'

Over the years, Peter Robinson had grown accustomed to surprises from Dalglish but this was astonishing. The two directors looked stunned. They still weren't sure whether he was joking. But he wasn't. He tried to explain.

'I'm tired. The pressure is incredible. I can cope during the week, but on match days I just feel as if my head is exploding.'

'Is this anything to do with last night's game?' asked White, searching desperately for a logical explanation. 'Because I could understand you feeling drained after that. I felt the same myself.'

'No,' replied Dalglish. 'I've been feeling like this for some time now. I did wonder about quitting at the end of last season, but I decided to soldier on. But I can't go on any longer. My health is suffering. I see so little of my family. They're growing up without my seeing them. In fact I want to go now. Today.'

White and Robinson had assumed that he was talking about leaving at the end of the season, but this latest bombshell rocked them back in their chairs.

'You want to go now?' exclaimed Robinson. 'I'm staggered.'

'But is there any other reason?' asked Noel White. 'Are you unhappy, here?'

'No,' replied Dalglish. 'You've all been very helpful over the years.'

'Have you had another offer from somewhere?' they asked him.

'No,' answered Dalglish. He set about trying to explain and elaborate on his reasons again, the unbearable strain.

'Is there anything we can do to help, give you more assistance, maybe a short break, even until the end of the season?' they suggested.

'No,' was the short answer. 'I want to go and I want to go now.'

The more they talked, the more White and Robinson pleaded. The more they searched for a solution, the more adamant Dalglish became.

After an hour or so, White told Dalglish that he would have to call a full board meeting. 'I'll try and arrange it for this afternoon. If not, it will have to be tonight,' he said. 'I think we should adjourn now and reflect.'

Dalglish went on his way, leaving Robinson and White to dwell on the implications of what had happened.

At noon, the phones rang in the offices and homes of Liverpool's various directors. It was Peter Robinson. There would be an emergency board meeting at 4.00pm at Anfield, he told them. It was extremely important that they attend. Robinson said no more. They were all mystified.

At four, just as Anfield generally closes down for the day, a fleet of smart cars pulled into the parking spaces opposite the main entrance. There were nods and smiles as each of the board members made their way upstairs towards the boardroom. There was still talk of the previous night. 'My heart hasn't stopped pounding yet,' joked one director. 'How could we throw it away like that?' added another. They wondered why the meeting had been called at such short notice, but they were all too polite and experienced to speculate on the reasons.

The directors convened in the boardroom and wasted little time in beginning their meeting. White thanked them all for coming: 'The reason I have had to ask you all to come at such short notice is that at our regular meeting this morning between myself, Peter Robinson and the manager, Mr Dalglish informed us that he wished to resign as manager of Liverpool Football Club.'

There were gasps around the table. Dalglish was as much an idol to most of them as he was to any young lad on the Kop. 'I couldn't believe what I was hearing,' said one director. 'My mind kept harping back to the day Shankly resigned. I wasn't a director then, but this is what it must have been like.'

Noel White and Peter Robinson expanded on the meeting they had held with Dalglish that morning and his reasons for quitting. Everyone was flabbergasted. It just didn't seem like Dalglish.

'What was puzzling,' said Noel White, 'was that he waited twenty minutes into the meeting before telling us.' It was almost as if he decided on the spot, there and then, twenty minutes into the meeting, as an afterthought. We had been given no hint of what was to come.'

'Was there anything said during those twenty minutes that might have upset him?' asked one director.

'Not a thing,' said White. Peter Robinson concurred that it had been a perfectly amicable meeting.

White explained that Dalglish had told him that he had considered quitting before the season began and that the pressure had been increasing as the season unfolded.

'But he only signed a new contract six months ago,' pointed out one director. 'That was supposed to bind him to us for three more years. Why did he sign if he knew he had doubts?' Nobody could answer.

Someone also pointed out that Dalglish had accepted a hefty signing-on fee, an inducement to stay with them.

'There must be some other reason,' suggested another director. There were nods around the table.

'I think we should call him in and talk with him, see if we can persuade him to change his mind,' said John Smith, though in his heart he probably knew that once Dalglish had made a decision there was no changing his mind. He was a stubborn man, single-minded. That was what had attracted John Smith so much in the first place. He admired his self-confidence, his assuredness, even when they had had their differences.

Dalglish was ushered into the room and pulled up a chair next to Noel White. He looked nervous and tired.

'I've told the board about our meeting this morning and your request to resign as manager. Has anything happened since then to make you change your mind?'

Dalglish shook his head.

'I've tried to explain your reasons to the board but I think you should perhaps tell them yourself in your own words.'

Dalglish began, his voice quiet, almost inaudible. He repeated that he had not been feeling well. During the week he could cope, but on a Saturday he found it unbearable. 'I feel as if my head is exploding,' he told them, just as he had told White and Robinson earlier that morning. He told them about the rash that had covered his body.

The board listened in silence.

As he talked, they could see he was under considerable strain. He looked worn out, lines etched on his forehead, his fingers grasped tightly in a ball, a distant look about his eyes.

He repeated that he wanted to go now, this day. As before, there were suggestions that he might take a break, perhaps resuming his post at the beginning of the following season. But Dalglish would have none of it.

He wanted to go immediately. After an hour it was clear that there was no persuading him. He had made his decision and, as John Smith always suspected, he would not change his mind.

It was agreed to leave an announcement until the following morning when an emergency press conference would be called. Noel White still hoped that he might change his mind overnight and that he could be persuaded against this potentially devastating course of action. Dalglish thanked him and the board for all their help over the years. He had always enjoyed his times at Anfield, he added, and the club would remain close to his heart.

Dalglish left the meeting and the directors stared dejectedly at one another. Most seemed convinced there must be another reason. It was hard to believe that Kenny Dalglish had been beaten by pressure.

For most of the directors it had been a trying six years: the Heysel tragedy, the disaster at Hillsborough and now the resignation of their manager. There had been the compensation of further honours, but now they had to begin the search for a new manager. In the meantime, they hurriedly agreed to ask assistant manager Ronnie Moran to act as caretaker boss until they had had time to consider their next move.

For months, Dalglish had been privately suffering, yet nobody had noticed. Scottish sports journalist Gerry McNee had been interviewed on a TV programme with him in Glasgow barely a week before his resignation, yet had spotted nothing untoward. 'He seemed the same old Kenny I had known for almost twenty years,' he says. Ian Hargreaves of the *Liverpool Echo,* who saw Dalglish most days, similarly had no indication that something was amiss. 'He might have been a bit more tetchy than usual,' he says. 'But he was just as full of jokes and smiles.' Most of his friends also claimed not to have noticed any changes. Dalglish had managed to hide successfully his own personal crisis. There were headaches, his head was spinning, he had come out in a rash. And on one occasion, it was said that he had driven into the Anfield car park and had been unable to get out of his car for some time, his body refusing to carry him the few yards into reception. It was a classic symptom of pressure.

In the dressing room, among the players and the bootroom staff, there was total surprise when Dalglish walked in that Friday morning and gathered them together to make his announcement. They sensed that something was in the air but guessed a new player had been signed. They all stood in silence and disbelief. It was a brief meeting. Dalglish thanked them for all their hard work and support over the years and wished them well in the future. He briefly explained his reasons for quitting, without going into detail. Dalglish was not a man for public confessions. There were no questions, just vacant stares of disbelief from the players. Heads were bowed. It was an uncomfortable moment; Dalglish was clearly upset. Nobody could believe what they were hearing. Then he was gone. He had been at Liverpool not far off 14 years, arriving from the Paradise of Parkhead at the Paradise of Anfield. But now even that was lost.

It was, no matter what anyone else might argue, a courageous decision that had not been arrived at hurriedly. Dalglish was well aware of the implications for the club and its supporters. It was hardly the ideal moment to be quitting his job. He must also have been conscious of its impact and the damaging potential for his own career. But, more importantly, he was aware of the detrimental effect that continuing would have on his health and consequently on his family. The pressures of Hillsborough, that end-of-season clash with Arsenal, and the never-ending quest for success, had taken their toll. It was probably no single incident or reason which finally pushed him over the brink but the culmination of five years in one of the country's most pressured jobs.

Dalglish is a renowned perfectionist. Second best is not sufficient for a man of his endeavours. As a player he had known little else but success, collecting championships in Scotland and England, European honours, international caps, cups; he was admired wherever he played. It seemed, as Don Revie once suggested, that he was blessed to win at everything. Yet most of his accomplishments had been achieved through dedication and sheer hard work. Dalglish may have had more than his fair share of skill, but without application such artistry could so easily have been wasted. The football parks of the world are littered with those who have thrown away their talents. Dalglish the perfectionist painstakingly strove for improvement whether as a player or manager. As a schoolboy, Ian Ross could remember how he played day and night with only a short break for meals. And at Celtic, Billy McNeill could recall his unquenchable appetite for the game, always practising his control until it was near perfect. He did not change much at Anfield. He would train hard in the morning, spend the afternoon resting in bed, being careful with his diet, avoiding drink and late nights. He was the ultimate professional, the kind of player every lad should look to, advised Jock Stein.

Dalglish was dedicated to his trade. As a manager, he carried that same dedication into his new job and, after just one season, he had achieved the League and Cup double. He was already at the top of the tree, among soccer's immortals. But what was there to do next? The only answer was to repeat the performance. And so he took Liverpool to within a whisker of two more doubles. By the end of 1988, when the Barnes/Beardsley axis gloriously swept Liverpool to the title, he had set himself impossible standards. The quality of football that season almost drowned him in accolades. The clamour for more was deafening; Anfield was bursting every game. Maintaining such phenomenal standards was an impossible task and yet still he persevered, discovering that there were indeed new boundaries and fresh challenges. But, like all perfectionists, Dalglish found delegation extremely difficult. Eventually it would tell. The bootroom, with its wealth of experience, was bypassed as Dalglish preferred to rely on his own wits and intuition.

Pressure is always relative. At least one Liverpool social worker was scornful when he heard of Dalglish's resignation. 'Pressure,' he scoffed. 'He should try being a single parent in a one bedroom flat in Liverpool 8. That's pressure.' Michael Parkinson in the *Sunday Telegraph* was equally dismissive: 'Pressure is something that nurses know about, or people who grind out a living in a factory or men who dig coal a mile underground. Pressure is being poor or unemployed, or homeless or hopeless. What it's not is being paid £200,000 a year to manage one of the world's great football clubs.'

It was a fair point. At the end of the day, Dalglish was a wealthy man who could easily back away from the precipice. The single parent, the unemployed, the poor simply have to get on with it; there is no escape. You could argue endlessly about which situation is the most pressured. The point is that much depends on the individual. Pressure is not just about the size of hurdles and problems, but how people respond. Some cope better than others. Some feel pressure in different ways.

Both Sean Fallon and Billy McNeill recall being surprised when they heard that Dalglish was to become a manager. 'At the time I didn't think it was the right move,' says McNeill. 'He is such an insular person. He was very single-minded; particularly about looking after himself. He also sets such high standards and goals for himself that I could never see him meeting them.

'As a manager; he would expect his players to be equally as dedicated. But they can't be. They're all different, they all have their own standards. You can't force them to be like you.' McNeill also points out that Dalglish 'is not severe and calculating. He is warm and caring. People do not appreciate the demands on a manager.'

Coping with criticism did not come easily to Dalglish. He was convinced that his reasoning was correct. Most of the time it was, yet once he had taken on the role of manager, criticism was inevitable. But to pick up a newspaper and digest the opinions of sports writers who had never played the game, let alone managed a football club, did not come easily. The most successful and self-confident of people can equally be the most anxious, and the most likely to be unnerved by press comment.

'Dalglish is no different from anyone else,' argues industrial psychologist Professor Cary Cooper, who has spent many years studying stress among businessmen and sportsmen. 'Given Dalglish's personality as a perfectionist, and as a sensitive man, it becomes more understandable. Managing Liverpool Football Club is probably one of the most difficult jobs in the country. The expectations are phenomenally high. You are continually living in a goldfish bowl with the press and everybody else wanting to squeeze your hand. The poor man can't even go out without being instantly recognised. For an introvert like Dalglish it would inevitably become wearing. Eventually, it takes its toll.'

Dalglish had set impossible standards from the start and maintaining them was always going to create its own pressures. 'It's often the case,' says Professor Cooper, 'that once you have attained the highest level you wonder where to go next. There is rarely an obvious answer. Many at the top simply have to get out, so that they can put life into perspective and see where their next move lies. It's a sort of mid-life crisis.

'For Dalglish that would have posed a particular problem. There are not too many other jobs open to him. Football is all he has known. He's from a working-class background, has had little formal education, and will have few qualifications. And that of course narrows his range of choices considerably.

'Make no mistake, we all go through some kind of mid-life crisis when we ask ourselves is this what we really want to do for the rest of our lives. Dalglish at forty is no different from other men, or indeed women, at that age. But having said that, it was considerably more than a mid-life crisis that he has been through.'

On top of the normal duties and ambitions of a manager, Dalglish had also experienced the disasters at Ibrox, Heysel and Hillsborough as well as the death of Jock Stein, a man as close to him as his father. It had all taken its toll. Dalglish, like so many, was desperately shaken by the events of Hillsborough and the subsequent weeks.

'For a family man it would have been doubly disturbing,' says Cary Cooper. 'Once you have children, death takes on a different perspective. He would have met with families whose children had died and he would have seen youngsters in hospital. He would understand the pain parents were suffering. He has a boy himself who could just as easily have been on that terrace. You can be assured those thoughts would have gone through his head. And don't forget that having four children of your own presents a lot of pressure.'

For weeks, Dalglish and his wife had helped counsel the bereaved, unstintingly giving their time and, with it, their emotions. The phone would ring in the early hours of the morning, there was an ever open door, funerals had to be attended and there were more than a couple of his own players in deep shock. The club was stunned, not quite sure how to respond, yet Dalglish bobbed to the surface, a symbol of dignity and humanity in everyone's hour of need. Dalglish himself probably never had sufficient time to recover fully from the trauma as he raced from one drama to another. He never showed the great depths of feeling inside him. Above all, it demonstrated that Dalglish was a deeply sensitive and decent man. Undoubtedly, the events that day destroyed his appetite for the game, as it did for so many in the city of Liverpool. Even after the long break, the spirit was never the same. Hillsborough changed everyone in Liverpool and Dalglish would never be quite so single-minded about football again.

It was hard to believe that a man so professional as Dalglish could quit just as his club was entering the most crucial part of the season. It was probably not unnatural that everybody should be searching for another, more sensational, explanation. The tongues were soon wagging. The most bizarre suggestion came in one paper which even reckoned Mrs Beardsley was behind it, that she had rowed with Marina Dalglish over why Kenny never picked her husband. It was an explanation not worth the paper it was written on. The truth, hard though it may have been to accept, was that Dalglish was worn out. The day after his resignation, with speculation reaching hysterical proportions, Dalglish phoned the *Liverpool Daily Post* and Radio Merseyside to elaborate on his reasons. 'I've told the truth,' he said, 'and if people don't believe me then that's up to them.' It was a cry from the heart. 'Why people have to speculate, I just don't know. I gave my reasons for going and they are one hundred per cent true. Anything else is ridiculous.'

But the speculation would never disappear entirely. Many men would have snapped earlier under the strain. Even the joking, extrovert Bill Shankly came to a point where he could take no more, while friendly Joe Fagan lasted just two years in the job before the pressure finally dragged him under. Fagan had decided to retire long before Heysel and carried the pain of that chaotic evening into retirement. Dalglish had to cope with it from day one and then had to live through Hillsborough. Although Bob Paisley struggled manfully through his reign at Anfield, it was to be at a severe price as his health rapidly deteriorated in the years ahead. And Dalglish's successor, Graeme Souness, would within a year of taking over at Anfield suffer a heart attack and face triple bypass surgery.

As a devoted family man, Dalglish would have listened to his wife, who would have been the first to spot the strain. They had been married since he was a young hopeful at Celtic and she was his first serious romance. At the end of the day, he knew that his first duty was to himself and his family. Marina Dalglish can, by all accounts, be just as strong-minded as her husband. One television journalist recalled going to the Dalglishes' house to conduct an interview. He arrived some time before the crew but Dalglish invited him in, gave him a beer and the two sat down to chat. Ten minutes later, Marina arrived home. 'I'm about to do a television interview,' explained Dalglish to his wife.

'Not looking like that you're not,' answered Marina, telling him to go upstairs and change. Dalglish promptly did as she said.

Marina's influence on her husband is considerable and Dalglish is equally protective, shading her and their four children from outside. He is a particularly private man, relaxing most with his family and close friends. And therein, perhaps, lies a further complication.

His old friend Les Donaldson remembers coming down to Liverpool to stay with him one weekend. 'We went to the match together and the whole time Dalglish was worrying about whether he was going to be able to get away from Anfield in time to see his son singing in the church choir. In the end he did, but it was a rush. I don't think he even had time to speak to the papers; he was so anxious to get there on time. It mattered to him so much.'

His friend Tommy Smith probably summed him up best when he said Dalglish 'is the type who bottles things up and keeps an awful lot to himself. He took a lot of responsibilities on himself as a manager – he did not spread the load. He is a caring person and the Hillsborough tragedy had a much bigger effect on him than many people realised.' Dalglish had few friends to share his burden, his life outside Anfield focused almost entirely on his family. He was a man with no safety valve, ready to explode as the pressures built up.

'It was a smart move to get out of Liverpool,' adds Professor Cooper. 'He was extremely brave. It takes a lot of courage to do something like that and he did it before anything happened. It was the best thing he could have done; had he not, it could have had dire consequences. It's a pity more people don't do what he did.'

It would undoubtedly have been painful for a man like Dalglish to stand up in public and admit that he could no longer face up to the strain. It was as courageous a step as any he had taken in his life. The full extent of what might have happened became all too apparent a year later when his successor, Graeme Souness, also discovered that managing Liverpool Football Club had become a job almost beyond human calling. For the moment, however, the storm in Dalglish's life had abated. But how much longer would he be able to keep away from football?

CHAPTER SEVENTEEN
The Man They Loved To Hate

I have come to the conclusion that Kenny Dalglish has been put on this earth by God to be a winner at everything. I honestly believe he has been blessed.
Don Revie

Who is the lonely figure in the knee-length red anorak, huddled nervously inside the dugout, his face taut and twisted, his hands clenched one moment, then fidgeting, tearing at his hair, shaking his head, gesticulating. Whoever he is, he is a man visibly suffering as he watches every kick, shot and effort before him. And then the next moment, he is off his seat, springing anxiously into full view, yelling, pointing and urging. Finally, he stands brooding and menacing alongside the touchline, his hands plunged deep into his pockets. If only he could be out there, on the field where he used to be. In his heart of hearts he has never ceased to be a player. But standing there, watching, there is nothing he can do.

Who is he? He's the man they love to hate. The scorn tumbles down the opposition terraces. 'Sit down, sit down,' they scream in unison. But he takes no notice. Not so long ago, they might have drooled over his delightful touches, the unqualified rapport with his team-mates. They may not have enjoyed his commitment as he set about destroying their own favourites, but they had to admire him and acknowledge that here was a player without equal. But that was another job, another era. The man in the red anorak was a manager now and he was seen as fair game for anyone.

As a player, Kenny Dalglish was almost above criticism. Talented and dedicated, he was the perfect professional. He had been shown a red card only once in an unusually long and distinguished career. He was an MBE, a Freeman of the City of Glasgow and twice Player of the Year. He had never known criticism, except perhaps for some of his Scottish performances. The sports writers had never blamed him for defeats, whether at Celtic or Liverpool. And when he did appear on the back pages, it was because of his exploits on the football field and not because of some dressing-room scandal. There were rarely any sensational exclusive interviews. Dalglish might have been fond of money, but he was not one to grab at the tabloid pieces of silver.

This happy arrangement could not last once he became Liverpool's player/manager. The comment and questioning began almost from day one. It was he who took the blame; everything rested on his slender shoulders. As American President Harry Truman would have pointed out: 'The buck stops here.' Dalglish may have had the Midas touch when it came to performing on the football field but could he have the same magical powers when it came to management?

Shortly after his appointment, the former Liverpool striker Ian St John perceptively warned that Dalglish would now have to come to terms with the brickbats. 'As a player he never received any criticism but as a manager he will be subjected to intense scrutiny, especially as manager of Liverpool. If things go wrong he will get the blame. If the team loses, he will not be able to avoid criticism, comments from the press, from the terraces. He will have to get used to it but it will be difficult.'. In the end it was to prove too difficult.

John Smith had seen in Dalglish an old-fashioned general, a man who could lead from the front. He had no doubt been given an insight by Bob Paisley, who had long realised that Dalglish was 'an outstanding motivator on the pitch, a man not afraid to lead the charge into the thick of the battle.' It was a precious commodity for anyone hoping to become a manager. Phil Neal, for all the personal problems Dalglish's appointment would throw up, eventually was to come to the same conclusion: 'He was a natural leader of the front line. The qualities of passion and determination he showed then are common to players at Liverpool, and they are his qualities in management.'

It was not, of course, a happy introduction to football management, given the events at Heysel. Within 24 hours of the board ratifying his appointment on the eve of their European Cup final against Juventus, Liverpool Football Club was plunged into the gravest crisis in its history. Any comments on whether Dalglish was suitable for the job needed to be put aside while the papers discussed other, more relevant and crucial, matters.

One of the first questions Fleet Street wanted answering was whether the players were aware of any deaths at Heysel before the game kicked off. Later that evening, the new manager was cornered and tackled by a battery of TV reporters. It was a legitimate question they were asking and one which the public had a right to know the answer to. Nobody at the club had initially seemed keen on confronting this particular issue, but Dalglish was forthright enough. 'No,' he replied. He had not known of the deaths. The answer came as a surprise. It seemed extraordinary that any player could not have known, especially when half of Europe watching on television was aware of the magnitude of the disaster. Yet here was Dalglish insisting that he had no prior knowledge.

It may sound inconceivable to many that Dalglish did not know, yet as I was actually standing on the fateful terrace that evening. I can confirm that even I was not aware of any deaths until an hour after the game had ended. I had even spent the entire second half standing, almost, alone and within 20 yards of the collapsed wall without any hint of the deaths that had taken place earlier. I had obviously witnessed the tearing down of the fence and the chaos that ensued, but I remained unaware that people had been killed. Astonishing though it may seem, it is often those closest to a disaster who are the last to know its full magnitude. And so it was with Dalglish and many others that night at the Heysel Stadium.

Chris Lawler, for example, who was on the bench and in the changing room that evening, explains how it came about that Dalglish did not know. 'I remember he was ill,' says Lawler. 'He had the flu and spent the whole time lying on the treatment bench, resting. It was a large dressing room with all sorts of small rooms running off it, including toilets and a bathroom. The treatment bench was away from the main area.'

Craig Johnston, a substitute that evening, was an eye witness to the caving in of the wall, but asserts categorically in his autobiography that no Liverpool player actually witnessed the deaths of any fans. 'Snatchy reports filtered down the stairwell that people were dying,' he wrote in his book. 'The estimated body count mounted – eight, 15, 20 – we didn't know what to believe.' Johnston adds, however, 'if we had known the full magnitude of the horror I think it would have been impossible for us to even go through the motions of playing, but we had not seen what those watching on television or the rescue crews had witnessed. The sophistication of long-range lenses and saturation television coverage had relayed the entire drama to a watching worldwide audience. We were right on the spot but we knew little of what had really happened.'

Mark Lawrenson is another who has written about that evening. He admitted in his autobiography that 'it was clear that something was seriously wrong'. Riot police had been in the dressing room, UEFA officials had notified them of a delay to the kick-off and Phil Neal had been sent off to make an appeal over the tannoy. But, insists Lawrenson, 'we still did not know the magnitude of the disaster'.

Although Dalglish did not know of the deaths, it later emerged that at least one of his colleagues had known. Phil Neal, Liverpool's captain on the night, has admitted that he knew something of the scale of the disaster while they were still in the dressing room. Neal had been asked to broadcast an appeal for calm and witnessed some of the carnage as he made his way to the PA position. But when Neal's book, *Life At The Kop*, was published in 1986, it not only stated that Neal had known, but questioned Dalglish's denial. Dalglish was so enraged that he took legal action to have the book altered. He saw it as a point of principle to continue to make it clear that he knew nothing of the deaths until after the match. Yet whether or not any players knew beforehand seems, in hindsight, to be of very little importance. The mood was ugly that evening; the game simply had to be played or an even greater catastrophe would have occurred. But for Dalglish it had hardly been the happy start he had imagined to his new career.

Over the next few days club officials found themselves placed under increasing scrutiny as the world's press descended on Merseyside. It was a new, revealing and uncomfortable experience for them. Misjudgements were made but they learned well and after the Hillsborough disaster did not make the same mistakes.

Once the dust of Heysel had settled, Dalglish's appointment as player/manager came under the expected spotlight of the press. The intrigue behind the appointment remained a mystery but his very selection raised a number of eyebrows. Everyone accepted that Dalglish was an impeccable player but there were questions about his suitability to manage. Bobby Charlton, it was pointed out, had a similar pedigree, a player with an outstanding record, but when it came to football management, he had been a sad failure. Others had discovered the same problems.

Had Liverpool made a serious error? Dalglish's tutor Bob Paisley did not think so. He tried to explain: 'Great players are normally like soloists in an orchestra. They perform alone and tend to look down on their teammates with lesser ability. But that was never Kenny Dalglish. He brought others into play. He understood that not everyone was blessed with the greatest of skill. He had patience.' Dalglish would carry that understanding and patience into management.

The tradition, established since Shankly's departure, of appointing the number two to the job, had surprisingly been disregarded. Ronnie Moran, the ebullient assistant to Joe Fagan, was the man everyone expected to be promoted, but he had been overlooked. He was not the only candidate.

Phil Neal was another who reckoned he was in with a chance of the top job. Neal was convinced that he would be offered the managership when Joe Fagan finally retired and recalled a conversation with chairman John Smith a few years previously when they discussed Neal's long-term future. 'Don't worry, Phil,' Smith is reported to have said. 'There'll be a job waiting for you here when you finish playing.' At the very least, Neal reckoned he would be joining the bootroom in some capacity, perhaps as youth team coach, and his hope had been that it would be as manager. Phil Neal's allegations have been generally dismissed as the natural reactions of someone who has been overlooked but there is evidence to suggest that he was right to be optimistic about his prospects. At least one other club director recalls Neal's name being touted as a future manager and felt some guilt when Dalglish was appointed. It may also explain some of the questioning by the board when John Smith informed them of Dalglish's appointment.

The pundits had other questions about the appointment. Dalglish was not only wholly inexperienced in the ways of management, but he had been appointed player/manager. How could he manage *and* play at the same time? It was one thing to be player/manager of a third or fourth division club, but to be player/manager of one of Europe's top clubs was an entirely different matter. There were few, if any, precedents. And how could Dalglish be expected to deal with players who a few weeks previously had been his colleagues? Who was the boss on the pitch – the captain or the manager? They were reasonable questions being asked as much by the terraces, and the Kop in particular, as by the press.

Sean Fallon, his old boss at Celtic, also had his doubts. 'Dalglish was something of a loner,' he admits. 'He didn't really show leadership qualities, so I was a wee bit surprised when Liverpool appointed him.'

Another man who was astonished was Billy McNeill, his former Celtic captain. 'I didn't think it was the right move,' he says. 'Kenny was an insular person. I was very surprised when Liverpool appointed him. He had been so single-minded in looking after himself, I didn't know how he would manage looking after others.' But McNeill admits that he was helped by an unrivalled structure and backroom set-up at Anfield which certainly made Dalglish's job much easier.

Few were better positioned to scrutinise the changes affecting Dalglish than Mark Lawrenson. 'We were in the firing line after Heysel but if the heat was on for us, it was at boiling point for him.' And at no time was the pressure any more intense than for Liverpool's first game, at home to Arsenal. The world's press seemed to be at Anfield. Some players were visibly nervous but if Dalglish had any worries he did not show them. Liverpool won 2–0, Anfield was respectful, and Dalglish had overcome his first public hurdle.

But there were also private hurdles. The appointment of Dalglish had left club captain Phil Neal very upset. When he heard the announcement in Brussels that Dalglish had been given the job he so coveted, he was heartbroken. It was hardly Dalglish's fault but Neal's relationship with his new manager was never going to be easy. 'I remember vowing to myself that I would never call him boss,' wrote Neal in his autobiography. 'It was psychologically very important to me to maintain some independence.' Neal also claims that he was not the only one apprehensive about the forthcoming season and the prospect of working with Kenny. 'No one had any idea about just how he was proposing to play things,' he added.

For some weeks, the tension simmered beneath the surface as Neal threw himself into preparations for his testimonial and hung on to his number 2 shirt. But once his testimonial was out of the way, the rifts re-emerged. Neal met with chairman John Smith to discuss his future and, after their meeting, emerged to tell waiting pressmen that there appeared to be no long-term future at Anfield for him. The next day, Neal was called into Dalglish's office and stripped of the captaincy. Dalglish told him he should not have spoken to the press. Neal responded by saying that he was only telling the truth. There did not appear to be a future for him at Anfield, especially now that he was having the captaincy taken from him. Dalglish was adamant; Alan Hansen was to be the new captain. Neal had inadvertently provided Dalglish with the ideal excuse to sack him. Dalglish was well aware that Neal's first division career was drawing to a close. With Steve Nicol challenging hard for the number 2 shirt, Neal's position was already under threat, which was hardly an ideal situation for the club captain. Clearly, Dalglish needed a younger man in the job, but he had found it difficult to face the agonising decision of asking Neal to hand over the captaincy. Within months, Neal had gone, moving on to manage Bolton Wanderers.

It had been a testing dilemma for Dalglish, perhaps the most difficult in his first months. It was clear that Phil Neal's playing days were drawing to an end and the execution would have had to be applied sooner or later. Neal was the one senior player who could rival Dalglish for experience and the decision not to appoint him as manager had been taken by the board. Nevertheless, Dalglish still had to live with the consequences of Neal's disappointment. But, as Mark Lawrenson testifies, 'You need a mean streak to succeed as a manager.'

Dalglish had therefore proved he had what it took when it came to dealing with problem situations and upset players. There would be flare-ups with other players as well. Ronnie Whelan, for one, was furious after being left out of the Cup final line-up against Wimbledon. 'But,' says Whelan, 'Kenny doesn't mind if you argue with him. But you can argue until the cows come home and you'll never win.' A lesser man might give in under the onslaught but not Dalglish. He once told a young reserve that he might be the 12th best player at Anfield but he was also the 12th best player in the first division.

He had carried his dedication from the field and into the office. He seemed to be able to cope with the players, who always showed him enormous respect. Although they might not like being left out of the line-up (players are never dropped at Anfield), their anger rarely lasted more than a day or two and few ever went on to demand a transfer.

But just as some questioned Dalglish's ability to take over Britain's leading club, there were those who argued that managing Liverpool Football Club was, in fact, comparatively easy. All he had to do was keep the machine ticking over and there was plenty of money to buy in the talent, if and when the machine ever spluttered. But tell that to Ron Atkinson, Gordon Lee, Malcolm Allison and a host of other first division big spenders whose forays into the transfer market brought headaches instead of honours. It's not how much money you have but how you spend it that counts.

But Dalglish was not one to sit back and occasionally apply a little oil to the cogs of the machine. He was his own man, he had his own way of doing things and they did not always comply with the Liverpool tradition. Changes were made as he endeavoured to stamp his own mark on the club. Some in the corridors of Anfield did not like it, but if they wanted Dalglish as manager they had no choice. Yet rarely did the players ever question the way he operated. In time, Dalglish would become the most powerful of all Liverpool managers. And if you judge a man by his results, there can be little question that Dalglish was as successful as any of his esteemed predecessors. His rapport with the Kop was even more finely tuned as a manager. They may have questioned him, at times, having their own opinions about tactics, but they never betrayed him. To the very end, they remained loyal to their hero.

If scoring goals is a hazardous occupation, then football management must surely rank as the most uncertain of all jobs. There is no career path to becoming a football manager. It's one of those occupations you fall into, like becoming a politician or a journalist. There may have been a time in the almost forgotten past when you did not have to serve an apprenticeship as a player, but those days were well gone. And, even after an apprenticeship, there is no guarantee of a job. There are only 93 managers in the entire Football League and well over 1,500 professional footballers. The odds are not favourable. Even a star-studded career, leading your country out at Wembley, is no guarantee of a job. Quite what the qualification is, can be anyone's guess. Appointments usually defy logic: the man in the right place at the right time, luck, a run of good results, someone the chairman likes. It can be any number of factors.

Former Arsenal manager Terry Neill and Professor Anthony Clare once attempted to sum up the qualities needed for this, the most daunting of all occupations. First, it required man management abilities. A manager had to be able to lead, keep players from one another's throats, rule over a happy camp. Then there were the obvious technical skills. He may not have to be a former international, but to win respect he had to know what he was talking about. On top of this, a competitive instinct is vital. Then there is the need to motivate the squad before games and boost morale after defeats. That, in itself, is a rare commodity. And, of course, one cannot forget teambuilding, with the skill needed to spot potential, know who to buy and who to sell. Nor is it quite as simple as buying 11 star names, assuming you have the money; teams have to gel. And not only does personnel selection mean players but also coaches, trainers, scouts, physios and so forth. Then there are the diplomatic skills needed to deal with directors, sponsors, the press, and agents as well as the hangers-on. And finally, the manager has to ensure that his transfer dealings help balance the books. In what other occupation would you have to pay £1 million for a member of staff? And in what other job would you be so rigorously judged by results? Then, after proving that you have all, or some, of these superhuman qualities, you are in a job that has the shortest career span of any occupation. Few last more than two years at any club.

Professor Cary Cooper, an industrial psychologist at the University of Manchester, Institute for Science and Technology, points out that in any other business such skills would never be expected of one person. They would be shared by a team: a personnel manager, an accountant, a commercial director, a public relations officer and so forth. What's more, they would have been trained for these roles over a number of years. Football managers receive no such training, rarely have academic qualifications, and, as in the case of Dalglish, can be plunged in at the highest level without any experience, training or evidence that they are even capable of carrying out the job. It was rather like plucking someone from the assembly line at Ford and appointing them chief executive of the company. No major business would even contemplate handing an inexperienced executive an open cheque book. Yet many a football manager will go out and spend millions within months of his appointment.

So how did Dalglish fare, given the demands of his job? When it came to man management, he proved himself immediately, imposing his authority from the start. Phil Neal was not the only one to discover a tougher, no-nonsense Dalglish, taking his promotion seriously from the first moment. But if Phil Neal felt that he was being treated harshly, others felt that Dalglish was simply doing his job. Mark Lawrenson accepted the dressing down he received for not turning up for training at the start of the 1985/6 season, despite being injured at the time. He soon knew where he stood with the new manager.

The severest test for Dalglish was undoubtedly in maintaining the high standards that had already been set at the club by his predecessors. Yet Dalglish would even improve on their record, although he would never have the opportunity to test his wits against European opposition. By steering Liverpool to the double in his first season, Dalglish achieved immortality. But this meant that for four more seasons there would be intense pressure as Liverpool chased further honours. In his second season, there was disappointment as his team failed to capture any of the major trophies. He had to rebuild the side and stamp his own identity on the teamsheet, a very tough challenge.

In came Barnes, Beardsley, Houghton and Aldridge to create one of the most exciting line-ups English football had seen since the days of Best, Law and Charlton. In his third season, with the League championship safely wrapped up, the gods decreed mercilessly that Wimbledon should win the FA Cup. A second, unique, double eluded him. A season later, Dalglish would again come within a whisker of the double, this time losing by an injury-time goal to Arsenal. It was another cruel blow in what, after Hillsborough, had already been the cruellest of all seasons. There is no doubt, therefore, that he maintained Liverpool's position as the premier club in England.

There were those who suggested that, as he left Anfield, he faced what would have been another tough battle, replacing an ageing team. Some even reckoned he had sized up the problem and, deciding that there was little he could do about it, quit while the going was good. But that was not Dalglish's style.

While he may have done well winning trophies and keeping a happy squad, Dalglish did have his problems. Relations with the press were always strained. Even the local papers found him a prickly customer. Ian Hargreaves, veteran football writer with the *Liverpool Daily Post and Echo,* remembers his first meeting with Dalglish after his appointment. 'It was preseason. I rang him up and said we ought to get together, have a chat, get to know each other. He said, "Fine." So I went in. "Well," he said, telling me to sit down. "You know nothing about football, I know nothing about journalism. So we should get along well." My colleagues thought it somewhat rude. I thought it was quite funny.'

Post-match press conferences at English football grounds are always an informal and haphazard affair. In America, where sports journalism has been elevated to a status undreamed of here, reporters are welcomed behind the scenes. After any American sporting event, the dressing-room door is thrown open and the coterie of pencil-clutching journalists are ushered into the inner sanctum where they can chat to whoever they like about whatever they want, the players free to comment at will. In other sports, players and managers appear at organised conferences seated behind desks and microphones. Even at the World Cup, there are organised press conferences with managers duty-bound to appear.

But at post-match conferences in England, football managers frequently do not bother to turn up, especially if they have been on the wrong end of a miserable afternoon. At some grounds, the press have to gather outside the dressing room, waiting for a head to appear around the door so that they can snatch a quick quote. At other grounds, they congregate in cupboard rooms, clutching their pads and scalding-hot cups of tea. The facilities are nearly always archaic. In Dalglish's case, he would arrive at the, post match conference, slump into his seat, arms folded, legs outstretched, crossed at the ankles, his head buried into his chest. If there were no seats, he would stand, surrounded by reporters, mumble a few epithets, and then retreat as quickly as he could, leaving the journalists scratching for a quotable comment or a story behind the result. There were always long silences, the reporters being reluctant to ask the first question for fear that his answer would make them look foolish.

Dalglish, like many footballers, had little time for the press. They were an annoyance, hardly aficionados of the game, more concerned with its personalities, headlines and sensations. Many a manager refuses even to allow his players within quoting distance of the press without prior permission. Dalglish certainly told his players never to let the press know that they were injured. It was part of a game he played, basically designed to keep everyone, especially the opposition, guessing. Players were named in his squad for a game even when they had relatively little chance of playing. It may have been done with all the best intentions for Liverpool Football Club, but you could hardly blame the reporters for not taking kindly to the strategy.

Yet, compared to many players and managers, Dalglish was rarely on the receiving end of Fleet Street's ravings. It was only in his final months that serious doubts were raised about his tactics, and even then it seemed churlish, with Liverpool blazing a trail at the top of the first division. At times there were attempts to improve relations and get-togethers were organised, but the following Saturday it would be back to normal. Yet Dalglish was never actually hostile to reporters, he never threatened them nor barred them from the ground, as has happened elsewhere. He was polite, albeit in his own way. And after Hillsborough the press saw a very different Dalglish.

If he felt hard done by, he would retaliate when the opportunity arose. A few days after Liverpool had been knocked out of the European Cup by CSKA Sofia, Granada Television concluded their weekly football programme with some slow-motion footage showing the crucial goals that ended Liverpool's reign as European champions. As presenter Gerald Sinstadt said goodbye and the footage began, so too did a recording of 'The Party's Over'. It was tongue in cheek but not many people west of Manchester saw the funny side of it. Granada, and in particular Gerald Sinstadt, would live to regret it. The joke went down like a lead balloon on Merseyside. Every time Sinstadt appeared at Anfield, he was sure of some barbed Scouse comment. They have long memories in Liverpool and once Liverpool had returned to their winning ways in Europe, the Kop began to sing: 'Gerald Sinstadt, Gerald Sinstadt. How's the party going now?' But the ultimate revenge came from Dalglish. After another European victory, Sinstadt and the Granada cameras went in search of Dalglish after the game for the usual comment. Dalglish appeared holding his young son Paul in his arms. After a few quick words Dalglish, nodding towards his son, said: 'I think you've got something to say, haven't you Paul?' Without further prompting, young Paul looked Sinstadt in the eye and asked: 'How's the party going Gerald?'

Similarly, there were times when Dalglish could show remarkable generosity towards those in the media. Stuart Jones of *The Times* recalls how his mother wrote to Dalglish, asking him to pass on her gratitude for all the letters she had received from Liverpool fans following the death of her husband, BBC radio commentator Peter Jones. Dalglish immediately phoned her son early the next morning and asked if he could publish his mother's letter in the club's next programme. 'Of course,' replied Jones. A little later Dalglish rang back. 'I think we should hold the letter over for another week if you don't mind,' he suggested. 'There will be a much bigger crowd at that game and more fans will see your mother's letter.'

It was not only the press who were on the receiving end of the sharp tongue of the Liverpool manager, as at least one other boss found out. After a particularly bitter confrontation between Manchester United and Liverpool at Anfield one Saturday, United manager Alex Ferguson was holding forth to the press after the match, commenting on the number of dubious penalty decisions Liverpool were awarded in front of the Kop. Dalglish, overhearing his comments as he walked past clutching his baby Lauren, pointed to her and told stunned pressmen that they might as well talk to his daughter, adding, 'You'll get more sense out of her.' Ferguson was left fuming.

But Dalglish could also use the press and on more than one occasion they would do him and the club a favour. When, for instance, Craig Johnston was repeatedly dashing to London to see his severely injured sister in hospital, Johnston called all the newspapers to ask them not to publicise the family's tragedy, he was astonished to discover that Dalglish had already beaten him to it. His reason was not that he needed an excuse for Johnston's absences, but he wanted to ease the family's burden over a traumatic period.

Dalglish was always protective of his players. Early in John Aldridge's Anfield career, the *Sun* newspaper ran a story claiming that Aldridge was about to be swapped for Oxford United's Ray Houghton. Aldridge had not long come to Anfield from Oxford and had been in and out of the side for some months at the expense of Ian Rush. When Aldridge read the story he was deeply depressed and moped around his house all day. At nine that evening the phone rang. It was Dalglish. He had arrived back from holiday that minute and was calling from the airport. He had just seen the paper and wanted to let Aldridge know that there was no truth in the story whatsoever. With Rush gone, Dalglish told him, he would be in the side at the beginning of the season. There was no need to worry. Aldridge was much relieved and appreciative of his call. Dalglish may not have always handled the press and others well but when it came to players his man management could barely be faulted. Dalglish was a player's man.

When Clement Attlee was Prime Minister he always asked for his newspaper to be brought to him opened at the cricket pages. Under no circumstances did he wish to read the political columns; they would only depress him and, at worst, influence him. Dalglish would have done well to have taken a leaf out of Attlee's book.

But while many players publicly slam the press, they privately snatch their money when it comes to a ghosted, back page exclusive or revealing dressing-room tittle-tattle. To his credit, Dalglish was never one for taking up such offers. He knew their game only too well – a juicy headline, a muckraking quote or a hail of abuse being poured on some opposition player or manager – and deliberately avoided supplying their headlines. It made life difficult for the journalists, especially those from the tabloids, but that wasn't his problem. Things were slightly easier for the local Liverpool papers, who cared more for football than transfer speculation or demands to drop players; and left any criticism of the city's teams to the letters page.

While he might not have taken the tabloids' money, this is not to suggest that Dalglish was not fond of it. On the contrary, Graeme Souness testifies that when it came to talking wages his colleague soon donned a Govan shop steward's badge. Bob Paisley also once said purely jokingly that when it came to adding up the goals bonus at the end of the season, Dalglish occasionally claimed a few that others reckoned they had scored. Dalglish may argue that 'money disnae matter', but the facts seem to suggest otherwise. There is no denying that he is a wealthy man. Eight years as Liverpool's highest-paid player and five years as player/manager and then manager have helped see to that, as well as another lucrative contract at Blackburn. When he quit Liverpool in February 1991, he was earning about £200,000 a year. He also received a signing-on fee of £250,000 when he agreed his final, three-year contract with Liverpool, just seven months prior to resigning. On top of that, Dalglish would also be earning money from various sponsorship deals, endorsements, appearances, books, videos and so on. It is not unreasonable to suggest that these alone would add up to at least a further £50,000 a year. A TV commercial for the NatWest bank in 1990 was reputed to have earned him £100,000. Dalglish also has a number of business interests, including a proposed hi-tech golf centre at Southport.

On top of all this, he has also enjoyed the fruits of two testimonials. His final one, a game between Liverpool and Real Sociedad, earned him £150,000, while an earlier testimonial in 1986 for Scotland, between a Tommy Docherty XI and an Alex Ferguson XI at Hampden Park had already brought him £60,000. Yet in Liverpool, a city of high unemployment, poor housing and desperate poverty few seemed to begrudge Dalglish his wealth.

The most damaging complaints levelled at Dalglish during his final season surrounded his tactics and the dropping of England international Beardsley. Against Spurs it was a plan that paid off, but against Arsenal it proved a disaster. Shankly would never have tailored his team to suit the opposition, claimed the press. But Shankly himself had commented: 'I never drop players, I just change the team around.' Perhaps Dalglish should have reminded them.

During Dalglish's final season at Anfield, there was much talk that his Liverpool side was past its peak, and there didn't seem to be any youngsters coming through to replace them. There was an easy answer. They were waiting but not quite ready. Brian Glanville, in the *Sunday Times,* wrongly accused Dalglish of ignoring a youth policy. The fact was that Dalglish could hardly throw raw recruits into the battlefront when virtually every game they played was crucial. Yet, more than any other manager at Anfield since Shankly, Dalglish was deliberately instituting a youth policy. He appointed Steve Heighway as youth development officer and began to spend time himself with the apprentices.

When he had first taken over as manager, Dalglish was reportedly astonished and ashamed to realise that he did not even know the names of many of the apprentices. He set about rectifying it. 'He was tremendous with the youngsters,' recalls former chief scout Geoff Twentyman. 'They all respected him and were keen to learn and he was equally keen to show them.' He went out and paid some substantial fees for youngsters: Jamie Redknapp arrived from Bournemouth, Nicky Tanner from Bristol Rovers, Steve Harkness from Carlisle United and Don Hutchison from Hartlepool. At the same time, his backroom staff set about unearthing the local talent with more zeal. Yet before Dalglish could realise their potential, he was gone. By the end of the following season, injuries would have forced his successor, Graeme Souness, to successfully blood many of them. But sadly, outside of Anfield, Dalglish was never given the credit for his initiative.

There are doubtless those who actually enjoy football management; the agonising, the insecurity, the tactical debates, the obsessive hours, the dealings with press, directors and fans. Despite all his success, Kenny Dalglish almost certainly did not number among them. He had proved that he had the Midas touch as a manager but at heart he was a player who preferred to be out on the pitch where he could best influence events. Being in the dugout, unable to participate, was painful. He was a bundle of nervous energy, itching to be off his seat. Most of the time he was, attempting to direct operations from a vantage point on the touchline, where he no doubt felt that fraction closer to his players. He was visibly desperate to be among them. The day Dalglish hung up his boots was a dramatic moment. He had given up what he was best at, what he loved most. Once he had stopped playing, his influence over team affairs was limited to training sessions, buying and selling players and tactical talks. When kick-off time arrived on a Saturday afternoon, he could only wish his players luck, offer a few, final words of advice and then steal away to the dugout. It was the most crucial 90 minutes of the week and yet everything was out of his hands. All that he could do was to sit back and watch the drama unfold.

CHAPTER EIGHTEEN
Money Talks

Money is like muck, not good except it be spread.
Francis Bacon

Jack Walker was a self-made millionaire. Slightly thickset, with short, cropped hair that was greying at the sides and a round buttery face, he barely looked his age. He was one of a number of millionaires in Blackburn. Walker made his money out of steel. He was alleged to be the 24th richest man in Britain. Up in Blackburn, they'll tell you he once pushed a cart around the town loaded with scrap metal. But nobody knows if that's really true or just one of those apocryphal tales.

Jack Walker's empire began back in 1945, just after the war. He was still young but he and his father managed to raise £80 to set up a small sheet-metal and car-body repair business in the bombed-out back streets of Blackburn. It soon grew. By 1950, it was reporting a turnover of £6,000 per year, a not insubstantial sum in those days of post-war austerity. After a period of national service and the death of his father Charles, Jack's brother Fred joined the business and, by 1956, its turnover had mushroomed to £80,000 a year. But it was still primarily the same business as it had always been. But that year they made a momentous decision to diversify. It was the days of Harold Macmillan and 'you've never had it so good'.

There was a worldwide shortage of steel. There was rapid industrial expansion sweeping across Europe. There was money to be made. A band-wagon was on the roll. Walker decided to get into the business of buying and selling steel. He would become a stockholder, buying in steel, charg-ing a commission and then selling. Walker had found his forte. By the mid-1960s, they had outgrown their Blackburn works. In 1968, they pur-chased a 54-acre site on the scarred eastern fringes of Blackburn and, in 1970, the Duke of Edinburgh opened their new one million square feet plant. At the time, it was reckoned to be the largest steel stockholding site in the world.

In 1989, the business was boasting sales of £623 million a year, employing 3,400 workers in locations throughout the UK. Walker Steel was hugely profitable. The company soared from success to success. Walker moved to the Channel Isles to become a tax exile and, from an elegant two-storey, stone-built luxury home on Jersey known as Mount Cochon, he issued his orders via the telephone. He had the knack of knowing when to buy and when to sell. It was a simple formula. He bought in at a cer-tain price, stored it in his warehouse and then, when the price went up, he sold. Simple, basic economics. You didn't need an LSE degree to under-stand.

He had also acquired a number of other businesses. There were sub-sidiary interests in property, manufacturing, insurance and an airline known as Jersey European Airways. Since taking it over in 1986, he had already trebled the number of its passengers, while turnover had rocketed from £9 million to £26 million.

Then, in 1989, as the market hit its peak, Walker surprisingly sold his steel company to British Steel for the astonishing sum of £330 million. It was the biggest private company sale in British history and it made Jack Walker a multimillionaire. He was suddenly flush with money. It seemed that everything Jack Walker touched turned to gold.

Step into the boardroom at Ewood Park, home of Blackburn Rovers Football Club and you will see a club with a glorious past. Close your eyes and through the mists of time floats Victorian England. On match days, a welcoming fire crackles in the grate, a bucket of best Lancashire coal piled up nearby. A spread of steaming hot pies and cream cakes adorn the crisply laundered tablecloths that cover the large oak table. A thousand arguments have raged here. There is hot tea by the gallon served by ladies with hard Lancashire dialects and consumed by smart-suited gentlemen with avuncular smiles and soft northern accents. The room is panelled in oak, the ceiling latticed. Trophies, shields and mementoes rest ornately on walnut cabinets, all highly polished and boasting famous victories of yesteryear.

Little has changed in this small corner of England. Outside, Archibald Leitch's famous stand, opened on New Year's Day 1907, towers over its cosy surrounds. And in Kidder Street, at one end of the stadium, you can still see the tramlines and cobble stones. They once made a famous TV commercial here about bread. Brass bands and meat pies, that's what Ewood Park football is about. Or at least it was until Jack Walker arrived with money to spend.

In this tiny outpost of East Lancashire, they still pride themselves on thrift. Times have been hard here. There was mass unemployment during the 1930s and the town's cotton industry was wiped away in the 1960s, so they have every reason to be careful with their cash. And at Ewood Park they've hardly splashed it about either. When Dalglish's old Merseyside sparring partner Howard Kendall was manager here, they asked him to reduce the amount of milk in the players' tea and to post his letters second class. But all that was about to end.

Shortly before 2.00pm on a pleasantly warm October Saturday, Kenny Dalglish stepped from a car outside the Blackburn Rovers ground. Jacket slung casually over his arm, his tie wafting in the breeze, he was besieged by a waiting army of photographers, TV cameramen and journalists, all of whom had been gathering in the Nuttall Road for well over an hour. He could hardly have chosen a better Saturday. There was no first division soccer because of impending internationals and not a game in the second division worth covering. It meant all eyes were on Blackburn, something which had not happened for years. Since midnight, the BBC had been carrying the story in their main news bulletins. There was now little doubt. Kenny Dalglish was about to become the new manager of Blackburn Rovers.

The story had been rumoured for at least a month, but nobody really believed it. Surely it was a flier. Jack Walker was rightly being ambitious, but he did not really have a hope of persuading Dalglish out of semi-retirement. Walker might have had the money, but so too did any number of other clubs. Celtic had been searching for a new manager after sacking Billy McNeill and, not unnaturally, Dalglish's name was linked with his former club. But it never got further than newspaper talk. And when Graeme Souness was named as the new boss at Anfield, everyone expected Dalglish to step into his shoes at Ibrox. But for the second time in their history, Glasgow Rangers failed to come knocking on the Dalglish door. Then Aston Villa were rumoured to have made a bid, followed by the hardest story of them all, an approach by Olympique Marseille, the French champions and European Cup finalists. But nothing had come of that, though Dalglish did meet with Bernard Tapie. And now here was second division Blackburn Rovers with the cheekiest approach of all.

It was a quarter of a century since Blackburn Rovers had last been in the first division. That was back in 1966, the year England captured the World Cup. Five years later, they went tumbling into the third division for a few years before promotion again catapulted them into the second division. But it didn't last long and within four years they were back down. This time it was short-lived and the following season they returned to second division soccer. And that was where they where on Saturday 12 October 1991, the day Kenny Dalglish walked through the main door.

They had been there since 1980, narrowly missing out on promotion on at least half a dozen occasions. Like Liverpool in the late 1950s, they simply could not make that final leap back to the big time. What it needed was a genius to inspire confidence, renew pride and make the town and club believe in itself. Liverpool had Bill Shankly, now Blackburn had Kenny Dalglish.

One of the four big Bs of Lancashire, Blackburn – along with neighbours Bolton, Burnley and Blackpool – had fallen on hard times. Their success and fame went hand in hand with the fortunes of their local economies. During the 1980s, Burnley almost lost its place in the Football League, while Bolton and Blackpool both struggled with undignified spells in the fourth division. The days when Matthews, Finney, Lofthouse, Adamson and Ronnie Clayton plundered the fields of the Football League seemed a distant dream away.

Blackburn had been a cotton town but as the mills closed during the 1960s and 1970s, so the town waned. At its peak in the late 1920s, there were over 200 mills here, with two thirds of the working population employed in textiles. But today, no more than a handful of mills remain. The municipal elegance and pride in the town has all but disappeared. What was once a monument to King Cotton and Lancashire endeavour is now a sad reflection of a past era. Similarly, Blackburn Rovers was a football club with a glorious past but little future.

The Rovers had once been the pride of the Football League. With their neighbours Blackburn Olympic, they had pioneered professional soccer in England and helped transform it from the aristocratic game of the Eton playing fields to the working-class game of northern England. In the millstone grit valleys of Blackburn, Darwen and Accrington, the modern game of soccer evolved.

Blackburn Rovers were formed back in 1875, long before the Football League had even been dreamed of and had entered their first FA Cup competition in 1879. Three years later, they reached the final, only to be beaten 1–0 by the Old Etonians at the Kennington Oval. A year later, Olympic succeeded where Rovers had failed, and so paved the way for the modern game of soccer by beating the Old Etonians 2–1. The Cup came north for the first time. Football would never be the same again. The proud era of the Old Etonians, Oxford University, the Royal Engineers and the Old Carthusians had ended. The men of Lancashire had arrived. A year after Olympic's success, Rovers went even better, winning the FA Cup three years in succession, a feat which to this day remains unique. And in 1890 and 1891, they again won the Cup. Five times in eight years Blackburn Rovers had been winners.

In 1888, the Football League was formed, with Blackburn Rovers one of the founding members. They twice won the League championship, in a second glorious spell shortly before the First World War. But since those Victorian days, Rovers had won the Cup only once prior to Dalglish's arrival. That was in 1928 when they defeated Huddersfield Town 3–1, an occasion fondly remembered by that great walking son of Blackburn and the Lake District, Alfred Wainwright, as 'the greatest moment of my life'. Such is the affection the Rovers can evoke. But there has been little to cheer about since. They made it to Wembley in 1960 with a team that boasted England internationals Ronnie Clayton and Bryan Douglas, as well as Derek Dougan and Peter Dobing, but still lost 3–0 to those other famous cup fighters Wolverhampton Wanderers. Since then, nothing.

Kenny Dalglish must have driven past Blackburn a thousand times, racing up and down the M6 between Glasgow and Liverpool. It's not a natural stopping-off point and certainly not one where you would have expected Dalglish to bury his roots. But after seven months out of football, it was time to return. He had played some golf, improved his swing a little, even hit a hole in one, 197 yards on the 16th green at Hillside in

Southport using a five iron. But while golf was a passion, it was not his lifeblood. Speaking on radio about his interest in golf shortly after his resignation, he let slip a revealing point. 'I enjoy the challenge and the company,' he said. 'And you can't blame anyone else in golf except yourself.' It was Dalglish the private man, preferring his close friends to any wider circle and it was Dalglish the perfectionist preferring to shoulder the blame rather than having to rely on others.

He had begun to miss football almost from the start. It was impossible for him to pick up a paper without glancing at the back pages. After a long family holiday, he returned with the season winding to its climax. He even reappeared at Anfield and joined the team on the coach travelling to Highbury to play a friendly against Arsenal to benefit Ray Kennedy, the former Arsenal and Liverpool player suffering from Parkinson's disease. The club welcomed him, everyone commented on how relaxed he looked, and he chatted amiably about his holiday with the family. Dalglish's recuperation was well under way.

Liverpool lost the League title, managing only seven wins in their remaining 14 games, six of those ending in defeat. When Dalglish had quit they were three points clear of the Gunners at the top of the table and had lost only two games. When the season ended, they trailed Arsenal by seven points. Ronnie Moran stepped into the breach briefly and let it be known that he was a candidate for the job. But the results never worked in his favour. Alan Hansen was another contender, but he quickly ruled himself out and announced that he was retiring as well, injuries having finally caught up with him. He was looking for a career outside football. And, of course, there were other names being bandied about, including John Toshack, Joe Royle, Steve Coppell and even George Graham. Most of it was wild speculation, conjured up in the minds of journalists rather than based on any hard fact.

Liverpool always had their eyes on another man. The name of Graeme Souness had been one of the more obvious suggestions, but Souness appeared to rule himself out of contention. He had a seat on the board Ibrox, a substantial shareholding and a six-figure salary. He also had a close friendship with Rangers' owner David Murray and together they had guided Rangers to three League championships. When Liverpool approached Souness, they discovered that he was indeed keen to return to Anfield, though not until the season had ended. But it was naïve of both Liverpool and Souness to think that they could keep such a deal under wraps. News eventually leaked out before the end of the season and an angry David Murray summoned Souness to a showdown meeting. They agreed to part company immediately. And so, Souness returned to Anfield to take charge as the season wound to its inconsequential end.

Dalglish was pleased to see his old friend back at Anfield and wished him well. They met, chatted about football and enjoyed a meal together. All the time, offers were pouring in to Dalglish. He began writing a weekly column in the *Sunday Scot*, the paper owned by Murray, chairman of Glasgow Rangers, and signed up with ITV as a pundit. But when he appeared for a live Manchester United game, the ITV phone lines were jammed with complaints from United supporters. He was still too closely identified with Liverpool. He also began negotiating to sell his biography, but the price was high and interest was patchy. And of course there were the offers from within the game.

By the beginning of the new soccer season, Dalglish was itching to get back. He turned up at Anfield and sat in the stands; he was seen elsewhere. He even telephoned a few of his TV friends, and asked if any of them wanted him as a TV pundit. He was bored. Then, on 2 September, Blackburn Rovers sacked their manager Don Mackay. During the close season they had spent heavily on new talent. They had made an audacious offer for Gary Lineker, but Spurs turned them down. Ironically, they had bought David Speedie, Dalglish's final signing at Anfield, for £500,000, but results had not matched expenditure. Mackay was the unfortunate scapegoat.

The problem was that while everyone knew that new owner Jack Walker was flush with money, few took his ambitions seriously. He all too easily seemed like another chairman who promised much but would deliver little. Attempting to sign star names looked good in the local press and even warranted a few headlines in the tabloids, but at the end of the day everyone knew that the likes of Gary Lineker were never going to go to Ewood Park. To be taken seriously, Walker had to make a signing that would convince everyone that he meant business, that it was not all bluff. He had to begin at the top. With Mackay gone, he now had to enlist a manager of the highest quality, a man who could reverse the fortunes of Blackburn Rovers and convince the footballing world that Jack Walker meant business. In Jack Walker's mind, there was only one man for the job.

The job was advertised, but Walker already had the name of Kenny Dalglish pencilled in. Within days, an approach was made. It was the beginning of September and Dalglish was on holiday. He was eventually tracked down in Monaco. He listened politely to the offer but said he needed time to think about it. But he was sufficiently interested to leave the door open. He was still not certain that the time was right to return to football management. And his wife, especially, had to be convinced. He had to be sure it was the correct move. After all, Blackburn was a second division club and, unless money was available, it would remain a second division club. Like everyone else, he had his doubts. He would be taking an enormous gamble. If he failed, it could damage his reputation irrevocably. But if he succeeded, it would only enhance his standing. Big-spending businessmen intent on reviving the fortunes of local football clubs have come and gone in the past with a depressing regularity. In the end, the businessmen had usually disappeared, leaving behind a burden of debts, unfulfilled hopes and broken promises.

After walking out on Liverpool at the most crucial point in the season, he had already cast doubts over his own professionalism. Dalglish was all too aware that many a club chairman would be wondering if he might do the same again. Who was to say that the same pressures might not bring about the same result. And there are pressures of one sort or another at every football club, no matter what position they enjoy. At least at Blackburn, Dalglish knew he would face different challenges. There would not be the continual strain of having to win every game. That was the problem of success. Every game Liverpool played was a cup final, there was no letup. Life would be easier at Ewood Park, although there would still be a demand to win promotion. Yet winning promotion would be made considerably easier by the amount of money promised for transfers. In the end, Dalglish figured it was a gamble worth taking.

Dalglish was interested enough to meet up with Walker. He was immediately impressed but told him, 'I can't build a first division outfit from nothing. If that's what you want, it will cost you.' But Walker meant business. He agreed and repeated that money was no problem, he was ready to put his money where his mouth was. Above all, he wanted success for Blackburn Rovers. There would be £3 million a year available for transfers and he intended spending a further £12 million on making Ewood Park a 24,000 all-seater stadium. Dalglish still needed time to consider.

There were further board meetings. Some directors were keen to approach Steve Coppell, the young, intelligent and highly successful manager of Crystal Palace. But Walker insisted that as long as Dalglish was available, he wanted him. By now, September was drawing to a close and Dalglish seemed no nearer making a decision.

But money was talking, though for Dalglish it was not the overriding factor. He was being offered a three-year contract, said to be worth £1 million – even more than the £200,000 a year he was reputedly earning at Anfield. But what probably influenced Dalglish more than anything was Walker's determination and dogged persistence. He refused to take 'no' for an answer, was prepared to accept almost any condition and was ready to invest a considerable amount of his own money in the Ewood Park club.

The negotiations had dragged on for five weeks. Walker did not want to force the Scot's hand, but Dalglish was insisting on a contract that would protect him from the kind of pressures that had occurred at Anfield. Dalglish had one further crucial condition. He wanted to appoint his own assistant, someone of the highest quality. Walker agreed even though Dalglish warned him it might prove expensive. The deal was at last sealed. It was the beginning of October. Blackburn had hoped to make the announcement on Friday 11 October, but there were still minor snags. Finally, on Saturday 12 October, Walker was confident enough to know that Dalglish would take his place in the managerial chair that day. A press conference at Ewood Park prior to Blackburn's meeting with Plymouth Argyle was duly arranged for 2.00pm.

To many people in football, it was surprising that Kenny Dalglish should have struck up a friendship with Ray Harford. It was even surprising to Harford. They appeared to have little in common. Even their football appeared to be at loggerheads. As tacticians they seemed miles apart. Harford, as manager at Luton and then Wimbledon, was not renowned for the style of play he had encouraged. Working with limited, assets he believed in nullifying the opposition, using the long ball, striking from the back rather than the midfield. Dalglish had always been one to develop and encourage flair, preferring ball players to workhorses, signing players like John Barnes and Peter Beardsley. Unlike Dalglish, Harford had not enjoyed a particularly distinguished playing career. Never capped, he had neither been involved in European football, played on the world's great stages, nor alongside major talents. A Yorkshireman, he had instead done the rounds of the lower divisions playing with Charlton, Exeter, Lincoln, Mansfield, Port Vale and Colchester before turning his hand to management. He was a roustabout, a journeyman player. But on his travels he had picked up valuable experience that would put him in good stead as a manager.

Yet despite their different approaches, Dalglish and Harford seemed to respond to each other. Dalglish telephoned regularly. Harford was never quite sure why. They would gossip, talk football, mull over ideas, maybe even swap opinions about players. At the end of their conversations, Harford would replace the receiver and wonder quite why Dalglish had called him. The answer soon became apparent.

Dalglish clearly rated Harford's opinions and talents as a coach and had struck up a liking for the man. They seemed to get on well. If ever he was to be offered another job in football he knew who he would want as his number two. Here was a man he could trust, a man he could delegate responsibilities to. And so, when Jack Walker asked Dalglish to take over at Ewood Park, Dalglish already had the name of Ray Harford marked down. Walker needed little convincing when he suggested Harford. It was going to cost Walker, but so was the whole adventure. In for a penny, in for a pound, was Walker's opinion. Harford also needed little persuading, even though he was going as number two, rather than number one. But the chance to work alongside Dalglish, maybe work a miracle at Blackburn, was an opportunity not to be missed.

And so Dalglish and Harford arrived that muggy October Saturday afternoon at Ewood Park. At a press conference held before Blackburn's clash with Plymouth Argyle, Dalglish once more faced the world's press. But this time it was a far different man from the haunted, agonised face that had stared across a table at them back in February at Anfield. Ray Harford sat to his left, Blackburn's chairman Bill Fox at his right with Jack Walker, the club's president, alongside him. A year before, few people outside rarefied business circles would have known the name Jack Walker. But now everyone knew him. Such is the pulling power of soccer.

Looking tanned and relaxed, Dalglish described his feelings in one word: 'recharged'. Seven months had passed. It had been a holiday, he said. And now he was ready to start work again. Wouldn't anyone after a seven-month break? he asked, a twinkle in his eye. 'Seven months ago, football was not the most important thing in my life,' he added. 'I'd had enough and needed to recharge my batteries. But the time is right to come back.' He confirmed that he had been made other offers but insisted that he could have continued without football. He told another interviewer that he had been 'living in a goldfish bowl of Merseyside soccer.' There had been too many weights on his mind. 'There were scars that take time to heal,' he said.

But why second division Blackburn? inquired one brave journalist. 'They've impressed me,' he answered. 'They're ambitious and want to get into the Premier League.'Whether that can be done immediately is something I cannot guarantee. But I will guarantee this,' he added, 'I will give one hundred per cent to the job and so will everybody else at the club.'

Bill Fox admitted that he was delighted with the signing of Dalglish. 'We at Blackburn Rovers,' he said, 'want to make it to the Premier League. And we want to make it next year. It is now imperative that we move forward quickly.' They were ironic words, given Fox's own position as president of the Football League and his well-known antipathy to the setting up of the Premier League.

Many had wondered if Dalglish would ever return to football, or concentrate instead on his multifarious business activities. The reply was revealing. 'I've been part and parcel of football since I was sixteen,' he said. 'I didn't have much of an academic education. If you are going to make yourself a life you have to do it in the industry in which you are best equipped. Football is the one most suited to Kenny Dalglish.' And he added with a wry grin, 'Anyhow, the wife wanted me out of the house.'

There had been a plan to present Dalglish on the pitch before kick-off but time was running out and chairman Bill Fox was opposed to such hype. A game of football had to be played. Instead, Dalglish pulled on his fashionable overcoat and took his seat in the directors' box alongside Jack Walker, though not before he had acknowledged a tumultuous welcome from the 10,000 crowd. Blackburn promptly put on their best display of the season, thrashing Plymouth 5–2. Dalglish had arrived. Sixty-four days and £2.5 million later Blackburn were top of the second division.

CHAPTER NINETEEN
Welcome To The Cotton Club

From a volley, a sidekick,
A graceful leaping head flick:
Subtle, supple, cunning, quick
Dalglish, sheer football magic.
Alan Bold

It was Don Revie, the former Leeds United and England manager, who reckoned that Dalglish was, in some way, blessed, born to be a winner. And so it proved to be yet again at Blackburn Rovers, the Cotton Club of East Lancashire. No sooner had Dalglish settled into the manager's chair than the odds on Rovers gaining promotion had been slashed. But it wouldn't be easy. In the end, Blackburn would squeeze their way into the newly created Premier League with the narrowest of victories, thanks to a Wembley penalty and the abiding fortune of Kenny Dalglish.

Dalglish's arrival set Blackburn buzzing. Gates soared from an average of 8,000 to over 11,000, up 30 per cent, the biggest rise in the division. The club's souvenir shop was awash with customers and Blackburn's famous blue and white shirts were more widely in evidence on the streets of the town, proudly worn by kids and teenagers alike. The local paper featured a colour pullout and the advertisers were eager to cash in on the Dalglish name. Within weeks, Jack Walker announced plans for a £12 million facelift to Ewood Park, turning Archibald Leitch's grand old design into a 24,000 all-seater stadium that would once more be the pride of the Football League. The big time was coming back to East Lancashire and old boys Ronnie Clayton and Bryan Douglas had to admit a little envy. 'It would be nice to be part of it again,' sighed Clayton.

Expectations were soaring. Yet you could hardly fault Don Mackay's team. They had sweated towards the playoffs three years in succession and, even though they had wasted all three opportunities, it was still an admirable achievement. Mackay's team had cost next to nothing, a bunch of second division vagabonds, compared with what was about to arrive, and it was only since Jack Walker had taken over that any serious money had been spent. Yet during his four years in charge, Mackay had tempted Steve Archibald away from the glamour of the Nou Camp for a short loan as well as the popular Argentinian Ossie Ardiles. Mackay had shown ambition without resources. But his more audacious forays into the transfer market, to try to sign Gary Lineker and Teddy Sheringham, had only produced a few sniggers in the national press. He had even agreed a fee with Everton for Mike Newell only to be embarrassingly rejected by the player. Jack Walker was getting a little weary of his side being called the 'nearly men'. Mackay might have demonstrated a flair for good Lancashire housekeeping, but the truth was that Blackburn Rovers were still little more than a good second division outfit. What's more, the 1991/2 season had kicked off with a barrage of miserable results. Five games in August and not one victory. Mackay had to go.

Dalglish had little time to settle. Although the faltering start to the season had been transformed under caretaker manager Tony Parkes, ten league games had already gone and Blackburn were still wasting in midtable; at one point they had sunk into the relegation zone. Dalglish promised not to act rashly; everyone would have a chance to prove themselves. But something had to be done quickly, a view that was firmly consolidated after Rovers went down 2–1 at Swindon in Dalglish's first game in charge. Within a week, Dalglish and his assistant Ray Harford were spotted in the stands at Bloomfield Road casting an eye over a young Blackpool defender. Days later they splashed out £500,000 on Alan Wright. It was possibly the best slice of business Dalglish would transact all season. It seemed to do the trick instantly. On his debut against Grimsby, the callow youth played as if he had been sporting a Blackburn shirt all year as Rovers chalked up their 1,000th win in the Football League and edged into seventh spot.

By now Dalglish was being linked with every big name in soccer. Ian Rush, Bruce Grobbelaar and Steve McMahon from his former club were reported to be top of his list, while Chris Waddle, Bryan Robson, Paul McStay and a galaxy of other stars would also be linked with him over the next few months. The papers reckoned Blackburn were awash with money. Dalglish was even said to have made a sensational £3 million bid for Southampton's highly rated Alan Shearer. Much of it turned out to be nonsense and Dalglish wondered out loud where they picked up these tales. But there was an element of truth in some names and before the autumn was out Dalglish had taken his spending well over the £2 million mark with the signing of former Ewood favourite Cohn Hendry from Manchester City, Mike Newell from Everton and the experienced Gordon Cowans from Aston Villa.

Results during Dalglish's early days were mixed. After Grimsby came a 1–0 win over Brighton followed by an ignominious 3–0 hammering at Southend. Even the *Blackburn Evening Telegraph* was forced to admit Rovers had been 'abysmal'. Other papers wondered if Dalglish hadn't taken on more than he had bargained for. Dalglish remained confident. 'We can do a lot better,' he urged.

Cohn Hendry's arrival in early November brought some desperately needed strength and organisation to the defence, while a 2–0 win at Charlton, albeit somewhat flattering, helped wipe out the memory of Southend. A debut goal from £1.1 million Mike Newell in a 3–0 win over Barnsley the following week also gave rise to optimism, as Dalglish's blend of youth, experience and proven ability began to pay dividends. Even a goalless draw at Newcastle brought a smile to Dalglish's face. 'The best since I've arrived,' he claimed, heaping praise on his side. And just to prove that he wasn't only interested in big-name signings, he paid a small fee to Drogheda in the League of Ireland for the youngster Gary Tallon. But the cheque book was never far away and the £200,000 signing of Gordon Cowans from Aston Villa at the end of November brought Jack Walker's personal spending to £5 million since he had bought the club, There was more to come.

Cowans's arrival looked a masterstroke. Experienced, authoritative, busy; all he had needed was a change of scenery. It looked as if he might do for

Blackburn what Gordon Strachan was doing for Leeds. In his first game against Middlesbrough, Blackburn turned on the style, overpowering their promotion rivals 2–1 at Ewood Park, with Newell again on target. 'The best yet,' insisted Dalglish. 'The game was a credit to every player.' What's more, 15,000 turned up to applaud. Blackburn was agog. Even the cynics, those who had puffed with delight at the men of the 1950s and early 1960s, were coming back to the terraces. Blackburn were beginning to threaten and had climbed into fourth spot. It was only the end of November and a 3–1 win at Oxford United a few days later shot them to within a whisker of the top of the table.

But the early excitement was soon tinged with sadness. Bill Fox, chairman of the club for ten years and associated with Rovers since 1938, died suddenly on 9 December. After a brief stay in hospital, he had collapsed at his home, just as everyone thought he was on the road to recovery. Fox, who was also president of the Football League, had been instrumental in persuading Jack Walker that Dalglish was their man and had backed Walker's tireless efforts to tempt the Scot out of retirement. At his funeral, Walker wept openly while Dalglish found himself following yet another funeral hearse as it made its final journey.

Days later, Blackburn clambered to the top of the table for the first time in three years with an emphatic 3–0 win over Bristol Rovers. Bill Fox would have been proud. But after a goalless draw at Wolves on Boxing Day where David Speedie missed a late chance, and a 2–1 defeat by promotion rivals Ipswich, Blackburn's grip at the top hooked to be less than secure. On New Year's Day, they made amends for their poor Christmas showing with an impressive 2–1 victory in a top-of-the-table clash with Cambridge. And there was more transfer activity as Russell Beardsmore was signed on a month's loan from Manchester United with a view to a permanent move. But it was a deal that never worked out. After just one appearance, Beardsmore returned to Old Trafford.

Early January and in the FA Cup non-leaguers Kettering Town were the victims, beaten 4–1 after making Blackburn fight every inch of the way. Back in the league, Blackburn's lead over the chasing pack stretched even further when Bristol City came to Ewood Park and were cuffed 4–0, with Mike Newell bagging a couple more. But at Portsmouth a week later, Rovers looked unusually edgy as they tossed aside a comfortable two-goal lead and in the end had to hang on frantically for a 2–2 draw. Fratton Park roared for the first time in years; it was the beginning of their season. But for Blackburn the jitters were starting to show. Yet two weeks later, all seemed to be well again as they beat Swindon 2–1.

The bookies had long given up taking bets on Blackburn. There was little doubt that they were going to be promoted and probably as champions. One local bookmaker calculated that he stood to lose £43,000 if they won the second division title. He claimed to have mixed feelings. But the success of Blackburn and the presence of Dalglish, especially, had its drawbacks.

Blackburn were now the team everyone wanted to beat. They were crowd-pullers wherever they played – 23,000 at Newcastle, 18,000 at Molineux, 17,000 at Ipswich, 20,000 at Portsmouth. For most clubs, the arrival of Blackburn meant the biggest gate of the season, guaranteeing a cup-tie atmosphere. It had always been like that at Liverpool, where everyone had grown up in a pressure cooker atmosphere. But at Ewood Park it was something new and not everyone was accustomed to the burdens of success.

Dalglish himself had learned well from his Liverpool experience. The man who once ruled the Anfield dugout, twitching and fidgeting so anxiously, was now a smartly dressed executive, resplendent in the comfort of the directors' box seated next to his benefactor, Jack Walker. It was Ray Harford and Tony Parkes who barked the orders from the bench. Dalglish was learning to delegate. He had every confidence in his colleagues. It was even suggested, perhaps tongue in cheek, that Dalglish could go on holiday for a week and his absence would not have been critical.

Dalglish had also learned, wisely, to keep the press at arm's length. Interview requests were frequently turned down. Even the popular ITV show, Saint and Greavsie, was refused a request to send a photographer to snap Blackburn's latest signings. Other TV companies were also turned away as Dalglish cleverly kept the spotlight off himself and his players. Yet on a Saturday the press box overflowed, such was Dalglish's pulling power. After the match and after watching Granada's Goals Extra, he would meet with reporters in the little terraced house over the road that had become a makeshift press office.

'He was always on his guard,' says one local journalist, 'Careful not to say anything that might be conjured into a headline or anything sensational.' It was very different from the press briefing he held on a Friday with the local journalists. Just the two Lancashire radio stations, the two local papers and a freelance or two were invited, with Jimmy Armfield of the *Daily Express* getting the occasional welcome. Dalglish trusted them but remained suspicious of the nationals, particularly the tabloids and one or two reporters especially. 'He was always friendly with us,' claimed another local journalist, 'though he never revealed much about his team plans. He usually just talked about the opposition. On a Friday he was always far more relaxed with us than he ever was on a Saturday.'

Behind the scenes, training remained much as it had before. Dalglish was out on the pitch with Harford, Parkes and reserve coach Asa Hartford, enjoying himself. As ever, he was more at home in a pair of football boots and shorts than sitting at a desk. He was popular with the players, especially the younger ones. 'He quickly learned all our names,' remembers one of the youngsters. 'It may not sound particularly important but it was to us.' Even the older players were in awe, eager to testify to the respect that Dalglish commanded. 'At the Saturday afternoon team talk,' vouched the experienced Gordon Cowans, 'everyone sits around and listens, in total silence. You don't often come across that.' Colin Hendry seconded him. A confidence soon began to ooze through the club.

In the fourth round of the FA Cup, Blackburn missed out on the plum draw. There was first division opposition, but it was no Manchester United or Liverpool. Instead, it was Notts County, struggling at the foot of the first division. What's more it was away. Yet it was a useful proving stage for Blackburn, a chance to show that they were ready for the big time. Sadly they failed their test, losing 2–1, but perhaps more importantly, losing David Speedie, sent off with County skipper Phil Turner after a head-butting incident. Speedie vehemently denied the charge. 'It was handbags at forty paces,' he joked. 'And anyhow, if I had butted him he wouldn't have got up.' Dalglish sided with him and launched an unusually bitter attack on the referee and officials.

'You can't even talk to referees now,' he complained. 'If you get into the dressing room and try to speak to them, they ask you to leave. And if you start talking to them you don't get an answer. Football is about players, it's not about officials.'

They were harsh words; they were also unwise ones and Dalglish was lucky to escape the wrath of the Football Association. Speedie was less lucky, banned for three matches: It was his second suspension of the season; this time his presence was to be sorely missed and could have cost Blackburn dearly.

Out of the FA Cup, Blackburn could at least concentrate their thoughts on the league and quickly returned to their winning ways with three outstanding results. First came a 3–2 win at Grimsby; then a 2–0 victory over Derby County to notch up their tenth successive home win and finally a 3–1 defeat of Kevin Keegan's Newcastle, the two famous Liverpool number-7s sizing each other up again. As usual, Dalglish won. But the man who really stole the limelight was David Speedie, slamming in a thrilling hat trick to bring his season's tally to 19 goals.

With Speedie absent for the next three matches through suspension and Newell injured, the cracks inevitably began to show. A goalless draw at Middlesbrough was followed by a 2–1 defeat at Cambridge. Given the quality of opposition, both results were perhaps excusable but a scrappy 1–1 draw at Ewood Park with Oxford United saw their lead at the top dangerously slashed. Dalglish had already plunged into the market in early February, signing another old Ewood favourite, the bubbly defender Chris Price, for £125,000 from Aston Villa. Now he moved in yet again, this time recruiting Tim Sherwood of Norwich for £500,000. But the most expensive buy was QPR's American striker, Roy Wegerle, signed for £1.1 million as a replacement for Newell, who looked to be out for the rest of the season. Wegerle made his debut at Bristol Rovers as David Speedie returned to the attack. But it did little good, Blackburn went down 3–0. They had now taken only two points out of a possible 12.

On the field and on the terraces, panic was beginning to set in. Dalglish tried to remain calm. 'The luck will turn our way,' he argued. 'All we have to do is show the same kind of commitment that we showed in the second half against Bristol Rovers.' He was probably right and at home to Southend a week later they clinched a heartening 2–2 draw, thanks to a late Speedie equaliser, and still clung to their top spot. And when Brighton were beaten 3–0 at the Goldstone, with Colin Hendry at his lucid best, the crisis appeared to have been averted. But it was about to return with a vengeance.

The chasing pack were sniffing blood. A week later, Rovers crashed 2–0 at home to Charlton. Dalglish was furious and even the local papers were forced into posing a few questions. Peter White in the *Blackburn Evening Telegraph* wondered if Dalglish really knew his best 11 players. The team never seemed to be settled, with so much chopping and changing all the time. 'With so many options in a huge squad, sometimes you can't see the wood for the trees,' he suggested.

Dalglish had heard it all before at Anfield, where the criticism had been far more pronounced, far more vocal and more public. It was coming back to haunt him and over the next few weeks he must have wondered why he had ever bothered accepting the job at Ewood Park. Blackburn were under siege, and when Barnsley beat them 2–1 they were off the top with just six points from a possible 24. It was hardly promotion form.

Then, worst of all, on a cold night at bottom-of-the-table Port Vale, they crashed 2–0. Dalglish was fuming; words rattled off the dressing room walls, heads drooped on chests. 'There are a lot of people around who would love to see Blackburn Rovers fail because of jealousy,' he told them. 'The national press put the club on a pedestal and then can't wait to boot it away.' He was angry. 'We are all in it together,' he argued, 'and we have to stick together.' Days later, he even took them off to a secret Scottish hideaway but it still failed to do the trick. In their next fixture, they were beaten 2–1 at Watford, with his own players contributing to Watford's good fortune. By now they had dropped into fourth place and when Wolves came to Ewood Park and won 2–1, Blackburn were in serious trouble, equal fourth with three other clubs. Five successive defeats; the new Premier League looked a million miles away. Dalglish had even forsaken the comfort of the directors' box for the chill and drama of the dugout. He was to remain there for the rest of the season.

Blackburn were in danger of being washed away. Jack Walker's dream of the Premier League was fast disappearing. Dalglish and Harford conferred but remained convinced that their side had the ability. All that was missing was luck. It was roll up your sleeves time and hold your nerve until luck returned. Against Wolves they had lost to an injury time goal and had seen a perfectly reasonable penalty claim turned down. The question was whether luck would return in time.

Some good fortune did come their way. Mike Newell's injury proved not to be so serious and he was back for the visit of Leicester. But even that was not enough to turn the tide. Blackburn lost again, 1–0, and all hope of automatic promotion disappeared. They now had to compete with five other teams for the playoffs. Two days later, on Easter Monday, they forced a 2–2 draw with a lively Tranmere Rovers side at Prenton Park, with Newell hitting the target, and their luck seemed to be changing. Three games to go, could Blackburn at least force their way into the play-offs? The days when they were odds-on favourites for automatic promotion had long passed. Now they needed a minimum of six points from three games and, with two of those games at home, there was every hope. First came Millwall, with Newell and Atkins setting up a 2–1 win. Yet it still looked a tricky task, especially with FA Cup finalists Sunderland about to visit Ewood Park. At the foot of the table, the Wearsiders were fighting for their hives and every player was also playing for his Cup final place. As expected, Sunderland battled every inch of the way and it took a thumping, right-foot drive from Scott Sellars four minutes from time to keep Blackburn's hopes alive as they drew 2–2. There was one more league game left, a visit to Plymouth, who would be relegated unless they won. It was where Dalglish had come in almost seven months previously, arriving at Ewood Park on that pleasant autumn afternoon to see Rovers trounce Plymouth 5–2. It was make or break for Dalglish and Blackburn. Some tabloids even suggested that Dalglish's job was on the line but there was never any truth in it. Yet it went without saying that the last thing anyone at Ewood Park fancied was another season in the second division. David Speedie for one was not going to allow that to happen. Just when he was most needed, Speedie popped up with the goods, slamming in a hat trick in a 3–1 win.

Blackburn were into the playoffs by the skin of their teeth. A few weeks earlier, as they crashed to their sixth successive defeat, it had looked a hopeless, if not lost, cause. But, just as dramatically, the timely return of David Speedie had catapulted them into a semi-final against Derby County. But Speedie's part in the drama had only just begun. The man Dalglish had signed to resurrect Liverpool's flagging season a year previously was about to fire Blackburn into the Premier League. Dalglish had come in for considerable criticism after signing the tough little Scot at Anfield. They had said he was too old, too costly and, what's more, he was a Scot when what Liverpool needed most were young, English legs. The criticism had grated. Speedie owed him, and he was about to repay him the debt. It was Blackburn's fourth appearance in the playoffs, something of a record, though their record of three successive defeats was hardly an enviable one.

The drama hadn't finished. At Ewood Park in the first leg, on a pulsating night, Derby stormed into a two-goal lead within 15 minutes with strikes from Gabbiadini and Johnson. It looked to be all over for Blackburn. Then Sellars made it 2–1 in the 35th minute and, just before half time, Newell pounced to drag the two sides level. But the second half belonged to one man: David Speedie. Two goals inside five minutes halfway through the half settled it for Blackburn. By then they were rampant and might well have had six. As it was, the score remained at 4–2 and few doubted that Blackburn were into the final, though they still had to visit the Baseball Ground.

Dalglish took to the dugout for the return leg. It was just as well, as his side were about to come under fire. Derby might not have beaten Blackburn for 15 years, but in the 23rd minute they shot into a one goal lead. Derby powered forward, Speedie was booked along with two other Blackburn players and it began to look as if Blackburn were about to lose their nerve. But then, minutes after the interval, Kevin Moran charged up-field to scoop a loose ball into the back of the net: 1–1. A minute later, Speedie was upended in the area only to see the referee wave play on. A revitalised Blackburn were surging ahead confidently, but not for long. In the 73rd minute, Ted McMinn restored Derby's lead and it was all change. For the next 15 minutes, Blackburn were on the rack as Derby searched frantically for a third goal that would take the game into extra time. They struck the bar, Rovers kicked off the line, Gabbiadini was felled in the area, chances fell here, there and everywhere. But at the end of the day, the gods were with Blackburn. They were through to the final.

A heatwave had struck the land; two weeks of dripping heat. The sun locked high in the May skies, glaring and dazzling, and the temperature on the pitch at Wembley as Rovers and Leicester walked through the dark concrete tunnel into the blaze of light was close on 85 degrees. Rarely can the old stadium have been so stifling and airless on a May afternoon. In the space of a fortnight, Liverpool, Barcelona, Sampdoria, England and Brazil had graced its lawns and now Blackburn Rovers. Blackburn were up there with the best of them, just like the old times. But Dalglish was not leading his men out. That task was given to coach Tony Parkes. Dalglish, in blue T-shirt, shorts and trainers, took a back seat, maintaining his now customary low profile. With Liverpool he had always led his men out, proud and smart, marching his team into the cauldron of Wembley. But these were different days. He knew the cameras would have been pointed at him, their lenses peering and invading. It was to be avoided. And anyhow the popular Parkes deserved much credit. So Dalglish made his way quietly to the bench, Ray Harford at his side.

In the first half, both sides edged towards each other nervously, shy of risking too much, waiting instead for the moment when a guard had been dropped. But there were few such occasions. And then, with Dalglish looking at his watch, rehearsing his halftime talk, David Speedie was sent sprawling as he broke into the box by Steve Walsh's right arm locked across his chest. There was no question that it was a penalty and referee George Courtney, about to bow out of football, pointed without hesitation to the penalty spot. Ironically, it was Courtney who had awarded a penalty against Rovers three years previously in the final game of the season at Crystal Palace, a penalty that denied Blackburn promotion. This time Mike Newell stepped up and coolly fired the ball into the corner of the net, the goalkeeper diving in the opposite direction. What a moment to score. Seconds later, the whistle had gone and Dalglish was rewriting his dressing room oration.

If the first half had been all sweetness and shyness, the second half was fury and thunder as Leicester charged at Rovers. Three times Blackburn cleared off the line, but Moran and Hendry held their nerve, heading up-field, flicking the ball forward, even kicking it into touch, anywhere for safety. There was no doubt that Leicester were unlucky. Even in the last minute they found the strength and the opening to almost upset Blackburn's day. By then, Rovers might well have been two up had Newell not missed a second penalty, after he himself had been upended by the goalkeeper. Again Newell stepped up, stroking his spot kick towards the corner of the net. But this time Carl Muggleton guessed correctly; diving to make a comfortable save. Dalglish's heart wobbled. Was this to be a turning point? No, Blackburn hung on and after two minutes' stoppage time, George Courtney finally blew an end to a long, hard season. Newell's 46th-minute strike had been worth its weight in gold. Dalglish beamed, the old familiar smile of Wembley victory etched on his face. Up in the stands, benefactor Jack Walker hugged Marina Dalglish. The lad had done it again. What's more, he had come through 90 personally testing minutes unscathed. He had learned his lessons well. The Midas touch had not escaped him.

There were many who would have liked to have seen Dalglish take a fall: those who reckoned he was buying his way into the Premier League, those who thought he was overrated, those who had never forgiven him for his successes at Anfield. Alan Hansen for one was convinced that the knives were out for Dalglish. Former Blackburn manager Don Mackay graciously reminded people that while money was an important component, more important was the way you spent it. Even on Merseyside, there were a few who did not wish to see him succeed. There were more than a handful of managers in the top division who also dreaded his return. But he was coming back. In three months' time, he would be there again, no doubt yelling, wincing, pointing, or nervously fidgeting from the bench or the touchline, revisiting his old haunts: Highbury, Old Trafford, Goodison and, of course, Anfield. The thought of Dalglish in the opposition dugout at Anfield was barely imaginable. But he would be there and, no matter what the sentiment, Dalglish would forever remain the professional.

As Dalglish excitedly congratulated his Blackburn players in the Wembley sunshine, a television journalist asked him if he was pleased he had proved himself. Dalglish looked him in the eye. 'I don't need to prove myself to anybody,' he replied. And nor did he. It summed up the man perfectly.

CHAPTER TWENTY
The Return Of
The Prodigal Son

Arte et Labore
Motto, Blackburn Rovers Football Club

Who would have guessed? Just 22 months after walking out on Liverpool Football Club, Dalglish was back at soccer's citadel. But this time, on a winter's afternoon that was beginning to turn raw, he was not heading for the home dressing room or for his traditional spot in the dugout. Instead he was closeted in the visitors' dressing room and bound for the opposition bench. Nor was he returning with one of soccer's more fashionable clubs.

When Dalglish quit Liverpool they had a three-point lead at the top of the first division while Blackburn Rovers, a club with a rich heritage but seemingly little future, were struggling to stay out of the third division. The contrast could hardly have been more marked. Yet, almost two years later, it was Blackburn who had title aspirations while Liverpool languished in mid-table anonymity.

It was not the first time Dalglish had been back to Anfield. He had returned to see the occasional match before joining Blackburn, and had even accompanied his second team to the ground for a game against Liverpool reserves. But this time it was different. This time he was facing his public, the fanatical Liverpool supporters, more than 16,000 of them crammed into the Kop. Anfield was a cauldron with the total attendance a little over 43,000, making it the biggest gate at any Premier League game since its inception. And, of course, the press were eagerly anticipating his return to the club with which he would always be associated. For days the back pages had talked of little else. What would Dalglish feel? How would the fans react? Could his new side surprise soccer's supremos? The papers were full of the expected sentimentality.

Dalglish reacted in his usual taciturn manner. 'I haven't a clue what sort of reception I shall get,' he told his local paper, adding that 'this is the first time that I have been back to Anfield in opposition. It's also the first time since August 1977, when I joined Liverpool, that I shall be hoping that they lose.'

It was the day every Liverpool fan had pencilled in their diaries since the fixtures had been published back in July. Inside Anfield, Dalglish was warmly greeted. Old friends shook his hand, the tea ladies gave him his usual brew, former playing colleagues joked with him. There were smiles, slaps on the back and even a photograph with the new Liverpool manager. It was just like being back where he belonged – but of course that was no longer the case. Once the backslapping was over, he had to go to the strange surroundings of the visitors' dressing room to prepare for taking on and defeating his former colleagues.

But that was all behind the scenes. The moment everyone had been anticipating was when Dalglish emerged from the tunnel and climbed the steps that would bring him out on to the Anfield pitch. It was a walk he had made a thousand times, occasionally nervous, always cautious but never with quite the trepidation of this shivery Sunday afternoon. And this time there would certainly be no superstitious touching of the 'This is Anfield' sign.

And, waiting to greet him were the paparazzi, the largest pack of photographers Anfield had seen in years. Dalglish left it until the final moment, seconds before the kick-off, then suddenly the flashing lights told their story. King Kenny was about to make his entrance. For Liverpool fans it was impossible to know how to respond. Every eye in Anfield was focussed on the tunnel. And as the former manager appeared, a roar erupted from the Kop. But it lasted only a few seconds, perhaps more out of the novelty of the occasion than out of enthusiasm and, after a quick chant of his name, came an equally brisk call for the new manager. Football fans can be fickle, and it was that kind of season for Liverpool.

There were still many with conspiratorial memories who had never fully forgiven Dalglish for deserting their cause. Since he had abandoned Anfield, Liverpool's fortunes had ebbed. When Dalglish left they had been top of the league, three points ahead of Arsenal. They had not been in pole position since. True, they had gone on to win the FA Cup under new manager Graeme Souness but now, as Christmas 1992 approached, Liverpool were in dire trouble, battling against the unthinkable: relegation. It was hardly Dalglish's fault, yet there were plenty who were ready to point the finger of blame at the ex-manager, rather than look at the present incumbent. Even Souness had been quick to point out that he had inherited an ageing team. Dalglish was their scapegoat, an easy target.

Dalglish came not in search of fuss, nor accolades. No way was he ever going to stride across the Anfield pitch and take a salute in the way that Malcolm Allison once had when returning to Maine Road. Dalglish was now in charge elsewhere. His heart may have still belonged to Liverpool, but Jack Walker paid his wages now and that was where his loyalty lay.

In the cauldron of Anfield there was only ever going to be one winner that day. Liverpool and the Kop were hyped up for the occasion. In the second half, they stormed into the lead with a goal from substitute Mark Walters, though a sudden stunning goal from Alan Shearer quickly levelled the score. Mark Walters added a second with just six minutes remaining and the Kop went home happy to have put one over their former hero. It only added to the belief that heroes are built for toppling.

Yet Dalglish was more than magnanimous towards his old colleagues. 'They were generous to me when I played here and when I managed here and they carried it on today,' he said. 'I said at the time when I left the club that Liverpool would never leave me although I was leaving them. I don't see any reason why I should be thinking any differently after today.'

For Dalglish, the ordeal was over. He may have lost on the playing field, but he had passed another test. He had faced the Kop for the first time and had overcome all the hype that surrounded his return to Anfield. It had been a personal battle for him. Now he could get back to concentrating on Blackburn's assault on the Premier League title.

Dalglish had already set the new Premier League alight in its initial season. The first league table revealed Rovers at the top. After a 3–3 draw at Crystal Palace, Blackburn had picked up wins against Arsenal, Manchester City, Coventry, Nottingham Forest and then, most spectacularly, against Arsenal again, this time at Highbury. It was an exciting start and it was eight games before Blackburn suffered their first defeat, when Dalglish took his side to Goodison Park. It would then be another nine games before they lost again. In between came a spectacular 7–1 thrashing of table topping rivals Norwich City and a goalless draw against eventual champions Manchester United. Blackburn were on their way, already being tipped as potential champions. While Dalglish was firing up his side in the dressing room, the one man who was firing them up on the field was Alan Shearer.

Shearer was the name on everyone's lips, the natural successor in the England side to Gary Lineker. He was powerful and possessed a natural goalscorer's instinct, although still only 21. Dalglish had long been an admirer of the Southampton number 9. Even at Liverpool he had taken more than one glimpse at the young man but with an abundance of shooting power at Anfield he had hesitated at the likely asking price. He had made enquiries throughout the 1991/2 season, but Southampton were not selling and with Blackburn still in the second division there would have been little hope of persuading Shearer to join them. But now it was different. Blackburn were in the Premier League and as ambitious as any club. However, by the summer of 1992, the price was even higher. Southampton were demanding a record transfer fee.

With just about every club in the league coveting the young striker, Southampton decided to cash in their asset. Manchester United were first off the mark and were told it would cost them in the region of £3.5 to £4 million. Alex Ferguson was taken aback but still approached his board. They were hesitant, so was he. Then there were the wages. Not only would Shearer end up as the most expensive player in Britain but also as possibly the highest paid. United pulled out of the race, reluctant to disrupt their pay structure. Southampton knew that, with Blackburn interested, they could stick with their £4 million demand. It was a game of poker but there was never really any doubt that Shearer would wind up at Ewood Park. Jack Walker had the money and Dalglish had the ambition.

Dalglish met with Shearer and had little trouble in convincing the Southampton man that his future lay north of Manchester. 'It wasn't the money,' Shearer later insisted. 'It was the prospect of working with Dalglish that persuaded me to come here.' However, Dalglish was in a position to resolve any of his financial concerns. Within days Shearer was a Blackburn man, signed for a British record fee of £3.3 million, smashing the previous record by half a million pounds.

But as Shearer walked in one door, out of the other walked an angry David Speedie, cast aside by Dalglish. Speedie was devastated. After scoring 23 goals in 36 games to help shoot Blackburn into the Premier League, Dalglish told him that he was no longer wanted. He was going in part exchange for Shearer, as Southampton manager Ian Branfoot was insisting that Speedie be part of the deal. Dalglish's hands were tied. If he wanted Shearer he had to part with Speedie. There was a heated exchange between Dalglish and Speedie, but in the end Speedie had to accept that his manager had little option. It would not be the only time that season when a player was transferred against his will. Roy Wegerle was another who would react angrily at having to quit Ewood Park.

Shearer was not the lone new face at Ewood Park during the season. Dalglish was dealing in the transfer market like a frantic trader on the Stock Exchange. Eleven players were signed, among them Stuart Ripley from Middlesbrough for £1.2 million, Swede Patrick Andersson from Malmo for £800,000, Kevin Gallacher from Coventry for £1.5 million and Graeme Le Saux from Chelsea for £650,000. Also joining them were Lee Makel, Wayne Burnett, Nicky Marker, Simon Ireland, Norwegian Henning Berg, and Australian goalkeeper Frank Tahia. The total cost of his deals for the season reached a staggering £9 million. Few clubs throughout Europe could outgun Blackburn in the transfer market.

Meanwhile other players were unloaded. Besides Speedie, out went Paul Shepstone, Scott Sellars, Duncan Shearer, Chris Sulley, Simon Garner, Lee Richardson, Keith Hill, Craig Skinner, Nicky Reid, Stuart Munro, Steve Agnew, Chris Price, Steve Livingstone and, most surprising of all, Roy Wegerle. The total income from his 15 sales was £3.3 million, giving him a season's loss in the transfer market of £5.7 million.

Walker's bank account and Dalglish's dealings in the market had given Rovers the edge in signing quality players over even Liverpool, Arsenal and Manchester United. If Dalglish wanted a player, Walker had the money to guarantee his signature. It would become even more apparent at the end of the season. Week after week, Dalglish was linked with the best: Frank Rijkaard, David Platt, Les Ferdinand, Des Walker, Craig Short, Geoff

Thomas and even the Moscow Dynamo goalkeeper. They were all rumoured to be on Dalglish's shopping list or on their way to Ewood Park.

Jack Walker's commitment to Blackburn's finances soon became clear when the club's latest annual report was published at the beginning of 1993. Not only had the company's capital share value been increased from £80,000 to £25 million but Walker now owned 99 per cent of all shares in Blackburn Rovers. The company had been signed over to Rosedale (JW) Investments Ltd which, in effect, was now Rovers' parent company. Walker had pumped in just over £12 million to cover what was an overall loss on ordinary activities before taxation of £7.9 million. The deficit had been caused primarily by the club's extravagant dealings in the transfer market, yet the figures only related to the year ended 30 June 1992, before the signing of Shearer, Ripley, Gallacher and company. Walker might have regarded it as business, but it was hard to see it as anything other than an expensive hobby. It was clear that Walker's commitment would have to be ongoing. Take Walker's millions away and Blackburn Rovers might disappear under a mountain of debts.

And nor did the deficit take into account Walker's proposal to build a new 30,000 all-seater, super stadium at Ewood Park, a ground which he claimed would be fit to house the championship. Work had already begun on building a new stand at the Darwen End and, at the close of season, the opposite end was scheduled for demolition. After that Nuttall Street would go. There was even talk of a railway station being constructed next to the ground. The estimated cost for the entire project was £12 million. Jack Walker had become the Berlusconi of British football; and every small club longed for its own Jack Walker.

From the start Shearer was explosive. There were two goals on his debut and one in the following match. Between mid-September and mid-October he netted in six successive games, scoring a further eight goals to give him a total of 13 even though the season had barely kicked off. There was no stopping Shearer, and suddenly his £3 million-plus price tag seemed cheap, with Blackburn having swept stylishly to the top of the table. Dalglish had only been at Ewood Park for 12 months and they had shot from the depths of the second division to the head of the Premier League. From the very beginning, Blackburn were up with the pack chasing honours. Along with Manchester United, Norwich and Aston Villa they vied for pole position, rarely out of the top three until disaster struck at Christmas. Two weeks after going down to Liverpool, they defeated the reigning champions Leeds United, but lost Alan Shearer with a knee injury. He returned a few weeks later, playing for just 30 minutes against Cambridge United in the Coca-Cola Cup only to limp off and end up on the operating table. It was to be the last time he would play that season. Shearer had netted 22 goals, 16 in the Premier League, plus another six in the Coca-Cola Cup, to make him the league's leading goalscorer for much of the season.

Blackburn battled along bravely at first, but then came a miserable spell towards the end of January when they lost four games in succession, three in the league – including a 2–5 hammering at home by Coventry – and a 2–4 pummelling in the first leg of the Coca-Cola Cup semi-final at Ewood Park that left them with an impossible mountain to climb at Hillsborough.

As the season wound to its conclusion, Dalglish found himself the subject of unexpected press speculation that once again centred around Liverpool Football Club. The traumas of Liverpool had continued unabated throughout the season. They had struggled in the lower half of the table for much of the time and had dramatically crashed out of the FA Cup at the first hurdle, knocked out by second division Bolton Wanderers at the usually impregnable Anfield. Liverpool had also gone out of the Coca-Cola Cup at an early stage, leaving the Merseyside club with nothing to fight for except their pride.

It was the worst campaign Liverpool had experienced since the early 1950s and Graeme Souness was having to shoulder the blame as the new manager. The knives were being publicly sharpened and Souness looked all set to be on his way from Anfield. It seemed such a foregone conclusion that the press were already speculating on who his successor might be. Even the normally cautious Liverpool papers had confidently reported his sacking. And, of course, the name on everyone's lips was Kenny Dalglish. Speculation was further heightened when Dalglish was spotted in Spain one weekend at Marbella's exclusive Harbourside Bar in animated discussion with the Liverpool chairman David Moores and a fellow director, Terry Smith. The press believed that this was a secret meeting set up to iron out details of Dalglish's transfer back to Anfield. The truth was much more mundane: it was no more than a golfing weekend that had been arranged months before.

It was inevitable that Dalglish should have been seen as a possible successor to Souness and it may well have been that Liverpool did make an approach but it was never a realistic possibility. Dalglish had a new life and was perfectly content with it: the agonies of Anfield were behind him and he had settled into the homeliness of Ewood Park. Blackburn were making steady progress; Jack Walker was more than satisfied with his young protégé and Dalglish had assembled around him a team that were capable of staking a claim to honours. What's more, he had a backroom staff that allowed him the luxury of taking off to Spain for a weekend without the worry of what might happen in his absence.

Had Dalglish been tempted by the idea, his friends and family would have soon dissuaded him. He had learned from the experience of Howard Kendall, who had dramatically returned to Everton, the scene of so many past glories, but had struggled to rekindle the same success. Dalglish himself was quite clear in his own mind. When asked by pressmen if he was about to return to Anfield his reply was short and to the point: 'Are you joking? What's it got to do with me?'

Had he gone back, he would have found a very different Anfield to the one he left. There was a new chairman, new training routines and a set of players he would have barely recognised. Even the famous bootroom had been torn down. The old-style Liverpool of Shankly, Paisley and Fagan had all but disappeared. Dalglish may have begun a quiet revolution during his term as manager, but Souness had initiated an earthquake.

Dalglish and Blackburn had one more starring role to play that season. They had a date at Old Trafford with Manchester United when United were due to be crowned the first kings of the Premier League. It was hardly the kind of occasion for a visiting side. It would have rankled even more with Dalglish not only to see Liverpool's fiercest rivals handed the new trophy, but also, as a Blackburn man who had contested the title for so long, to see someone else crowned. Just over 40,000 packed inside Old Trafford for the party and, although Blackburn threatened to spoil the fun with an early goal, the guests ran out 3–1 losers. And, in scenes that would have made even Anfield proud, United stepped up to receive their award after 26 years.

Dalglish put on a brave face. He congratulated United manager Alex Ferguson and his team and then typically explained that he reckoned Blackburn's achievements were every bit as impressive as those of United. 'It was our first season in the Premier League,' he explained, 'and we have contested the title. We finished fourth and that is an incredible achievement, in my opinion even better than United's achievement.'

Dalglish had laid the foundations of a side for the future and, had Alan

Shearer not been so cruelly injured over Christmas, Blackburn might well have gone on to contest the title more keenly. There are those who would point to Jack Walker's money, suggesting that this was the sole reason behind Blackburn's success, yet Alex Ferguson had spent as much in building his championship side. Nobody was making the same accusation against him.

Blackburn had ended the season in glorious style, winning eight out of their last ten games. Their season had been much the same as the previous campaign, beginning on a high note with a rocky patch in the middle before ending impressively. With Shearer ready to return for the 1993/4 season, Blackburn would be a hefty proposition for any Premier League side. But, in truth, they were probably a player or two short of a championship side. What was needed was a quality midfielder to create chances through the middle for Shearer. Dalglish had already been told by Walker that he had an open chequebook to sign the right man.

Dalglish's career had come a long way, from the humble block of flats overlooking Ibrox to a multimillion-pound purse at Blackburn. En route as a player he had collected European Cup medals, a century of goals north and south of the border, league championship and cup winning medals in both Scotland and England, plus a record number of caps for Scotland. And, as a manager, he had pulled off the Double in his first season. For one so young, it was an impressive list of campaign medals. But the battles had taken their toll. War weary, he had backed away from another stressful season at Anfield.

But there was no doubting that he was now a changed man. Eight months out of football and the more relaxed, cosy world of Blackburn had recharged his batteries. Everyone noticed it, even the journalists usually at the sharp end of so many of his barbed comments now found an almost happy-go-lucky character, joking, grinning and signing autographs. And nowhere had all this been more evident than that day at Anfield when Dalglish returned with his new charges. The man doing most of the worrying that day was not Dalglish but his successor, Graeme Souness.

Dalglish was still a private man, still capable of a cutting comment to a journalist, still reticent about naming his side before 2.00pm, still as controversial with some of his team selections and still as stubbornly convinced as to the sense of his own ideas. But the experience he had gone through at Anfield had probably left him a wiser and more thoughtful person. In his 18 months at Ewood Park, he had taken Blackburn into the

Premier League, had topped the table for a time and almost taken the club into Europe, as well as taking the side to the semi-finals of the Coca-Cola Cup and a quarter-final replay in the FA Cup. It had been the most astonishing period in the club's 117-year existence. All that remained now was for him to prove that he could fill the old Ewood Park boardroom with trophies in the same way as he had filled the trophy rooms at Parkhead and Anfield. Few doubted that he would.

CHAPTER TWENTY-ONE
The Five-Year Plan

Four thousand holes in Blackburn, Lancashire.
The Beatles

When Dalglish and Jack Walker shook hands on their partnership that warm October afternoon before the cameras at Ewood Park, there was no public talk of how long it might take to put Blackburn back at the top. Walker wisely did not want to put any pressure on Dalglish and had there been any suggestion that he had a fixed plan in mind, Dalglish would have immediately bolted for the door. But privately Jack Walker reckoned on taking Blackburn to the top in five years. It was an ambitious plan, especially with Blackburn still hovering in the middle of the old second division. Indeed, had his plans been made public, many might have dismissed them as the rantings of a rich man, a man with too much money in his pocket who didn't really understand what he was taking on. So, as the press squeezed around Walker and Dalglish, nobody was putting a date on how long it might take. 'It will take as long as is necessary,' insisted Walker.

Walker had promised to finance the rebirth of Blackburn and so far had been true to his word. When Dalglish wanted money to buy players,

Walker had signed the cheques without blinking. Walker's money and Dalglish's magic were doing the trick. So far they had won promotion to the top division and in their first season had finished in fourth place, even showing enough potential early on by briefly topping the table. Champions Manchester United, however, were reminding them that success does not come overnight.

As Dalglish reflected on the season, he recognised that he needed to strengthen his squad if he was to make a genuine tilt at the title. Players had to go and new ones had to be recruited. What he needed more than anything was a strong midfielder, a player who could win the ball and move it forward with pace. And so the hunt was on that summer for a quality midfielder. But Blackburn would have to wait. It would not be until October that Dalglish finally won his man, David Batty of Leeds United. Batty would cost Blackburn £2.75 million, making him the second most expensive player at Ewood Park. Weeks earlier, Dalglish had also recruited Paul Warhurst from Sheffield Wednesday for £2.65 million. Warhurst was another midfielder, but unfortunately he was to be injured early in the season, missing virtually the entire campaign.

Most followers of the game were aghast at Dalglish's spending, but he was not always successful. Occasionally, players would not quite fulfil expectations. Some were recruited to do a specific job and, when better players became available, were discarded. Roy Wegerle and Steve Livingstone had both been moved on in March 1993, bringing in £1.7 million. And before the season was out Dalglish would have spent heavily in the market again. Failures were quickly rejected. Players like Scott Sellars and David Speedie, whom he had inherited, were soon sold while his own signings – Gordon Cowans, Roy Wegerle and Alan Wright – were moved on as soon as they had served their purpose. Dalglish had learnt from his Anfield days that if a better player became available, you had to be in the market for them. If the new man was no better than the player you already had, there was no point in bothering. The tabloids would link Dalglish to almost every transfer-listed player in the land, as well as anyone who showed a spark of talent. But Dalglish's forays into the transfer market were not reckless. Dalglish knew the value of money far too well ever to waste it.

The injury to Alan Shearer had undoubtedly robbed Blackburn of the chance to make a more serious challenge for the title during the 1992/3 season, though even in his first season the former Southampton man had netted 22 goals. Much more was expected of him as the 1993/4 season kicked off and nobody would be disappointed.

Blackburn were off to a flyer, chalking up an impressive 2–1 win at Chelsea in their opening fixture. But in the next game, at home to Norwich, they came down to earth with a bump. The Canaries, in confident mood, ran out 3–2 winners at an Ewood Park resembling a building site. Walker was now investing his millions, not just in building a team, but in constructing a stadium fit to house a team of champions. New stands were shooting up to make Ewood Park an all-seater stadium. But at the ground that evening Walker must have wondered if it was all worth it.

The defeat by Norwich was a depressing result, but at least there was something to cheer as Shearer returned from his long-term injury, coming on as a second-half substitute. A few days later Rovers were at home again, this time with a Lancashire derby against another small-town club, Oldham. Blackburn won 1–0 and then travelled down the road to Manchester City where Mike Newell and Kevin Gallacher gave them a comfortable 2–0 victory. It might even have been more but for Newell missing a penalty. From there, Blackburn travelled to Newcastle. Andy Cole soon put United ahead but Alan Shearer, back on his own patch, came on as a substitute and proved that he was back to form by latching on to a long ball to net his first goal of the season. It was to be the first of many. Blackburn settled for the draw, with the league table at the end of August putting them in sixth place behind leaders Manchester United.

September began with a 1–1 draw against Arsenal at Ewood. Dalglish had again opted for a cautious approach, leaving Shearer on the subs' bench, though caution looked to have been cast aside a few days later when he paid out a massive £2.65 million for Paul Warhurst. Next in line for Rovers was a trip to the manager's former stamping ground, Anfield, and this time it was with more success than the previous season. Liverpool, after a bright start, had hit a bad patch, which was not helped by Mike Newell, who scored the only goal of the game from a corner. Anfield might not have been the fortress it used to be, but it was still a noteworthy occasion for any team to come away with all three points.

September continued with defeat at West Ham as the Hammers introduced three new signings, including Lee Chapman, who scored on his debut. That was followed by a 1–0 win over Bournemouth in the Coca-Cola Cup, a game marked by Alan Shearer's appearance from the very start and, of course, an Alan Shearer goal. A few days later he was on target again, equalising against Sheffield Wednesday at Ewood Park as Wednesday stole a 1–1 draw. It was a result that left Blackburn in eighth place, some way behind United. If Dalglish was worried he didn't show it. The side was still evolving and it was still only two years since he had rolled up at Ewood Park himself.

With Shearer now buzzing up front, October produced an improved run of results. Bottom-of-the-table Swindon were brushed aside, although at the cost of losing new recruit Paul Warhurst with a broken leg. Then came a disappointing goalless draw with Sheffield United at home, followed by a more thrilling 3–3 draw at Leeds United. Blackburn, two goals up at one point, allowed Leeds back into the game with a penalty and then a last-minute equaliser. David Batty came on for Leeds that day as a substitute. Little did he know that not only would it be his last appearance for Leeds, but that days later he would be signing for Blackburn.

Batty duly made his debut in a Blackburn shirt in a 1–0 win at Ewood over Tottenham Hotspur, with Spurs keeper Erik Thorstvedt denying Blackburn time and again. Shearer hit his ninth of the season but it still left Rovers trailing Manchester United by a massive 11 points. The Premiership race already looked to be all over. Days later Dalglish was spending again, this time signing Tim Flowers, the agile Southampton goalkeeper, for £2.4 million – a record for that position. It took Dalglish's spending at Blackburn to more than £20 million. Flowers had looked set to join Liverpool, but a last-minute bid by Dalglish soon had Flowers rethinking. Current goalkeeper Bobby Mimms, who had been at Ewood Park prior to Dalglish's arrival, had served the club well but, as Dalglish knew, an outstanding keeper could mean the difference between finishing first or second.

Ironically, Flowers made his debut against his former club Southampton at Ewood Park, with Shearer putting Blackburn ahead from the penalty spot before volleying one of the goals of the season from a Gallacher cross to give Rovers the three points. Shearer struck two more a few days later in the frost and mist at Ewood, but it still left Blackburn trailing United by 15 points.

December began with defeat in the Coca-Cola Cup by Tottenham, followed by wins over Chelsea, Oldham and Manchester City in the Premiership, before Rovers travelled to Old Trafford on Boxing Day to take on United. Blackburn might have begun the day as underdogs, but in the end they came away cursing themselves after giving away a last-minute equaliser. Kevin Gallacher had earlier put them ahead, slipping the ball through Pallister's legs before slamming it through Schmeichel's legs as well. Dalglish was thrilled by this, but much less thrilled at United's scrambled goal. The year ended with a 2–0 win over Everton and two more Alan Shearer goals.

On New Year's Day, a crowd of over 40,000 turned up at Villa Park to see Blackburn's multimillion pound outfit, now one of the attractions of the Premiership. And nor did they disappoint, with Shearer again on target, as Rovers snatched a 1–0 win. Yet, despite all their endeavours, Dalglish's men were still 13 points off the top of the table, though by now they had climbed into second spot and looked to be United's most dangerous rivals. There were also wins at Sheffield United and over Leeds at Ewood Park. Sheffield United had had the temerity to go ahead, but in the end a couple more Alan Shearer goals and two players being sent off was just too much for Sheffield. Shearer also hit a brace against Leeds. In early February, he was on target again in a 3–0 win over Wimbledon, though Jason Wilcox's long-range thunderbolt into the top corner was a goal to remember. On the debit side, Blackburn lost Tim Sherwood with a dislocated shoulder.

But if there was success in the league, Blackburn's cup luck deserted them yet again. It was fraught from the beginning as Portsmouth held them to a 3–3 draw at Ewood. But in the replay Blackburn romped home 3–1 to raise everyone's hopes. In the fourth round, they were drawn against Charlton Athletic and, after a goalless draw in London, it looked odds-on that Rovers would go into the fifth round. But Charlton had other ideas and, in one of the shocks of the competition, Blackburn went down to the only goal of the game.

Dalglish was as puzzled as anyone. All he could do was to shrug his shoulders and urge his players to put it behind them. And so they did, bouncing back with a 2–0 win against Tottenham, thanks to Alan Shearer's 50th goal for the club. Blackburn were going well and in mid-February notched their 10th league win in 11 games when they beat Newcastle United 1–0 at home. A few days later against Norwich, a team that earlier in the season had given Rovers something of a footballing lesson, Rovers scrambled a 2–2 draw. Chris Sutton scored twice for Norwich; Dalglish sat up and took notice. Kevin Gallacher scored both for Rovers but four days later was stretchered off at Highbury with a broken leg that ended his season. Rovers lost 0–1, their first defeat in 13 games, leaving them seven points off the top of the table.

A week later, United were beaten while Blackburn defeated Liverpool 2–0. Suddenly United's lead, 16 points in January, had been cut to four, breathing new life into a title race that had looked to be all over. A 2–1 win for Rovers at Sheffield Wednesday brought not only the return of Mike Newell after a three-month absence with injury, but a last-minute goal to give Rovers another three points.

Alan Shearer had briefly lost the goal-scoring touch, but in the next match against Swindon he hit his first in six games and his 29th of the season to level the score after Swindon had shot into an early lead. Sherwood added a second and then Shearer settled the outcome with his 30th of the season, bringing the gap with United down to three points.

But then, just as Rovers were building up to a genuine challenge, came disaster when they travelled to Wimbledon. Dalglish had never been over fond of Wimbledon. They had robbed him of a second Double when they beat Liverpool in an FA Cup final and have always been one of those clubs likely to spring a surprise, especially on their own ground, and against quality opposition. Rovers began well enough, going into the lead, which they held until half time. But, in an astonishing turnaround, Wimbledon stunned Rovers with four quick goals in the second half.

It was only Blackburn's second defeat in 17 games and there was little Dalglish could say except that every game against Wimbledon is like a cup game. Fortunately, Blackburn were entertaining Manchester United a few days later at Ewood Park and this gave them a glorious opportunity to cut the gap at the top back to three points. At half time, the score remained goalless but then a minute after the break Shearer struck with a stunning header to put Blackburn into the lead; later he added a second. If only Blackburn had not crashed at Wimbledon.

With Easter approaching, the season was winding towards its conclusion. It turned out to be a good time for Rovers, with further wins over Everton and Aston Villa. A week later, with the championship reaching its climax, Blackburn travelled to Southampton. The south coast side, hovering in the relegation zone, were playing for their Premiership lives; Rovers were playing for the title. On this occasion, it was the relegation team that won. Not that Blackburn didn't have their chances, but they came and went. You need a little bit of luck to win the title and that day the luck was with Southampton, who were awarded a fortunate penalty. Le Tissier tucked it away and Blackburn's hopes evaporated. 'That penalty was the turning point of our season,' complained Dalglish later. Southampton went on to win 3–1, effectively ending Blackburn's challenge for the title.

Demoralised by the result, Blackburn, needing to win their next game to maintain any hopes, could only draw with QPR at Ewood. Shearer opened the scoring but, with seven minutes remaining, QPR equalised. A win at Upton Park followed but then there was another defeat, this time at Coventry. The title was United's. Blackburn had collapsed in the final weeks of the season, losing their nerve when it finally counted. They ended their campaign in second spot, eight points adrift of United.

Defeats at Southampton and Coventry and draws with QPR and Ipswich had cost them the title. They had simply not been able to sustain their challenge when it mattered. Dalglish might have been bitterly disappointed, but he tried to be philosophical. 'They gave of their best,' he said, 'and at the end of the day the least that you can ask is that everybody gives of their best.' But while Dalglish was dispirited, Jack Walker was delighted. He was only three years into his plan and yet his side had pushed United to the end. There could also be no denying that United were a fine side, scoring a hefty 80 goals.

At the end of the day it was that goal tally which told the tale. In comparison to United's 80 goals, Blackburn had scored a mere 63. While Blackburn's defensive record was the second best in the league, five teams had scored more goals than Blackburn. Shearer had performed magnificently, hitting 34 in all (31 in the league), but what was clearly needed was someone else to share the burden and score more goals. To win the league title you needed to be scoring 70 goals or more. Dalglish required another striker and the summer would have to be spent scouring the land for a suitable recruit. Fortunately, Dalglish would not have to wait too long.

There were a number of contenders – Ian Wright at Arsenal, Les Ferdinand at Queens Park Rangers, even Andy Cole at Newcastle. They were all possibilities, although the chances of Jack Walker's money ever luring any of them away from their respective clubs seemed highly unlikely. The obvious man was Chris Sutton, the Norwich striker. Sutton, who had made his debut for Norwich in 1991, had since become a regular in the Canaries' side, making more than 100 appearances. He had ended the season with 28 goals (including 25 in the league), scoring a couple against Rovers in both games during the campaign. Already capped at Under-21 level by England, he had impressed throughout the season and was now knocking on the door of the full England side. Sutton had pace, good distribution and an eye for goal, talents that would supplement the skills of

Shearer. Together they would make a potent strike force, one that any defence in the league would find nigh impossible to handle. The long injury to Shearer during the previous season had also proved the need for a second, top-rate striker. Vital points had been lost early in the season as Shearer made a gentle return from injury.

And so the pursuit of Chris Sutton began. Norwich were initially reluctant to part with their jewel, but when a sum of £5 million was mentioned even Norwich had to sit up and listen. It was too good an offer to turn down. Sutton was keen to join Blackburn, and the thought of £5 million in the bank was just too much for Norwich. It was a huge fee that smashed the British record of £3.6 million paid for Alan Shearer. What's more, Dalglish was paying out for a striker who was still largely unproven. But then everyone, including United manager Alex Ferguson, had said the same about Alan Shearer. And they had all been proved wrong. Dalglish was confident about Sutton. Ray Harford backed him up and Jack Walker had no hesitation in signing the cheque. Walker's five-year plan still had another two years to run but by now both he and Dalglish were beginning to feel that their dream really was within their grasp.

CHAPTER TWENTY-TWO
The Rovers Return

Always look on the bright side of life.
Monty Python song

The trouble with the successful is that they always crave more success. There can never be one too many sweet moments. They may, on occasion, become complacent but one more success is never to be rejected or squandered. Kenny Dalglish might have won as many honours and medals as any footballer in British history but the hungry search for yet another prize had always gone on. It was like a drug.

Four years earlier, Blackburn had been battling against relegation to the third division and now they were on the brink of the Premiership title. It was a remarkable turnaround and, although many would put their success down to Jack Walker's millions, Dalglish's ingenuity, respect, and knowledge of the game, were equally important.

But what Dalglish had done, more than anything, had been to transform this sleepy, half-forgotten corner of Lancashire into a football giant. Prior to his arrival at Ewood Park, attendances had hovered around the 8,000 mark as Blackburn struggled in the second division. Even in Blackburn, nobody was much bothered about Rovers, a club with a glorious past but little future. It was the club of Bob Crompton, Jessie Carver, Syd Puddefoot, Ronnie Clayton and Bryan Douglas; it was the club that had been founding members of the Football League, a giant of Victorian football. But, in 1994/5, as Blackburn pushed for the title, attendances were not far short of 30,000; not bad for a town that boasts a population of little more than 130,000.

Previously, on Monday mornings in this busy East Lancashire town, the talk was usually of United, Liverpool and Everton, rather than Blackburn Rovers. But since Dalglish had pulled his car up outside Ewood Park, all that had changed. Rovers was never a club that attracted its support from the neighbouring towns and cities like the Manchester and Merseyside giants. The coaches have never pulled up in their dozens here, bringing in the fans from Wales, the Midlands and the south. Blackburn Rovers is a one-town team and, as three o'clock draws near, you can spot the supporters pouring out of the two up, two down terraced houses that surround the ground, flocking in their thousands towards Ewood Park. Not so long ago, the kids of this town would have been sporting the red of United and Liverpool, but now it's the blue of Blackburn, another sign of changing times and what Kenny Dalglish has done for this town. Make no mistake, Dalglish's influence stemmed considerably further than Ewood Park. Corner shops, local pubs and industry have all benefited from the spin-off of Blackburn's success. The achievements of the football club have done more to uplift the town's image than any multimillion pound advertising campaign could ever have brought. And it's not just an economic revival; there's a renewed pride as well. Dourfaced Lancastrians have become reinvigorated.

Blackburn Rovers is a friendly club, part of the community, realising its responsibilities. It has the stamp of Mr Blackburn, honest Jack Walker, about it. It has none of the expectations, pedigree or city life pressures that had bedevilled Dalglish's former clubs, Celtic and Liverpool. 'It's a nice, homely, little club,' reported David Batty a few weeks after signing for them. There's no danger of Blackburn ever getting caught in the merchandising merry-go-round that has engulfed a club like Manchester United. Most weeks, 2,500 tickets are distributed to local schools at £2 each. Catch them while they're young, get them hooked, is the motto. It makes a lot of sense. Kenny Dalglish was never going to always be there and one day Blackburn would not be top of the Premiership. But if the youngsters have been hooked, then there's a good chance that their enthusiasm will not wane. Even Blackburn's large Asian population had been impressed, with cricket bats and whites carefully stored away in favour of footballs and Blackburn strips.

Of course, it was not all down to Dalglish. None of this would have been possible without Jack Walker's fortune. Even Dalglish could not have built such a successful team on a shoestring. In today's multimillion pound football industry, it takes a few million pound players to shape a winning team. The critics will, of course, point a finger at Dalglish and say it's only because he had the money. But so too did Alex Ferguson, spending more than £20 million to win the title, and later spending £7 million on one player alone. Not to mention Graeme Souness, who, in his 33 months at Liverpool as Dalglish's successor, shelled out just over £21 million on a bunch of players that catapulted the club into oblivion. Spending money is easy; spending it wisely is a little more tricky. Just ask the likes of Trevor Francis, Roy McFarland, Ron Atkinson, Malcolm Allison and John Bond. Dalglish may not have always spent wisely but he bought players for the moment, to do a particular job. Fortunately, he had the financial resources to allow him that luxury as well as to make the occasional mistake. But there can be little doubt that in signing the likes of Alan Shearer, Chris Sutton, Tim Flowers and David Batty, he was prepared to spend where others hesitated. Shearer could so easily have joined United's ranks but Alex Ferguson was reluctant; while Flowers seemed bound for Anfield until Dalglish stepped in.

In all Dalglish paid out a fraction under £30 million to take his team from the middle of the old second division to the peaks of the Premiership. In the process he sold £7.7 million worth of players, giving him a net transfer deficit of just over £22 million. His spending may well have exceeded that of Souness and Ferguson but, in fairness, he did kick off a division lower. Both Ferguson and Souness were spending at the top.

In Jack Walker, Blackburn had not just a Mr Moneybags but the club's biggest fan. Walker was no glory-seeker, no would-be politician in search of a wider stage and a popular image. He was just a Blackburn lad who happened to make good, someone who had been supporting the club through thick and thin since he was a youngster in short trousers. And when he'd made his crust, he simply decided to plough some of it back into the community. And what better way than giving the town something to be proud of, something to cheer, something to put Blackburn back on the map.

The enthusiasm of the man at the top had filtered downwards to the manager, the players, the ground staff, even the tea ladies. You would have to go a long way to find a more community-spirited club in the Premiership than Blackburn. As they battled to lift the title that Sunday evening at Anfield, you could have heard a pin drop in the normally busy streets of Blackburn; everyone was crouched anxiously around their television sets and radios.

When Blackburn had last won the title, there had been too much talk of a worrying conflict in the Balkans for anyone to celebrate. Hundreds, maybe even thousands, who stood on the terraces in that spring of 1914 to cheer Rovers would die in the smoke and gunfire that was soon to shroud Europe. It would also prove to be the last of the Blackburn team of the masterly Bob Crompton, the defensive pivot Percy Smith and the elegant Eddie Latheron. And, of course, there was Danny Shea, the Alan Shearer of his era, whose huge £2,000 transfer from West Ham had raised more than an eyebrow or two, though his 27 goals in 36 league appearances that season quickly silenced the doubters.

There were other similarities with the 1990s. Even in those days, Blackburn boasted a wealthy benefactor. His name was Lawrence Cotton, a local man who made his money from textiles. Like Walker, Cotton dug deep into his pocket to finance the club, presiding over an ambitious rebuilding programme to turn Ewood Park into a 70,000 capacity stadium. That alone cost £33,000, while more than £12,000 went on new players. But it brought success, kept Blackburn on the map, and no doubt kept the mills and their workers busy.

It was Blackburn's second title triumph in three years, but the intervention of war that summer was to halt any further ambitions. The following season, the last for four years, saw Blackburn wind up in third spot. They would never be the same again. England international Eddie Latheron, still only 28, would die in the trenches of France while other colleagues enlisted for the march across Europe. By the time they came home, they were too weary to play football. They had sacrificed their best years. For the likes of Crompton it was a sign to pack in. The fans, too, had swapped the terraces for the trenches, many of them never returning either. Cotton recognised the problem; the club would need to rebuild, he was too old and so he stood down in favour of a younger man. The club hardly went into terminal decline, but it was to mark the end of a glorious era that had seen Blackburn emerge as one of the great forces in English football. They would finish no higher than sixth in the first division until Jack Walker and Kenny Dalglish took over. What was needed to break the spell was another Lawrence Cotton.

It was the final irony. Blackburn against Liverpool at Anfield in the match to decide the destiny of the championship. Stumbles against Manchester City at Ewood and then against West Ham at Upton Park had left Blackburn just two points clear of Manchester United. When the title was within their grasp, Blackburn seemed hell-bent on committing suicide. Dalglish must have wondered if his side were about to lose their nerve again. United, meanwhile, had simply gone on winning, chipping away at Blackburn's lead with every point won. And so, on the final day of the season, while Blackburn made the short journey down the M6, United travelled to London to take on West Ham, who had just secured their place in the Premiership for another season.

The scenario may have been complicated, but one fact was clear: Manchester United simply had to win if they were to take the title. No other result was good enough for them. But they would also have to hope that Liverpool could take at least a point from Blackburn. Many doubted if Liverpool would have the resolve seriously to challenge Rovers. The rivalry between United and Liverpool was as fierce as any in English football and there seemed little chance that Liverpool would ever do United any favours. Coupled with that was the fact that Blackburn were managed by their favourite son, Dalglish. The Scot may have deserted Anfield in his moment of crisis, but he was still revered on its terraces. Precisely a year earlier, in a gala that preceded the Kop's final game before the bulldozers moved in, Dalglish had been one of many former Liverpool stars to be introduced to the crowd. That afternoon the Kop saved their biggest cheer for the man who had brought them so much glory. It seemed inconceivable that Liverpool could now let him down in his moment of need. Not that there was ever any suggestion of dirty tricks. Liverpool manager Roy Evans quickly slapped down any such notion, calling it an 'insult to the professionalism of the club and its players'.

Anfield was packed for the occasion, the Kop enjoying one of its flag days, boisterous and good-humoured, while the Blackburn fans in the Anfield Road end basked in the spring sunshine. They had rolled into Liverpool in their thousands, anxious but determined to see their favourites claim their first title in 81 years. It was an occasion for Lancastrian pride. Babies, young children, they were all there hoping to witness an event they might never see again. After all, there couldn't have been many still alive who had seen the 1914 victory. The magnitude of the occasion made them tense.

The mood was catching. Almost from the whistle, Blackburn looked jittery, with passes wandering astray and little cohesion. They were a far cry from the side that had swept all before them for so much of the season. The nerves that had jangled against Manchester City, West Ham and Newcastle were now sounding loud enough for the Kopites to hear above their own din. Save for a first minute break, it was all Liverpool. But then, on 20 minutes, Stuart Ripley latched on to a Shearer pass, broke down the right and crossed for the unmarked striker to fire his 34th goal that season into the corner of the net. Liverpool had been torn in two by the raking stride of Shearer. It was Rovers and Shearer at their bulldozing best.

It was a goal that should have calmed Blackburn, especially when news filtered through that West Ham had taken the lead against Manchester United. But, instead, they became edgier, ready to settle for their slender goal lead, rather than striving to improve upon it. Liverpool, meanwhile, pressed on, at times half-heartedly and with none of the gusto and fire that had destroyed Manchester United at Anfield a few weeks earlier. And yet for all their lack of conviction, it was Liverpool who were dominating the game, proving to the championship pretenders that it takes more than a season to learn how to pass the ball with style.

At half time the scores remained the same but as the second half wore on, Liverpool, still casual at times, seemed the more likely to score. Seven minutes into the second half, a groan swept around the ground. Blue-shirted youngsters clutching radios to their ears buried their heads in their hands. From 200 miles away, the news came down the airwaves that United had equalised. But still Blackburn were hanging on to their one goal lead. There was really no need to panic yet. But when, in the 64th minute, John Barnes sidefooted Mark Kennedy's cross past Tim Flowers there was total disbelief. The Kop was dumbstruck, not sure whether to cheer or cry. Blackburn's grip on the title was hanging by a thread.

United needed just one more goal to wrest the championship from Blackburn. Dalglish, who, for so much of the season, had appeared relaxed, was now showing the strain, back in the business of pressure football. Down at the Anfield Road end they turned their backs on the game, unable to watch as the tension mounted. And yet Rovers, despite the precariousness of their position, seemed unable to rouse themselves in the white-knuckle climax of the last 20 minutes. Yet still the score remained locked at Upton Park. Then, three minutes into injury time, came the unthinkable. Liverpool were awarded a free kick when Steve McManaman was felled outside the area. With everyone wondering what was happening at Upton Park, Jamie Redknapp stepped up and let fly with a shot that streaked beyond Tim Flowers into the net. Blackburn were behind. But as they looked in disbelief, their world set to crash before them, came word from the East End that the final whistle had sounded and United, for all their last-minute heroics, had been held to a 1–1 draw. Blackburn were champions. They had been beaten, but who cared? They had lost the battle but they had won the war.

Anfield erupted, a mighty chorus of 'Always look on the bright side of life', the Manchester United song, swelling in unison from the Kop as the Liverpool supporters taunted their old enemy in mocking style. It was not long before the Blackburn supporters joined in. The party had been 81 years in the making and nobody was going to stop them from enjoying it. A giant inflatable bottle of bubbly bounced carelessly over the heads of the Blackburn supporters.

Dalglish appeared, arms raised, striding on to the pitch to hug his players one by one. He had become only the third manager in modern football to lead different clubs to the title. The Kop roared its approval, ready to forgive even if it could never understand why he had ever wanted to desert them. It was also Dalglish's 14th championship in England and Scotland, four of those coming as a manager.

'Everyone knows my feelings for Liverpool,' said a breathless Dalglish, the strains of the afternoon showing on his gaunt, pasty face. 'If we could not win it at Ewood Park, this was the best place to do it. Like other teams, we've had our problems this season, but we've conducted ourselves with dignity. A lot of things that should have gone our way didn't, but our attitude has been impeccable.' And then it was off to join in the party.

Even Jack Walker appeared on the pitch, determined to savour the moment and get his hands on the trophy. After all, it had cost him enough. The players graciously handed it to him. 'It was the proudest moment of my life,' he confessed.

The following evening, the party continued, this time at Ewood Park, as more than 30,000 crammed into Blackburn's new palace of dreams, a modernistic, muscular structure that looks so out of place in the surrounding, narrow, cobbled streets. It is a potent reminder that steel was the very commodity that brought Jack Walker his riches in the first place. Walker had spent £30 million on rebuilding the stadium that a few years ago had been collapsing. Where once there had been leaking roofs and grass sprouting on the terraces, today there are executive boxes, restaurants and unrestricted views in an all-seater stadium. They'd come to see the side, admire the new facilities and say 'thank you' to Jack. Almost everyone in the town's population seemed intent on joining in the fun. They had been queuing since 4.30pm for an event scheduled to begin three hours later. They sang, jigged, and whooped the night away. Premiership boss Rick Parry made another formal presentation of the cup, while Dalglish, named Manager of the Year that afternoon, also received his trophy. It was the best party they'd had in Blackburn since VE-Day 50 years earlier.

Yet from the start it hadn't always looked like Blackburn's season. They kicked off their campaign back in August at Wembley in the Charity Shield, the traditional pre-season curtain-raiser. Having won the Double, the honour of playing champions Manchester United fell to Blackburn. Dalglish was back on the ground that had become his second home when he was with Liverpool. But it was something of a new-look Blackburn that day. Gone was David May, who had bolstered the Rovers defence for much of the previous season, sold to United for £1.4 million during the close season. Unfortunately a glut of preseason injuries meant that Rovers were well below strength, with Chris Sutton one of those missing. David Batty was also absent and would not reappear until the climax of the season nine months later. Not surprisingly, a rampant United ran out 2–0 winners. Losing to their nearest rivals was hardly the confident opening Rovers needed.

Blackburn's shaky start continued a week later with a 1–1 draw at Southampton, Alan Shearer finally equalising after earlier missing a penalty. Then it was back to Ewood Park, now boasting a resplendent new stand, for a 3–0 win over newly promoted Leicester City. Chris Sutton opened his account for the club with a diving header, while Norwegian Henning Berg made it 2–0 before Shearer tapped in a third. Days later, again at Ewood, Sutton struck with a vengeance, hitting a hat trick as Rovers romped to a 4–0 victory. Sutton looked to be the perfect foil for Shearer. While defences were busy tracking the number nine, Sutton was stealing in to mop up the loose chances. At £5 million, Sutton's record-breaking transfer had raised more than a few eyebrows but as his partnership with Shearer began to flourish and pay dividends the hefty price-tag looked to be cheap. The first league table of the season showed Blackburn in second place.

Next came a goalless draw at Arsenal and a 3–0 home win over Everton, followed by one of the biggest disappointments of the season, a 0–1 home defeat in the UEFA Cup against the Swedish club, Trelleborgs.

Dalglish, with three European Cup-winner's medals and years of experience, could offer few explanations. It seemed inconceivable that his £20 million outfit could collapse so pitifully against a team of part-timers. Yet there was always hope in the return leg. As it turned out, there was no coming back as Blackburn could only salvage a 2–2 draw. It was a huge disappointment for Dalglish to see his side eliminated from Europe almost before the competition had begun. It also, as the papers were quick to point out, underlined the gulf between Blackburn and the rest of the continent. They still had much to learn, but if there was any compensation it at least meant that they could now concentrate on winning one of the domestic tournaments.

Back in the league, Blackburn's fortunes continued to fluctuate. There were wins over Chelsea and Aston Villa before Norwich City beat them at Carrow Road. Then came a creditable 1–1 draw with highflying Newcastle at St James' Park, followed by a fortunate 3–2 win over Liverpool at Ewood Park and a 2–4 defeat by Manchester United, also at Ewood Park. Yet again United had the better of Blackburn, even though Rovers had twice been in front. The turning point came in the 44th minute when Henning Berg was dismissed for a foul, which led to Eric Cantona scoring United's first from the spot. Dalglish was left with a few questions to answer as his side slipped from second spot into fourth.

But that defeat was to mark a low point in their league endeavours. Rattled by the result, they put their heads together and came out more full of resolve than ever that they would bring the title to Ewood Park. It was followed by ten wins and one draw in their following 11 league fixtures, before they next met United, when they again lost. It was to be a run that would eventually shoot them into the top spot. Perhaps the most impressive result had come immediately after the defeat, as they ran out 2–0 winners at Nottingham Forest with Sutton scoring twice. That was followed by a 1–0 win over Sheffield Wednesday that lifted them into second place, a 2–0 victory against Tottenham, a 3–1 win at Ipswich and a 4–0 win over QPR at Ewood Park, with Alan Shearer hitting a second-half hat trick.

Sandwiched in between had been a 2–0 win in the Coca-Cola Cup over Coventry. But then came a bitter disappointment in the competition as Blackburn lined up against Liverpool. It was undoubtedly the clash of the round, especially with Liverpool showing signs of returning to their old ways. But even Blackburn could not have expected the onslaught that was to come. Liverpool simply swept them aside, finally running out 3–1 winners in front of a packed Ewood Park.

But if there were any worries that Blackburn might collapse, they were quickly eased as they crushed Wimbledon 3–0 at Selhurst Park without ever looking convincing. That was followed by a 3–2 win over Southampton, with further wins over Manchester City, Crystal Palace and West Ham.

Blackburn were firing on all fronts and topping the table. Liverpool, who had looked impressive early on in August and September, had faltered, while Newcastle, who earlier in the season had built up a handsome lead at the top of the table had also stumbled, along with Nottingham Forest. It looked to be developing into another two-horse race between Rovers and United. Chris Sutton was proving more than worth his £5 million price tag. In the first 22 games of the season he had scored an astonishing 17 goals, the same number as his partner Alan Shearer. They were christened the SAS (Sutton And Shearer) strike force.

Over Christmas, the club had to make do without Dalglish, who was rushed to hospital with appendicitis and needed an emergency operation. At the time, it caused a few anxious moments but within a few weeks he was fully recovered and back at Ewood. Ray Harford took over and Dalglish was barely missed.

Dalglish had looked relaxed all season, a far cry from the brooding man who had sulked out of Anfield. With Ray Harford sharing his load, and with none of the expectations that had dogged his days at Anfield, he could afford to smile, though he still kept his distance from the press. He had even forsaken his seat in the stand for a permanent place by the dugout, usually leaning against a wall.

Blackburn ended the year still in top spot, just one point ahead of United. The New Year brought the third round of the FA Cup, and a visit to Newcastle United. They could hardly have asked for a tougher tie, but in the event came away from the North East with a 1–1 draw. A week later, with home advantage, Blackburn were expected to complete the job. Instead, Newcastle sneaked away with a 2–1 win and Rovers were out of the Cup. Out of three cup competitions by mid-January, Blackburn now had only the Premiership to play for. A week later, they travelled to Old Trafford for a showdown with United.

Rovers went into the game with a five-point lead over their rivals, but by the end of the afternoon it had been slimmed down to a mere two points as United celebrated a 1–0 win in front of over 43,000. It was Blackburn's first league defeat since United had beaten them at Ewood Park back in October and it was the third time United had got the better of them that season.

As the season wore on, the gap between Blackburn and United fluctuated, with Blackburn at one time as much as eight points clear, though United, games in hand, always posed a threat. But, again, after the United defeat there was no hangover as Blackburn trounced Ipswich 4–1 with Alan Shearer hitting another hat trick. Controversy surrounded Blackburn's next fixture, as they took on Leeds United at Ewood Park. Tim Flowers was dismissed after just two minutes for a professional foul. Four minutes later, Rovers were awarded a hotly disputed penalty and Shearer put them ahead. Then, with just five minutes remaining, Leeds were awarded another disputed penalty that led to an equaliser.

Early in February Rovers lost at White Hart Lane, but it was only to be followed by another fine run, this time ten games without defeat, taking in seven wins and three draws. It was a run that almost certainly clinched the championship for them.

Then came the end-of-season disaster as nerves began to gnaw away at confidence. Sutton had also lost the goal-scoring touch, claiming only a handful of goals during the spring months, though thankfully Shearer was still hitting the target regularly. Injuries had not helped the Blackburn cause either. Midfield dynamo David Batty missed virtually the entire season with a foot injury, returning just in time for the end-of-season celebrations. Stuart Ripley also missed vital games, while Jason Wilcox was absent from the title run-in. Kevin Gallacher, who had broken his leg the previous season, returned to the side in late April to face Crystal Palace only to be stretchered off with a hairline fracture shortly after scoring. That was the end of his season.

With the title almost in their grasp, Blackburn looked to have scooped up another three points at Leeds but a last-minute equaliser from the home side brought a swift halt to any early celebrations. As if that was not bad enough, it was to be followed by a nightmare of an evening as relegation-threatened Manchester City came to Ewood Park on Easter Monday and walked off with all three points. Twice Rovers had been in front only to throw away their lead. City eventually won 3–2 and the whole of Manchester celebrated. City were safe; United were back in the fight. Dalglish was furious, even though Rovers still clung to their narrow lead at the top of the table. But sense was restored three days later when Crystal Palace were the visitors. On paper, Rovers' end-of-season run-in had looked manageable but with so many of their opponents now battling to stave off relegation, easy fixtures had become a fight for life. Palace were also staring relegation in the face and, although they put up a brave fight, Kevin Gallacher's winner left them facing the drop into the first division.

Next in line was a trip to West Ham to face yet another side in danger of the drop. By now Blackburn were showing plenty of nerves and, with West Ham battling for their Premiership life, the Rovers went down 0–2. It was hardly championship form. Eight points had been thrown away in four games to leave the title on a knife edge.

When Newcastle United came to Ewood Park with only two games remaining, it was a case of Rovers having to win. Defeat would have seen United coast past them. As it was, Shearer was on hand to record his 33rd goal of the season, though it was Tim Flowers who was the hero, saving Blackburn time and again. And so the title decider was set for Anfield.

Dalglish worked at taking the pressure off his players. 'Bottle doesn't come in to it,' he told journalists, 'I think it's all down to playing now. We are just pleased to have got into this position.' Dalglish even turned out for a Blackburn side against the press, oozing conviviality and cheerfulness with those he seemed to spend most of his time avoiding. It was a far cry from his behaviour at Anfield four years previously.

It was to be one of the most remarkable finales in the history of the championship. Forty-one games played and yet there was still drama ahead. Three minutes into injury time and the fate of the title remained uncertain. Only when the final whistle was blown at Upton Park did Blackburn know for certain that they were champions.

There would be some who begrudged Dalglish his success and even more who would begrudge Blackburn their title. They called it a 'manufactured' side. True, Blackburn were not as dashing as United at their best, nor as clinical as the Liverpool of Dalglish. But Blackburn were efficient. They scored more goals than anyone, won more games and ended up with more points. They had not bought the title as some suggested. Rather they had played the modern game more effectively. Walker had proved an astute businessman, investing in the market on the word of a man he could trust. Where once he bought and sold steel, now he bought and sold players. Maybe there wasn't really much difference. He had set targets and achieved them.

Jack Walker had reckoned on five years to take the title and here he was completing the job in four. It had been costly but it had been worthwhile. That afternoon he had gone through a thousand nightmares, convinced that when United equalised against West Ham, and Liverpool drew level with Rovers, the title was about to slip away from him. But Walker had not accounted for the Dalglish luck. He may not have been feeling fortunate, but Dalglish was. 'I had a feeling we'd win it. I felt we were going to be lucky today,' said the man who seemed to have been blessed with more than his fair share of luck, the man with the Midas touch.

But behind the smiling face and the celebrations, all was not well with Dalglish. The strains of the championship chase had caught up with him. The final months of the title race had reminded him mercilessly of the real pressures of football management: the disaster against Manchester City, the stolen win over Newcastle, and then the final drama at Anfield. He was working a relentless seven days a week, responsible for paying out millions of pounds for players, and filled with the urge for success. He knew that it would get no easier. What's more, it would be harder the next season: European football, expectations of more domestic trophies. It didn't all end with the title triumph. You couldn't suddenly rest on your laurels. There is always one more trophy to be won.

He'd been lucky and it only served to underline how much luck was involved in football management. It was time to get away from the pressures; time to see the chairman.

Walker was sympathetic and certainly did not want to lose his man. A new post would be created, that of director of football. Dalglish could take a back seat and let Ray Harford deal with the first team on a day-to-day basis. It was the ideal solution. But as they announced it to the press, it seemed likely that Dalglish's days as a touchline manager were over. Success may be sweet, but it carries with it burdens that are not always so welcome.

CHAPTER TWENTY-THREE
History Repeats Itself

I don't want to continue as manager. I don't want the team responsibility or heavy day-to-day involvement.
Kenny Dalglish

History has an uncanny habit of repeating itself, even when it comes to something as seemingly innocuous as football. Yet at the beginning of 1997 few, and certainly not Kenny Dalglish, could have guessed that not only was he about to slip into the dugout again, but he was also set to step into the boots of Kevin Keegan once more.

Dalglish had become little more than a glorified onlooker at Blackburn after he stepped down from the manager's job. He may have been called director of football but as one insider put it, it was with a small 'd' and a small 'f'. Theoretically he was just a phone call away from Ray Harford, who had succeeded him in the managerial chair, but Harford rarely bothered him, while Dalglish didn't want to poke his nose in too much. He'd go to the training ground a couple of times a week and work out with the youngsters. He'd also watch a few games here and there, but that apart, there wasn't a great deal for him to do. After winning the title he'd had a break, enjoyed some skiing and even been paid an advance of around £200,000 to write his autobiography. But, as the months wore on, he found himself feeling more and more sidelined. The problem was that his new job had never been properly defined. No one was quite sure what he was supposed to be doing.

'I was available but I didn't want to interfere with or hamper Ray Harford in any way, shape or form … I didn't want to impugn his authority,' he later claimed. There were various jobs for Dalglish to do, but he was never in the thick of it. He claimed in his autobiography he wasn't even consulted about the transfer of Alan Shearer to Newcastle. When he heard he was staggered.

By August 1996 he had had enough of his consultancy role. There was no satisfaction in the job. Most people could have told him that from the start. In, truth, it was little more than a well-paid sabbatical. He called Blackburn chairman Robert Coar from his house in Spain to tell him, and was informed that the club had come to much the same decision. In fact, Coar said, they had already sent a letter to his Southport home telling him that their relationship had run its course. The two men agreed that it had not worked out. Dalglish was leaving Ewood Park.

But suspicions lingered that there was more to the story. The word in Blackburn was that the club had tired of paying him £300,000 a year for little in return. Dalglish had not travelled to Europe with the club, where his expertise might have proved invaluable. What's more, he was on holiday in Spain as the football season kicked off. If there was any mutual consent in the parting, it was more on the club's side.

It wasn't long before the offers were rolling in. The most attractive came from Scotland, from Rangers, the club he had supported as a boy. Rangers, which had seen its European ambitions blitzed season after season, decided that Dalglish, with all his experience and knowledge of the European game, might be able to help. Rangers chairman David Murray offered Dalglish the chance to be involved. But again there was confusion over his role. The papers made out that Dalglish was being lined up eventually to take over from Ibrox boss Walter Smith. But there was no truth to that suggestion and nor would he have any day-to-day involvement with the club. Instead, he would be a glorified super-scout, checking out young players wherever he fancied, home and abroad. He would also carry out spying missions to assess Rangers' European opponents. In fact, he would not even be on the Rangers payroll. Instead, he was to be employed by one of David Murray's many companies, Carnegie Sports Management, for whom he was also expected to do some consultancy work. This seemed to involve playing golf with the captains of industry and generally impressing people by his presence. Dalglish thought long and hard about it, but in the end decided to give it a try. Before he had even unpacked his briefcase, events were to overtake him.

They say you can usually define the importance of events by whether you can remember where you were when you first heard the news. Kenny Dalglish was heading up the motorway on the way to a funeral when his drive was interrupted.

His mobile phone was ringing. The cold, sharp weather of the previous week had disappeared and the mid-morning sun was dazzling through the windscreen. It was a friend on the line.

'Have you heard the news?' he spluttered.

"No, what news?' asked Dalglish.

'Kevin Keegan's resigned as manager of Newcastle,' came the answer.

Dalglish could barely believe his ears. Nor could half the nation. Dalglish thought it was a joke. Within minutes he was on the line to Terry McDermott, Keegan's number two at Newcastle. His former Liverpool colleague confirmed the story: Keegan was going. Yet it seemed incredible that he should quit Newcastle when they were still fighting for the league title. There had been rumours in one of the Sunday newspapers that Keegan had offered his resignation on Boxing Day after Newcastle had been beaten by Blackburn. But, according to the paper, it had been turned down. Nobody gave much credence to the story at the time. Now the Newcastle Club Call line was announcing that Keegan had handed in his resignation, the club had accepted it and the hunt was on for a new manager.

The thought of managing Newcastle did not occur to Dalglish immediately. Why should it? He was happy living on Merseyside. He had a new job that would allow him enough involvement with football and time to be with his family. It seemed an ideal compromise. His son Paul was also back on Merseyside, having signed for Liverpool after a brief spell with Celtic that had left him homesick for his beloved Liverpool.

Yet before the evening was out, the newspapers and the bookies were already installing Dalglish as favourite to take over from Keegan. To many it seemed a fanciful idea. Dalglish, after all, had quit Liverpool citing stress as the chief factor. Then he had sensationally quit Blackburn Rovers as manager to take a backseat job as director of football, and a year later had confirmed in various newspapers that the explicit reason for his resignation as manager was because he 'did not want the demanding day-to-day involvement of management'.

What's more, he already had a job. He could go where he wanted, still live on Merseyside, host a few events, play a little golf, and pick up a nice wage packet at the end of the week. What more could a man want? In Dalglish's case, clearly a great deal more.

It didn't take Dalglish long to decide that he was interested in the job. Newcastle were a big club with as fanatical a following as any in the country. It was the kind of place he liked, a touch like Glasgow and Liverpool: friendly, loyal and tough, a city where adversity breeds backbone. Kevin Keegan had taken the club from the depths of the first division to the top of the Premiership but had failed by a whisker the previous season to land the title. Keegan had shown that Newcastle was a sleeping giant, rather like Liverpool had been when Bill Shankly took over in late 1959.

There had been something of the Shankly about Keegan, a rapport with the fans, a determination to make the side succeed for their sake not his own. But equally there was also something of the maverick. Like Shankly, he was an emotional man who wore his heart on his sleeve, threatening to resign on occasion and liable to walk out on a club, not really interested in the money. Keegan would be a hard act to follow, but the more Dalglish thought about it, the more he was attracted by the thought. And there was also the opportunity to lead a third club to the league title, something no other manager in the history of the game had ever achieved in England. Dalglish was soon relishing the prospect. The papers were also trying to track him down, wanting to know if he was interested. Dalglish remained tight-lipped. But noticeably he did not deny any interest.

Meanwhile, the Newcastle chairman Sir John Hall was pursuing Bobby Robson in Spain. It was clear that Robson, a long-standing friend, was his favoured choice, but the Barcelona manager owed a loyalty to his new club. He had always wanted to manage the Spanish giants and had twice turned them down in the past. Now, after only six months in the job, he wasn't going suddenly to return to English football. 'Right job, wrong time,' he reluctantly told Sir John.

The way was now open for Dalglish. Hall seemed hesitant but then over the weekend Alan Hansen, on BBC Television's *Match of the Day,* let it be known that Dalglish would be interested in the Newcastle job. Coming from someone so close to Dalglish, you had to assume that there was more than an element of truth in what he was saying. On the Monday Hansen was again singing Dalglish's praises, this time in the *Daily Express,* suggesting that Dalglish was the only man for the job and that 'he won't crack again'. Journalist Henry Winter, who months earlier had ghost-written Dalglish's autobiography, suggested in a prominently-placed article in the *Daily Telegraph* the same morning that Dalglish was 'ready to answer Newcastle's call'. If ever there was a hint that was it. That morning Dalglish got the call. He confirmed his interest and availability. 'Let's meet,' suggested Newcastle.

Within hours Dalglish was motoring up the M6 again, towards Preston and an afternoon meeting with Newcastle representatives at the Tickled Trout Hotel, just off the M6, alongside the River Ribble. At the meeting, vice chairman Freddie Fletcher, Sir John's son Douglas and Freddie Shepherd tested Dalglish out. Dalglish impressed them. He was sharp, knew what he wanted and was keen to take the job if it was offered him. Hall, not surprisingly, questioned him about his decisions to quit Liverpool and Blackburn. He wanted to know why and would it happen again? Dalglish assured him that he would not walk out on them. Two hours later, Dalglish left and returned home to Southport to await their response. The Newcastle representatives talked for another hour.

Sir John Hall, basking in the Spanish sun, still harboured hopes that Bobby Robson would change his mind, that a renewed offer might tempt him back to his birthplace. But really he was clutching at straws. A decision had to be made; the flotation of the club on the stock exchange was imminent. They could procrastinate no longer. The rest of the board had already moved firmly in the direction of Dalglish. Hall told them he wanted one more conversation with Robson, a last chance to see if the Barcelona manager might change his mind. By Tuesday night, however, it was clear Robson was staying put. 'Get Dalglish,' he ordered. 'I'll be on the first flight home.'

On the Wednesday morning Dalglish's phone rang. It was the call he was awaiting. Did he want the Newcastle job?

Dalglish had already talked it through with Marina. He'd told her he was keen and they had discussed the fact that it would mean moving. There was no way he could commute from Southport. They would have to move house. It wasn't the ideal time for an upheaval but then, when is? In many ways they had been lucky. They had moved areas only once, when he came to Liverpool from Celtic in 1977. They had been almost 20 years on Merseyside, an area they had grown to love. But it was now almost six years since he had quit Anfield and much had happened since. It was time to move on.

'Yes,' replied Dalglish, 'I'm interested.' It didn't take long to finalise the details. It was reported that Dalglish would be paid almost £1 million a year. A press conference was hastily arranged. By early afternoon the news had leaked out that Dalglish was coming to St James' Park. One Liverpool legend was taking over from another. It was like the summer of 1977 all over again, when Dalglish moved into Anfield to pull on Kevin Keegan's number 7 shirt. Blackburn's millionaire owner Jack Walker was left puzzled. 'I cannot understand it,' he said, perplexed by the whole business, remembering that Dalglish had quit managing Blackburn claiming that he wanted to avoid just such a job.

Dalglish seemed to be making a habit of working for some of the richest men in the country, from Littlewoods heir David Moores at Liverpool, to Jack Walker at Blackburn, and now to Sir John Hall at Newcastle. Hall had made his fortune from property, by turning a derelict Gateshead site into the MetroCentre shopping mall. It cost £100 million to build, with the Church Commissioners as partners. Hall later sold his stake to them for an undisclosed amount but enough to boost the assets of his property company, Cameron Hall Developments, to well over £100 million. Money was also sunk into the 7,500 acre Wynward Estate, which he bought from the Marquess of Londonderry for £3 million in 1987. With extensive development already taking place on the site, Hall's estimated fortune has risen to around £130 million by 1996. A lifelong football fan, he finally won his battle for control of Newcastle United in 1992 and since then was reckoned to have invested more than £70 million in the club. In fact, it was the bank which had loaned the money, with Hall acting as collateral.

'The Geordie nation is on the march' he told everyone at the time, and you had to admit that Hall was the one person largely responsible for putting the region back on the map. Not since the misty days of city boss Dan Smith have Newcastle had a Mr Geordie quite like Sir John Hall. But it had cost the club. Keegan had spent a small fortune on players, while the directors were also preparing to float the club on the stock exchange in order to raise the money to build a new 60,000 all-seater stadium that would satisfy the fans' unquenchable thirst for tickets.

Hall had poured a substantial part of his own fortune into the club. He alone had been largely responsible for persuading Kevin Keegan to return to St James' Park where, as a player, he had inspired Newcastle to promotion. Keegan, having quietly retired to the Spanish sun, had never wanted to be a football manager, but Sir John set the challenge and Keegan responded, signing up in February 1992 as Newcastle struggled in the then second division. Without Keegan, the once-great Newcastle might even have crashed into football's lower basement. They hadn't boasted a trophy in years. In the 1950s they were FA Cup giants, but the fact was that they hadn't won the championship since the days of Hughie Gallacher in 1927. It was a long time and the North East was hungry for success.

Nor was it the first time that Keegan had come to their rescue. Back in 1982 he had signed for Newcastle as a player, ending his illustrious career in black and white stripes two years later. But with his job done and Newcastle back in the top division he retired and went off to Marbella and the sun. Until the call from Sir John Hall brought him dashing back.

It had been a glorious homecoming. Gates soared at St James' Park, just as they had when he had arrived as a player. Suddenly there was a new spirit. But there were hiccups. 'It wasn't long before Hall and Keegan were at loggerheads. Keegan wanted to buy Brian Kilcline from Oldham for £250,000. Hall baulked at the price, pleading poverty. Keegan promptly walked out on the club, talking of 'false promises'. It turned out to be the best thing he could have done. Hall begged him back and promised him whatever money he wanted. Over the next few years, Keegan took Newcastle to promotion and then to the top of the Premiership. But it was all so tantalising as Newcastle failed to get their hands on the silverware they so desperately wanted.

At one stage during the 1995/6 season Newcastle had been ten points ahead of Manchester United and the chasing pack. But the jitters had got the better of them and, as the season wore to its weary conclusion, Newcastle's confidence evaporated and they were caught by United just before the finishing line. Keegan was distraught, his frustrations ending in an embarrassing end-of-season slanging match with Alex Ferguson that did neither Keegan nor Newcastle United any good. They kissed and made up but Keegan never really got over it. He had been beaten and he didn't like it. He was never a good loser.

He wanted to go then and was adamant that he would not change his mind, but Hall's son Douglas, who was taking on more responsibilities at the club, persuaded him to give it another season. Neither Keegan nor the board were altogether convinced. Keegan really wanted out and the directors had already begun to draw up a shortlist of potential new managers, fearful that he would resign yet again. More than one member of the board had had enough of Keegan's tantrums. They soldiered on, momentarily delighted when they beat United to the signature of Alan Shearer, even though it cost them a staggering £15 million.

For a time it looked as though Newcastle had all the aces. Yet they got off to the worst of starts, humiliated at Wembley in the Charity Shield by a Manchester United side in exhilarating form. It may not have really mattered but to have been so embarrassed in front of 80,000, plus a European television audience of millions, hurt deeply.

Newcastle's early-season league form was little better. They struggled in their opening encounter at Goodison and then lost a second game a week later at home. It was a mixed bag of results that didn't promise much. The major highlight was the 5–0 thrashing of Manchester United at St James' Park in October. It would live in the memory-banks of Geordie fans forever. Briefly they topped the tables but could not sustain it.

The early-season performances only confirmed what Keegan already knew: the problem was in defence. Under his guidance Newcastle had been an attacking side, happy to concede goals in the sure knowledge that they could always score more. But there were one or two teams around who could stem Newcastle's rampaging forwards and then catch them on the counter. Keegan had given as much as he could. The only football he knew was cavalier style, and it hadn't worked.

As Christmas neared, Keegan wondered if his side really could go one better than the previous season. Whatever happened he could not take the pain of being second best again. On Boxing Day Newcastle slipped up once more, this time at Blackburn. It was their sixth league defeat of the season. Keegan could take no more; he'd had enough. He told John Hall that he wanted to quit but Hall, as persuasive as ever, made him change his mind. It was now only a matter of time. A few days later they thrashed Spurs 7–1 at St James' Park and everything looked to be rosy again. Over the New Year, Keegan made an appointment to see Sir John. Both men knew what was going to happen. Then, on the morning of Tuesday 7 January, came the dramatic statement from St James' Park. The Keegan era was over. History was about to repeat itself.

A week later at 6pm on Tuesday 14 January, Dalglish was being paraded at St James' Park as the new manager of Newcastle United Fans had gathered outside the ground while Sir John Hall had flown in from Spain, a little disorientated by the speed of events, but taking his place calmly next to Dalglish. Terry McDermott sat the other side as the press conference got underway. Of course there were still some predictable questions to be answered. 'Would he walk out on Newcastle as he had at Liverpool and Blackburn,' wondered the press, and just about everybody else. Dalglish answered before they even asked the question. He'd left Liverpool because he could not do the job, two disasters had taken their toll, but even then he had left them with silverware on the table.

As for Blackburn, 'I left them for footballing reasons,' he explained intriguingly. 'Reasons I could not make public because I was trying to protect Ray Harford a little bit. There were problems internally that I couldn't accept as a manager.'

His answers seemed to silence the critics. Yet in his autobiography Dalglish had claimed that when he quit as manager of Blackburn he told the chairman Robert Coar that 'I don't want to continue as team manager. I don't want the team responsibility or heavy day-to-day involvement.' Yet here was Dalglish, less than six months after publishing that statement, taking up one of the most pressurised jobs in British football. You had to wonder why.

Over at Blackburn they were staggered by his decision to join Newcastle and at Ewood Park chairman Robert Coar was flabbergasted by Dalglish's claim that there had been some kind of division. Nobody seemed to know what he was talking about, and it all left a bad taste with the fans. 'The warmth has gone,' said one club insider. 'You can't take away the fantastic success he achieved here, and we will always hold him in regard, but we feel let down.' Coar was also quick to warn Dalglish off poaching any Blackburn players.

There was much the same feeling over on Merseyside. When he'd left Liverpool there was respect and sympathy. Then, when he'd joined Blackburn, there was no threat: he had gone to a lower division club. Furthermore, he'd kept his home on Merseyside and was a still regular visitor to Anfield. But now he was selling up; severing his ties with the area for good. It was the final goodbye to Liverpool. But there was worse; Dalglish was joining a club challenging Liverpool for the championship. 'It's all about money,' grumbled one Scouser to another. Even the Kop seemed to be losing the traditional warmth it reserved for its old boys.

One wondered if Dalglish had fancied a job back at Anfield – helping with the kids, overseeing future developments, a seat on the board – there had been plenty of stories that he was keen to return. It was just the kind of role that might have suited him. But if he was expecting something it hadn't been forthcoming. Maybe that was why he was now so readily cutting his ties with Merseyside.

Within 24 hours Dalglish was back in the thick of it, taking a bow before the St James' Park crowd, and then retiring to the dugout to sit alongside Terry McDermott as Newcastle took on first division Charlton Athletic in a Cup replay.

Yet, despite one raucous chant of his name, it was a subdued welcome from the normally noisy Gallowgate crowd. They seemed confused. Their hero had gone and now somebody else was in his place. They might have been delighted that Dalglish had joined them, but they were still mourning Keegan, the local favourite.

Dalglish decided it was best if Terry McDermott chose the side that day. McDermott knew the players, the system. The two men went back a long time, to the glory days of Liverpool's European success and Dalglish knew he could be trusted. Indeed, the presence of McDermott and another former Liverpool man of that era, Mark Lawrenson, at St James' Park, may well have been a crucial factor in Dalglish's decision to join Newcastle. Dalglish sat back to watch but it didn't make for comfortable viewing. Newcastle struggled, finally scoring a winner in extra time, the problems of the past week lying heavily on their shoulders.

A few days later Dalglish, in charge for his first Premiership game, took his new side down south to face Southampton, managed by his old Liverpool roommate Graeme Souness. It was a crucial test for Newcastle, who could ill afford to let league leaders Liverpool and the other contenders pull away from them.

This time it was Dalglish choosing the side. He decided to leave the mercurial Frenchman David Ginola on the bench, adding to the growing speculation that some of Keegan's expensive foreign imports might not last the rest of the season at St James' Park. Dalglish was never one for temperamental players. He appreciated skills as much as anyone but expected total commitment as well. Colombian Faustino Asprilla as well as Ginola knew that they would be under the spotlight.

Initially, Ginola's absence seemed to do the trick as Newcastle swept into the lead and then added a second after the interval. With just eight minutes remaining, Newcastle were two goals ahead and coasting to victory but then a fatal error by goalkeeper Shaka Hislop allowed Southampton back into the game, his mistake compounded by a mighty last-second volley from the unpredictable Matthew Le Tissier that sizzled past a helpless Hislop.

Yet again Newcastle had thrown away a comfortable lead. This result starkly illustrated Newcastle's underlying problem: their defence. The Dalglish magic was slow in coming. On Sunday 26 January Newcastle entertained Nottingham Forest at home in the fourth round of the FA Cup. With Forest fighting relegation and having propped up the league for most of the season, the odds had to be on Newcastle. Eventually, on the hour, Les Ferdinand edged them into the lead but then, typically, Newcastle leaked a couple of goals and were out of the Cup.

A few days later, Everton visited St James' Park for what looked a comfortable three pointer for Newcastle. In the end it was, but for 74 minutes it looked as if Newcastle were about to slip up yet again. Everton even had the temerity to take the lead after two minutes and looked to be capable of adding to their score as they fluffed numerous chances. Some of the Gallowgate faithful were describing the first half as their worst 45 minutes for years. There were even boos directed at the players as they left the field. Dalglish was not impressed. If any of them hadn't heard the sharp end of Dalglish's tongue before, then they were in for a new experience. Whatever he said to them in the dressing room, it worked. Asprilla came on and, in an inspired display, began to make Newcastle grow in confidence. But it took a long time for the goals to come. Eventually, they arrived in the last 16 minutes as they fired in four to win 4–1. On paper it looked easy but in reality it had been a struggle for much of the evening.

Leicester were the next visitors to St James' Park and as Newcastle shot into a three-minute lead it looked like the Magpies were in for an easy ride. But rather than finish Leicester off, Newcastle huffed and puffed and in the second half their defence collapsed before a sudden Leicester barrage. Leicester were suddenly 3–1 up with just 13 minutes remaining, and it seemed United were about to go down and lose further touch with the league leaders. But then Shearer struck, scoring first from a free kick to make it 3–2, then minutes later he was there again and finally in injury time he completed his hat-trick to send the Gallowgate End wild. It was a famous victory, yet it only covered up what should have been glaringly obvious: Newcastle's defence was a shambles. Dalglish had left Ginola out of the line-up, but in the second half brought him on. Ginola's trickery had helped but you had to ask so many questions about their defence.

Given these problems, it was no surprise that it wasn't long before

Dalglish was being linked with just about every star name in Europe. More realistically he was said to be in for the Crewe midfielders Danny Murphy and Gareth Whalley. Mostly, it was just newspaper talk but there was enough evidence to suggest that Dalglish was not at all happy with what he had seen at St James' Park and that he was moving to plug some of the gaps. He was being spotted here, there and everywhere, with chequebook at the ready. Paul Kitson was soon on the move, shifted to West Ham for £2.2 million while David Ginola was rumoured to be hankering for a move to Italy.

Whatever the comings and goings, Dalglish knew that he had a challenge on his hands. Newcastle were still in Europe, scheduled to meet Monaco in the UEFA Cup quarterfinals, but they were losing ground in the Premiership; a 1–0 home defeat by Southampton at the beginning of March left them in fourth place, nine points behind Manchester United, albeit with a game in hand. Meanwhile, Alan Shearer was likely to be missing for some weeks as he re-entered hospital for another groin operation, and Les Ferdinand was also injured, thus greatly reducing Dalglish's attacking options. In the circumstances, it would take an almighty effort to catch United and Liverpool. So Newcastle's season slithered to its sad end in March as they lost 1–0 at home to Monaco in the UEFA Cup and then a week later were beaten 4–3 at Anfield in the Premiership. On paper that game, as nail-biting as the previous season's, looked close, but in reality Newcastle had been embarrassed for 80 minutes. Five-nil might have been a more appropriate scoreline.

Eight days later, Monaco rubbed salt into the wound, winning 3–0 in Monte Carlo, to dump Newcastle out of Europe. Even Sir John Hall was said to have been incensed by the lack of fight in the side. On the bench you could sense that haunted look in Dalglish's eyes again as the strains of management began to tell. Running Newcastle was not going to be easy. Keegan had instilled in them an urgency to attack; now they were being told to defend. Ginola had already clashed with Dalglish and soon put in a transfer request. They had finished the season in second place, seven points behind champions Manchester United and were into the Champions League.

Winning the title had not been possible in his first season, but given time, there was enough cash and ambition at St James' Park to turn Newcastle into a true giant, and to make them one of the most feared and respected clubs in Europe. The main question was whether Dalglish could still work the magic and take them one step further.

CHAPTER TWENTY-FOUR
When The Boat Comes In

Wish me luck as you wave me goodbye

Brian Clough used to argue that it was sometimes better to have lucky footballers than brilliant ones. And it was undoubtedly true that wherever Kenny Dalglish had landed, personal – as well as club – fortune followed accordingly. But suddenly lady luck was about to desert him.

Success had tracked Dalglish ever since he was a seventeen year old at Parkhead. He'd gone on to win League and Cup honours in Scotland as well as starting what would be a glittering international career. Then at Liverpool lady luck had been even more generous as he picked up League and Cup silverware on top of three European cups. As if all that wasn't enough he had then settled into a managerial career of similar success, clinching a League and Cup double in his first season.

Hillsborough had briefly interrupted that journey but after an anxious break from the game he had returned to inspire the rise of Jack Walker's Blackburn from first division anonymity to Premiership champions.

Now at Newcastle he was charged with fulfilling the dreams of thousands of success-starved Geordie fans. Keegan had whetted their appetite for glory with his all-attacking, all-entertaining approach and after years of play-ing second fiddle to the big boys of Manchester, Merseyside and London, the fans of Newcastle were itching for silverware.

In his first season Dalglish had already clashed with the mercurial David Ginola, leaving him on the bench on a number of occasions, much to the annoyance of many fans who regarded Ginola as a potential match winner. He may have been but he was also something of an extravagance. Ginola had already slapped in a transfer request and it was obvious to any seasoned Newcastle observer that his days were numbered. Dalglish had decided that major surgery was needed. The defence was leaking goals and there were far too many players swanning around and not pulling their weight. The pony-tailed Frenchman seemed to fall into that category.

And so in the summer of 1997 Dalglish began a clear-out that would unwittingly lead one day to his own exit. First out was Lee Clark, sold to North East rivals Sunderland for £2.5 million, then Robbie Elliot went to Bolton for £3.5 million. He was followed by David Ginola and Les Ferdinand going to Tottenham for a combined £8 million. Another favourite, Peter Beardsley, went to Bolton for £450,000 while the tempera-mental Colombian Tino Asprilla would later go to Parma for £6 million.

It was probably the biggest sale in the club's history, bringing in a mas-sive £20 million. But it didn't go down well with too many fans. In particular they would cringe at the sales of favourites Ferdinand, Ginola and Asprilla. In hindsight, however, neither Ginola nor Ferdinand con-tributed much to their new clubs. Ginola was never a Dalglish type of player. He may have had flair but he was not a battler. Dalglish liked play-ers who gave 100 per cent and all too often Ginola would stray out to the touchline waiting for the ball to land at his feet, neglecting any defensive responsibilities or ambitions to go searching for the ball. Given that Newcastle were trying to emulate Manchester United, perhaps a pertinent question that fans should have been asking was whether any of the players sold by Dalglish would ever get into an Alex Ferguson side. The answer surely was a resounding 'no'.

With £22 million in his kitty Dalglish then went on a spending spree. In their places came Jon Dahl Tomasson for £2.5 million and Alessandro Pistone of Inter Milan for £4.5 million while Shay Given, Temuri Ketsbaia, Stuart Pearce, Paddy Kelly, Brian Pinas, John Barnes and Ian Rush all came in on free transfers. Financially it was a good deal. Dalglish had spent a mere £7 million, leaving £15 million to go into the club's treasure chest. On paper it looked good but on the field his signings would provide mixed fortunes. Over the years Given proved a valuable signing as did Pearce and Ketsbaia. Pistone, however, was little short of a calamity, as was Jon Dahl Tomasson, who always seemed unnerved by the St James's Park crowd. Within the year Dalglish had sold him. Interestingly, Tomasson ended up at AC Milan and went on to make outstanding performances for that club as well as for Denmark.

What Newcastle fans really craved were big names and nobody had heard of either Tomasson or Pistone while Pearce, Rush and Barnes were undoubtedly players past their best and not surprisingly were being given away free by other Premiership clubs. Dalglish's dealings seemed during that summer to lack real ambition. The fans wanted to see big names join-ing Newcastle, not has-been players or his old friends from Liverpool. And nor was there much evidence of players being signed to shore up the beleaguered defence.

Since his arrival Dalglish had brought plenty of players in but not one of them could possibly be described as a signing that would make their Premiership rivals sit up and take note. On the other hand there were proven first-team players leaving by the exit door. It all led to the accusa-tion, which persists even to this day, that Dalglish had dismantled Kevin Keegan's star-studded attacking side.

The word was that Dalglish had been told by the board that he need-ed to raise money in order to improve the club's financial position following its flotation on the London stock market in April 1997. If this is true, then the £22 million which Dalglish raised would have been an enormous boost to the club's liquidity.

The chances are that Dalglish might have escaped a torrent of criticism had he suddenly not struck bad luck. In the same week as striker Les Ferdinand left for north London, Alan Shearer was to suffer an horrendous injury during a pre-season friendly at Everton that would sideline him for most of the season. The England striker had fractured his fibula and badly ruptured ligaments. Suddenly, from boasting two of the best strikers in the Premiership, Newcastle now had nobody. Rush and Barnes could more than have filled their boots in the past but with the pair of them already over the age of thirty, there was no chance of them performing at that kind of level again. It was a grim start to the season and it would inevitably get little better.

By November, and after eleven games, Newcastle had already lost three and drawn three. By the end of the year they had lost eight and were well out of contention for any honours. But at least in Europe, Newcastle were showing some spirit. In their Champions League qualifier they edged past Croatia Zagreb and were drawn in a group alongside Dynamo Kiev, PSV Eindhoven and the mighty Barcelona. Nobody gave them much hope but in their opening game against Barcelona at St James's Park, Newcastle gave one of their finest-ever performances as they stormed into a 3–0 lead courtesy of a Tino Asprilla hat-trick and an outstanding display by Keith Gillespie. Asprilla may have looked out of sorts in the Premiership but in Europe he was on fire. Barcelona pulled two goals back late in the game but there was no questioning Dalglish that night. He was the toast of Tyneside and expectations were suddenly soaring.

Unfortunately, Newcastle's European ambitions were soon to evaporate as Tino Asprilla suffered an injury that left Newcastle even more depleted. After a useful draw in Kiev they then lost both games against the Dutch and lost 1–0 on a rain-soaked night in Barcelona. Newcastle were out of Europe, although a 2–0 win over Kiev at St James's Park restored some pride.

If Newcastle had been holding Dalglish's spending back during the close season, there were no constraints as the season wore on. Some might describe it as panic buying. In January he spent heavily, signing Andreas Andersson from AC Milan for £3 million, a player who fitted the profile of what the fans wanted, a big name coming in from Serie A. Then came Andy Griffin from Stoke for £1.5 million and Gary Speed from Everton for £5.5 million. This was more like it; Newcastle looking ambitious. But again it proved to be a mixed bag. Andersson was a disappointment although Griffin and Speed went on to give good service.

In March he plunged once more into the transfer market, taking Paul Robinson from Darlington for £250,000, Stephen Glass from Aberdeen for £650,000, and Nicos Dabizas from Olympiakos for £2 million. Glass, who was a promising Scottish youngster, never quite made the grade although Dabizas would turn out to be one of Dalglish's best buys.

Back in the league there was no improvement. If anything, matters got worse as Newcastle slid dangerously close to the relegation zone, though they managed to pick themselves up sufficiently to claim thirteenth place.

In the FA Cup they almost suffered humiliation in a tie that was fraught with pitfalls from the start. Having defeated Cup giants Everton in the opening round, Newcastle were then drawn away to non-league Stevenage

Borough. For any big club, the prospect of visiting a non-league side is greeted with mixed feelings. It may be what the romance of the Cup is about but at stake is also the ultimate embarrassment.

Even before the game kicked off there were problems. Dalglish had visited Stevenage and came away worried that the ground was unsafe. Memories of Ibrox, Heysel and Hillsborough still loomed large in his mind. Dalglish expressed his concerns and so too did the club but the latter did it in such a way as to annoy many football fans. The club portrayed the game as a rags versus riches Cup tie, suggesting that such matches should always be played on the bigger ground. Pressure was put on Stevenage to transfer the match to St James's Park but Stevenage stubbornly refused to budge. Newcastle's approach smacked of arrogance and Dalglish was left to clean up the mess. It was a public relations disaster. But it could equally have been a disaster of another sort as any Newcastle fan could testify that day as the stands shook ominously to the stamping of the Toon Army.

In the end Newcastle survived, though not without a scare and not without having to return to St James's Park for a replay. But everyone was happy, especially the directors, who got what they had always wanted, a full house with plenty of money flowing through the turnstiles and entry into the fifth round draw. Although drawn away to Tranmere Rovers Newcastle progressed smoothly through to the quarter finals where they faced Barnsley who had obligingly defeated Manchester United in the previous round. Another easy win and Newcastle were into a semi-final clash with first division Sheffield United at Old Trafford. A single goal from the now recovered Alan Shearer was enough to put Newcastle into the final where they faced Premiership champions Arsenal, out to clinch the double.

For the first ten minutes Newcastle looked quietly confident but as the game wore on, Arsenal upped the pace and in the end a disappointed Toon Army traipsed away from Wembley feeling that their side had barely exerted themselves. They had lost 2–0. Dalglish's name might have been briefly chanted in the early banter of the fans but by the late afternoon he had become chief villain for his failure to inspire anything that could be described as a genuine effort. It was a dreary end to a season that had at times looked promising. The excitement of that famous victory over Barcelona had augured well but in the end had produced little. In the League, the delights of the previous season had never been matched while in the Cup there had been a rude awakening at Wembley. Newcastle had achieved nothing. If anything they had gone backwards and for most fans the fault clearly lay with Dalglish.

The excitement generated by Keegan's attacking side had all but disappeared. In its place was a dour, hard-working, uninspiring mix. Nobody was impressed, least of all Dalglish, who in the summer of 1998 was given another bagful of money to spend, in spite of a growing clamour for his head. In came another Greek, this time the £500,000 George Georgiadis from Panathinaikos – French World Cup winner Stephane Guivarc'h arrived from Auxerre for £3.5 million, another Frenchman Laurent Charvet came from Cannes for £750,000, while in August German international Dietmar Hamann was signed from Bayern Munich for £4.5 million along with Nolberto Solano from Boca Juniors for £2.5 million. It had been an expensive summer with a total of almost £13 million spent. The only player of any note to go was the disappointing Jon Dahl Tomasson who went to Feyenoord for £2.5 million. At least Dalglish had not lost any money on that deal.

And yet, for all the spending, Dalglish's signings would continue to baffle and fail to live up to expectations. When Stephane Guivarc'h was signed there was a buzz about the city but he would prove a huge disappointment. At least Hamann and Solano would prove to be quality signings although Hamann would be offloaded to Liverpool for a neat profit a year after being signed.

One signing Dalglish could certainly have done without making was that of his own son Paul, whom he had signed in the autumn of 1997. He may not have cost a penny but to fans, and a suspicious local press, it smacked of nepotism. His son had already failed to make the grade with Liverpool and there was nothing to believe that he would succeed at Newcastle. But the damage had already been done. Fans and the local media shook their heads in disbelief.

Having lavished so much money in the transfer market, expectations were high. In their first game Newcastle drew 0–0 at home with Charlton. The writing was on the wall. As Dalglish left the pitch it was to the unfamiliar sound of boos ringing in his ears. It was not a sound he was accustomed to. To be given such a reception from what were supposedly his own fans was a humiliation. Though it is equally true to say that there were few occasions when the Tyneside crowd had ever chanted his name. He had never been held in the same regard as his predecessor.

After the game there were heated words. Newcastle had been taken to the edge of success under Kevin Keegan and whatever promise there had been had now fast disappeared. There was frustration, anger and bitterness from the fans, the board and the local press.

One Liverpool fan who happened to be living in Newcastle and a visitor to St James's Park that day remembers it with sadness. 'It was appalling to see Liverpool's great hero having to stand there and listen to those boos. It was desperately sad.'

A week later Newcastle travelled to London to face Chelsea. Dalglish needed a win if he was to ward off his critics. But he didn't get one. Instead they drew 1–1. And that was it. After the game rumours abounded that Dalglish and chief executive Freddie Fletcher had had words in the corridor. Whatever happened, the love affair between Dalglish and Newcastle was over although there would continue to be a dispute over whether Dalglish had actually been pushed or had walked. Dalglish claimed that he had been sacked and as such demanded proper compensation. Inevitably he was criticised by the fans who saw this as yet another act of arrogance.

Dalglish may have had his enemies upstairs and in the local press, but in the dressing room there was considerable respect for him. Nicos Dabizas still reveres him. 'Kenny was a very likeable man,' he says, 'and I'll always have the utmost respect for him. He was very straight. He kept a low profile and always respected his players. He never criticised a player to the media and all the players liked him for that. He made Newcastle feel like one big family, like we were all in it together.'

So what went wrong? 'It just didn't work out for him,' Dabizas says. 'It came as a huge surprise when he left, because we'd just managed a 1–1 draw at Stamford Bridge, which was a good result. No one expected him to go at the time.' But go he did.

What remained bizarre – and almost unforgivable for a plc – was that the Newcastle board should have allowed the manager a spending spree of almost £13 million during the close season, only to sack him days into the new campaign. The board had simply panicked and caved in to public pressure. They then went on to appoint Ruud Gullit as manager, a man who would then start to undo everything Dalglish had done and spend just as much in the process.

It should have been obvious that the new signings would take time to settle and come together, particularly foreign players who need not only to learn a new language but to adapt to the more competitive nature of English football. Hamann and Solano would both prove to be exceptional signings while Charvet was one of Dalglish's better buys. Given more time. even Guivarc'h may have matched his transfer fee.

In the months ahead the fans would point to the presence of Lionel Perez at United as a continuing reminder of their former manager, who brought him in on ludicrously high wages from Sunderland. In the two years since he was signed he had made well over £500,000 out of Newcastle without ever kicking a ball in a competitive game for the club.

Dalglish had overseen a massive turnover in staff. In all, 34 players had arrived while some 22 players had departed. Most of these were on free transfers or loans but massive fees had been paid for the likes of Pistone, Speed and Hamann. In total Dalglish had spent £33.3 million in bringing in his 34 players while earning £27.5 million in selling 22 players. It was a net loss of £5.8 million that certainly did not put him among the most spendthrift of managers. Indeed, he was not that far off balancing his books. But his critics could point to the doomed signings of ageing former colleagues John Barnes and Ian Rush while the signing of his own son Paul was, at best, ill judged.

Yet there were successes: Shay Given, Stuart Pearce, Gary Speed, Nicos Dabizas, Andy Griffin, Laurent Charvet, Didi Hamann and Nobby Solano were all admirable signings, with many of them still plying their trade in the Premiership years later. And if Newcastle fans thought that by getting rid of Dalglish and appointing Ruud Gullit in his place, they had got the better of the deal, they had a rude awakening.

When Dalglish had arrived at St James's Park he had been astonished to discover that Keegan had disbanded the reserve side, leaving the club short of fit and reliable substitutes. And nor was there any sub-structure of youth development. Both cost-cutting exercises had left Dalglish so short that on the night they played PSV, he didn't have enough players to fill the bench. Dalglish had consequently been forced to build a squad, bringing in some players who might not be world-beaters but who at least were reliable. When he left St James's Park, Newcastle had not only a reserve side but a well-structured youth system in place that was already reaping dividends.

Dalglish never enjoyed a particularly friendly relationship with the local press. Newcastle was a small village and the local media an even smaller gathering. One journalist, although sympathetic to Dalglish, recalls many an uncomfortable meeting with him. Dalglish always remained an outsider, and many among the local media wanted one of their own – a

Geordie – rather than an interloper. Although Dalglish did invite the Newcastle football writers to Christmas lunch in 1997 he never sought to charm them, as Keegan had done, and as a result his relationship with them never moved beyond the strictly professional. The failure to woo the local media would ultimately leave Dalglish short of vital friends.

Newcastle chairman Freddy Shepherd agrees that Kenny was never comfortable with the local media. 'But I never knew why,' he adds. 'Socially we got on well. Kenny was a good pal. I had some great times with him. I didn't hear anybody say it was a bad choice when we appointed him. We may have got it wrong but so did the supporters as well – they all thought the same as us. The supporters were behind us 100%.'

Behind the scenes there was also much politicking, something Dalglish had never really experienced during his days at either Liverpool or Blackburn. But at St James's Park it sometimes seemed to be every man for himself. Dalglish had also arrived just as the club was going into a public flotation on the London Stock Exchange. It was a difficult time and a far from easy board to work with. Sometimes it seemed more obsessed with being the biggest club in the North East rather than taking in the wider picture.

In the end Newcastle maybe just needed someone of their own ilk, a Geordie as passionate as them, someone who could understand the mood of the Toon Army and who lived the same dream as they did. Eventually they would get such a man but not before another painful few years.

CHAPTER TWENTY-FIVE
Feet Of Clay

SUPER CALEY GO BALLISTIC, CELTIC ARE ATROCIOUS
Sun

It may have seemed inevitable that Dalglish would, some day, wind up back at Celtic. It was surely written in the tea-leaves and anybody with an ounce of footballing sense could tell you that Kenny really belonged to Glasgow. It was where he belonged and one day he would, for sure, return. It certainly came as little surprise to most Liverpool fans but, ironically, few Celtic supporters had ever anticipated that their legendary striker would return. Indeed there were many still bearing a grudge that he had left them in the first place. But in June 1999 return he did.

His job at Parkhead however was not to be as manager but in a newly created post, Director of Football, making him Celtic's football overlord. Yet instead of being greeted with lavish enthusiasm, his appointment was received more with a mixture of curiosity and hope. Even the board had been divided with Fergus McCann, the man who saved Celtic from bankruptcy in March 1994, vigorously opposed to Dalglish's appointment. Chief Executive Allan MacDonald, a personal friend of Dalglish, had won the day.

'Kenny Comes Home', read the generous headline in one Glasgow paper. Other newspapers were less enthusiastic. Columnist Gary Keown in the *Sun* was scathing. 'Am I alone in thinking the only thing dragging him back to Glasgow after 22 years south of the border is the rustle of the folding stuff ?' He wasn't the only one. Among the fans there were widespread reservations. Memories of Dalglish's time at Newcastle were still fresh, as was Dalglish's flirtation with his childhood favourites, Rangers, immediately prior to his appointment at Parkhead. At Rangers he had become some kind of 'super scout', leaving many Celtic fans wondering what on earth he was doing hooking up with the 'enemy'. Anything more than just European scout would certainly have proved disastrous, but for the moment it was respectfully brushed aside. Judgement at best was reserved.

But there was no denying that Dalglish was returning to his roots and to his first love, Celtic Football Club. No matter the slight hiccups in between at Newcastle and Rangers. What really mattered was that after an absence of twenty-two years the prodigal son was back in town.

In the intervening years Kenny had kept his ear well to the ground. He knew precisely what was going on inside Parkhead and was well abreast of the feuding inside the boardroom. He was even said to have warned Lou Macari against taking up the manager's position when it was offered him. It was also rumoured that Dalglish had been sounded out about a return to Parkhead when he was still managing Blackburn but Dalglish, still with a young family, was well settled on Merseyside and in no mood for a return north. And anyhow, Celtic's finances at the time would never have been sufficient for them to offer Dalglish a tempting enough contract.

Early in 1999 however Dalglish had become involved in a consortium, along with the Glaswegian pop singer Jim Kerr and others, to persuade Celtic's managing director Fergus McCann to sell his shares to their consortium. The idea may have been knocked back by McCann who always doubted that they ever had sufficient money, but it alerted his successor, Allan MacDonald, to the idea that Dalglish was keen to become involved in the club in some capacity or other. After some discussions a suitable role was found for him: that of Director of Football. The announcement was made in June 1999.

Parkhead, and Glasgow, for that matter, had changed significantly since Dalglish had last worn the green and white hoops. The drab tenement blocks of the city had been largely restored and the grand gothic buildings which in the eighties had taken on an air of vandalised gloom had been renovated to their former glory. A fresh spirit of optimism was about Scotland. With its new degree of independence it had become a more confident nation, no longer wallowing in its past or as subservient to its southern neighbour. And even at Parkhead, The Jungle, once the most feared terracing in all of Scotland and most of Europe, had been replaced by a gleaming double-decker stand as swanky as any in England. Corporate facilities and executive boxes all symbolised football's new relationship with money. But in 1999 it was Rangers who were the dominant force in Scottish football.

Dalglish had taken on an awesome task. Expectations were high and his first job was not an enviable one. It was the most crucial of all. He needed to appoint a new coach, someone to take charge of first team affairs. As Director of Football, Dalglish's role was to oversee the footballing activities of the club, rather than that of the first team. From the start Dalglish had a name in mind.

Dalglish had always been a fan of John Barnes, even before he arrived at Anfield, where Dalglish had signed him for almost a million pounds from Watford. At Anfield Dalglish had been able to closely study his approach to the game. In team talks Barnes always had something to contribute. Dalglish would give his talk, then ask if there were any questions. 'He always had an opinion,' remembers one insider. 'We'd be all ready to make off for a shower and go home when up he'd chirp and we'd be there for another half hour or more.' At times it could get on players' nerves as they reluctantly sat down once again to hear what Barnes had to say. 'But it was always constructive, always aimed to help. He was very thoughtful in whatever he said.'

But whatever Barnes did say, it usually made sense. There were even some who predicted that sooner or later Barnes would become manager of Liverpool. If that was the case, his appointment at Parkhead was to scupper that plan once and for all.

It had been the same at Newcastle. Barnes regularly got involved with the coaching, particularly with the reserves. He and Kenny would chat for hours and Kenny seemed to like his ideas. Barnes was an intelligent lad. He was thoughtful and articulate and much admired for the way he had conducted himself over the years in the face of the racist bully boys of the terraces, particularly when he had first come to Merseyside.

That Dalglish should suddenly pluck him out of nowhere and appoint him as coach was still a huge surprise to everyone. For a start, Barnes had no experience of managing. He had not even been a coach. To suddenly throw him into one of the highest profile jobs in management was an enormous risk. But Dalglish was adamant and believed that Barnes could do a job.

Barnes, however, was privately less than enthusiastic. He called his friend and former team-mate Jan Molby and told him that he had been offered the Celtic job. 'Are you going to take it?' asked Molby. 'Not sure,' he replied. A few days later Barnes was appointed. Whatever happened to change his mind during those few days must have come largely from the silver tongue of Dalglish. Barnes was to be Celtic's seventh manager in ten years. When Celtic announced the appointment they described it as 'the dream team'.

Barnes' other major problem was that he did not know anything about Scottish football. He'd never played there, didn't know half the clubs, had never visited the grounds, knew none of the players, and so forth. And no way could Barnes have ever fully understood the pressures of managing one of the big Glasgow clubs. To compensate for his lack of knowledge the former Aberdeen player Eric Black was retained as number two with another Liverpool old boy, Terry McDermott, also being drafted in.

It is also true to say that Dalglish had only a limited knowledge of the modern Scottish game. He may have known the clubs and where they played but that was from twenty year previously. Much had changed and of course the personnel had changed drastically. Dalglish no longer had an extensive knowledge of the players and nor was Celtic any longer the homely club of the 1970s where Jock Stein would answer the phone or be found at the front door enquiry hatch helping to solve some fan's problem. Celtic was now a corporate club, a plc and a major business. Dalglish was still essentially, a football man, and not the type to feel comfortable with the suits.

In hindsight the appointment of Barnes was disastrous, and it is surprising that Dalglish, himself should, even for one minute, have thought that it could work. It had never worked in English football. The nearest was the Brian Clough/Peter Taylor partnership at Nottingham Forest during the early eighties but there was only ever one boss in that relationship. Dalglish had even tried it himself at Blackburn but that had ended in an unmitigated disaster. He had also been close enough to Anfield to see that the Roy Evans/Gerard Houllier partnership did not work.

Dalglish had the pick of managers and coaches, yet he had chosen someone without any experience of managing and someone without any knowledge of the Scottish game. Both men were also coming into a club that had been in turmoil for longer than fans cared to remember.

Another problem was ex-manager Jozef Venglos. Having relieved him of his job, nobody was quite sure what to do with him. Rather than pay him off, Celtic opted for the worst scenario of all; they appointed him European Technical Adviser, whatever that was supposed to mean.

Celtic had made a similarly confused decision some seasons earlier when Dutch coach Wim Jansen was appointed as manager but at least he had the experience of Jock Brown as general manager. History was about to repeat itself.

Dalglish may have been the main influence in appointing the coach but many wondered exactly what Dalglish's other jobs were. He wasn't the manager, he didn't choose the team, he didn't sign players and he didn't take most of the press conferences. So what precisely did he do? Good question. Well, he did a little bit of scouting, he joined in some training sessions and watched opposition teams but most of what he did seemed to be peripheral, playing a supporting role to his protégé John Barnes. He also went to most board meetings, with Barnes reportedly only attending one during his time at Parkhead.

And yet for all the concern, Celtic made a promising start to the season, beating Aberdeen 5–0 at Pittodrie in their opening match and St Johnstone 3–0 at Parkhead a week later. Then came a surprise 2–1 defeat at Tannadice Park to Dundee United. There were further wins in August and September, including a 7–0 drubbing of Aberdeen at Celtic Park. It all looked good and yet despite the bright start questions were soon being asked by the parochial Glasgow press as well as many fans.

The rot began to set in late in October when they lost a second game, this time at home to Motherwell. Then came Rangers a fortnight later in the league again. Celtic went 2–1 ahead but bad luck was to strike as Paul Lambert was injured in a penalty area collision that cost Celtic not only a penalty but also the lead and the services of one of their most inspiring players. They eventually lost 4–2 and ended up seven points behind their Glasgow rivals and were now looking well and truly out of the running for the league title.

Barnes told the papers, however, that he was sure that Celtic could still land second spot. But what he did not fully understand was that second spot was simply not good enough and if Celtic was behind Rangers it was tantamount to disaster. Perhaps Dalglish ought to have put him wise.

It didn't get that much better. A Christmas-time draw at home to Rangers and then another 1–1 draw, this time at Kilmarnock, was followed by an embarrassing 3–2 defeat at Parkhead to Hearts. It was getting worse.

It hadn't been any better in Europe either. Again, after a promising start that saw Celtic cruise past Cwmbran Town of the Welsh league and Israeli side Hapoel Tel Aviv in the early rounds of the UEFA Cup, Celtic came up against tougher opposition in French side Lyon. Although Celtic lost only 1–0 in the away leg, it was a game that was to be remembered for an injury that left striker Henrik Larsson writhing in agony on the pitch. Larsson had broken his leg and Celtic were left to cope for virtually the rest of the season without their talisman and the one man who might have been able to keep their campaign alive. Not surprisingly, they also lost the return 1–0 leg and were out of Europe.

Barnes gritted his teeth and put on a brave face to the Glasgow press, claiming that there was still everything to play for that season. But in truth both he and Dalglish knew that anything other than league or European success came a long way down the pecking order.

To offset the loss of Larsson, Barnes decided to bring in the former Arsenal striker Ian Wright who had been winding down his career at West Ham and Nottingham Forest. It was a gamble that did not pay off. Wright was well short of the mark and played just a handful of games before joining Burnley.

Having gambled on Ian Wright, Barnes took an even bigger gamble with the signing of Rafael Scheidt, a Brazilian centre back who was signed for a reported £5 million. It doesn't take much to imagine what his name soon became. Barnes had not even seen him play but decided that with Stubbs being ill, he needed someone to fill a potential gap. In the event Scheidt ,who played just three times that season, was exactly what his name suggested. Barnes was lampooned in the Glasgow press over the signing.

As if that was not enough the greatest humiliation of them all came on 8 February 2000 when the delightfully named Inverness Caledonian Thistle were the visitors to Parkhead in the Scottish Cup third round. It was supposed to be an easy game against one of the minnows of Scottish football. Celtic could, in theory, have put out their third team and still have won. Perhaps they should have done for what followed was to go down in the annals of Scottish Cup footballing history as one of the greatest giant-killing act of all time, if not the greatest. Barnes and company must have cringed as Celtic conceded not just one goal, not just two, but three goals, to lose 3–1. And at Parkhead as well. Dalglish, who was away on a scouting mission at La Manga in Spain had missed the debacle but was urgently summoned back to Parkhead for an inquest with a furious Allan MacDonald.

Ironically the game had been postponed for ten days after high winds had damaged guttering in the Lisbon Lions stand. Who knows how differently the story may have ended if the game had not been postponed.

At half time there was the most almighty bust-up in the dressing room, even by Scottish football standards. Tempers flared, fists flew and Mark Viduka hurled his boots against the dressing room wall, refusing to come out for the second half. The row became legendary. It was that bad and the absence for the second half of the only man who seemed to be able to find the net certainly did not help Celtic's cause. Black, who had been brought in as the previous manager's number two, had retained his position under Barnes and was at the centre of the row. He did not last much longer.

'SUPER CALEY GO BALLISTIC, CELTIC ARE ATROCIOUS' ran the memorable headline in the Scottish edition of the *Sun* the next day. It was a genius of a headline that, much to the chagrin of Celtic fans, would be remembered by football fans forever. Perhaps only once had Celtic suffered such a humiliation. They were the laughing stock of Scotland, and, especially in the closeted world of Scottish football, in Glasgow itself.

That was it. Enough was enough. Celtic were out of Europe and the Cup and already ten points behind Rangers in the league. The John Barnes experiment was not working. And on 10 February 2000 he was ousted as head coach. There was little sympathy. Certainly the fans were not begging for him to be given a second chance or more time. He had been given ample resources, bringing in nine new faces and even paying a Scottish transfer record fee of £5.75 million for West Ham's Eyal Berkovic. Admittedly there had been injuries, in particular to Larsson, but the fans were not looking for excuses. They'd had enough; John Barnes had failed to deliver and that was that.

The fans could never quite fathom his tactics. Barnes had played a 4-2-2-2 system – it was something he had helped perfect at Anfield under Roy Evans where it had been similarly criticised for its lack of progress and ambition. But perhaps most importantly Barnes had failed to realise the importance of beating Rangers. If you couldn't win the title, then the very least that was expected was to come away with something from the Old Firm games. Yet to have faced Rangers twice and to have taken no more than a single point off them was too much even for the most loyal of Celtic fans. Had they beaten Rangers just once, then perhaps he would have been given more time but failing to beat Rangers was, for the fans, simply unforgivable. Not that it got any better later that season as they lost twice more to their oldest rivals.

There was little Dalglish could say. He had felt the humiliation as much as any Celtic fan. If the fans were going to blame Barnes, then equally they were blaming Dalglish.

'I had a lot of meetings with Kenny,' says Barnes. 'Kenny was probably a little bit disillusioned with the whole situation himself. I was his appointment so he was under pressure as well. So Kenny and I had a bit of a siege mentality. We would talk to each other a lot about the situation. We were hoping to keep on to Rangers' coat tails for as long as possible.'

Most days Dalglish would join in training along with Barnes and Eric Black, after which he and Barnes would settle down to watch videos of players that were potential signings. Defining Dalglish's job was far from easy. He was neither one thing, nor the other. His job title may have sounded powerful but in truth it wasn't. The one major function he had was to recommend the appointment of a manager to the board. John Barnes was very much his appointment and when Barnes failed, Dalglish too had to accept much of the blame. Equally, had Barnes succeeded, no doubt some of the accolades would have rubbed off on Dalglish.

What was a Director of Football supposed to do? In truth, Dalglish was little more than a figurehead, brought in to satisfy the fans; the prodigal son returning to cast his magic on Parkhead. Had Dalglish been a lone appointment as manager then perhaps he might have been able to weave some of his old magic but given the convoluted set up at Parkhead, it was never clear who was really in charge of what. Some members of the local press suggested that Dalglish spent more time on the golf course than on the training field.

Barnes wondered if others at Celtic had anticipated that Dalglish would have more input into team affairs. But it was certainly not the way Dalglish had read the situation, nor John Barnes. 'I don't know whether other people thought that, and maybe they did, and that's why they felt that Kenny should have been doing more but I wouldn't have come under those circumstances.'

The fact is that Allan MacDonald had the highest regard for Dalglish and if Dalglish said that he wanted Barnes as his manager/coach, then

MacDonald backed him to the hilt. Doubtless there were other directors who thought differently. There were those, directors as well as fans, who reckoned Dalglish should have been taking more training sessions as well as helping to choose the side. But that was neither Dalglish's nor Barnes' definition of Football Director.

With Barnes gone and the season end still three months away, Celtic took the sensible option by asking Dalglish to assume the role of acting manager until a successor could be found. Not that Dalglish was overjoyed at the prospect. He was said to be still seething over the treatment dished out to Barnes. But it was either accept or join Barnes through the exit door. He had little option but to just get on with it.

It all began well enough. Four days after the Caley debacle, they notched up a 3–0 win over Dundee. It was noticeable that after the game, Dalglish shook each player's hand as they left the pitch, then turned and gave a salute to the Celtic supporters. In the CIS League Cup semi-final a few days later, Celtic beat Kilmarnock 1–0 and in the final went on to defeat a poor Aberdeen side 2–0. And yet, despite bringing some silverware back to Parkhead the name that was being chanted by the fans was not that of Dalglish but of one of his predecessors, Tommy Burns, who had been brought in by Dalglish once more to help out. If that win in the Cup suggested brighter days had arrived, then a week later reality returned as Celtic lost 4–0 at Ibrox. By the end of the season they trailed Rangers by a record 21 points in the Premier League.

Even before the season was over the number one item on the directors' agenda was to appoint a new manager. Had Dalglish wanted the job then he probably could have had it. But there were doubts on both sides. As for Dalglish, did he really want all that hassle, could he be bothered with all the board room bickering and did he need all that press scrutiny? As for the directors, they must have wondered if the fans really wanted him. Perhaps the latter was the most important consideration of all.

The fans' love affair with Dalglish had cooled. He was no longer the God that he had been. He might have had successes at Liverpool and at Blackburn but his days at Newcastle were a closer memory. And his one season at Parkhead had been a disaster. One of the problems was that he didn't seem to stay anywhere very long. He had quit Liverpool unexpectedly and abruptly, and had then left Blackburn after less than five seasons. Newcastle had been even shorter, just over a season.

The fans also were never fully aware of precisely what his input had been at Parkhead. His heart was no longer in it. Other names were being mentioned anyhow. Had the entire board come to Dalglish and pleaded with him to take the job, no doubt he would have done so but it was clear that some did not want him. Even Allan MacDonald, for so long a Dalglish admirer, was conducting a public search for a new manager with Guus Hiddink the favoured candidate. Dermot Desmond, the new powerbroker at the club had other ideas. He'd phoned Liam Brady to tap the Irishman's knowledge of the English football scene and Brady had recommended the Leicester manager Martin O'Neill. And so it was that O'Neill swept aside Tommy Burns, Guus Hiddink, Kenny Dalglish and any other name that might have been mentioned to become the new Celtic boss.

Dalglish had also had his problems with the Glasgow media, who could be just as parochial as that in Newcastle. Editors demanded a major Celtic or Rangers story every day. The ultimate as far as they were concerned was to have a Rangers or Celtic story on the front page and the back page. Although there had been enthusiasm for Dalglish when he arrived, some members of the press were less than enthusiastic. They had looked at his more recent record and seriously wondered if he could still deliver.

Dalglish had never been comfortable with the press at the best of times. As manager of Liverpool, his first day in office had meant dealing with the Heysel disaster. After that he was always suspicious even though he was managing the best team in Europe and one that kept on winning. But generally the Liverpool press gave him little trouble. Then at Blackburn he was dealing with just a couple of local journalists. He learnt to trust them and was always said to be friendly and forthcoming. And as long as Blackburn kept on winning few troublesome questions were ever asked. But at Newcastle it had been a different story. Not only was the North East press more critical but it was also more demanding and when Newcastle lost their way it could be ruthless. Dalglish reacted by retreating and pulling up the drawbridge. And it was the same in Glasgow.

Angered by the criticism he was getting in the Glasgow media, Dalglish arranged for the usual Friday press conference to take place in Baird's Bar, a well known Celtic pub in the Gallowgate district. Dalglish, believing that he was being continually misquoted and misrepresented in the press, reckoned that if the conference was held in public then the fans would hear what was being said and could compare it with what they read in the papers the next day. Unfortunately, it turned out to be a public relations fiasco and did not go down well with the Glasgow press who had to sit over pints being eyed suspiciously by the punters coming in for their lunchtime drinks. A second press conference which took place in the social club ended with *Sunday Mail* journalist Hugh Kevins having to be escorted off the premises after one of the watching punters had taken a dislike to him. The story hit the headlines the next day and Dalglish was pilloried for it.

There may have been a time when the Glasgow press waltzed cheek to cheek with Celtic but the days when Big Jock Stein terrified local journalists were long gone. The press were now far more intrusive, far more critical and far more powerful.

But at least Dalglish spoke the language. As for John Barnes, it was impossible. He'd never played in Scotland, didn't know anyone and never went out of his way to win over many journalists. He was on a hiding to nothing and his prickly attitude to some journalists who found him 'difficult' and 'awkward' made it all the worse.

Dalglish's position had become untenable. It was known that the incoming O'Neill did not want anyone overseeing his activities. O'Neill was his own man. He had to be the 'gaffer' in name and deed. It was to be his job and his responsibility alone and no way would he even consider the job if there was anyone else interfering in the footballing activities of the club. After a brief crossover period Dalglish diplomatically took his leave of Parkhead though wrangles over his pay off would drag on for some time.

Since leaving Celtic Dalglish has taken a backseat. If you frequent the right golf courses, you'll see him in an afternoon, usually with a former Liverpool team-mate, still trying to perfect his swing. He can also be spotted at Anfield watching a game or two and from time to time rumours surface that maybe one day he will return in some capacity or other. But nothing concrete has ever emerged. He can also be seen as a regular TV pundit, particularly when Liverpool play, and while other former Liverpool players have often been critical of the club and its management, Dalglish has always kept a diplomatic and loyal silence. Liverpool fans respect him enormously for that. What's more, Dalglish always talks sense and always authoritatively. He's a football man, not a suit. He understands the game from the players' prospective.

But in the main Dalglish is now a peripheral figure in the world of football, no longer formally associated with any club. And nor, it seems, does he wish to be. Whenever important soccer jobs are on offer the name of Dalglish is no longer touted on the back pages, and you won't find him filling in an application form or dashing off a CV to some club in dire straits. Although nothing is ever certain in life the chances of Dalglish returning to big-time football seem distinctly remote.

When fans called for the head of Liverpool's Gerard Houllier late in 2003, Dalglish's name was generously mooted as a possible successor on one website. But the fans soon e-mailed in to put an end to that suggestion. He had been out of it for too long, they all argued, going back never worked, and anyhow the game had now moved on. It wasn't that Liverpool fans had fallen out with him, it was just that they were being realistic.

No doubt Hillsborough still haunts him and over the years he has kept in touch with the Hillsborough Justice Committee and is usually in attendance when the annual memorial service is held at Anfield. These days the press corps talk about Dalglish's warmth and charm and how he's a changed man. 'Not at all like the suspicious and uncomfortable manager he used to be with us,' was the way one leading Glasgow journalist put it.

Mention the name Dalglish to most young football fans today and they are just as likely to think that you are talking about his daughter Kelly, now a regular SKY TV sports presenter. His son Paul, who played at Anfield, Newcastle and Norwich, though with little success, is still involved in the game.

And yet you can't help thinking that Kenny Dalglish is a talent being neglected and wasted. Surely, somewhere in football, there is a role that he could play, perhaps with youngsters, perhaps with the national team. It would be a sad day if this was to be the end of the Kenny Dalglish story.

APPENDIX

THE DALGLISH ROLL OF HONOUR

Born: Glasgow, 4 March 1951 Kenneth Mathieson Dalglish
1966 Played for Scotland Schoolboys
1967 Joined Celtic on provisional contract
1968 Turned professional

Celtic career
Debut as substitute v Hamilton Academical, 25 September 1968, Scottish League Cup quarter-final second leg

Celtic statistics
Competition Appearances Goals League 200(4) 112 Scottish Cup 30 11 Scottish League Cup 56(4) 35 Europe 27(1) 9 TOTAL 313(9) 167

Honours with Celtic
Four Scottish championship medals – 1971/2, 1972/3, 1973/4, 1976/7
Four Scottish Cup-winners' medals – 1971/2, 1973/4, 1974/5, 1976/7
One Scottish League Cup-winner's medal – 1974/5
August 1977 transferred to Liverpool for a British record fee of £440,000

Liverpool career
Debut v Manchester United, August 1977, Charity Shield at Wembley

Liverpool statistics
Competition Appearances Goals League 342(13) 118 FA Cup 37 13 League Cup 57(2) 27 Europe 46(1) 10 TOTAL 482(16) 168

Honours with Liverpool as a player
Five League championship medals – 1978/9, 1979/80, 1981/2, 1982/3, 1983/4
Three European Cup-winner's medals – 1977/8, 1980/81, 1983/4

Four League Cup-winner's medals – 1980/81, 1981/2, 1982/3, 1983/4
One European Super Cup-winner's medal – 1977/8
May 1985 appointed player/manager of Liverpool

Record with Liverpool as player/manager and later manager

League champions 1985/6, 1987/8, 1989/90
Runners-up 1986/7, 1988/9
FA Cup-winners 1985/6, 1988/9
Runners-up 1987/8
League Cup runners-up 1986/7
Resigned as manager of Liverpool Friday, 22 February 1991

Blackburn Rovers career

Appointed manager of Blackburn Rovers Saturday, 12 October 1991
Record with Blackburn
Promotion to the Premier League 1991/2
Premiership runners-up 1993/4
Premiership champions 1994/5
Appointed director of football 25 June 1995
Resigned as director of football at Blackburn Rovers 21 August 1996

Newcastle United career

Appointed manager Tuesday, 14 January 1997

Record with Newcastle

Premiership runners-up 1996/7; qualified for Champions League
Finished thirteenth in Premiership 1997/8
FA Cup runners-up 1997/8
August 1998, Dalglish sacked after two games

Celtic career

Appointed Football Director, June 1999
Takes over as caretaker manager, February 2000

Record with Celtic

Runners-up in Scottish Premier League 1999/2000
League Cup winners 2000
Dalglish leaves Celtic, June 2000

Scotland career

Scotland Schoolboys: Two appearances, 1966
Scotland Youth: Six appearances, 1968/9
Scotland Under-23s: Five appearances, three goals

Scotland senior team

Debut as substitute v Belgium at Aberdeen, 10 November 1971
102 appearances (national record)
30 goals (equals national record)

Other honours

MBE
Freeman of the City of Glasgow
Footballer of the Year 1978/9, 1982/3
PFA Player of the Year 1983
Manager of the Year 1985/6, 1987/8, 1989/90, 1994/5

Other records

Dalglish was the first Scot to win 100 international caps
The first player/manager to win the League Championship
and the FA Cup
The first player to score 100 goals in both the Football League
and the Scottish League
Only the third manager this century to lead two different clubs
to the League championship

INDEX

The index is arranged alphabetically except for subheadings, which appear in approximate chronological order.